DATE DUE

PRINCE OF LIBRARIANS

PRINCE OF LIBRARIANS

The Life and Times of Antonio Panizzi
of the British Museum

EDWARD MILLER

THE OHIO UNIVERSITY PRESS
Athens Ohio

The Ohio University Press
Athens Ohio

Printed in Great Britain

CONTENTS

LIST OF ILLUSTRATIONS

INTRODUCTION

IT would be perfectly true to say that the British Museum Library as most of us have known it is Panizzi's creation. He is generally regarded as the Museum's second founder. Undoubtedly he was an administrator of genius and as so often happens with men of genius he was also in Arundel Esdaile's phrase, *felix opportunitate vitae*.

Mr. Miller in the present book emphasizes the same point: 'His long reign as Keeper of Printed Books coincided with a new and widespread interest in every aspect of knowledge. The new spirit of the age would never have been content with the old easy-going, slothful Museum of the early years of the century. Reformed, willy-nilly, it would have to have been. It was its supreme good fortune to have been reformed from within.'

Panizzi was subjected to pertinacious attack throughout his Museum career and even after his retirement, but he was throughout resolutely *tenax propositi* and he never flinched from what he considered to be his duty towards the institution he served, and the library, as the result, is his creation. If change is now on the way, it is as much as anything due to Panizzi's insistence on the inescapable importance of the quality of the services to be offered by a great national library.

I am very glad that one of my colleagues of the present day has written a new book about Panizzi and drawn attention once more to the wide sweep of his activities, to his bold generous spirit, to his impatience of arrogance and incompetence, to his pugnacious striving for the good of the British Museum, to which he gave his unstinted loyalty.

This could not have been an easy book to write and Mr. Miller deserves the warmest commendation for undertaking it and carrying it through so successfully.

SIR FRANK FRANCIS
DIRECTOR AND PRINCIPAL LIBRARIAN

British Museum
London WC1

ACKNOWLEDGEMENTS

THE author wishes to express his gratitude to Sir Frank Francis, K.C.B., Director and Principal Librarian of the British Museum, for kindly consenting to write a foreword to this life of one of his predecessors, to Mr R. A. Wilson, formerly Principal Keeper of the Department of Printed Books for his encouragement and to the following for help and advice: Mr L. J. Gorton, Mr P. V. Blake-Hill, Mr R. S. Pine-Coffin, Dr D. E. Rhodes, Mr R. Williams, Mr I. R. Willison, and especially to Dr C. B. Oldman, without whose valuable assistance this book would never have been written. The author would also like to express his appreciation for help rendered by the staff of the Director's Office, of the Departments of Manuscripts and of Printed Books, British Museum, and by the staff of the National Library of Scotland, and to his wife for her invaluable assistance at all times.

Grateful thanks are also due to the Earl of Clarendon for permission to quote from the letters of the fourth Earl; to Mr A. C. Gladstone for permission to quote from the Gladstone Papers; to the Countess of Ilchester and to her daughter, Viscountess Galway for permission to quote from the Holland House Papers and for permission to reproduce the portrait of Panizzi, formerly at Holland House; to the Trustees of the British Museum to make use of the Committee minutes, the official papers of Sir Anthony Panizzi as Keeper of Printed Books, the diaries of Edward Edwards, and other papers now in their custody and for permission to reproduce the remaining illustrations used in this book.

Acknowledgements are also made to the following for their kind permission to quote from published copyright material:

Messrs Allen & Unwin; Avv. Aldo Bacchi Andreoli; Messrs John Baker; Messrs Ernest Benn; The Keeper, Department of Western Manuscripts, Bodleian Library; The Brown, Picton and Hornby Libraries, Liverpool; Messrs Chapman & Hall; Messrs Constable; The President, Deputazione di Storia Patria per le Province Parmensi; The Controller, H.M. Stationery Office; Loescher Editore; The Librarian, Manchester College, Oxford; Manchester University Press; Messrs John Murray; The Director, Museo del Risorgimento, Modena; The Trustees, National Library of Scotland; and University College, London.

I

THE BACKGROUND

THE ITALY into which Antonio Genesio Maria Panizzi was born on September 16, 1797,[1] was a broken and disrupted country. That very year, Napoleon Bonaparte had dictated to Austria the peace of Campo Formio, signed within a few weeks of Panizzi's birth.[2] By offering to the Hapsburgs the thousand-year-old Venetian Republic he had obtained for France the whole of the rest of northern Italy. The old stable order of things was changing, as revolution and counter-revolution succeeded each other with bewildering rapidity. The somnolent, if perhaps decadent, Italy of the eighteenth century, the Italy of the Grand Tour and of the paintings of Tiepolo and Guardi, had vanished and a new and very different society was taking its place.

To a large extent, the period that was vanishing had been one of languid torpor, a period in which the country slowly recovered from the devastating wars and invasions of the previous centuries. The end of the war of the Spanish Succession in 1714 had closed the long period during which Italy had been a helpless victim, over whose prostrate body France and Spain had struggled for the mastery. By the terms of the Treaty of Utrecht, the map was redrawn in the pattern to which it largely adhered, despite the interruptions of the Revolutionary and Napoleonic régimes, until the formation of the united kingdom in the years 1859 and 1860.

Without some understanding of this older Italy and the violent stresses to which it was being subjected during the childhood and youth of Antonio Panizzi, it is difficult, if not impossible, to

1*

comprehend fully the character and ways of thought of this remarkable man.

It must always be remembered that eighteenth-century Italy
was not one country, but several. If when he used the taunt
Metternich was cruelly wrong in describing Italy as a mere geo-
graphical term, fifty years earlier undoubtedly he would have been
right. There was little, if anything, in common, historically,
racially and even linguistically, between the superstitious, secre-
tive Neapolitan, the easy-going, art-loving Tuscan, the industrious,
litigious Lombard and the Venetian, whose lovely city was the
holiday capital of all Europe. To these must be added the wretched
inhabitants of the misgoverned Papal States and the subjects of the
smaller and even more provincially-minded petty princelings, such
as the d'Este family, for centuries the rulers of the tiny state of
Modena.

Throughout the countryside, an increasingly impoverished
and decadent nobility ruled over a sullen mass of ignorant and
illiterate peasantry, whose hovels and habits shocked even
eighteenth-century standards of hygiene. Only in the towns, and
particularly in those of the north, do we get the beginnings of an
educated middle class, with new aspirations and a new outlook on
the world around them, but, as yet, very small and powerless compared with the same classes in the old centralized monarchies
north of the Alps, and whose material circumstances and prospects
were still very modest.[3]

That such a class was able to come into existence at all was
largely due to the policy of the Hapsburg rulers of northern Italy.
They brought a new prosperity and order to the lands over which
they ruled in a spirit of enlightened and efficient autocracy. To an
increasing extent, authority there was being placed in the hands of
native-born Italians and the imperial example was followed by
other progressive rulers within the peninsula.[4]

The rest of Italy, particularly the Papal States, where even the
best intentioned Popes, such as Benedict XIV,[5] were completely
defeated by the combination of a particularly corrupt and impoverished nobility, clerical government and widespread disease
and abject poverty, remained untouched by these ideas. Indeed,
to a very large extent, the Italian people, strongly attached to their
local customs, everywhere returned to them gladly, as soon as an

Austrian or Spanish reformist prince gave up the legislation aimed at suppressing them.

The catalyst which was soon to resolve this problem was also to come from abroad, not from the bureaucrats of Vienna, but from the salons of Paris. French prestige, both literary and social, was as high in educated circles in Italy as elsewhere in Europe and among all men of any pretence to education French influence, both that of the *encyclopédistes* and, in clerical quarters, that of the Jansenists, was very strong.

Each little sovereign strove in his own way to emulate the glories of Versailles,[6] whilst among the emerging middle classes and the more enlightened members of the aristocracy, Voltaire, Diderot and many others were profoundly affecting the climate of opinion.

To these social, religious and literary influences was soon added another, more profound and perhaps more lasting on the course of Italian history. This was Freemasonry, brought to Italy in the wake of English noblemen doing the Grand Tour, and which soon spread widely in aristocratic circles. Towards the end of the century, it seems to have become increasingly middle class, less social and more political in its outlook. From 1789, if not before, Freemasonry became permeated with French revolutionary thought. The Lodges, which earlier had been social gatherings of a somewhat questionable nature, were now turned into 'clubs', on the French model, and began to serve as propaganda 'cells' for the Revolution.[7] But the influence of Freemasonry in Italy was limited by an important fact. It was never 'patriotic' and remained strongly francophil and non-nationalistic. As the effects of the French invasions and occupation became widely felt, its influence waned and its place was, to a large extent, taken by the new nationalistic societies, such as the *Carboneria* and its many derivatives. But this development was later, and on the eve of the revolution only Freemasonry existed in Italy as a ready-made channel for the new ideas. The exact relationship between Freemasonry and the *Carboneria*, even so late as Panizzi's youth, remains, however, involved and obscure, difficult, if not impossible to disentangle, both to contemporaries and to subsequent historians.

As the revolution apparently triumphed, the whole political map of Italy changed, as if by magic. In the wake of the French armies now pouring into Italy, new republics, almost overnight, sprang up like mushrooms. The ancient, oligarchical republic of Genoa became the Ligurian Republic; Reggio, Mantua and Bologna formed themselves into the Cispadane Republic; Milan, Brescia and other northern cities into the Transpadane. At the suggestion of the conqueror, Bonaparte, these last two petty republics combined and, provided with a constitution by their patron, formed the Cisalpine Republic. However, within eighteen months, these states were swept away by the triumph of the Austro-Russian armies, many of their supporters executed or hounded down by mobs, infuriated at the behaviour of the French armies and sadly disillusioned at the pillaging propensities of their liberators. Within a short while, all was as it had been, only to be once more overthrown by Napoleon's victorious return and the final expulsion of the Austrians from the greater part of the penin-sula in 1801. With the establishment of the Italian Republic, sub-sequently the Kingdom of Italy, all northern Italy entered upon that period of relative internal peace and tranquillity which marked Panizzi's boyhood.

This period, which lasted for some thirteen years, the whole of his boyhood and youth, gave to the most populous and most advanced areas of Italy a new experience and a new outlook, which vitally affected the minds of all thinking men of this and of the subsequent generation. For the first time, a large expanse of the country was under one ruler, with the same currency, the same laws and regulations. Instead of the old, indescribable muddle of traditional customs and privileges, varying from state to state, from the advanced, enlightened criminal code of Tuscany to the medieval horrors of Naples and the Papal States, there was one legal code, modern, fair and scientific. Modern systems of educa-tion were introduced, with new subjects and a new outlook, though in this field, too, improvements had been initiated, here and there, under the old dispensation. New industries and new industrial processes were being set up, making Milan and almost all the north, the centre of a growing prosperity. Above all, there was the feeling, widespread among the middle classes that, at last, there was a chance for them. With noble and clerical privileges abolished, the eager, thrusting new men, lawyers, doctors, business men and civil servants, felt that the century was theirs. They occupied most of the higher places in the civil administration, lately virtually closed to them, and their sons largely officered the new Italian armies that were fighting for the Emperor with great gallantry on distant fronts.

They might hate the French, as the lower classes certainly did, for their misconduct, their arrogance, their pillaging and looting and, with their new-found nationalism, resent the occupation of their country by any foreign power. But to Panizzi and his generation, looking back, this time seemed a golden age compared with the black reaction, the bitter disappointment that was to follow; the age in which the seeds of Italian nationalism took root and began to flourish. It is always particularly difficult for English people, a nation state for almost a thousand years, to fully appreciate the often misguided, yet deeply felt, nationalism of those countries, whose history has condemned them to long centuries of subjection and division. Yet without a sympathetic appreciation of these powerful emotions, we shall fail fully to understand such men as Panizzi and many like him, in this century as well as the last, to whom a fervent, deeply felt and conscious patriotism, together with an undying hatred of the oppressor, was one of the mainsprings of their existence. It was to be Panizzi's task to help make this plain to an often callous and indifferent English public, to enlighten the self-centred and prosperous mid-Victorian Englishman, as to what went on beyond the narrow confines of his own shores.

To many Italians, the French occupation, a heavy drain on the country, both in men and money, was, nevertheless, felt to be something external and alien to their true way of life. The essence of this feeling was crystallized in the secret societies which sprang up all over Italy, during the first decade of the century. Passionately anti-French, demanding the expulsion of all foreigners and the achievement of national unity under a constitution, the secret societies, especially the most powerful of them, the Carboneria, worked unceasingly against the French overlords. Off-shoots, for the most part, of the older Freemasonry, they were uncompromisingly political and nationalistic. The often, to us, almost comic mumbo-jumbo of their various initiation rites made a powerful appeal to the spirit of the age and no one who had undergone them, however halfheartedly, would be likely to forget the objects of the society: the freedom and union of all Italy. Although they directly affected comparatively few, they held fast to the idea of independence and spread that idea and all that it implied among every class. Realizing that there seemed to be little immediate hope of independence, they steadily undermined the administration, penetrating, even, into the highest ranks of the civil service and of the army, preparing for the day when the hated French would go.

Go they did and very suddenly. Brought down by the overthrow of the French Empire, the French administration collapsed almost overnight and few Italians rallied to its defence. But it was not the constitutional state of the nationalist's dreams that was to replace it, but the settlement imposed on a prostrate Italy by the Great Powers assembled at Vienna. The Grand Duchies and principalities were restored, Lombardy and Venice remained part of the Hapsburg Empire, and the old way of life, clerical and noble privileges, the antique codes of law, the multiplicity of customs and coinages, all the paraphernalia of the *ancien régime* was to be restored and the last twenty years were to be as if they had never been. It was in this time of bewildering change, of sudden reversals of fortune, that the young Panizzi grew to manhood. It had on him a most profound effect, which was to determine radically the course of his whole life and to influence his conduct, even into old age. To the end of his days, Panizzi never forgave the Austrians, who had imposed such a settlement upon his beloved Italy. To undo this work, he devoted his life. All else might alter, he might become, as he did, more English than the English; nothing dimmed his hatred of Austria and of her tyranny.

NOTES TO CHAPTER 1

1 It seems certain that Panizzi was born on September 16 and not on the following day. September 17, 1797, is given as his birthday in the obituary notice in *The Academy* of April 19, 1879: 'Antonio Panizzi . . . was born . . . on September 17, 1797, not on the 16th as is usually stated and, as until a very recent date, he himself believed.' The same date appears to have been inscribed on his coffin [*The Times*, April 14, 1879]. There seems to be no justification for this. It was certainly not known to the authorities of his native town, Brescello, since on April 16, 1872, they sent Panizzi birthday greetings, for which he duly thanked them. [Add. MS. 36, 725 ff. 490, 491.] The matter seems to be settled by an entry in the parish records of S. Maria Maggiore, Brescello, quoted by Friggeri, p. 63. 'Die 17 7bris 1797. Panizzi Antonius Genesius Maria natus heri a undecimi.' The following day the child was baptized, by special licence, at his parent's house. [See also the copy of the entry at Add. MS. 36, 714. f.1.]

2 October 17, 1797.

3 During the eighteenth century, the middle classes, even in mercantile Venice, were not reckoned as being more than one-fifth of the total population. Elsewhere, except possibly in Milan, it would have been a far smaller proportion.

4 Such were the Hapsburg Dukes of Tuscany, who had succeeded the last of the Medici. Similar reforms were attempted by Charles III of Naples and by the Este rulers of Modena.

5 Prospero Lambertini, 1675–1758. Pope from 1740 to 1758.

6 The Dukes of Modena, for instance, built the charming palace of Rivalta, celebrated for the brilliance of the receptions given there to visiting notables.

7 An example of the varied strains to be found in Italian Freemasonry of the period is shown in an illustration given in Dito, p. 168. Among the mythological personages and various symbols which decorate a diploma for the rank of Master in the Carbonari are the Instruments of the Passion and such republican emblems as the Fasces and the Cap of Liberty.

BOYHOOD AND YOUTH

PANIZZI was born in Brescello, a small town in the Duchy of Modena, which had long been the centre of the territory of the three communes of Brescello, Landbigione and Boretto. Each little town had its own *podesta*, or chief magistrate and its own municipal council and the three separate councils united to form a single general council for matters of common interest and for negotiations with the ducal governor of the district. In Brescello itself was the residence of the Governor, the legal and administrative departments and the archives of all these communities.

There lived, also, for obvious reasons, the lawyers and other professional men, who gradually came to occupy most of the positions of influence in the other two councils as well. So Brescello came to consider itself and, indeed, was so considered, as the capital of the little territory and through it flowed, for what it was worth, all the public, economic and intellectual life of the neighbourhood.

From its situation close to the crossings of the Po and as, moreover, the most remote territory of the Duchy, closer to Parma, and even to Mantua, than to its own capital of Modena, Brescello had always been favoured with particular attention by the Ducal Government, an interest which its inhabitants repaid by a reverent, almost obsequious attachment to the reigning house of Este.[1]

This loyalty was still widespread at the end of the eighteenth century and found expression in a genuine devotion to the native ducal family in the person of the reigning sovereign, Hercules III, a mild and benevolent autocrat, to whom Panizzi himself was later to pay tribute.[2]

The Este family had ruled them now for many centuries[3] and the loyal Brescellese saw no reason to change. So when, on September 3, 1796, a letter was received from the Senate of Reggio, urging them to unite with that town under the new republican régime, they spurned the offer with deep protestations of loyalty to the ducal family. But change they must! On November 20, 1796, two envoys arrived in Brescello from the Committee set up in Modena to organize the new government, suppressing the three former communes and establishing a single municipality for the whole area, in which the rival town of Boretto was to have the preponderant influence.

This municipality lasted until May 17, 1799, when the former podesta and council were restored by the Austrians, once more in possession of Modena. The Council, thereupon, recorded its delight at being liberated from a government, 'so heavy and troublesome',[4] by the victorious allied armies and offered to the Imperial Junta at Modena its most humble submission, respect and obedience.

But their modest triumph was short-lived. All too soon for them, Napoleon's shattering victories had in 1800 chased the Austrians and their allies once more out of northern Italy and Brescello reverted, most unwillingly, to the authority of the republican administration at Reggio. In September 1800 the old council was once more dismissed and a new and more radical municipal administration set up, in which, as before, the hated Boretto was made the dominant partner. It is not really surprising, therefore, that the worthy inhabitants of Brescello, despite their frequent protests of loyalty to the Italian Republic and to the subsequent Kingdom of Italy, remained singularly devoted to the memory of their old rulers and dreamed of revenge on upstart Boretto. To their delight, they saw their hopes at last fulfilled when the newly restored ducal authorities, by a decree of January 12, 1815, made their beloved little town a commune of the second class and, added joy, tacked on to it bits of Boretto itself and other nearby districts.

Panizzi's boyhood would have been filled with news and discussion of this jealous struggle between the two little towns. A loyal son of Brescello, he, too, would have hated the upstart citizens of Boretto and, with his elders, rejoiced to see the final triumph of his native town. Like most men, Panizzi always looked back with a certain nostalgia to his childhood days in little Brescello. His inability to see it again for so many years deeply grieved him and great was his joy when, at long last, he was able to revisit once more the haunts of his boyhood.

The Panizzi family had for several generations occupied an honoured, if modest place, in Brescello, as members of the tiny middle class of doctors, lawyers, lesser clergy and more prosperous tradesmen, which was slowly growing throughout the eighteenth century in northern Italy. It was, in many ways, a very humble middle class, sandwiched uneasily between the aristocracy, who filled all the higher positions in church and state, and many less elevated into the bargain, and the great mass of half-starved and ignorant peasantry. They were distinguished mostly from those classes above and below them by an assiduous devotion to work, simple tastes and an exemplary family life, virtues which were shared in full measure by young Antonio.

Our Panizzi's grandfather, another Antonio, after whom his grandson was presumably named, was a lawyer in modest circumstances, amongst whose ancestors were other lawyers, doctors and minor clerics. He had obtained a foothold in the local governing class by his marriage with Guilia Scardovi, of a family already wealthy and soon to be preponderant in the neighbourhood. Of this marriage was born, amongst several other children, a daughter Anna on April 10, 1745, and a son Luigi on March 27, 1764. Anna married, in 1765, Andrea Cugini, a minor bureaucrat and small landowner. The couple moved shoftly afterwards to Reggio, where they succeeded in bettering themselves. A clever and determined woman, on the death of her husband Anna Cugini obtained for herself and her two sons, Giuseppe and Sebastiano Cugini, the citizenship of Reggio.

Her elder son, Giuseppe, an ingenious and cultivated man, distinguished himself by his ardent and successful partisanship of each successive government, being Republican, Bonapartist and monarchist in turn. At length, this wily and amiable Vicar of Bray so captivated the restored Duke, that he was given high office in Reggio and, at length, ennobled, made podesta of this, the second city of the Duchy.[5] Giuseppe Cugini was an able man, a bold and resourceful politician, always at the centre of things, in close touch with the ruling circles of the little state, but always mindful of his mother's relatives, back in distant Brescello.

His young uncle, Luigi Panizzi, had married, on December 4, 1796, Caterina Gruppi, daughter of Dr Luigi Gruppi, another lawyer and prominent member of the communal council.[6] Almost alone in this very legal complex of closely related families, Luigi Panizzi was no lawyer but a pharmacist, whose house and shop was situated on a road which led from the main square of the little town down towards the embankments of the River Po.

To the young couple was born at Brescello, on September 16, 1797, their first child and only son. Antonio Genesio Maria. A second child, a daughter, Margherita, was born in 1802. Luigi Panizzi and his wife lived quietly at Brescello during these stormy years. Never very prosperous, Luigi seems to have been a modest, retiring man, without much drive or ambition, unlike his eldest sister or only son, quite content with his comparatively humble station in life, never moving or wanting to move far from his native town during the whole of his long life.[7]

The young Antonio, however, was a bright and promising lad, called 'Tognet',[8] an abbreviation of 'Antonio', by his family and friends and 'Orcion' or 'big ears' by less respectful playmates. He was soon at school, going first to a '*scuole di grammatica inferiore*', under a certain Don Pietro Panizzi, no close relative, Brescello being full of Panizzis, and, next, to the local high school or '*scuola di grammatica superiore*'. Clerical influence, despite the republican tendencies of recent years, was still strong in the lower strata of the educational system, and the young Panizzi, like all the other pupils, duly took his turn at serving at mass. He was already a most promising youngster. On May 19, 1810, the mayor of Boretto, as head of the local administration, transmitted to his superior, the prefect of the department of Crostolo, a report on the senior school at Brescello. In the 'humanities' class of Father Manfredi there were thirty-six pupils, of whom the top two were Giuseppe Levi-Minzi and Antonio Panizzi, his lifelong friend.

Panizzi was soon to move on. Already, on November 30, 1809, being just turned twelve, he had had his name put down for the '*ginnasio*' or grammar-school in Reggio and in the following

November, he went there, studying rhetoric under Angelo Fica-relli. Already his future career was planned for him. In his family of lawyers on both sides, any bright boy was destined for the legal profession. In these years of the Italian Republic and of the King-dom of Italy, more and more places were being filled in the government service by the up-and-coming middle classes. A clever lad, well grounded in the law, might go far, as his Cugini cousins were already demonstrating. Bonapartist Italy depended on the middle classes to officer its armies, to run its ever more complex bureaucracy and to administer its code of laws. In 1810, few could have foreseen that the whole position was so soon to change. Luigi and Caterina Panizzi must have had few doubts and have been prepared for any sacrifice to launch their only son on what promised to be a lucrative and influential career.

Antonio was now lodging at Reggio in the house of his cousin Giuseppe Cugini, so much older than he as to be regarded rather as an uncle. Cugini and his amiable wife, a Frenchwoman from Lyons, and their four young sons treated the boy as a member of the family, and made the years that Antonio spent there some of the happiest in his whole life.[9] The Cugini, as has been said, were somewhat higher in the social scale than the Panizzis and at their house, young Antonio first began to meet men and women of culture and influence, laying the foundations of those social graces which were in after years to stand him in such good stead. Giuseppe Cugini was fast working his way up the ladder, whilst his relative, Luigi Panizzi, tended to stay where he was, or even to sink downwards.

Antonio's close friend, young Levi-Minzi, another bright boy, from one of the several Jewish families at Brescello, had also accompanied him to Reggio, and both were soon distinguishing themselves. All Panizzi's reports were endorsed 'colla massima assiduata'.[10] Successes came to him in the logic and moral philo-sophy classes and, in the following year, 1813, he obtained addi-tional distinctions in literature and history. He was undoubtedly fulfilling all the hopes and expectations of his fond parents.

Contrary to what was believed by Louis Fagan, Panizzi's first biographer, his professor of rhetoric at Reggio was not Gaetano Fantuzzi, but, as we have seen, Angelo Ficarelli.[11] Fantuzzi had indeed been professor of rhetoric in 1806, but during the years

Panizzi was at Reggio, he has been forced on medical grounds to give up teaching, and had occupied himself exclusively with the communal library. Fantuzzi was a devoted librarian, putting the library, which had been badly neglected, in order and adding greatly to its contents. Young Panizzi went there constantly and became very friendly with its custodian. He now had his first initiation into what was to be his life's work, and, in later years, affectionately recalled the man who had first introduced him to the world of books.

But school days and the happy years in the Cugini household were now drawing to a close. In 1814, that fateful year for Italy, the young man, now aged 17, entered the University of Parma. Much has been made of Panizzi going there, rather than to Modena and it has even been regarded as a deliberate slight to the new régime and a reason for Duke Francis' subsequent hostility. But quite apart from the extreme improbability of the highly re- spectable Panizzi family doing anything so unlikely as to flaunt deliberately established authority, or for the new ducal govern- ment, in its first months of power, to have any knowledge of so petty a matter, it was very much the usual thing for those citizens of Brescello who succeeded in obtaining higher education, to go to nearby Parma, rather than to distant Modena. It must be remem- bered that Brescello and its neighbourhood formed a Modenese enclave in what was otherwise Parmese territory. With a good horse, one could be in Parma in about two and a half hours, little more time than it took to get to Reggio, whilst it took more than half a day to reach Modena, where the ducal university was situa- ted. The Brescellese had always frequented Parma, which to them had always had a certain elegance and refinement not to be found in their own capital. The conditions of the last few years, with frontiers and passports swept away, had encouraged that tendency and, even though Parma was now once more 'foreign' territory, there seemed no reason to change. Luigi Panizzi would have considered it perfectly natural to send his promising young son to a university which had always had a fine academic reputation and which had been recently reopened after being closed for some years by the French.

Doubtless, young Antonio looked forward more to going to Parma, already regarded by many as dangerously 'liberal', rather than to stuffy and reactionary Modena, but it is not likely that such considerations ever entered his father's head.

The year 1814 had been one of many changes, changes which were to affect the whole course of Antonio Panizzi's life and which, even at that time, with his strange future unknown to him, must have stimulated and appalled a clever, high-spirited youth of seventeen. For in the short space of a few months, the political scene, which Panizzi had known since childhood, in the midst of which he had grown up, and which must have seemed to him immutable (as the background to one's daily life always does especially to the young) had dissolved, and a new and to many, including Panizzi himself, strange and repellent way of life had taken its place. At the beginning of 1812, halfway through Panizzi's years at Reggio, the Napoleonic Kingdom of Italy must have seemed as if it would endure, if not for ever, at least, for many decades. Its titular king, Napoleon, was married to the daughter of the Austrian Emperor and Europe seemed to be at his feet. Within a few months, all had gone. The Russian campaign, in which Italian troops had fought bravely and well, had destroyed the veteran armies, and the battles of 1813 and early 1814 in Germany and along the French frontiers had clearly shown that the end of the Napoleonic dream of a united Europe, under French hegemony, could not be far off.

In Italy, the Viceroy, Napoleon's stepson, Eugène Beauharnais, did what he could, but, undermined by Carbonarism and indifference, the régime collapsed. Italian public opinion was weak and divided, and there were no generally accepted Italian candidates for the vacant throne. Neither Beauharnais himself nor Murat, King of Naples, were regarded as suitable by more than a small minority. Riots at Milan between the rival factions gave Austria an excuse for action. Marshal Bellegarde, the Austrian Commander-in-Chief, was ordered to occupy the city and Italy's fate as an independent nation was sealed.

To the statesmen of Europe meeting at Vienna, Italy was of secondary importance, an area in which Austria might be compensated for losses elsewhere. Although not successful in getting all she desired, Austria's gains were immense. Lombardy, the heart of the 'Kingdom of Italy' and the most progressive province, and Venetia, the old Republic of Venice and its outlying territories, were formally incorporated in the Hapsburg Empire. Tuscany, Modena and Parma were granted or returned to members of that house, whilst Austria considered that, within these minor states, she was the mistress of the lives and property of all Italians.

In almost every territory, however, the new rulers were enthusiastically welcomed. To many, they stood for peace, a return to the old ways – of powerful appeal to a largely peasant population – an end to the salt tax and to the hated conscription. Their shortcomings were not at once apparent, and all, even the most liberal, hoped for the best.

Not least was this so in the little Duchy of Modena, where there had always been a strong feeling of loyalty towards the former dynasty. Its most recent sovereigns had been, on the whole, just and progressive rulers and the new-fangled 'French' ways were regarded, not only at Brescello, with widespread suspicion and hostility. Their Duke was Francis IV, the first of the Austro-Este dynasty, generally held to be the most able and ambitious of the new rulers. These characteristics he seems to have inherited from his mother, sole surviving child of Duke Hercules III, who had been married off to one of the numerous sons of the Empress Maria Teresa. The young Archduke Francis had spent the war years travelling in the Balkans and the Near East, where he had vainly endeavoured to stir up a local rising against the French, and in trying to induce the British authorities to back his claim to the throne of Italy, a claim in which his mother in Vienna had singularly failed to interest the all-powerful Metternich.

The new Duke's arrival at Modena, on July 15, 1814, was hailed with fireworks and the usual adulatory verses, which were repeated when on July 27 he paid his first visit to Reggio, the second city of his dominions. Panizzi, just finished with his studies there, and about to start at Parma the following November, must have seen something of the celebrations; the professors at his late school addressing their Prince in terms of the most gross flattery; the triumphal arch; the Podesta offering the Duke the keys of the city; the little girls of good family, dressed in white, scattering flowers before the ducal party, and everywhere the cheering crowds. His Cugini cousins, their republican and Bonapartist past conveniently forgotten, were warmly attached to the new régime.

Giuseppe, in particular, was now embarked on that career which was soon to lead him to high office,

But to an ardent young patriot, like Panizzi, and one with ambitions in the law, there were already some discordant notes in the chorus. By a proclamation of August 28, 1814, the Duke had decided to liberate his subjects from a code foreign to their customs and 'contrary, in every part, to the public interests of the state, to the well-being of family life and to the maxims of our holy Catholic religion', that is, from the Napoleonic Code, which had, for the first time, given them a just, equable and modern legal system. Also announced was a return to the earlier laws, particularly to the *Codici do leggi e costituzioni* of 1771, known as the *Codici Estese*. Francis had already abolished civil marriage and certain laws regarding ecclesiastical benefices. Only a few years later, Panizzi was to declare, in no uncertain terms, his hatred of and contempt for this act, which set back the clock for, at least, a generation and deprived the Modenese, at a critical moment, of the protection of a code of law in which they could trust.

In August 1814, also, came the first of a series of anti-semitic decrees designed for the purpose of sending the Jews back to the ghetto and laying upon them heavy and invidious restrictions. These, too, must have infuriated Panizzi, for not only was he always violently opposed to any act which threatened individual liberties, but, moreover, his closest friend, Levi-Minzi, was a Jew.

But, for the moment, from November 1814 onwards, Panizzi was living in the freer and more liberal air of neighbouring Parma. The victorious powers had allotted this tiny Duchy to the young ex-Empress Marie Louise, daughter of the Austrian Emperor and wife of the fallen Napoleon. Parma had in addition during the late régime been formally joined to metropolitan France and had thus come under French influence more directly than most of northern Italy. Marie Louise, too, was a mild and benevolent ruler, far too mild in the opinion of her fellow sovereigns, especially in that of her former suitor and now near neighbour, Francis IV. She had little real interest in government, preferring to leave such matters to her favourite, Count Neipperg, who, on the whole, ruled justly and wisely in her name.

Panizzi greatly enjoyed his years at Parma. The town was a lively, bustling place, after Reggio and little Brescello. He was making new friends of a type and class he had rarely met before: Claudio Linati, a young aristocrat and soldier, Dr Martini and two other soldiers, Captain Antonio Bacchi and Major Ambrogio Berchet, all of them veterans of Napoleon's campaigns and all hating the new order of things. All were *independista* or 'liberals', as indeed, by now, was Panizzi. But the young Antonio did not neglect his studies and was soon regarded as a most promising student.

During these years, he became, moreover, very friendly with Angelo Pezzana, librarian of the Biblioteca Parmense. This worthy man, who must be considered as one of the principal formative influences on the mind of the young Panizzi, was a learned and enterprising librarian. He had recently acquired for his library many fine books, both ancient and modern, and was particularly good at inducing the Duchess to grant him the necessary funds. Still comparatively young himself, he delighted in having young people about him. He took a particular fancy to Panizzi, showed to him all the treasures of his well-stocked library, teaching him many things about fine printing and the delights of bibliography. Above all, he encouraged in the young man a love of books and an appreciation of what true librarianship really meant. The future Keeper of Printed Books and Principal Librarian of the British Museum indeed owed much to the skill, knowledge and enthusiasm of Angelo Pezzana.[12]

It would seem to be, most probably, that it was at this time that Panizzi became a member, if not of the Carboneria itself, an association which he, in later years, always strongly denied, at least of some other secret society, devoted to the cause of Italian freedom.[13] As we have seen, Carbonarism had developed as a counterblast to the older masonic societies, which were regarded as too tainted with French influence and not sufficiently nationalistic. It was strongest in Naples and the south generally and was throughout its existence a typical 'southern' movement, with obvious affinities with the later Mafia.

In the north, however, the secret societies that were beginning to take shape in the Duchies of Parma and Modena seem to have derived from various Piedmontese bodies, which, if not properly 'masons' in the full sense of the term, were at least 'masonic' in inspiration. The society of which Panizzi was almost certainly a member appears to have been formed round about 1819 to 1820 of a fusion of two or more of these organizations. It was known as the *Sublimi Maestri Perfetti*. The first 'church' seems to have been set up in Reggio, followed by a second at Parma in 1819 and then a third in Modena. As with the true Carboneria of southern Italy, its political goal was to give liberty, unity and independence to the Italian peoples and to expel all foreigners. In some respects, the *Sublimi Maestri* were a more radical body than even the Carbonari themselves. According to some, it was to exist for the express purpose of becoming a superior directing body, controlling all the secret societies, not only in Italy, but throughout Europe, and to urge them towards a more revolutionary and extremist policy.

Panizzi seems to have been one of the earliest to be initiated into this society, although his youth would have prevented him from being reckoned among the leaders of the new movement. The government of Parma, on the whole, was content to turn a blind eye towards the activities of the secret societies, unless prodded into some sort of action by the Austrian or Modenese authorities. Panizzi, now in his final year at the university, would have, therefore, seen very little risk in joining the *Sublimi Maestri*. To him, it was a step towards the supreme object of all these ardent and patriotic young men, the overthrow of the hated Austrians and of the régimes supported only by their bayonets.

At last, on August 8, 1818, Panizzi took his degree in jurisprudence and was henceforth entitled to call himself 'Doctor'.[14] He had now to earn a living and support his family, a task which his poor father, Luigi, seemed increasingly incapable of doing.

NOTES TO CHAPTER 2

1 When Panizzi visited the district in 1859 he found that this once wide-spread spirit of loyalty to the ducal house had long since vanished. [Add. MS. 44, 274. f.185.]

2 'Ercole III d'Este veggente sovrano . . . aveva apertamente e generosa-mente protetti gli studi d'ogni maniera.' [*Dei Processi*, p. 15.]

3 The house of Este was one of the oldest of the Italian reigning houses. The family had ruled continuously in Modena since 1527.

4 Statement of the Commune of Brescello to the Imperial Governing Junta at Modena, May 18, 1799. [Quoted in Bacchi, p. 11.]

5 Giuseppe Cugini was created a Councellor and Inspector of the Ducal Palace at Reggio on May 14, 1816; on December 17, 1816, Podesta of Reggio, which office he held to his death on January 23, 1823. Cugini was granted the distinction and title of *nobile di Reggio* on June 18, 1819, and subsequently the title was made hereditary. He had four sons, of whom the second, Emilio, became Bishop of Modena and the third, Prospero, was the lifelong friend and correspondent of his cousin, Antonio Panizzi. [Bacchi, p. 40.]

6 Caterina Gruppi's brother, Ferdinando, was a delegate to the Grand Council of the Cisalpine Republic and one of the two '*maggiorenti*' or prin-cipal officials of Brescello, where he died on April 21, 1813. [Bacchi, p. 16.]

7 Luigi Panizzi died on July 5, 1845, aged 81. His daughter, Margherita, married on October 17, 1825, Giuseppe Venturini of Gaetana. Many years later, Antonio Panizzi attempted to assist their son, Adolfo, a government employee, to secure a transfer to a better situation. [Bacchi, pp. 40, 41; Add. MS. 36, 724. f.47.]

8 Panizzi does not seem to have used this nickname much, except when corresponding with the Cugini family and other friends of his youth. He preferred 'Pan', an affectionate contraction of his surname.

9 Panizzi always remembered with gratitude the kindness he had received, as a boy, from Giuseppe Cugini and his wife, Sofia. In a letter of April 18, 1836, to their son Prospero, he wrote: 'To your lady mother say many things on my behalf and, in particular, tell her . . . of my feelings of respect and deep gratitude.' In a subsequent letter of August 30, 1845, to Prospero Cugini's wife, he wrote, 'I have had the extreme pleasure of making the acquaintance of the wife of one to whose father and mother I owe so much.' [Bacchi, p. 40.]

27

10 Atti de Liceo, 1810–11. November 8, 9, 1811. [Bacchi, p. 41.]

11 Angelo Ficarelli became subsequently Bishop of Reggio. In 1822 he braved the wrath of Duke Francis by pleading for the life of the young priest, Andreoli, and refused to unfrock him in order that he might be executed by the civil power.

12 Panizzi was always grateful to Pezzana and the other 'illustrious men', whom he met in Parma, who, 'young as I was did not disdain to honour me with their friendship and to instruct me, not by sterile precepts but by living examples.' Pezzana and his former protegé maintained a lively correspondence, mostly on bibliographical questions, for many years. [Boselli, p. 5.]

13 The exact relationship of these various secret societies to one another is still obscure, as are details of their aims and origins. The latest writer on the subject, R. J. Rath, concludes that the Carbonari derived from various earlier Masonic bodies and may be considered as a society of popular and liberal Freemasons, with the primary intention of arousing the uneducated masses against the French. Subsequently, they had as their principal objective the unity and independence of the Italian people and the expulsion of all foreigners. In the north, the *Sublimi Maestri Perfetti* seem to have fulfilled many of the functions of the Carboneria and acted as some sort of link between it and the Freemasons. It would seem to be almost certain that it was to this body that Panizzi belonged. He might, therefore, deny that he was, in fact, a Carbonaro and, yet, as a member of a higher order, admit novices into the more popular society.

14 In England, Panizzi never used the prefix. 'I now am divorced from Justinian and so mine is but an empty title, like that of King of Cyprus and Jerusalem taken by so many sovereigns at whom I take the liberty to laugh.' [*University College MSS*, no. 940.]

3

THE ANXIOUS YEARS

BACK home in Brescello, a fully fledged lawyer, scarcely a month had gone by when Panizzi was striken down by a severe attack of typhoid, at that date a most serious illness. For a while, his life was despaired of, but, thanks to his robust constitution, he soon recovered and started his legal practice in a room of his father's house. Panizzi in his early twenties was a striking figure, good-looking, tall and slim. In Berchet's sketch of him, made about this time, he looks a stern, somewhat humourless, young man, yet he was already renowned for his good company and love of parties. Equally remarked on was his incredible application for study, always reading, even, as was said of him a little later, when on his way from his father's house to his office. As in later years, his temper was at times uncertain and he never suffered fools gladly, but already his powers of judgement and clarity of thought were respected by all those that knew him.

Even before Panizzi had qualified, the Podesta of Brescello, Giuseppe Conti, in a letter of June 28, 1818 to the authorities at Reggio, had warmly recommended the young man for a post in the fiduciary service. On account, presumably, of his youth and lack of experience, he failed to obtain it, but helped, no doubt, by the growing influence of his cousin, Giuseppe Cugini, by now himself Podesta of Reggio and a man of note in government circles, and by his own increasing reputation as an up-and-coming young lawyer, he was on January 1, 1819, nominated *Amministratore del Comune di Brescello e della Congregazione di Carita* and shortly afterwards *Giudice dell'Annona*. It is difficult to define these various posts in equivalent English terms, but, very roughly, 'Town Clerk' and 'Inspector of Weights and Measures' gives some idea of their scope and importance.

Panizzi was also in private practice. His very first brief, which he won, incidentally, was concerning a dispute among several local smallholders and shortly after, his native town secured his services for a complicated case, dealing with the levels of certain islands in the River Po. This was judged before the courts at Modena and the young lawyer seems to have acquitted himself well. The authorities appear to have been impressed by this capable and talented young man and a bright future was forecast for him.

Panizzi had been most fortunate in now being befriended by the distinguished lawyer, Filippo Cocchi. Cocchi, a close friend of Giuseppe Cugini, had possibly met Antonio when he was living in his cousin's house at Reggio. On the young man himself becoming a lawyer, Cocchi had given him certain briefs and had chosen him to be his assistant in several important cases. Filippo Cocchi was very much the man of the moment. Comparatively young, only, in fact, ten years older than Panizzi, he had joined, in 1806, the government administration at Reggio and had quickly distinguished himself in both civil and criminal cases. By 1813, he had risen to the position of procurator and his future seemed assured. A few months later, on the fall of the kingdom, he had quickly perceived that the new régime, sadly lacking in men of ability, could make use of his great talents, both as a lawyer and as an administrator. By a mixture of obsequious flattery of the ducal government and by widely proclaiming his newly discovered religious beliefs and hatred of the former authorities, Cocchi successfully achieved the not too difficult task of transferring his loyalty to their successors. In this he was helped by a widespread recognition of his undoubted merits. He had his rewards. By a judicious mixture of flattery and skill, he succeeded in winning the confidence of the new men, particularly of Giuseppe Cugini, whose daughter he married and of Count Moretti, a personal friend of Francis IV, by means of whom he soon succeeded in becoming on intimate terms with the sovereign himself. In his heart, Cocchi may well have retained many of his former ideals. Henceforth, in public, he was to be the resolute and implacable servant of the Duke. During the next thirty years, he held a number of increasingly important legal posts, until at last in 1855 he became Minister of Justice, a post he held until the fall of the ducal government in June 1859. He died quietly on August 12, 1860 in his house at Reggio, surviving for little more than a year the régime he had served so long and so faithfully.

Despite their profound political differences, Panizzi always remembered in terms of the warmest affection his 'caro dr. Cocchi', longing to see him once again. He was deeply grieved when, at last, in 1860, he was told of the death of his old friend and benefactor. Cocchi, himself a basically kind and honest man, ready to intercede with the Duke for mercy on behalf of the victims of the harsh system he had to administer, always loved and admired his young colleague, whom, to a great extent, he had initiated into the legal profession and who, in the dangerous days to come, he protected and whose very life he may well have saved.

But this was then still all in the future. Thanks to the friendship of Cocchi and Cugini and to his own abilities, which had already been brought to the notice of Duke Francis, Panizzi seemed all set for a brilliant career in the highest government circles within the Duchy. But it was not to be his fate to spend his life in the narrow world of provincial Italy. Panizzi, always a man of essential probity, already had doubts and was deeply troubled in his mind. By his new appointments and by his friendship with Cocchi, Cugini and their circle, he had publicly adhered to that party, which was devoted to the Austro-Este family and which had, in consequence, a vested interest in the maintenance of absolutism and all that it entailed.

In the twentieth century, we have, unfortunately, a far better idea than had the Victorians as to what crises of conscience, what personal bitterness and frustration, can come to a man of liberal outlook, forced by circumstances to spend his life in the service of an arbitrary and tyrannical despotism. For Panizzi, like many another man in these circumstances, was now leading a double and dangerous life. In the public eye, he was a rising young lawyer, with powerful friends; a hard-working civil servant and a devoted follower of the reigning monarch. He himself knew that he was already an active member of a secret, and soon to be proscribed organization. To his house in Brescello, so conveniently close to the borders of Parma, now came many of his old university friends, all ardent patriots and conspirators, amongst whom were several well known to be Carbonari. Contact with his fellow revolutionaries was made still easier by the continuous coming and going through Brescello of many bound for the little district of Guastella, a detached portion of the Duchy, from which the quickest way to Parma was through Panizzi's native town.

Panizzi felt his difficult position, his divided loyalties, so keenly, that he took in June 1819, not six months after receiving his appointment, the dangerous step of writing personally to Duke Francis himself. In his letter, he begs his sovereign to relieve him of his functions as Administrator of the Commune and of his other offices. As an excuse, he pleads his own poverty and that of his father, the ill-health of both his parents, and his position as the only son, the mainstay of his family, which he can only hope to support by the constant exercise of his profession. His work as Administrator hampers his further study and so greatly impedes his progress in the law and gives him insufficient time for more lucrative private practice.[1]

All his pleadings and flattery of his royal master were largely in vain. The Duke recognized some force in Panizzi's arguments and agreed to relieve him of his duties in connection with the *Congregazione di Carità*. However, he must remain as *Amministratore communale* and the decision was communicated to the Governor of Reggio, to the Podesta of Brescello and so down to Panizzi himself. So ended the young lawyer's attempt to escape from the almost intolerable dilemma, in which, like so many others, he now found himself.

But with the natural resilience of youth, Panizzi seems to have decided to make the best of the situation. He threw himself with redoubled vigour into his official duties and own legal practice, while still keeping up his contacts with his liberal friends in Parma and elsewhere. He had, in addition, now been named as Inspector of the Public Schools in Brescello, a duty which he undertook with marked enthusiasm.[2] Despite the mental and physical strain of the double life he was now leading, Panizzi may well have thought he would be able to succeed in concealing from the government all trace of his secret political activities. After all, it was his public life, as a member of the ruling classes, as a fervent adherent of established authority, that really mattered. What he chose to do in his private life must have seemed to him to be his own concern and that of no one else.

But Panizzi was no longer living, as in his university days, under the mild and benevolent rule of the Duchess Marie Louise. He was living in one of those states that had long ago excited the scorn of Montesquieu, who declared, 'I would not be a subject of one of these petty princes for anything in the world.' He was, too, a subject of Duke Francis IV, a man, almost pathologically suspicious of new ideas, and whose hatred for the principles of the French Revolution, and of the secret societies that upheld them, was deep-seated and fundamental.

Still, had things gone on quietly, with the liberals dreaming of unity and liberty, joining societies, but doing little else to bring about the promised millennium, all might have been well. The government was growing more confident and less nervous, as Napoleon lived out his last years of exile in distant St Helena and absolutism seemed everywhere to be triumphant. Panizzi was careful, discreet and supremely confident of his ability to deceive the authorities. On his frequent journeys to Reggio and to Modena, he was always prudent and circumspect, both in speech and action. He passed his time in the company of such 'safe' men as Cugini and Cocchi, giving the secret police no possible reason to suspect him of treasonable activities. Home, in Brescello, it was ostensibly the same. The young Dr Panizzi was a respected citizen, devoted to the ducal cause and zealous, some thought over-zealous, in the performance of his official duties.

But behind this façade, this public life into which he threw so much of his superabundant energies, he lived another and very different existence. Some time early in March 1820, he had, it seems, been finally initiated into one of the highest grades of the *Sublimi Maestri Perfetti*,[3] probably by one of his friends from Parma, whom he used to meet almost every day at the Golden Lion at Brescello. His old friend Linati and new acquaintances, such as Guglielmo Borelli and Pietro Gisia, secretary of the Piacenza Chamber of Commerce, were frequent visitors and here, at the neighbouring Café Volta and at the houses of such good friends as Montani and Levi-Minzi, his companion now for many years. He could relax, admiring the peasant girls as they walked through the dusty piazza, pay discreet court to more well-brought-up young ladies in Brescello or Reggio, or, with due care and only amid those whom he could trust, talk far into the night, planning how they would achieve their dream of a free and united Italy.

The *Sublimi Maestri* had become a channel, by means of which the new ideas from the south might reach the northern lands and become more widely known. The secret societies, largely dormant since 1814, were now stirring. They had plans for establishing a strong and centralized monarchy in northern Italy. Even Francis IV began to take an interest in these matters and saw himself as the ruler of a powerful kingdom, rather than that of a petty duchy. For all over the peninsula things were getting rapidly worse. Backed by Metternich, the new governments asserted their power. The honeymoon, such as it was, was almost over. The Church was once more in a position of great authority, especially in educational circles. A student, in Reggio itself, had been sent to prison for forty days for a satire on the Jesuits and more prosecutions were threatened. Above all, economic conditions were deteriorating. Poverty was widespread and brigandage once more, as in the eighteenth century, an ever-present menace on the roads. This was so, not only in the turbulent, untamed south, but also in the more settled north. Both the mail and private travellers were waylaid and robbed, even in the Austrian dominions. The roads between Florence and Rome were so infested by brigands that in 1817 travellers were forced to go by the Adriatic route.[4]

In the midst of this rumbling discontent and dissatisfaction, the news from Naples fell like a bombshell. Naples, the most backward, the most reactionary of Italian states, whose short-lived Parthenopian Republic had been swept away in bloodshed years before, had revolted and the Carbonari were masters of the army, of the government and of the person of their wily old monarch, Ferdinand.

Throughout Italy, the effect of this coup was sudden and dramatic. Gabriele Rossetti,[5] bard of the Carbonari, chanted: 'In the balmy garden of Italy, bondage is no more,' whilst a more cynical, but doubtless more realistic, view was expressed by the Austrian minister, who considered that a revolution might rather have been expected in the moon than in Naples. In the north, the news, particularly that King Ferdinand had, on July 13, taken the oath to the constitution, was hailed, according to taste, either as a triumph of enlightened progress or else as a return to the worst excesses of the French Revolution. Francis IV of Modena, at any rate in public, had no doubts at all.[6] Whatever his secret hopes and plans may have been to succeed his father-in-law on the throne of Piedmont or to play at being a constitutional king of a united northern Italy, his reaction to the news of the revolt in the south was unmistakable. If only to hide from Metternich his own recent flirting with 'liberalism', the Duke, fired, too, with his quite genuine and deeply felt hatred for the principles of the Revolution, decided to crush without mercy any incipient carbonarism within his own dominions.

On September 20, 1820, Francis declared war on the societies. By a decree issued on that date, it was clearly laid down that membership of any society, such as the Carbonari or any other, constituted the felony of '*lèse-majesté*', conviction for which automatically carried the death penalty.[7]

But for the moment, he contented himself with comparatively few arrests. The Neapolitan revolt, condemned by the great powers, collapsed before the might of the Austrian army and the despots could breathe again. To Panizzi, however, the failure of the Neapolitan rising and the subsequent triumph of reaction was a bitter blow. With his customary enthusiasm, he had been recently engaged in breathing new life into the tiny masonic cell, which maintained a precarious existence in Brescello. Composed of a handful of minor communal officials and such-like, it had been in existence for some years, but its members were timid and cautious, fearful of drawing upon themselves the attention of the police.

Panizzi now succeeded in persuading three of its members, Alberici, Nizzoli and Cavandoli, to assist him with his secret Carbonari activities, though, with his customary discretion, only whilst at Parma. In Brescello itself, he dared only to initiate into the mysteries those whom he considered he could trust absolutely, his childhood friend and schoolmate, Giuseppe Minzi, his cousins, Francesco and Bartolomeo Panizzi, and one other close acquaintance. As an added precaution, he performed the necessary rites in his own house, and, indeed, in his own room, feeling, no doubt, that a small gathering there of men, either closely related or with personal or professional connections, would seem perfectly normal, and not arouse unnecessary suspicions.

For things were undoubtedly getting worse and more difficult, and it was every day harder for him to live his double life, and to contain, within himself, his true feelings and aspirations. And now a series of events was to take place, which was to shatter for ever the pattern of his old way of life.

At the beginning of 1821, some Hungarian troops, sent south to help suppress the Neapolitan uprising, were quartered in Modena. The local Carbonari decided to appeal to these troops not to fight against the Neapolitans, like themselves, victims of the same Austrian oppressor. They produced, therefore, a proclamation in Latin, a language which all educated Hungarians were supposed to be able to read, calling on the soldiers to mutiny and to refuse to fight against the Neapolitan revolution.

Whatever the effect of this manifesto on the Hungarians, and, as far as we know, it had none, its effect on the Duke was unmistakable. No doubt fearful of any Austrian suspicion of his own complicity in the matter, he fell savagely upon the patriotic organizations. Not only those persons suspected of having produced the pamphlet, but even those who admitted having read it or, even, of knowing what it contained, rendered themselves liable to immediate arrest. A large number of suspects, many of them palpably innocent, were quickly rounded up and incarcerated in the ducal prisons.

The new and dreaded head of the secret police, Besini, directed this reign of terror. Panizzi instances the case of a young boy of eighteen, imprisoned for two months amongst the worst types of murderers and other hardened criminals, without any charge at all ever being brought against him and there must have been many similar incidents.

The atmosphere, in both Modena and Reggio and throughout every town and village in the Duchy, was tense and heavy with menace. In March came news of the Piedmontese uprising, followed all too soon by the announcement of its disastrous failure. This was the signal for a new wave of arrests. Panizzi, as we have seen, had recently been appointed Inspector of Schools for Brescello, it was said on the personal initiative of Duke Francis himself. This move may well have been at the instigation of Cocchi, an attempt to bind even more tightly the brilliant young lawyer to the ducal cause. Panizzi, too, had personal worries, as well as the ever-present threat of arrest and imprisonment. He had recently lost his mother and the strain of looking after his young sister and his feckless father was immense.

As throughout the rest of the Duchy, feeling was now running high between those who blindly supported the government and those whose hopes were pinned on some form of constitutional change. Police spies were everywhere. The activities, moreover, of the Urbani, a locally raised militia, recruited from those known to be devoted to the cause of absolutism, were particularly obnoxious to Panizzi. He, rashly, castigated their doings, with ill-concealed contempt and, in turn, aroused the dislike and suspicion of these worthy upholders of law and order.[8]

Nevertheless, the young man still carried on, to the world, a devoted and hard-working public servant. He hoped for the best, but was increasingly less confident of his ability to survive these difficult days. For now arrests were being made with terrifying frequency, if merely to keep alive the prevailing atmosphere of anxiety and fear. Distinguished men were arrested in the theatre, in the streets, anywhere, often for the sole reason that they were considered to be suspected freemasons. The police, inspired by the example of Besini, were behaving with increasing brutality, both towards their victims themselves and towards their unfortunate families. By virtue of the 'sovereign will and pleasure' of Duke Francis, on March 14, 1821 a special tribunal had been set up to try all political offenders. Besini saw to it that it would not lack for clients. Under the restored Code of 1771, so bitterly attacked by Panizzi, the maxims of an outdated system of canon and civil law could always be introduced during the trial, at the discretion of the presiding judge alone, a system which was, at times, a complete denial of any form of justice to the poor wretches brought before the courts.

Already some of Panizzi's friends had been arrested, but suddenly the threat came nearer. One morning early in 1822, Conti, the Podesta of Brescello, received a visit from a troop of dragoons from Reggio. The officer in command handed the Podesta a sealed dispatch, with the inscription, 'Not to be opened, except in the presence of the Secretary of the Commune'. This was Alberici, the very man who knew the secret of all Panizzi's political activities. Alberici was summoned to the Podesta and the envelope opened. Inside was an order arresting Alberici himself, together with Nizzoli and Cavandoli, other members of the tiny masonic lodge at Brescello. Straight away, the unfortunate Alberici was carried off to Modena, to await the tender mercies of Besini, the other two men being rounded up four days later.

Panizzi was now consumed with anxiety. Would it not be better to flee at once, as his friend Linati had already done, rather than stay to face the now almost inevitable arrest? But where would he find refuge? The frontiers with Parma were closely watched. To go south into the Papal States was worse than useless and to cross the Po and go north, into Austrian territory, would be an extremely hazardous undertaking, a risk only to be run if all else failed.

So, for the moment, Panizzi decided to stay where he was to carry on with his official duties and to hope for the best. With his usual thoroughness, he took his precautions. Thanks to the good offices of his friend the Podesta, he had experienced no difficulty in renewing his passports, vital documents for any successful attempt to escape. In his application, Conti had taken care to stress Panizzi's position as a government official, his constant need, therefore, to cross and recross the frontiers for professional purposes and the importance to him of being able to visit freely such places as Parma, Guastella and Cremona.

Panizzi, both as a lawyer and as a patriot, was more and more scandalized by what was going on at Modena. The prisoners were now subject to frequent torture and were being tricked or frightened into making true or false confessions. Such confessions were, by a special ducal decree, judged acceptable to be received as evidence by the Tribunal. After having finished his inquiries, the infamous Besini, by another decree, was himself made a member of the Tribunal itself. He was thus able to have presented before him, as judge, sworn evidence, which he himself, as chief of police, had had extracted from the accused by torture or by other improper means. To Panizzi, and to all men of moderate opinions, this seemed a most monstrous act of injustice and tyranny.

But Besini was never to try his wretched victims. On the evening of May 14, while the hated Chief of Police, accompanied only by a secretary, was walking home, a man suddenly appeared, threw Besini to the ground, lifted up a corner of his coat, stabbed the Chief of Police with a stiletto and fled, leaving the knife sticking in the wound. None of the bystanders attempted to hinder the assassin, as he made his escape through the crowd. Within a few hours, Besini was dead, having indicated as his possible murderer a certain Ponzoni, who was known to hate him. (So, said Panizzi, did everyone else throughout the Duchy!) Despite the strong doubts of the examining magistrate, who took down Besini's dying accusations, the unfortunate Ponzoni was immediately arrested, and sent for trial. The circumstantial evidence offered by the prosecution, however, was so feeble and Ponzoni was able to produce so perfect an alibi for the time of the murder, that even the obsequious Tribunal felt unable to convict him. Nevertheless, the furious and implacable Duke would not permit the Court, even in these circumstances, to find Ponzoni not guilty and the wretched man was sent back to prison, where he remained until released in 1831. The real assassin proved to be a certain Morandi who, safely in London, openly avowed his responsibility for the deed.

Francis was out for vengeance. Infuriated by the murder of his trusty Besini and by the dilatory conduct of the trials of suspected Carbonari then proceeding in neighbouring Parma, the Duke determined on a vigorous counter-blow. Fortified, no doubt, by the presence of 1,000 Austrian soldiers, he made up his mind to hold a series of trials, which would show all Europe, and particularly Metternich, just how Carbonarism and all other treasonable activities should be dealt with.

He chose for the scene of his activities the little frontier town of Rubiera, garrisoned it well with Austrian troops and, as he thought, carefully chose the court which was to deal with the unfortunate prisoners. But it seems he had not chosen it sufficiently well for his purpose. On June 15 1822 a special Summary Tribunal was set up and attached to it, as legal adviser, was Domenico Giglioli from Brescello, one of the very men whom Panizzi, in his own house, had initiated into the mysteries of Carbonarism. It seems certain that Panizzi, with his usual skill and cunning, had managed to bring this about. Probably working through Cocchi and profiting by the difficulties the government were having in finding suitable lawyers, willing to serve on the

Court, the astute young conspirator had succeeded in introducing on to the very bench of judges a loyal informant, able to keep him constantly aware as to exactly what was going on at Rubiera.

Panizzi was already in a terrible position. If, after the death of Besini, he was less likely, on arrest, to be maltreated and tortured, it was almost certain that damaging revelations concerning his own secret activities would come out at the trial. He must, at all costs, know what was happening. Giglioli fully bore out all Panizzi's hopes and expectations. He had complete access to all the information and alleged confessions extracted from the prisoners by Besini and he was permitted to be present at the daily proceedings of the tribunal, even those held in secret. From the close contacts that the members of the Court and their officials, of necessity, had with each other in the confined area of Rubiera, Giglioli was able to gauge, with remarkable accuracy, the various currents of opinion as to the way the trials were going.

Above all, he had free access to the prisoners themselves and complete liberty to correspond with the Podesta of Brescello and so indirectly with Panizzi. It must have been, too, from Giglioli that Panizzi obtained the wealth of documentary material, which he soon afterwards incorporated into his book on the Rubiera trials, an impossible feat if he had relied entirely on his memory and on common knowledge. From Giglioli came warnings that Panizzi could pass on to his friends at Parma, who were being incriminated by secret evidence laid before the Tribunal at Rubiera. For the Modenese and Austrian authorities were, once again, making every effort to make Marie Louise and Neipperg abandon their casual ways and to proceed, with unaccustomed zeal, against their own revolutionaries.

But all was not going well for the Duke and his Austrian masters. All the confessions so far obtained from the prisoners had proved to have been obtained by force or by fraud, carried out by Besini and his creatures. Many of the prisoners testified before the court to the deceits and cruelties inflicted upon them whilst under interrogation and to the false promises and inducements held out to them to make them confess. The chief prosecutor, Vedriani,[9] an honourable man, determined as best he might to uphold civilized legal principles, demanded that the Tribunal should make it quite clear to the prisoners that such promises were valueless and quite unauthorized. His fellow prosecutor, Fieri, opposed this request and the matter was referred to Francis, who promptly denied ever having authorized Besini to hold out any such promises at all to the prisoners. Vedriani then insisted that the Duke's reply should be made known at once to the accused and that they should be given the opportunity of retracting, without prejudice, any confession so made, in expectation of favours to come.

The Tribunal, fearful lest any victim might escape and bring down upon their own heads the wrath of their terrible master, rejected the prosecutor's plea. Thereupon Vedriani threw up his brief in disgust and was succeeded by the more complaisant and more intolerant Fieri.

Though every difficulty was put in the way of the defending counsel, the palpable innocence of the accused, guilty, at most, of belonging to a society whose public objectives at least were moderate by any standards save that of the most savage reactionary, put the Tribunal in a dilemma. The guilt of the accused depended, in almost every case, on confessions forced from them by the most questionable means. The Tribunal, therefore, despite the demands of Fieri for no less than forty-two death sentences, felt bound to indicate that comparatively modest terms of imprisonment were all that were really necessary in the circumstances. The rumour of their leniency spread quickly through the Duchy and there was widespread rejoicing, not least, one must presume, in Brescello.

But there was still the Duke to be reckoned with. Beside himself with fury at the Tribunal's mildness, Francis summoned the terrified President before him. The sentences were thereupon quickly revised, the browbeaten and panic-stricken judges justifying their change of mind, because such was '*la sovrana mente e voluntà*', that very favourite phrase of Duke Francis. Nine of the accused were now condemned to death, most of the remainder to twenty years in the galleys, or virtually, to imprisonment for life; some few, mainly those who had been intimidated to betraying their own comrades, to shorter terms of imprisonment.

The trials, as Panizzi points out in his book,[10] clearly and unmistakably, had been a farce, a mere travesty of justice from beginning to end. Men had been condemned for offences which had not been proved, even to the satisfaction of the court itself. But

2*

such was justice under Francis IV of Modena. Of the death sentences, only one was, in fact, carried out, that on the unfortunate young priest, Andreoli. This young man, a teacher at Correggio, had particularly aroused the anger of the Duke, because in his view Andreoli had doubly abused his position, both as priest and as educator, in order to corrupt the young and to instil into them the pernicious and anti-Christian doctrines of Carbonarism. No mercy was to be shown to such a wretch, who had, moreover, added to his crimes by refusing to confess during more than eight months of imprisonment. At the very moment when, on October 16, the sentence of death was being read out to the poor man, the scaffold was being erected on the road between Rubiera and Reggio. The following day, at twelve, Andreoli, calm and resigned, was publicly beheaded, whilst a shocked and silent crowd watched behind the heavy guard of Austrian troops what that champion of the Catholic faith, Duke Francis, could do to a Christian priest.

Meanwhile, Panizzi, in Brescello, waited on events. All was now prepared for flight, if flee he must, gold in his belt, his passports in his pocket, a boat hidden close by lying ready. From Giglioli he had learnt that his neighbour, Alberici, had confessed, whilst the other accused, Cavandoli, had remained silent. It was evident, therefore, that the authorities, at last, knew all about his political activities in Brescello and elsewhere. In the meantime, he put a good face on things, doing his official duties as if nothing had happened and no man was more loyal to the Duke than he. Thus, on August 27 he played a prominent part in the visit of the Governor of Reggio to Brescello to mark the occasion of the victory of his native town over rival Boretto. This was necessary, not only to demonstrate his loyalty to the authorities, but also to subdue the malicious rumours and wild tales about him that were now flying about. Such gossip, he maintained, was due partly to his own austere and upright habits, which offended the weaker brethren and partly to the evil machinations of a personal enemy. Less kindly folk said it was his own fault, since his haughty manner and unwarranted severity had annoyed his fellow citizens, especially the poorer ones and had terrified the local rustics.

In these last trying months occurred also the incident of the ducal coach.[11] Francis was in the habit of sending one of his own private carriages on special missions to Brescello, among other places, with sealed orders to bring back to Modena for questioning or for other undisclosed purposes persons whose names were set out in the documents. Not unnaturally, the Brescellese viewed this particular activity of their Duke with suspicion and aversion, and none more so than Panizzi and his friends. It so happened that Panizzi and Giuseppe Minzi were strolling along the road to Reggio, when they saw in the distance the ducal coach bowling along towards them. Neither Panizzi nor Minzi had the slightest desire, at the moment, to visit their Sovereign and they strongly suspected that they might be high on his visiting list. They threw themselves, therefore, into the ditch at the side of the road and, luckily, escaped notice as the vehicle went by. What to do now? To return to Brescello at once was to find the carriage still there, possibly waiting for them. To return, in any case, by road, was to meet it, perhaps still empty, on its way back, to receive a pressing invitation to climb in and continue the journey with it to Modena.

The two friends decided, therefore, that for the moment, anyhow, they would cross into Parmese territory and see what would happen. Cutting across country on foot, they soon reached the comparative safety of the neighbouring Duchy, so relieved that they both fell down and kissed the friendly soil, overjoyed at their escape from the fate that had threatened them. A nice romantic touch, showing that the normally staid Panizzi was not unmoved by the spirit of the age.

However, they both soon realized that they must make a further decision. To remain longer on Parmese territory, without any credentials and in suspicious circumstances, was to invite discovery and arrest. After all, the carriage might not have come for them and they would be throwing away everything on mere speculation. The two companions, therefore, decided to return, with due circumspection, making careful inquiries before they reached home, as to the names of the two men the secret police were after. This they did and, arriving at Brescello round about dawn, were overjoyed to discover that Minzi and Panizzi were not, at least this time, the destined guests of the ferocious Duke.

It was obvious that the respite, at any rate for Panizzi himself, could not be for long. After the confession of his accomplice, Alberici, and even more, after the arrest, at the end of September, of his cousin, Francesco Panizzi, the whole of his treasonable activities were well known to the government. Francesco, not having Antonio's firmness and resolution, had at once broken down and promptly told the police all they wanted to know about the strange goings on in Brescello.

The escape of Antonio Panizzi has produced the usual crop of more or less highly-coloured and exaggerated anecdotes. Once he became famous, elderly survivors were called upon to produce their recollections of the romantic youth of the great man. Professor Enrico Friggeri, as a Brescellese presumably able to draw upon local traditions, in his address on September 26, 1897, on the occasion of the unveiling of a commemorative plaque on Panizzi's old home, tells one of these tales.[12] A troop of dragoons, sent secretly from Modena, burst into Luigi Panizzi's shop and, in a threatening manner, announced that they had come to arrest his son and sundry other Brescellese and carry them off to prison. Despite a thorough search, they were unable to discover their victim and returned, baffled, to Modena.

There seems to be no truth at all in this story. The orders for the arrest of Panizzi, together with those for the arrest of Giglioli and Levi-Minzi, were not issued till four months later, on February 18, 1823. On that date, indeed, a troop of dragoons was sent to Brescello, who arrested Giglioli and made a pretence of searching for Panizzi and Minzi, well knowing them not to be there. All other possible friends of Panizzi were already, by this time, either in prison or abroad, or no trace of their subversive activities had reached the attention of the government, then or subsequently.

Other tales of the events of these days are probably also mostly later inventions, thought up in Brescello a half-century or more later, to satisfy the romantic curiosity of visitors. Such is the story of the young lady, a close relative of someone in authority, who sent him a warning 'to have his new shoes ready'.

The version given by Fagan,[13] even though presumably based on first-hand evidence, also seems somewhat suspect. This is that on October 22 Panizzi received a message asking him to call at the Brescello police station, on some trivial excuse or other.

On entering the station, Panizzi was immediately arrested. Subsequently, with the collusion of the officer making the arrest, he was permitted to jump out of the window and to escape. No trace of any of these dramatic happenings can now apparently be found in the archives of Brescello, Reggio or Modena, as would certainly be the case if they had actually occurred. Little credence, also, may be placed in other tales of this period, which have appeared in various accounts of Panizzi's youth.

The solution of the mystery first advanced by Bacchi, seems, on the whole, the most plausible, and as close to the truth as we are now ever likely to get. Zatti[14] relates, and we must assume that here his informant was Panizzi himself, that on October 22 or possibly late on the evening of the 21st, Panizzi got a message, telling him that he must now flee the country. It seems certain that this message must have come from Filippo Cocchi at Reggio.

All through these long months, ever since the arrest of Alberici and his subsequent confession, Cocchi must have been watching the course of events with increasing anxiety, not only for young Panizzi, his friend and protégé, but also for himself. Once arrested, Panizzi might fatally compromise, not merely himself but others. In those days, no man's position was safe and Cocchi's own republican past and his present association with a suspected traitor could be brought up against him. All too easily, the Duke's friendship might be turned to mistrust. It must not happen. Panizzi, when it got too hot, must leave quickly and without undue fuss or disturbance. After all, once things had quietened down, he would probably in a few months' time be allowed to return. He could always be represented to Francis as a young fool, whose usual firmness of character and unquestioned loyalty to the throne, had been corrupted by evil companions. Pardoned by the gracious favour of the Duke, he would live to render invaluable services to the state of his birth.

If such were Cocchi's plans, they were doomed to failure. Panizzi's action, in publishing some months later his blistering attack on Francis and on all his ways, secured for him his sovereign's undying enmity, his own trial and condemnation *in absentia*, and completely precluded any possibility of his ever returning to Modena while the old Duke lived. It was not, in fact, until 1857, in the reign of the Duke's successor, that Panizzi was at last able to revisit his home and family once again.

However, for the moment, all went well. On October 22 Panizzi said good-bye to his father and sister. He told them little of his intentions, merely that it was better that he should go abroad for a short while. Such, possibly, at the moment, may well in fact have been his plan. Late in the afternoon, accompanied by Minzi, Zatti and Montani, his three closest friends, Panizzi walked quietly down to the banks of the Po. There, hidden among the reeds, was a boat. With him, he had his passports and other necessary documents, such gold as he had been able to obtain, and his notes on the Rubiera trials. A hurried good-bye to his three friends, whom he was not to see again for many a long year and he was off. He hastily crossed the river and, concealing the boat, made his way to the Austrian customs post at Viadana. There he approached the officials calmly and quietly, as one who had just arrived on the normal ferry from Boretto. His papers were in order and he was permitted to proceed on his way. Panizzi now took a carriage and was driven to Casalmaggiore, where he spent the night, the first night of his life-long exile.[15]

The following day he got as far as Cremona, where he had some sort of a brush with the Austrian police. It would seem that he had made arrangements with a friend to obtain accommodation for the night and also to hire another carriage. He was due to start from Cremona after lunch, when a summons was brought to him to call immediately at the police station. Suspicions had been aroused by his arrival from Brescello by a circuitous route, instead of by the usual direct road. Panizzi had been recognized as a known suspect by one of the numerous police spies who infested northern Italy and the authorities thought it would be wiser, therefore, to check with Brescello, just to make certain everything was in order. They wished, also, to search his baggage, in case he was carrying any prohibited literature, or other incriminating documents.

Panizzi was asked to wait at the police station while inquiries were made. After a short while, the officer who was supposed to be watching him, went off for a meal, leaving the suspect alone and the door of the room unlocked. Panizzi thereupon walked downstairs, out of the door, retrieved the greater part of his luggage[16] and hurried off to meet his friend, who was, by now, anxiously awaiting him.

Hence, for a time, we lose track of him. Aided no doubt by the local Carbonari and by friends he had made during his travels of the previous years, Panizzi went northwards, succeeded in crossing undetected the Austrian frontier and still carrying his precious notes on the Rubiera trials, arrived safely at Lugano, in Switzerland, some time in the late autumn of 1822.

There, in that pleasant town by the lakeside, he settled for a while. Either here, or possibly in Geneva, whither he next went, in order to avoid arrest by the cantonal authorities, Panizzi wrote and had published his book on the trials. He may well have been forced to produce it somewhat sooner than he had hoped to do, in order to defend himself against the accusations that were now being freely made against him by certain of the refugees from Parma, that he, Panizzi, had betrayed them, staying quietly at home whilst the trials were proceeding, when they had been compelled to flee abroad to avoid arrest.

As can well be imagined, the publication of this little book aroused the implacable anger of Duke Francis and of the Modenese government. It is extremely rare, only two copies of it being known to exist. One of these, Panizzi's own copy, given by him to Louis Fagan, is in the British Museum, whilst a second is in Italy. During his lifetime, Panizzi was always most reluctant to acknowledge his authorship and succeeded in destroying most of the surviving copies. When questioned, he would merely reply, 'Better say nothing about it.'[17]

In his book, he bitterly attacks not only the conduct of the trial itself, but also the whole train of events that led to it. All that had happened in Modena since 1814 is held up to searching criticism and ruthlessly condemned. At last he can expose those things which had sickened and disgusted him during those years of enforced silence: the restoration of aristocratic and clerical privileges, the denial to the middle classes of their due position in the state, the corruption of education and of the law and, not least, the inefficiency and venality of the ministers themselves, and, by implication, of Duke Francis. Only Filippo Cocchi is nowhere mentioned. That good friend, to whom he owed so much, must never appear in such a telling indictment. He then describes, in detail, the events of the last two years, culminating in Besini's reign of terror, his murder and the setting up of the special Tribunal. Here again Panizzi has to be careful. He must do nothing to incriminate Giglioli, whose arrest was, nevertheless, ordered on February 17, together with that of Minzi and of Panizzi himself.

Mockingly and bitterly, Panizzi then exposes the chicanery and double-dealing that went on during the trials. He shows that the whole method of conducting them was improper from start to finish, the wretched prisoners illegally condemned even under the existing laws, a monstrous disgrace both to legal rectitude and to common humanity. Towards the end, Panizzi gives the formal judgements of the Tribunal, with an acute and sarcastic commentary on the sentences imposed on the unfortunate accused. He mentions, with especial bitterness, the wretched Alberici, '*il perfido Alberici*', whom Panizzi considered was the first to betray him, who got fifteen years, whilst his more 'guilty' companions, Cavandoli and Nizzoli, who had stoutly refused to make a confession, escaped comparatively lightly.

The effect of all this was sensational. Cocchi must have wept at his young friend's rashness. For now there could be no lying low for a few months and a quiet return to Modena. The Duke would never forget and never forgive. Panizzi was a marked man thenceforth and there can be little doubt that, if Francis had been able to lay hands on him, he would have suffered the same fate as Andreoli.

In the meantime, the Modenese government started proceedings. On February 17, the Duke ordered the arrest of the errant Dr Panizzi, as well as of Doctors Minzi and Giglioli. On the following day, a high official of the secret police, accompanied by two officers and a troop of dragoons, arrived in Brescello. They arrested Giglioli, searched his home and his office and made inquiries as to the whereabouts of the other two wanted men. It was, of course, well known that neither were there. Minzi was in Florence, ostensibly to practise in a hospital: Panizzi had fled the country, since it had been revealed by the publication of the sentences of the Tribunal, that he had belonged to a proscribed sect.

Old Luigi was asked where his missing son might be. He replied that he did not know. He was then asked how long Antonio had been gone. 'Some five months,' replied his father. 'And where?' 'To Lombardy on a legal case. I have had no news of him since and I do not know where he now is.' Whether true or false, the old chemist was certainly not going to tell an officer of the secret police all about his beloved Antonio. So the latter, after ordering Luigi to inform his son that he was to present himself for trial, went back to Modena, his dragoons bearing in their midst poor Giglioli, so lately himself an official of the court.[18]

For some months the Government did nothing. This delay proved to be most annoying for Panizzi. Unfriendly voices amongst the other refugees hinted that this was another example of his double dealing, proof that he was, after all, in collusion with the authorities, if not an *agent provocateur* put among them to betray them.

However, on September 2, 1823 the Government at last moved. By this time, Panizzi had been in England for some four months, safe from the clutches of the angry duke, and contemptuous of the legal flummery which now pursued him. The solemn farce was duly carried out. A summons was issued ordering Antonio Panizzi to present himself before the Special Tribunal within fifteen days, to answer the charges preferred against him. A notice to this effect was attached to the door of the Palace of Justice at Modena, a copy being also affixed to the door of his father's house, his last known place of residence. The specific charges of which Panizzi was accused were that he, as a member of a proscribed sect, had assisted at the reception into the Carbonari of his cousin, Francesco Panizzi and of Domenico Giglioli, in his own room of his own house at Brescello and that, subsequently, twelve days after, he had assisted at the reception into the Carbonari of Bartolomeo Panizzi at the house of Francesco.

The evidence at the ensuing trial was clear and decisive. However much one may suspect the motives of the witnesses, especially those of Francesco Panizzi, who had been promised a free pardon if he turned 'King's evidence', it is abundantly clear that, in the eyes of the Duke and of the Modenese authorities, and, indeed, as the laws of his country then stood, Antonio Panizzi was guilty as charged. No one could, therefore, have been surprised when, in October 1823, the Tribunal pronounced sentence and condemned the contumacious doctor of law, Antonio Panizzi, to the penalty of death, to be duly carried out in effigy, to the confiscation of all his goods, and to bear the cost of his trial and execution.

The sentence was confirmed by the Duke fourteen days later, and a copy nailed to the door of his house in Brescello. This symbolic act must have seemed to poor Luigi the end of all his hopes for his beloved son, whom he must now have mourned as one dead before his time.

But Panizzi was very far from dead. Writing from Liverpool, on

May 8, 1824, to Giuseppe Terni,[19] the presiding judge, he strongly attacks the whole conduct of his trial and repudiates any suggestion that he had been a Carbonaro, without precisely denying that he had belonged to some other secret society. The letter, if written in somewhat flamboyant terms, does show, most clearly, Panizzi's hatred of the despotism under which he had so long lived, his relief at being rid of the necessity of disguising his real feelings and his joy at being, at last, free of all fears, living amidst a nation *'libera è generosa'*. It must have given Panizzi great satisfaction to write this letter to Terni and to realize that he was done with Modena and its cruel and treacherous Duke for ever.

Panizzi did not stay long at Lugano. It was almost certainly here that he finished the *Processi di Rubiera*. The speed at which it was produced would indicate, however, that much had been written previously in secret. Ordered by the Ticinese authorities to leave, he next went to Geneva, where there were already gathered a number of exiles. Amongst them was a certain Giovanni Conti, who was to give evidence against Panizzi at the latter's subsequent trial. He then related that Panizzi had talked of writing a book on the Rubiera trials, an undertaking from which, Conti declared, he had tried in vain to dissuade him. On Conti's departure from Geneva to surrender to the authorities, a move of which Panizzi allegedly approved, they parted good friends. Conti does not seem to have ever actually seen Panizzi's book, and it seems possible that Antonio, always a prudent man, was justifiably suspicious of one whom he knew was about to return to Modena, and did not take Conti very deeply into his confidence.

Panizzi was now in desperate straits for money. He had scarcely anything on which to live, the scanty funds he had been able to bring out with him being, by now, almost exhausted. He tried to support himself by giving Italian lessons, an almost hopeless task in a city swarming with Italian refugees. He was ready, he declared, to become a serving man or to go for a soldier, anything rather than to return.

Soon he and all the other refugees had to move on. Despite its traditional policy of freely granting asylum to all and sundry, Geneva was forced by the combined pressure of the Austrian, French and Sardinian governments to order the exiles to leave. Panizzi, with a few friends, now determined to make his way to

England, the one country too powerful to heed the demands of the continental monarchies and still ready to welcome any exile to her shores. One member of the party, Bezzi, went ahead to explore the route. At Gex, some eleven miles from Geneva, he was stopped, searched and bundled back into Switzerland.[20] The way through France being thus barred, Panizzi and his friends travelled up the Rhine, through the Netherlands and so, at last, to England. In May 1823, Panizzi arrived, penniless, in London, six months after he had first left Brescello. He was in the country which was to make him famous, which he was to grow to love, even more, perhaps, than his native land, and which, except for short visits, he was never afterwards to leave.

NOTES TO CHAPTER 3

1 The text of this letter is given in Bacchi, pp. 19, 20.

2 Panizzi acquired this additional post in 1821. Friggeri, [p. 11] records the local tradition that even then he was extremely strict with his pupils. As in later years he demanded complete obedience but made himself loved and respected by his wit and by the keenness of his intellectual powers. A former pupil recalled having seen the youthful inspector take the master's place and expound, with remarkable skill, on some difficult passage in the classics.

3 Panizzi is said to have become a Carbonaro, or, much more probably, a member of the *Sublimi Maestri Perfetti*, towards the close of his stay at Parma. According to Friggeri [pp. 19, 67], he was enrolled as a member of the *S. Vitale* Lodge, but this is, admittedly, only a tradition.

4 Wealthy foreign travellers, such as Byron and his friend, Hobhouse, travelled, whenever possible, with an escort of gendarmes. The poet and his companion also carried a personal armoury of four brace of pistols, two swords, two sword sticks and a dagger.

5 Gabriele Rossetti, 1783–1854.

6 Francis IV, 1779–1846, himself, may well have belonged to one of the secret societies, the Concistoriali. The objects of this organization, which had been founded by Cardinal Consalvi, Secretary to Pius VII, was to drive out the Austrians, to set up a strong northern Italian Kingdom, with Francis as its ruler and to divide the remaining Austrian or Austrian controlled territories among the three other 'national' sovereigns, the Pope, the King of Naples and the King of Sardinia. It was said that Francis was sternly rebuked by Metternich, with whom he was already on bad terms, for his connection with the Concistoriali. It was to prove his loyalty to the cause of absolutism that he proceeded against the members of other societies with such harshness and vigour. [Dito, p. 289.]

7 The text of the decree is given in *Dei Processi*, p. 132.

8 Bacchi, p. 61.

9 Panizzi always kept in touch with both Cocchi and Vedriani, both of whom he much admired. They were both among the recipients of Panizzi's edition of Boiardo's poems which he sent to his private friends. In 1845 Cocchi succeeded in meeting his old friend at Mantua and, shortly afterwards, at Parma. Panizzi always spoke of him in tones of respect and affection and bore him no ill-will for his life-long service to the ducal family.

10 *Dei Processi*, p. 128 et seq.

11 Fagan, I, p. 40.

12 Friggeri, p. 19.

13 Fagan, I, p. 41.

14 *Quarterly Review*, vol. 151, p. 463 *et seq.*

15 More details are given in a letter from a cousin, Luigi Panizzi. The latter, then a schoolboy, had quarrelled with another lad on that very day. Antonio Panizzi was summoned to deal with the matter. He replied to say he was too busy to come. That evening, he crossed the river with the help of a friendly boatman, Giuseppe Monici, and 'took refuge . . . in the house of Signor Sanfelice, who accompanied him to Casal-Maggiore and thence to Cremona'. Luigi Panizzi also asserts that his cousin was warned by a certain Tavani or Tavoni, who had orders to arrest him. [Letter in the Museo di Risorgimento, Modena. Quoted by Brooks, p. 13.]

16 *Dei Processi*, p. 6. The friend was, presumably, the Sanfelice mentioned in Luigi Panizzi's letter.

17 Fagan, I, p. 26. See also the letter of Louis Fagan in *The Times* of April 19, 1879.

18 The documents on the trial of Antonio Panizzi are given in Brooks, Appendix I. The sentence of the Court is also in Fagan, I, p. 46.

19 Brooks, p. 189.

20 Fagan, I, p. 43.

4

ENGLAND: THE EARLY YEARS

THE England in which Panizzi found himself in May 1823 was outwardly a cheerful, bustling place, very different from the Italy he had just left. The mood of reaction and bitterness which followed the ending of the great wars was now passing and men's thoughts turned once more to the possibilities of reform by peaceful means. For the moment, however, the young man can have had few thoughts, save how to stay alive in this new and most strange country, of whose language he so far spoke not one word. Desperately poor,[1] his courage must often have failed him. Doubtless, like his friend Pecchio, his first impressions were those of overcast skies, of 'an eternal cloud of smoke, which involves and penetrates everything', so that the smoky appearance of the very houses in London gave the appearance of a city that had been burned.[2] In May, perhaps, this gloomy appearance was not so noticeable. The size of London, already with a million and a half inhabitants, was, doubtless, overwhelming for one brought up amid the little towns and villages of northern Italy, and the strangeness and foreignness of it all must have made him heart-sick for Brescello and the quiet banks of the Po.

We do not know where Panizzi spent his first days in that city he was to love and to know so intimately. Perhaps, again like Pecchio,[3] in a cheap lodging house, with fragile wooden partitions, the walls and floors so thin, that one heard every word spoken by one's neighbours. He was so desperately poor, he may well have slept in the open, like many another homeless vagabond. Panizzi, in later life, recalled that he was only able to allow himself fourteen pence a day for his food and there may well have been times when he had not even that. Scarcely more than a boy, with the healthy appetite of youth, he would gaze hungrily through the windows of the London cookshops, envious of the fortunate diners within.[4] His few friends and acquaintances could do little to help. In 1823, London was full of refugees, Spanish, French, Greek, Italian and even Haitian, all living in extreme poverty and all largely dependent on the charity of sympathetic Englishmen.

Of all these little bands of refugees, the Italians, however, were perhaps the most distinguished and the most close-knit group, who had, already, in many cases, links with the world of learning and fashion. Italy was still, of all foreign countries, the one most highly regarded by any educated Englishman, and to such men as Lord Holland, Fox's nephew, a second home from which they parted with reluctance.

Very soon after his arrival, Panizzi became acquainted with Santorre Santa Rosa, an acquaintance that speedily ripened into friendship. Santa Rosa, a Piedmontese nobleman, some fourteen years older than Panizzi, had been exiled for his share in the rising of 1821. After much hardship, he had arrived in England some six months previously, armed with introductions to various prominent sympathizers with the cause of Italy. Santa Rosa was a man of exceptional charm and nobility of character, so that 'whoever lived under the same roof with him could not avoid being the better for it',[5] and very soon became a favourite amongst the little circle of his fellow refugees and with their English friends and patrons. Thomas Campbell,[6] the poet, was particularly enchanted with him, a great tribute to the Italian's essential simplicity and sweetness of character, for Campbell, a man of highly nervous disposition, was very slow to make friends and easily upset by displays of temperament. During the few years Santa Rosa stayed in England, Campbell and he became firm friends and the poet would listen entranced to the other's tales of European politics and of the intrigues and machinations of the politicians of the day.

It would seem to be most probable that it was Santa Rosa who, in the summer of 1823, first introduced his young fellow countryman, Antonio Panizzi, to Campbell. They may have met, however,

at Digamma Cottage, Regents Park, where Ugo Foscolo,[7] the poet
and doyen of the Italian refugees, was now living. Foscolo also
owned the adjoining Green Cottage, in which Santa Rosa was
staying. The house of Foscolo, the most celebrated Italian poet of
his day, was naturally a centre for all his fellow exiles and one to
which every newcomer was eventually brought.

Panizzi, who, of course, must have known of Foscolo by repute,
was soon introduced to him. They met very much as master and
disciple. Foscolo was a man of European reputation, whilst Panizzi
was still young and completely unknown. Panizzi, too, an earnest
and rather prim young man, must have been somewhat shocked
by Foscolo's way of life and the odd set-up at Digamma Cottage.
There lived, not only the poet, but the mysterious young lady
Floriana, in fact his illegitimate daughter, together with various
other females, whose good looks perhaps compensated for their
conspicuous lack of other virtues, those 'Three Graces', whose
goings-on were the talk of London society.

It was this shifty, Bohemian existence of Foscolo, his debts and
his duels, his serving wenches and the whole atmosphere of seedy
mystery, which surrounded him, that appalled the precise young
lawyer from provincial Brescello. Though he always acknowledged
his debt to him, and revered Foscolo, both as a great man and as a
great patriot, Panizzi's profound distaste for this sort of life, and
the harm which he undoubtedly felt it did to the reputation of the
refugees, always seems to have caused him to feel a certain repul-
sion mixed with his admiration for the memory of this celebrated
poet, but often foolish man.

Panizzi himself, his own immensely practical mind reinforced
by the noble example of Santa Rosa, was determined on another
and quite opposite course. Not for him the life of a great gentleman, such as Foscolo led, against a background of duns,
prostitutes and endless debt. He would be poor, hard working and
eminently respectable, until better days came. There was little or no
opportunity for such as he in London. Even Santa Rosa, for all his
reputation and aristocratic connections, was finding it impossible
to live there, and it was clearly obvious that Panizzi must look
elsewhere.[8]

What made him think of Liverpool, we do not know but
probably it was because there lived William Roscoe, whose fame,

as the principal patron of Italian literature in England, must have been well known to Panizzi. Whether it was Foscolo or some other friend who now urged him to seek his fortune there, it was a decision which was to have momentous consequences for the penniless refugee.

Not only was Liverpool the home of Roscoe, whose lives of Leo X and of Lorenzo de Medici were already well known throughout Europe and whose personal sympathy for liberal causes assured any exile of a warm welcome, it was a prosperous, fast-growing city, which already justly regarded itself as the capital of northern England. Grown rich on the profits of the slave trade, it was a gracious and elegant city, in Wesley's opinion, 'one of the best built towns I have seen'. It had not yet acquired, to any large extent, its sordid slums, the result of mass immigration from Ireland, which were to render it notorious later in the century. It had been the scene of the famous election struggle between Brougham and Canning. It had such prominent citizens as Roscoe himself, John Gladstone, the father of the statesman, William Shepherd and many others. Other, younger men, who were to make their mark in the future, were William Ewart, founder of the Public Library movement and Grote, the historian of Greece. It had a Philosophical Society and numerous other literary and political associations flourished. In short, it was to no gloomy, provincial backwater, but to a vigorous and progressive community, with strong literary and musical traditions, that the young Italian, doubtless with a certain trepidation, turned his face northward in the summer of 1823.

He had but little to go with, save his own courage and an infinite capacity for hard work. He had had to borrow the money to pay his fare and the two-day journey northwards must have seemed very long and dreary. However, he had certain advantages, not counting his own great talents. Letters of introduction to Roscoe senior from Foscolo and from Thomas Campbell to William Roscoe junior[9] were in his pocket, and he faced the future with all the confidence of youth.

At Liverpool he was warmly welcomed by Roscoe, a kindly man, with a particular sympathy for the young and struggling. Soon Panizzi was an intimate of the Roscoe family circle. Both Foscolo and Campbell had written of the young man in the warmest terms, as one who had suffered much in the cause of Italian liberty. Foscolo had suggested that Roscoe might derive much interesting information on the subject of penal reform from conversations with the young lawyer. Roscoe, who was deeply concerned with this subject, undoubtedly must have found Panizzi well informed. After all, he had himself only recently written an account of the notorious Rubiera trials and had just had the unusual experience of being himself condemned to death and executed, if only in effigy.

Panizzi had also received a bill for his execution. The local Inspector of Taxes at Reggio, hearing of his escape and arrival in Switzerland, forwarded a demand for 225 francs and 25 cents, including a fee for the hangman. In due course, after his arrival in Liverpool, Panizzi sent a satirical reply, dated from the Realm of Death, the Elysian Fields and signing it 'The Soul of A. Panizzi'. Safe in Liverpool, he could afford to laugh at the miserable pedantries of the government of the 'microscopical Duke'.[10]

Old Roscoe, now poor and ailing, became warmly attached to the clever young Italian and his affection was equally warmly returned. Henry Roscoe, in his biography of his father, says: 'There was no one who became more sincerely attached to him or for whom he felt a higher degree of esteem and affection than Mr Panizzi . . . To the kindness and attentions of Mr Panizzi, which rather resembled those of a son than of a stranger, he owed many happy hours.'[11] This tribute to Panizzi's lovable nature, which few suspected behind his often stern exterior, was paid in 1833, years before the young refugee had, in turn, become famous. He never forgot the sympathy and affection he had received from the old scholar, in those first days in Liverpool, poor and friendless as he was, in a strange city. In 1853, the distinguished Keeper of Printed Books of the British Museum was obliged to refuse with the greatest reluctance the invitation of the Centennial Committee to be a guest of honour at the Roscoe celebrations in the following March. 'The veneration in which I hold the memory of that illustrious man and the grateful recollection of the warm and affectionate regard with which I was honoured by him'[12] were powerful inducements for him to accept the invitation. Pressing duties alone prevented him from once more travelling north to pay a last tribute to his old friend and patron.

Panizzi did not disappoint Roscoe's high hopes. Though, as Santa Rosa wrote shortly after Panizzi's arrival in Liverpool, it was unfortunate that there were two teachers of Italian already there, thanks to Roscoe's patronage and his own great talents, he prospered. He hated teaching, especially the hard grind of teaching beginners, yet brought to it all the strength of his powerful mind. The sheer hopelessness of it all, for a time, depressed him and his health, too, seems to have been affected by the rigour of his first northern winter. His pupils were, at first, few and widely scattered. He would trudge on foot through the snow or rain to give his lessons to a pupil in a distant suburb or outlying village and then return to Liverpool to do another job. We do not know what this second occupation was. Panizzi was young and strong, and, as we have seen, had said before, he would turn his hand to anything rather than be dependent on charity, sentiments he reiterated again and again. Fagan is discreet, but it is surely not impossible that it was some sort of manual labour he was now undertaking to supplement his scanty fees. Santa Rosa writes to comfort him, not to lose heart and, above all, not to think of returning to London. His friend further urges him to make himself a master of both Italian literature and history. By teaching these subjects, Panizzi would attract both more pupils and also interest a higher type of student. Above all, he must persevere and keep in touch with his countrymen in London.[13]

Heartened by Santa Rosa's kindly advice, Panizzi regained his confidence. His English was improving, though as yet by no means perfect and his circle of acquaintances was widening. As well as his letters to Roscoe, he seems to have had an introduction to William Shepherd, also probably supplied by Foscolo. The Reverend William Shepherd,[14] who remained on close terms with Panizzi long after the latter's departure, once more for London, was a Unitarian minister, then in his middle fifties, who had known Roscoe for many years and was now running a small school at Gateacre, near Liverpool. His interest in Italian literature having been aroused by Roscoe, he had published in 1802 a life of Poggio Braccolini and remained a warm friend of Italian liberalism and of the exiles for its cause. Another friend, this time more of his own age, was Francis Haywood.[15] Haywood, just three years older than Panizzi, was a man of some substance, who lived at Edge Lane

Hall. Panizzi and he were to remain very close friends for many years. No man was more dear to the Italian than was Francis Haywood and his comparatively early death was a terrible blow. Panizzi had met Haywood at the home of John Ewart, the son of old William Ewart, Gladstone's godfather and brother of William Ewart the younger.[16] Young William Ewart had also a strong interest in legal matters and, subsequently, as MP, was to be the originator of many bills on capital punishment. He, too, would have found much to interest him in the conversation of the young refugee lawyer from Modena and in his knowledge of continental systems of jurisprudence and of the reforms of Beccaria and other Italian penologists.

Life then was, at last, becoming a little easier for Panizzi. Still poor, he was, at any rate, more sure of a settled income from his teaching and was occasionally able to supplement it.[17] He had written an article for the *Edinburgh Review* on the Holy Alliance, for which he received a draft for twenty guineas,[18] a most welcome sum for an impoverished young teacher. He had written his article in Italian and then had had it translated into English, probably by one of the younger Roscoes, who translated for Foscolo from time to time. Panizzi's own English was, however, rapidly improving, as was his knowledge of Italian literature and history. Remembering Santa Rosa's advice, he had made a special study, in particular, of the Italian literature of the Renaissance and in the spring and autumn of 1825 he was able to deliver a series of lectures in English on the poets of this period. His notes for these lectures are written in admirable English and already show a considerable command of the language. In his opening remarks, Panizzi apologizes for his 'rash confidence' in addressing the 'numerous and most respectable audience of ladies and gentlemen' in their own language, but suggests that it is of very little consequence whether 'my diction be so correct or my pronunciation so pure if I am but intelligible'.[19] Despite the handicap of his accent – and Panizzi never succeeded in overcoming this – the talks seem to have been well attended and to have given 'universal satisfaction'. Doubtless, his experience in the courts here stood him in good stead, but, nevertheless, it was no mean feat to deliver these talks to a foreign and by no means uncritical audience.

These lectures at the Royal Institution were always of a high standard. Since its founding by Roscoe and a few friends, many distinguished men had been invited to speak and it was a tribute to the position which Panizzi was winning for himself in Liverpool society, that he, too, should deliver a course of lectures there 'with a talent and felicity beyond all praise'.[20]

Panizzi seems to have liked Liverpool and, after the first months, to have been very happy there. 'I have known Liverpool so long and so well and have had so many occasions of experiencing the hospitality of its inhabitants,' he said at his lecture, 'that my heart cannot allow me to think that you came to hear me, as you would have done a stranger.'[21]

Already, he seems by this time to have had a growing number of pupils of both sexes, for knowledge of Italian language and literature were still considered as an essential part of the education of any well-brought-up man or woman, and he must have been glad that he had followed Santa Rosa's advice and persevered in his efforts.

Alas, the friend, from whom he had obtained such comfort and assistance, was no more. Santa Rosa had long been depressed by his life in exile. Despite the many kind English friends by whom he was surrounded and the love and admiration of his fellow exiles, he felt that he was wasting his life teaching Italian. He was, moreover, worried about his wife and children, left behind in Piedmont. His quiet life in provincial Nottingham seemed to him to be a betrayal of his ideals, when so much, everywhere, remained to be done in the cause of freedom. The thoughts of all lovers of liberty had now turned to Greece. Byron, to the horror, mingled with admiration, of the romantic youth of all Europe, had died of fever at Missolonghi on April 19, 1824. Santa Rosa, amongst many others, now longed to go to Greece, to strike a further blow for freedom. Some time in the summer of that year, he had come to London to see the Greek deputies and to ask for the command of a battalion. He had said nothing of his intentions to any of his friends and great was their surprise when he suddenly announced his intention of leaving. On November 1, 1824, Santa Rosa sailed for Greece. He had been deluded by false promises from the Greek deputies of positions of responsibility on his arrival. In reality, they had advised their government not to employ the Piedmontese exile, lest by so doing they should compromise their relations with the Holy Alliance. From a worldly point of view, their duplicity was, perhaps, justifiable, but it was a cruel treatment of the noble-hearted Santa Rosa.

Once in Greece, the poor man was quickly disillusioned. Put off by empty promises, he quickly realized he was not wanted. Despite the efforts of his friends to persuade him to return to England, Santa Rosa decided to enlist in the Greek army as a private soldier. Within a few weeks, on May 8, 1825, he was killed at Sphacteria.

Panizzi heard the news with a heavy heart. His friend Giuseppe Pecchio had in turn gone out to Greece and had succeeded in meeting Santa Rosa, a few days before the latter's death, and had brought back to England the last tidings of their dead friend. With Santa Rosa's death, the unity of the little band of exiles seems to break up. Some, like Pecchio and Panizzi himself, settled down in England, more or less comfortably; others, like Claudio Linati,[22] the friend of Panizzi's student days at Parma, became wanderers over the face of both Europe and the New World, seeking to find, somewhere, consolation for their life of exile; others, again, like Foscolo, the man with the greatest reputation of them all, sank down into degradation and death.

Panizzi, too, had had his moments of doubt, and considered whether or not to leave England for the United States but fortunately he was now, as we have seen, becoming settled in Liverpool and enjoying the hospitality of an ever-growing circle of acquaintances. Always the most generous of men to those still poorer than himself, he had lent Linati 300 francs to help the latter establish himself in Brussels, a sum which, at this time, he must have found exceedingly difficult to afford.

Whilst Panizzi, therefore, was enjoying for the first time a modest prosperity and the friendship of such as Haywood, the Roscoes and many others, the wretched Foscolo was, by now, only a shadow of his former greatness. Dogged by poverty and ill-health, threatened with blindness, he seems to have lacked, to an increasing extent, any capacity to manage his affairs in an orderly manner. His daughter Floriana was now endeavouring to keep house for the irascible and prematurely ageing poet. In January of 1825 his two cottages were sold to pay his debts, debts for which he had been arrested the previous November, and had then gone into hiding. After a brief respite, while he worked at his proposed edition of Dante, he had again been forced to sell up his home and live in various cheap lodgings throughout London, under the assumed name of Emerytt.

It was whilst living in one of this series of hideouts, that Foscolo heard once more from Antonio Panizzi, the young man whom he had befriended nearly three years before. In a letter dated February 25, 1826, and sent from his new home at 93 Mount Pleasant,[23] to which his improved financial position had enabled him to move, Panizzi wrote to his old patron: 'I do not know whether you remember me . . . I have never forgotten nor will forget that you so kindly favoured me with letters . . . Thanks partially to their recommendations, I am so well treated and welcomed by all that, were it possible for me to forget our own country, I should certainly not forget Liverpool. If the misery of selling articles and verbs were not such as to freeze one's blood, I might say that I live yet I only vegetate; even this is due to you.'[24] Panizzi goes on to say that he had been in London, the previous June, with one of the younger Roscoes and had tried vainly to contact Foscolo, through Pickering, his publisher. He is full of praise for the poet's *Discorso sul Testo di Dante*. Panizzi, the previous month, had visited the Bodleian at Oxford and had there closely examined no less than thirteen manuscripts of the *Divina Commedia*. He now offers to send Foscolo the minute description of them which he has made, if such would be of any help to his old friend. Panizzi further mentions other Dante manuscripts, which he hopes to be able to see in the near future, including several in the possession of 'Signor Colke di Olkam' – an indication, by the way, of Panizzi's still uncertain mastery of the English tongue.[25] Roscoe was on friendly terms with Thomas Coke and had frequently visited his magnificent library at Holkham in Norfolk. He now introduced Panizzi to the great man, who very kindly offered to send the young Italian scholar his precious Dante manuscripts, so that Panizzi might study them at home. This was, indeed, a sure indication of the position he had now obtained in Liverpool society, and a deserved tribute to his own merits and integrity.

Foscolo replied almost immediately. His was a pitiful letter, full of complaints. The poet was now living once again at a permanent address, though still in the depths of poverty. His misery was possibly, however, not so great as he himself liked to make out and as some of his biographers have believed. He was helped by generous friends, both English and from among his fellow-exiles and by the love and devotion of his daughter. It seems to be true, however, that in July 1826 Foscolo was indeed living in a slum, amidst dirt and squalor, the noise of drunken men and screaming women and children, surroundings which must have been a sore trial to the fastidious and aristocratic poet. A timely cheque enabled him to move to better quarters, as he tells Panizzi in his letter.[26] Antonio was now full of schemes to help his former patron. He urged Foscolo to visit Liverpool, where he would be assured of a warm welcome by his numerous admirers, not least by Panizzi himself.[27]

To pay for the expenses of the visit, he urged that Foscolo should give a series of six lectures to last three weeks at the Royal Institution, where Panizzi himself had lectured the previous year and for which the Institution was ready to offer £50. Already, he writes, there were about thirty subscribers. Then there was Manchester, where there was a literary establishment of the same kind and the further possibility of giving more lectures there. Panizzi is full of ideas and enthusiasm; he will take charge of everything. 'Come and write, never mind the postage . . . I am not in want.'[28]

But Foscolo, sick and tired, and always reluctant to speak in public, did not come. He was still full of plans, of writing a novel based on his own amorous experiences, of translations from the *Iliad* and of articles for the *Edinburgh* and *Westminster Reviews*. But now his health was failing. There is a further letter from Panizzi on October 11, perhaps a little less friendly than the last, but still anxious to help. He suggests that Shepherd might make an excellent translator for the projected novel, though he has not yet seen him about the idea.[29]

Panizzi was always quick to take umbrage at any supposed slight on his native land. As one of the younger generation, which had taken a personal share in the struggle for liberty and unity, he knew the true worth of his compatriots and objected most strongly to Foscolo's attack on the Italian people in the *Lettera Apologetica*, which the poet now proposed to publish. 'What is the use,' the younger man exclaimed, 'of bringing shame on our country,' and pleaded with his old friend to omit all such strong language.

Old Montagu House.
The gatehouse, screen and residences seen from Great Russell Street, looking west

Antonio Panizzi, aged about twenty. From the sketch by his friend, Ambrogio Berchet. Probably drawn during their university days at Parma. Given by Panizzi to Louis Fagan.

Wax portrait of Antonio Panizzi, aged 53, by R. C. Lucas.

Foscolo demurred, in no uncertain terms, and some sort of a break seems to have occurred between them. The poet was now dying. In a last letter to Panizzi, he asks the latter to come and stay with him at his new house at Turnham Green, to which he had moved towards the end of the previous year.[30] In April, on the advice of friends, he had sent in an application for the Chair of Italian Literature at the newly founded London University. Campbell, however, told him that he would be little more than a teacher of languages and he withdrew his application. At any rate, it was now too late. Dropsy was killing him, despite the two operations which he had undergone. On September 10, 1827, Foscolo died and was buried quietly in Chiswick churchyard, close to his last home.

Panizzi was soon told of his death. To help poor Floriana, now left in wretched circumstances, the little fortune bequeathed to her by her grandmother being long ago spent by her unscrupulous father, Foscolo's few remaining books were purchased privately by his friends. Panizzi, with his usual kindness and generosity, bought as many as he was able and presented them to those he knew to be admirers of the great Italian poet.[31] One of those to whom he gave a book was T. B. Macaulay, the historian. He appears to have done this as a sort of apology for an incident which had occurred at their previous meeting. Macaulay thanked Panizzi for his gift and the incident, whatever it was, was regarded as closed.[32] Nevertheless, though acquainted for many years, the two men were never really friends and Macaulay always seems to have retained a certain mistrust of the Italian.

It was not long before this that certain events had occurred which, by a curious chain of circumstances, were to alter completely the whole course of Panizzi's life. Among the many friends and acquaintances that Panizzi had made in Liverpool was the distinguished lawyer and politician, Henry Brougham.[33] Panizzi was already, it seems, shedding some of his youthful radicalism,[34] but was, nevertheless, fascinated by the older man's magnetic personality.

As long ago as 1812, Brougham had been invited by Roscoe and some of his fellow merchants to stand for Liverpool and had consented to do so, along with Thomas Creevey,[35] the diarist. Commercial Liverpool admired Brougham for his successful struggle

3

to get repealed the Orders in Council against trade with neutral countries, even if not in time to avoid war with America. Likewise they hated him for his long campaign to abolish the slave trade. Half the world's slave trade had been centred on Liverpool and the wealthy merchants detested Brougham, 'with a hatred hardly natural for branding them with the name and fate of felons'.[36] Brougham and Creevey, after a tremendous struggle, lost to Canning and the other Tory, Gascoyne,[37] but Brougham had remained on friendly terms with Roscoe and his other Liverpool acquaintances.

Since that date, Brougham had become a national figure by his defence of Queen Caroline and, in radical circles, the most popular man of his day, whilst disliked and distrusted by the Tories and by many of the Whigs. It remains true that, whatever misgivings even some of his friends may have had about 'Old Wicked Shifts', as Creevey called him, he was for at least fourteen years after the Queen's trial the most widely acclaimed man in all England. A man of incredible energy and talents, yet he was never fully trusted by anyone. To Hobhouse, as to many, he appeared 'daily a more extraordinary man the more I see of him'[38] and even such old friends as Campbell, who had known him for so many years, were still under his spell.

It can well be imagined what impression Brougham must have made on young Panizzi. To the lawyer of Brescello, he was one who was considered to be a master of his profession, one of the greatest advocates living; to the young radical, he was the great champion of all oppressed, whether Queen or slave, rich or poor. It is probable that they first met at the house of Francis Haywood or else Roscoe or Shepherd may have introduced them. Judging by the remarks in Panizzi's letter to Foscolo of August 2, 1826,[39] he was, by then, already acquainted with Brougham; but it was a celebrated scandal and the ensuing trial that first really brought them together; and a chance acquaintanceship ripened into a lasting friendship that was destined to be of inestimable value to Antonio Panizzi.

Amongst those to whom Panizzi had taught Italian were the pupils of the girls' school near Liverpool, run by the Misses Daulby and their mother. As early as April 1825, or possibly even 1824, he had been teaching there, for in a letter of uncertain date, the Misses

Daulby 'present their compliments to Mr Panizzi', and ask him to give one of their pupils her lessons at the usual hour.[40] One of the girls at this highly respectable school was a Miss Ellen Turner, the daughter of a certain William Turner, a wealthy landowner and manufacturer of Strigley in Cheshire. She had been there for some five or six years and was now fifteen years old, an attractive and high-spirited girl. She had been one of Panizzi's pupils and he seems to have taken a certain interest in her.

On March 7, 1826, Miss Turner was abducted by a trick from her school and carried off to Gretna Green. There she went through a form of marriage with her captor, Edward Gibbon Wakefield,[41] the future colonizer of New Zealand, but, at that time, a handsome young widower, whose fertile brain had engineered the whole ingenious plot. Ellen was undoubtedly thrilled by the romantic adventure which had befallen her and by the dashing appearance of the mysterious stranger, who had appeared from nowhere to carry her off. She, therefore, consented to the marriage, as well as being deceived by certain stories of her father's supposed financial difficulties, which this marriage would, it was said, alleviate.

The young couple then went off to Calais, where they spent a week together 'as brother and sister',[42] until fate overtook them in the persons of two of Ellen's uncles, a solicitor and a Bow Street Runner, who had succeeded at last in tracking down the fugitives. Ellen was induced to return at once to England. Wakefield followed shortly afterwards and was committed for trial, together with his mother and brother, who had assisted him in the plot.

The scandal aroused extraordinary interest, both among the general public, on account of its romantic overtones and, among lawyers, by the niceties of the legal problems involved. If Ellen Turner was truly married according to Scots law, she was Mrs Wakefield and could not give evidence against her husband. The prosecution's case, therefore, would fall to the ground. On the other hand, if the marriage was invalid, since the facts of the case were not in doubt, the doom of the Wakefields was sealed.

Brougham was amongst the counsel appearing for the Crown, with Sergeant Cross[43] as his principal, whilst the defence was conducted by Mr Scarlett,[44] afterwards Lord Abinger. Panizzi and Brougham travelled together for the trial, which was held, after many delays, at Lancaster on March 23, 1827.

Brougham realized that the question of the validity or otherwise of the marriage was the key to the prosecution's whole case and that he must shake the expert evidence of the Scots lawyers. The young Italian, with his knowledge of continental legal systems, was of inestimable value to Brougham, who completely routed the Scots advocate, McNeil,[45] by his quotations from Roman law, the Edicts and Novels of Justinian and other learned sources. Though the marriage was declared to be valid in law, yet the presiding judge ruled that Ellen Turner's evidence might be received. Edward got three years in Newgate, his accomplices lighter sentences and the marriage was declared invalid by a special act of Parliament.[46]

Brougham must, it seems, have been deeply impressed by the knowledge and sturdy common sense of this young Italian teacher, for very shortly afterwards, he was instrumental in giving Panizzi his great chance. Others, such as Thomas Campbell, who had known and liked him on his first arrival in London, may have helped. It was Brougham's interest which was to be decisive.

As early as 1821, Campbell had discussed with his friends the idea of a University in London. No one not a member of the Church of England, no Dissenter, Catholic or Jew, might go to Oxford or Cambridge and this was now felt to be an intolerable restriction on the opportunities for higher education of so numerous a section of the community. Campbell had early enlisted Brougham's powerful assistance. The latter, who perhaps saw the scheme as a stepping stone to high office, rapidly displaced Campbell as the driving force behind the idea for the new University. Brougham had undoubtedly a deep and genuine interest in educational matters, but he was never averse from being in the centre of affairs. He now became Chairman of the newly established Council and for the next few years gave the undertaking most of his time and attention.[47]

In 1827 the first appointments to the various professorships were announced. It would seem that Campbell had first thought of Panizzi's friend Pecchio as a suitable candidate for the professorship of Italian, but the latter, having just married, gave up the idea on hearing that the post was one of small financial value. As we have seen, the dying Foscolo was briefly interested, but soon withdrew his application. Panizzi himself had recommended that his Piedmontese friend, De Marchi, who was at that time teaching in Edinburgh, should get the post and another candidate was Gabriele Rossetti, the father of D.G. and Christina Rossetti. In July 1827, De Marchi wrote to Panizzi that he was unlikely to apply for the professorship, an assurance he repeated a month later, when he heard that Panizzi had recommended him for it and in a further letter of August 1, 1827, assured Panizzi that he would himself use such influence as he possessed in his favour should Panizzi now wish to apply for the post.[48]

But a more powerful influence than De Marchi's was being brought to bear on behalf of the young Italian from Liverpool. Brougham, though no longer Chairman of Council, his place having been taken by the Duke of Sussex, the 'liberal' member of the royal family, was still one of the most influential figures behind the scenes. Impressed by what he had seen and heard of Panizzi's knowledge and acumen, he warmly espoused his cause. Panizzi himself was, not unnaturally, a little hesitant. He was at last doing well in Liverpool. He had made good friends there and had won for himself a position of comparative importance in intellectual circles. This University appointment, like the University itself, was a new and untried gamble. Men, whose knowledge and experience he respected, had already rejected it and London was a strange and unfamiliar world, in which he would have to carve out a position for himself anew.[49]

To help resolve his doubts, in February 1828 Panizzi paid a visit to London to see Horner, the Warden of the new University. Horner[50] received him kindly and they discussed what his duties would be. Panizzi had a strong objection to teaching beginners and expressed the view that he should have an assistant, on whom such tasks would devolve. Panizzi, as always, knew his own mind, and strongly voiced his feelings on the subject to Horner. In his subsequent letter of thanks,[51] he suggested that a certain Pistrucci should be his assistant, who was, he assured the Warden, 'a reasonable man . . . not a sturdy pedant or a conceited coxcomb'. Pistrucci also had the advantage of being a Roman, and thus, his accent would be a good one for beginners to imitate. Panizzi further goes on to give an account of the method of teaching Italian which he had himself found to be the most successful. He obviously felt that his system was the best available, far superior to any known other.

Panizzi's formal appointment to the Chair of Italian Language and Literature at the University of London was dated February 16, 1828, but he does not seem to have taken up his duties there until the following autumn. He must first close up his affairs in Liverpool, and say good-bye to all the friends, the Roscoes, Shepherd, Haywood and many others, whom he had made during the last five years.

In a letter to Horner,[52] acknowledging his appointment, Panizzi returns to the question of his having an assistant. He lays down firmly what he considers to be the respective duties of himself and of such an assistant. With his usual directness and clarity of thought, he suggests to the Council that, in conjunction with the other professors, a uniform plan should be adopted for the study of all modern languages and literature. Here was already evident that rationalization, that desire to eliminate all unnecessary hindrances to efficiency, that was to be so notable a feature of his years at the British Museum.

The Council did not approve of their new professor's suggestion and, unwillingly, Panizzi agreed that the responsibility for elementary teaching was his alone. He would be willing to undertake the unwelcome task himself for, at least, the first year, if such proved to be necessary. Subsequently, he reluctantly offered to renounce his claim to have an assistant, if the Council should so desire, but making it quite clear that he was indifferent to any pecuniary loss that he himself might suffer, should such an assistant eventually be provided.[53] Panizzi was always indifferent to money, and, indeed, to any personal consideration whatever, when the question of efficiency was at stake. He never ceased to complain, however, of his profound dislike of teaching beginners.

At the moment, the newly appointed professor had nobody, whether beginners or more advanced, to whom he might lecture. The young Robert Browning was entered as a student of Italian, but his name was withdrawn before the classes began, as a private tutor had been found for him nearer home. Thus Panizzi was deprived of the privilege of guiding the first steps in the study of Italian language and literature of one who was, in after years, to do so much to make more widely known the land and people of Italy.

Panizzi had now left his Liverpool friends, armed with letters of introduction from Roscoe to all his London acquaintances. The letter which Roscoe addressed to Samuel Rogers,[54] the banker poet, is a warm and eloquent tribute to the high regard with which the old scholar now held his young friend. Brougham, too, did not forget his protégé. He introduced Panizzi to Lady Dacre,[55] the authoress and translator of Petrarch: 'This will be presented to you by Professor Panizzi, of whom my brother has already spoken to you and of whom it is quite impossible to say too much.'

Panizzi and Lady Dacre, from this time on, became firm friends and, by her position and influence and that of her husband, greatly helped his entry into London society. Another who wrote to congratulate Panizzi on his new appointment was W. S. Rose,[56] an acquaintance from his earliest days in England, and now settled, close to Pecchio, at Brighton. For a number of years, until Rose's death in 1843, Panizzi and he wrote to each other frequently and a warm friendship developed between them.

On arriving in London, Panizzi had taken up his residence at 2 Gower Street North, close to the University buildings and, hopefully, he set about his new duties. Unfortunately, for the moment, there seemed to be few, if any. No introductory lecture was delivered and, though Panizzi expressed to the Council his willingness to give instruction at any time that he might be required to do so, hardly any pupils were found to take advantage of his offer. He had five during the first year, eight in the next and, once more, five in the following year. To a man bursting with energy, such as Panizzi, this state of affairs was ludicrous. With his usual keeness, he now produced two little books on the teaching of Italian: *Extracts from the Italian Prose Writers for the Use of Students in the London University*, and, shortly afterwards, an *Elementary Italian Grammar*.[57]

But he had little real interest in teaching. He occupied his ample leisure by further research in the field of Italian renaissance studies and in the preparation of his editions of Boiardo and Ariosto, upon which his reputation as a scholar mainly rests.

In the meantime, there were financial and other troubles. On his appointment, the Council, doubtless under Brougham's influence,

and owing to the particular circumstances of his case, had agreed
to advance Panizzi a loan of £250 a year for the first two years,
'such advance to be gradually repaid by him when ever his receipts
from public and private teaching shall exceed £250'.[58] So far and,
it would seem, for the foreseeable future, his fees were nothing like
that and the £250 was almost his sole means of support. In October 1828, the Council decided that the Professors of Italian, German, Spanish and Oriental languages should be guaranteed £200
a year. By this decision, Panizzi was to be deprived of an additional £50, which he had been led to expect before giving up his
position at Liverpool. Not unnaturally, he protested, but was
given only the choice of accepting the loan of £250 or of the
guarantee of £200. The Council further laid it down that no
guarantee of any sum would be made after the session of 1829–30.

This immediately raised great difficulties for Panizzi. His fees
from his pupils were almost negligible and little further was to be
made from an occasional review. The spectre of abject poverty,
such as he had experienced during his first years in England,
raised its head and he bitterly regretted his decision to leave
Liverpool. where he was known and liked and had enjoyed moderate financial security, for the hazardous uncertainty of life in London. In March 1829, he outlined to the Council a plan for a course
of lectures on the Romantic Narrative Poets, hoping such a subject might attract a better attendance. The lectures were duly
delivered, but the audience was small and a further course attracted
only two people, 'who would not have attended if they had not
been my private friends'.[59]

In the following April, he asked the Council for permission to
give a series of lectures on Italian life in a place where ladies might
be able to come. Much of the current interest in Italian was to be
found among women and, once more, poor Panizzi hoped things
might be better. Permission was granted and the lectures were
given in Willis's Rooms, King Street, St James. About fifty people
enrolled for the course, all of whom, however, seem to have been,
once more, his own friends.

These were unhappy years for Panizzi, years of frustration and
bitterness, when, despite the pleasure he found in the company of
his new friends, the outlook seemed to be bleak and unpromising.
In the controversy which now arose at the University between the

Warden and certain of the professors, Panizzi loyally supported Horner. It was alleged that the latter was endeavouring to drive out of the University John Conolly,[60] the Professor of Medicine. Unlike his colleagues, the Professors of Spanish and German, Panizzi did not sign the letter of protest, which was sent to the Council. Indeed, he wrote himself to the Council defending Horner against the attacks on him which had appeared in the more scurrilous Sunday newspapers. He implied that these attacks were due to personal malice and that Proprietors and Professors alike should be grateful for Horner's efforts on behalf of the young institution.[61]

Perhaps had Panizzi been more busily engaged, he, too, would have felt as did his colleagues, for Horner seems to have interfered unduly with the work of the academic staff. Panizzi never tolerated any interference with what he considered to be his own domain and he, too, might well have fallen foul subsequently of the over-powerful Warden. Panizzi could always stick up for his rights and for those of others. About this time, he had written a letter[62] to a member of the Council, probably Lord Auckland, protesting against the professional staff having been asked to consent to their own dismissal at any time, without the need for any cause to be shown. Such an action aroused all Panizzi's hatred of injustice and must have seemed particularly galling to him in his present circumstances. But help was at hand and a new and brighter prospect suddenly revealed itself to him.

The whole question of Panizzi's financial future was still unsettled. The Chair had turned out to be 'a barren honour',[63] and yet he must live. In April 1831, the matter of remuneration was again raised. Panizzi now asked for the payment of the whole of the money due to him, without any deduction by the Council, since during the past year he had had no more than nine students. 'It is evident,' he wrote, 'that if the almost total failure of my class had been foreseen, neither would the Council have appointed a Professor of Italian nor would I have accepted the appointment.'[64]

Events were now happening which were to have a decisive influence on the course of Panizzi's life. On February 16, 1830, his friend Brougham had won a resounding victory at a by-election. He had been returned for a Yorkshire constituency, as Shepherd wrote to Panizzi two years later, against the wishes of both the

3*

Whig and Tory aristocracy.[65] The Whigs now realized that, however much they might dislike it, Brougham was necessary to them, as the link between the official party and the national movement for parliamentary reform, towards which they were now somewhat reluctantly turning.

At the general election in September, Brougham was triumphantly returned for Yorkshire and it was abundantly plain how much of the success of the Whigs was due to his great popularity. On November 15, King William sent for Lord Grey, the Whig leader, and after nearly twenty years in the wilderness, the Whigs were once more in power. Within a few weeks, Henry Brougham was Lord Chancellor, called to the Upper House as Lord Brougham and Vaux, to receive from the irrepressible Creevey the new nickname of 'Guy Vaux'.

As Lord Chancellor, Brougham had immense powers, denied to a mere barrister, however famous and prominent in opposition circles he might be. Obviously considering that, since it was he who had persuaded Panizzi to leave Liverpool, he was, in some degree, responsible for his present plight, Brougham, always a kindly man where his own interests were not threatened, decided to do what he could to help his young acquaintance. By virtue of his office, he was now one of the three Principal Trustees of the British Museum and considered whether it would not be possible for him to secure for Panizzi an appointment within that institution.

Another good friend of Panizzi, also not without influence and most willing to help, was Thomas Grenville,[66] a wealthy book collector and scholar. Panizzi first seems to have become acquainted with Grenville, when, in 1829, he was occupying his too ample leisure with the preparation of his editions of Boiardo's *Orlando Innamorato* and of Ariosto's *Orlando Furioso*. Grenville kindly permitted the young Italian to inspect the early editions of Boiardo in his library, a collation of which did much to restore the hitherto corrupt text of this particular work.

A warm friendship developed between the two, which lasted until Thomas Grenville's death in 1846. He was the youngest son of George Grenville, the friend and follower of the elder Pitt. He had himself held minor office in the Whig administrations early in the century, but had long ago given up his political ambitions to amass his incomparable collection of early printed books. He saw in Antonio Panizzi one whose love of books was equal to his own and one whose warm and affectionate nature and uprightness of character appealed greatly to the old man. In 1830, he had become an elected Trustee of the British Museum and was now only too pleased to put what influence he had at the disposal of his young friend.

It could well be that Grenville's influence was now of more advantage to Panizzi, even than that of Brougham. The latter was deeply distrusted on all sides, even by those most closely associated with him. Creevey considered him to be 'a tortuous villain', and this judgement, though harsh, would have been echoed by many. In time to come, Panizzi was to be widely regarded as one whose entry into the Museum had been engineered by Brougham in some underhand way, and he undoubtedly suffered from this association with the now highly unpopular ex-Lord Chancellor.

Even at this moment, when to many, the fact that this dangerous radical was now Lord Chancellor was in itself an affront, to such a sober and conservative body as the Board of Trustees of the British Museum, the recommendation of a candidate by old Thomas Grenville would carry at least as much weight as that of the newly created Lord Brougham and Vaux.

But, as the Archbishop of Canterbury, the Senior Trustee, pointed out in his evidence before the Select Committee of the House of Commons in 1836, Panizzi was, in fact, chosen entirely on his own record, as 'a man of great acquirements and talents peculiarly well suited for the British Museum; that was represented to me by several persons who were not connected with the Museum and it was strongly pressed by several Trustees of the Museum, who were of the opinion that Mr Panizzi's appointment would prove very advantageous for the institution; and considering the qualifications of that gentleman, his knowledge of foreign languages, his eminent ability and extensive attainments, I could not doubt the propriety of acceding to their wishes.'[67]

How fortunate it was to be for the Museum, for Panizzi himself and for the world of learning in general, that Archbishop Howley consented to make that appointment. His name once proposed, the appointment was speedily made. On April 25, 1831, Grenville wrote in haste to tell Panizzi the glad news: 'I am just come from a meeting of the Trustees of the Museum, and have the satisfaction of telling you that your name, when proposed to succeed to the vacant Assistant Librarian[ship], was received with high testimony to you, universally approved, and the Archbishop said he would lose no time in signing the appointment and in obtaining the Chancellor's concurrence. The appointment was £200 per annum for five days in the week . . . I am very glad of your success and think that your appointment will be of great value to the Museum.'[68]

Soon followed the official appointment, signed by the Archbishop and by the Lord Chancellor.[69] The Speaker, the third Principal Trustee, whose signature would normally have been on the document, was not included, since Parliament being dissolved, there was, constitutionally, no holder of that office. How very relieved Panizzi was to get it and to see these all-important words: 'Antonio Panizzi, LL.D. to be one of the Extra Assistant Librarians in the said Museum.'

As was then the custom, two persons had to stand surety for £500 each, in addition to the candidate's own bond of £1,000. Two friends of his Liverpool days were happy to do this for him, the ever-faithful Haywood and John Ewart, son of old William Ewart.[70] At last Panizzi had entered an institution, where, for the first time, he could make truly felt his great talents and his prodigious powers of organization.

NOTES TO CHAPTER 4

1 In a deleted paragraph of a letter of February 6, 1866, to Sir Robert Murchison, Panizzi wrote of himself as: 'A man who came to this country with not quite a sovereign in his pocket, knowing no one nor a word of the language.' [Add MS. 36, 723. f.321.]

2 Pecchio, *Semi Serious Observations*, p. 2.

3 Pecchio, p. 29.

4 Fagan, I, p. 43.

5 Pecchio, p. 169.

6 Thomas Campbell, 1777–1844.

7 Ugo Foscolo, 1778–1827.

8 A. Gallenga, *Episodes of my Second Life*, vol. 2, p. 22, gives an account of an interview he had with Panizzi at the British Museum in 1839, during the course of which the latter exclaimed, 'I lived here for two years at the rate of fourteen pence a day . . . I tell you; it is a starving trade [teaching Italian]. I had to go to Liverpool for my bread.' Brooks relates this story to Panizzi's time as Professor of Italian at London University, but it seems more probable that Panizzi is referring to his first years in England.

9 William Roscoe, 1753–1831. Letter to William Roscoe, the Younger, from Thomas Campbell, July 5, 1823 [*Times Literary Supplement*, July 8, 1944]. Letter to William Roscoe the Elder from Foscolo, August 12, 1823 [*Giornale storico della Letteratura Italiana*. Vol. XCII. pp. 214, 215.]

10 Fagan, I, p. 51.

11 H. Roscoe, *Life of W. Roscoe*, v. 2, p. 407.

12 *The Liverpool Tribute to Roscoe*, p. 8.

13 Santa Rosa to A.P., September 5, 1823. *Lettere ad A.P.*, p. 11.

14 William Shepherd, 1768–1847.

15 Francis Haywood, 1796–1858. A cotton broker, he translated Kant and other works from German. He was, in all probability, Panizzi's closest friend for the greater part of his life. He died at Feckenham, near Bromsgrove, Worcester, on May 29, 1858.

16   William Ewart, 1798–1868. Prominent radical MP. Promoted acts for the abolition of capital punishment and for the establishment of free public libraries.

17   Unlike many of his fellow refugees from the Italian states. Certain of these, in a petition to the Home Secretary, Peel, declared they were 'reduced to the last misery . . . We had sold even our . . . wearing apparel . . . to beg a piece of bread.' They seem to be, for the most part, men who had fought in Spain and do not seem to have included any acquaintances of Panizzi. [Add. MS. 40, 371. f.184.]

18   Add. MS. 36, 714. f. 14. [Jeffrey to A.P., September 1, 1824.]

19   Add. MS. 36, 728. f.2

20   *Liverpool Mercury*, November 11, 1825.

21   Add. MS. 36, 728.

22   Count Claudio Linati, 1790–1832. He died, still an exile, at Tampico in Mexico.

23   Panizzi had already moved there by September 25, 1825, since the letter of Jeffrey, enclosing the draft for twenty guineas, was sent to that address. Later he moved to 9 George Street, a little further from the centre of the city and, it would seem, in a slightly better neighbourhood and remained there until his final departure for London.

24   A. P. to Foscolo, February 25, 1826. *Epistolario*, vol. 3, p. 460.

25   *Epistolario*, vol. 3, p. 461.

26   Foscolo to A.P., July 27, 1826. *Lettere ad A.P.*, p. 36.

27   A.P. to Foscolo, July 29, 1826. *Epistloario*, vol. 3, p. 463.

28   *Epistolario*, vol. 3, p. 464. Fagan, I, p. 69.

29   A.P. to Foscolo, October 11, 1826. *Epistolario*, vol. 3, pp. 465–469.

30   The house, Bohemia House, had formerly been the King of Bohemia tavern, which was the meeting place for the Jacobite conspirators, who plotted there to assassinate William III in 1696.

31   The little note from Floriana, thanking Panizzi for his kindness, is Add. MS. 36, 714, f.95.

32   Fagan, I, p. 71.

33   Henry Peter Brougham, Baron Brougham and Vaux, 1778–1868. In 1835, Panizzi wrote that he had known him 'during a period of more than ten years'.

34   A.P. to Foscolo, October 11, 1826. *Epistolario*, vol. 3, p. 465.

35   Thomas Creevey, 1768–1838.

36   Add. MS. 40, 532, f.172. Brougham to Peel. August [1843].

37 George Canning, the future Prime Minister, 1770–1827. Panizzi was afterwards friendly with his son, Earl Canning, Governor-General of India.
Isaac Gascoyne, 1770–1841, soldier, MP for Liverpool, 1802–1830.

38 Hobhouse, Diary, May 28, 1825. *Recollections*, vol. 4, p. 52.

39 Letter in Biblioteca Labronica, Leghorn. Quoted in Brooks, p. 37. Text is in
Brooks, p. 198.

40 Add. MS. 36, 714. f.29.

41 Edward Gibbon Wakefield, 1796–1862. Wakefield had already been mixed
up in a similar adventure, when, in 1816, he had abducted an heiress, who
was a ward of court.

42 *Annual Register*, 1827, p. 316.

43 Sir John Cross, 1776–1842. Barrister and judge.

44 James Scarlett, first Baron Abinger, 1769–1844. Tory MP for various
constituencies. Attorney-General in the ministries of Canning and Wellington.

45 Duncan McNeil, 1793–1874, first Baron Colonsay, Solicitor-General and
Lord Advocate, subsequently on the Scottish bench.

46 7 & 8 Geo. IV Private Acts. c.66, *An Act to declare void an Alledged Marriage
between Ellen Turner, an infant and Edward Gibbon Wakefield*.

47 Creevey sarcastically referred to 'Brougham and the enlightened who are
founding Stinko miles college at the end of Gower Street'.

48 Add. MS. 36, 714, ff.84, 86. De Marchi had been a friend of Panizzi in his
Brescello days.

49 Pecchio seems to have been equally dubious. 'As to your chair, it is not only
doubtful that you will be richer, but very doubtful whether you will be
happier. That depends on your character. London contains so many things
irritating to the bile.' [*Lettere ad A.P.*, pp. 72, 73.]

50 Leonard Horner, 1785–1864. Geologist and educationalist.

51 A.P. to Horner, February 24, 1828. Original at University College, London. Text is given in Wicks, p. 266.

52 A.P. to Horner, April 19, 1828; April 29, 1828, as above. Wicks, pp. 267.
268.

53 A.P. to Horner, April 29, 1828. Original at University College, London.
Text is given in Wicks, pp. 267, 268.

54 Fagan, I, p. 73. Samuel Rogers, 1763–1855, banker, poet and connoisseur.
He was offered the Laureateship on the death of Wordsworth, but declined.

55 Add. MS. 36, 714. f.127. Brougham to Lady Dacre, March 3, 1829. Barbarina Brand, Lady Dacre, 1768–1854, poet and dramatist. In 1819 married, as her second husband, Thomas Brand, 21st Lord Dacre.

56   William Stewart Rose, 1775–1843. MP for Christchurch, Hants., 1796. Reading Clerk to the House of Lords and Clerk of Private Committees, 1800–1824.

57   *An Elementary Italian Grammar for the Use of Students in the London University.* John Taylor; London, 1828. *Extracts from Italian Prose Writers for the Use of Students in the London University.* John Taylor; London, 1828.

58   *Minutes of Proceedings of Council.* Brooks, p. 47.

59   A.P. to T. Coates, May 1, n.d. Quoted in Wicks, p. 269.

60   John Conolly, 1794–1866. Specialist in mental disorders.

61   A.P. to Council of London University, March 13, 1830. Quoted in Wicks, p. 269.

62   *Brougham MSS.* March 24, 1829. Quoted in New, *Life of H. Brougham,* p. 387.

63   So called by Keightley in his review of A.P.'s 'Orlando' in *Foreign Quarterly Review,* no. 29, vol. xv. 1835.

64   *University College MSS,* no. 2444. Quoted, Wicks, p. 133.

65   W. Shepherd to A.P., April 4, 1832. Add. MS. 36, 714. f.261.

66   Thomas Grenville, 1755–1846. An adherent of Fox in 1782 he had begun the negotiations which were to end the American war. First Lord of the Admiralty, 1806–1807.

67   *Select Committee on the British Museum,* 1836, para. 5511.

68   Add. MS. 36, 714. f.223.

69   Add. MS. 36, 714. f.224.

70   Add. MS. 36, 714. ff.229, 231.

5

DEPARTMENT OF PRINTED BOOKS

THE institution of which Antonio Panizzi had now become a comparatively humble official was already old. The Act which had created it and which was to govern its administration for more than two hundred years had been passed nearly eighty years before in the reign of George II. This gathered together several earlier collections and joined to them the great collection of books, natural specimens and curios which had been amassed during the course of his long life by Sir Hans Sloane, the eminent physician. Under the terms of his will, this had been offered to the Crown for £20,000. The Treasury, being unwilling or unable to raise such a sum, the Act authorized the newly appointed Trustees to raise the money by means of a lottery. This was done, in a fashion scandalous even by eighteenth-century standards, and sufficient money was raised to purchase the collections, invest another £30,000 and to purchase suitable accommodation, Montagu House, Great Russell Street, Bloomsbury. In this old building, with subsequent additions, were still to be found the national collections when Panizzi joined the Trustees' service.

During the subsequent years, the Museum had continued on its way, largely undisturbed by the changing world without. There was, as yet, little systematic extensions of the collection, save by the generosity of a few enlightened individuals. Funds were low and the staff, though scholarly and conscientious, were mostly elderly clergymen or physicians. Visitors and readers were few, and those grudgingly admitted, whilst, over all, brooded an air of self-satisfied stagnation.

With the turn of the century, things slowly improved. In 1799, Joseph Planta,[1] Keeper of Manuscripts, was appointed Principal Librarian, a post he held until 1827. Planta, a most capable and industrious man, of Swiss descent, presided over the fortunes of the Museum during a period of increasing strain and complexity. Large new collections of antiquities, such as the Elgin Marbles,[2] necessitated the erection of other buildings and important additions were also made elsewhere. Two men, who joined the staff about this time and who were to be closely connected with Panizzi for much of his official life, were Henry Ellis,[3] later Sir Henry, and the Rev. Henry Baber.[4] Ellis, who succeeded Planta as Principal Librarian in 1827, was to hold that office for nearly thirty years, until, at long last, he was succeeded by Panizzi himself. Baber, a kindly, gentle man, did much, as we shall see, to help the young Italian in his early days at the Museum. Keeper of Printed Books till 1837, he then retired to be succeeded by the most brilliant of his staff, Antonio Panizzi.

But in the first decades of the nineteenth century, these events were far in the future, though the first murmurings of the storms, which were later, almost, to overwhelm the Museum, were already being heard. To an increasing extent, the buildings and the collections, together with the service offered to the public by the Museum, were coming to be considered grossly inadequate. Education was spreading and a new and more critical tone was to be heard everywhere. To J. S. Mill in 1831, transition seemed to be the leading characteristic of the time. 'Mankind,' he wrote, 'have outgrown old institutions and old doctrines and have not acquired new ones.'[5] The rising middle classes and the new intellectuals were demanding that everything should be judged by its utilitarian purpose, and, by these standards, much of the British Museum was woefully inadequate. In the words of Brougham, the schoolmaster was abroad[6] and little of the old, comfortable way of life would remain unscathed by the new Benthamite enthusiasm.

The old house in Great Russell Street could hardly hope to escape from vilification by the radical reformers. Cobbett denounced it 'as a place intended only for the amusement of the curious and the rich'[7] and objected, most strongly, to any public money being spent upon it. Parliamentary grants, however, were still very small and grudgingly bestowed. To most people, the

Museum was a mere favourite resort of idle visitors, charmed by the sight of two large stuffed giraffes, which flanked the upper landing of the magnificent main staircase and by suchlike exotic sights. That this heterogeneous collection of antiquities, odd scientific specimens, manuscripts and a few rare books should ever become an institution devoted to scholarship of the highest standard and, moreover, be the home of the greatest library in the world, in which men and women of every nation and creed might read and work, was an ideal then held by few, if indeed, by any. It was one which needed the great gifts, the courage and single-mindedness of purpose of an obscure Italian exile, of a provincial language teacher to transmute it, by his genius, into an established fact.

The Department of the Museum to which Panizzi had now been appointed was the Department of Printed Books. In 1831, this was, perhaps, the least known and least regarded of all. Even among scholars, it was not highly thought of, but, already, important new material was being bequeathed to supplement the original founding collections. By the thirties, Panizzi considered that for rarities and for costly modern books it already surpassed any other library of its size. It was, however, still far smaller than several other comparable European institutions. As the National Library of the wealthiest and most powerful nation in the world, it could only be regarded as totally inadequate.[8]

It contained, at this date, no more than some 240,000 books, less than the Bibliothèque Royale, and less than the principal libraries of Munich, Dresden, Copenhagen, Vienna and Berlin.[9] The books were housed in a suite of rooms on the ground floor of Montagu House, to which the public were not admitted. These rooms were entirely inadequate for the growing needs of the Department. New buildings were, indeed, contemplated. As early as 1815, the Trustees had appointed a young architect, Robert Smirke,[10] to draw up plans for a new wing to the old house. In 1823, the gift by George IV of the magnificent collection known as the King's Library convinced Parliament that newer and safer buildings to house the contents of the Museum were essential. By 1827, no less than £120,000 had been voted to defray the cost of the new construction, and in the following year was opened the great room, specially designed to contain the royal bequest.

This, by far the most splendid the Department has ever received, was the library built up over the years by George III, a
discriminating collector. On his accession, his son had but little
use for it and was persuaded to hand it over to the nation.[11] With
it came a staff of three Assistants and two Extra Assistants. These
provided a most welcome addition to the staff of the Department,
since their duties were not confined to work on the royal library
itself.

Among the works acquired during the first decades of the nineteenth century was a series of tracts on the French Revolution.
This had been bought in 1817 on the recommendation of J. W.
Croker,[12] who subsequently sold to the Museum two further large
collections. The first set had recently been bound, but had not yet
been catalogued. Panizzi's very first task on entering the Museum
was to transcribe a list of duplicates, which was to be submitted to
the Royal Society for their selection, but soon he was given something more worthy of his knowledge and abilities. This was to
commence cataloguing the newly bound volumes of the first
series of revolutionary pamphlets. He was, however, prevented
finishing by pressure of other work and the tracts were, in fact, not
finally catalogued until the 1870s. It was while dealing with these
pamphlets, a large proportion of which are anonymous or pseudonymous and almost all of which present peculiar problems, that
Panizzi first began to devise those rules for the cataloguing of
anonymous books that are among his many claims to bibliographical fame. He had also, of course, been given other tasks. He
was engaged in current cataloguing, in setting in order the Bank-
sian Collection, and in arranging and cataloguing the many rare
books to be found in the King's Library. This was an occupation
of which he was particularly fond and one to which he brought all
his considerable powers of scholarship. He was still living in
Gower Street, for though many of the officers had apartments in
Montagu House, Panizzi was not, as yet, of that number.[13] He was
working hard six days a week, thoroughly familiarizing himself
with every aspect of his new profession.

Much of Panizzi's superabundant energy and undoubtedly pugnacious temperament was occupied, for the next year or two, by
his quarrel with the Royal Society, a quarrel from which the
young Italian emerged shaken, but unconquered.

In 1832, the Royal Society had come to the conclusion that a class or subject catalogue of the books in their library which had been lately compiled by one of their own members, should be revised and, if necessary, seen through the press by some more experienced cataloguer. In October, a Committee of the Council approved a suggestion that Panizzi should be approached and be asked whether he would be willing to undertake this task. That evening, Panizzi happened to meet at dinner Dr Roget,[14] Secretary to the Royal Society, who asked him whether he would do it. Panizzi agreed and was thereupon given by Roget a specimen proof sheet of the projected catalogue. He took it home and started to work on it, but, to his dismay, it was so full of errors of every description, that, in his own words: 'it was utterly incapable of correction'.[15]

Panizzi, therefore, wrote to Roget straight away, declining to have anything further to do with a work which would only 'be disgraceful to the Royal Society and to any person who should venture to meddle with it'.[16] Christian and surnames had been confused; titles misread, mistranslated and, frequently, so completely altered as to be quite incomprehensible. Childish mistakes of every possible kind had been perpetrated; a work on starfish had been entered under 'Astronomy' and many other absurd 'egregious blunders' of a similar nature were immediately apparent.[17]

Panizzi further wrote to Roget, either then, or, more probably, shortly afterwards, to suggest that the Society should authorize the compilation of an entirely new Catalogue and that, if the Society so approved, he himself would be willing to undertake it. On October 16, therefore, the Cataloguing Committee decided to recommend to the Council of the Society the employment of Panizzi on the compilation of a new catalogue at a fee of £30 per 1,000 titles of scientific books, the total sum to be paid not to exceed £500.[18]

When Panizzi met the Council a fortnight later, he proposed that of this amount, the first instalment would be paid when all the titles had been written; another third when the titles were ready for the printer and the remainder when the whole work was completed. The Treasurer, Lubbock,[19] who was in the chair, agreed verbally to the proposals, on behalf of the Council, but nothing seems to have been put into writing.

Unfortunately for Panizzi, his well-deserved criticisms of the original catalogue had aroused the dislike, even the enmity, of several members of the Committee and they were determined, in every way possible, to control and restrain the activities of their new cataloguer. On April 25, 1833, the Committee resolved the following: – all comments to be omitted; the Catalogue to be made up to April 1833; Panizzi to make only such alterations as might be suggested by the Committee and the 'revise' to be sent to each member. And so, in the following October, 'cabined, cribbed, confined',[20] Panizzi set about his already unwelcome task. 'Heaven forbid that I should ever be supposed guilty of having approved it,' he exclaimed, 'or be suspected capable of selecting such a plan had I been at liberty to execute the work as I pleased. I agreed to carry their plan into execution on my own responsibility.'[21]

The agreement between the Council and Panizzi was, as has been mentioned, only verbal. Not unnaturally, however, he placed his full confidence in the integrity of the officials of the Society, especially in that of Lubbock, the Treasurer, and Chairman of the Cataloguing Committee, who, personally, had given Panizzi the assurance that the Council would agree to his proposals.

Relations between Panizzi and the Council now rapidly deteriorated, as the Cataloguing Committee attempted more and more to interfere with the progress of the work and as Panizzi, even more firmly, resisted their attempts. At length it was agreed, after much argument, that, in the future, any proposals that the Committee might make concerning the work were to be regarded as suggestions only. Panizzi had won the first round.

In July 1834, Panizzi, having nearly completed the writing out of some 15,000 titles, requested that the first instalment, £150, of the payment due to him should be voted by the Council before adjourning for the long vacation at the end of the month. The cheque would not be payable before the end of August, by which time he reckoned his task would be completed. This reasonable request was opposed by Lubbock on the grounds that Panizzi had probably not written more than eight to ten thousand titles. This was an estimate made by a Mr Robinson, the Society's clerk, and, in consequence, the Council voted a payment of only £100. Panizzi, who had, by the end, written considerably over 20,000 titles, was furious. He refused to accept the smaller sum and wrote

to Lubbock, reminding him of their agreement. He requested that
the titles should be counted and the full amount due to him paid.
After some prevarication by Lubbock, as to what exactly he had
said and what it implied, the titles were counted and found to be as
Panizzi had maintained. A second cheque for a further £50 was
therefore sent to Panizzi. To satisfy his sense of honour, he kept
both cheques until the beginning of September, by which time all
the titles had been written. Only then did he present the two of
them for payment.

By July 1835, the titles were at last ready for the printer, and so,
on July 4, Panizzi applied to the Council for the second instalment
of his fee. He had already, in the previous November, refused an
offer of a further £150 on the grounds that the titles were not yet
ready. Panizzi was sticking firmly to the terms of the agreement.
In his letter to the Council, he now agreed to accept the £150
already offered and asked for a further £150, making a total of
£450 received by or claimed by him. The Council seems, at the
time, to have agreed to this and to have voted the necessary money,
although, one must suppose, with a certain reluctance, and with a
determination to rid themselves of this stubborn and somewhat
self-righteous paragon they had engaged.

Panizzi was, indeed, not yet finished with the Royal Society. He
again had to complain of the continued interference of the Cataloguing Committee and of insufficient access to the books he was
supposed to be cataloguing. The Council now took the step of
asking the opinion of several members of the Committee, who were
experienced bibliographers, as to the value of Panizzi's work.
Among these were Ellis, Forshall and Baber, all colleagues of his,
who knew him well and his true worth. They were unanimously in
his favour and strongly advised the Council not to interfere with
him in the execution of the plan of the Catalogue. Nevertheless,
this expert opinion was pointedly disregarded and it was resolved
that: 'Mr Panizzi be no longer employed on the formation of the
catalogue.'[22] Thus they hoped to be rid of their troublesome
protégé and of all his works. The over-difficult Panizzi would re-
lapse into a seemly obscurity.

But how wrong they were! Day in, day out, in private and in
public, letters, expostulations flowed from Panizzi's ever-ready
pen. A letter to the benign, but not over-intelligent, Duke of

Sussex,[23] the King's younger brother, who was the President of the Royal Society, outlined in telling detail Panizzi's case against those whom he now regarded as his enemies.[24] Similar letters were addressed to other public figures. He was not a trained lawyer nor an Italian, with controversy in his blood, for nothing. In evidence before the Select Committee of the House of Commons in 1836, he speaks scathingly of the Royal Society and of its precious catalogue: 'The worst of all [types of classed catalogues] is the plan I have been obliged to adopt for the Royal Society . . . which will beat anything for absurdity.'[25] This, and other similar remarks, were scarcely likely to endear him to the Fellows.

At long last, in 1839, the 'Catalogue of Scientific Books'[26] was published, but without Panizzi's notes, and, finally, two years later, the 'Catalogue of Miscellaneous Literature'.[27]

So ended after much controversy and with a narrow escape from expensive litigation, Panizzi's connection with the Royal Society. His friends congratulated him on the termination of the wearisome business.[28] He had proved himself to be a man of resource, courage and integrity, if not always of tact; a sound scholar and an accomplished bibliographer, but a man whom, at any time, it was dangerous to cross and one who would never submit to what he considered to be an act of injustice. The whole affair, which certainly reflected little credit on so august a body as the Royal Society, left Panizzi with a life-long distrust of scientists, which he was at little pains to hide.[29]

But whilst this long and acrimonious controversy was going on, Panizzi was steadily making a name for himself at the Museum. At last he could feel that he was engaged in a task which might well prove to be his life's work, and into it he threw all his great energy. He was working all the time, by candlelight, late into the evening, until this was prohibited for fear of fire, and during almost all his vacations.

'I am sorry that you seem to have excluded yourself from all holiday-making,' wrote his friend, W. S. Rose and warned him, 'Nature may give you long credit, but I know by experience that she is a severe creditor and insists upon compound interest.'[30] These wise remarks Panizzi had good cause to remember later in his life. The plea for him to take more care of himself was echoed by others of his friends. Lady Dacre vainly asked him to stay in the country with her husband and herself for a few days.[31] Nothing could deflect Panizzi from his work. For the moment, it seems, he had largely given up that social life of which he was always so fond and was no more to be seen at fashionable dinner parties.

On March 24, 1832, he had become a naturalized Englishman,[32] his sponsors being Lords Sandon and Auckland.[33] From this time forth, though never forgetting or being ashamed of his native land, he more and more identified himself with the country of his adoption.

In April 1834, his Keeper, Baber, proposed to the Trustees that Panizzi be appointed to direct the new catalogue, which it had recently been decided to bring out.[34] Early the following year, Baber reported that Panizzi's output of titles was far ahead of that of any of his colleagues engaged on the same work.[35] It was then discovered that Panizzi, as an Extra Assistant Librarian, was being paid less than the other Assistant Librarians. In consequence, in June 1835, the Finance Sub-Committee recommended to the Board that his salary should be increased by £75 per annum, as a mark by the Trustees of their sense of his value to the Museum, 'and also of the particular service, which, by his zeal and knowledge, he has rendered in an eminent degree to the advancement of the new Catalogue of the Printed Books.'[36]

When, however, on July 11, 1835, this unanimous resolution of the Sub-Committee was submitted to the General Committee, they refused to concur with its recommendations. What the real reasons for this decision were, we do not know. It was said that Forshall, the Secretary, who already disliked Panizzi intensely, had packed the General Committee and had also made certain that two of the members of the Finance Sub-Committee were not summoned to the subsequent meeting. The General Committee, therefore, would go no further than to say: 'Although entirely concurring in the opinion expressed by the Sub-Committee as to the zeal and ability with which Mr Panizzi had discharged the duties of his office,' they felt themselves to be precluded 'from adopting a rate of payment to Mr Panizzi differing from that which is fixed for the office which he at present holds in the Museum'.[37]

This turn of events so angered old Thomas Grenville, who now felt himself to be slighted, both as a member of the Sub-Committee, which had passed the earlier resolution and as a friend of the officer in question, that he immediately got up from where he was sitting, walked out and never attended another meeting of the Trustees as long as he lived.

Forshall, to rub salt in the wound, promptly forwarded to Grenville a copy of the relevant minute, which the latter duly passed on to Panizzi with the comment: 'It is at least an honourable testimony to the sense which they entertain of the value of your services in the British Museum and, as such, I send you the original minute . . . and beg you to keep it.'[38]

The old man was so deeply angered at what he considered to be the meanness and duplicity shown by the Trustees, that it is certain that but for his deep personal affection for Panizzi, he would never have left to the Museum his great library, now one of its most valued treasures.

Panizzi's colleagues in these early days were mostly men far older than he and of a very different stamp. Baber, his Keeper, whom Panizzi was soon destined to succeed, had entered the service of the Museum as early as 1807, having come thence, like Ellis, from the Bodleian. In 1812, he succeeded Ellis as Keeper of Printed Books and collaborated with him on the catalogue issued between 1813 and 1819. He was a kindly, amiable man and a sound, though not distinguished, scholar who had presided over his department capably and diligently during the difficult years of the post-war period. He quickly grew to appreciate the value of a man such as Panizzi, and, despite the latter's quick temper, seems never to have been on anything but the friendliest terms with his younger and more aggressive subordinate.

Panizzi's relations with his other senior colleagues were, on the whole, less harmonious. The Rev. Henry Cary,[39] the well-known translator of Dante, had entered the Museum as an Assistant Librarian in 1826. He was already fifty-four and had tried, unsuccessfully, the previous year for the post of Keeper of Antiquities. A quiet, scholarly man, loved and respected by all his friends, it was he who had first recommended Antonio Panizzi for a reader's ticket long before the young Italian had joined the Museum staff. Cary had recently lost his wife and had then suffered what would now be described as a nervous breakdown.[40]

During his subsequent long absence, most of his duties were

carried out by Panizzi, who thus, in practice, at a very early date, stepped into the position of Assistant Keeper and, as deputy to Baber, gave to that kindly but often somewhat dilatory man the vigorous support which he so often needed.

Even before the death of Mrs Cary, Panizzi seems to have interested himself in her husband's welfare. He had written to his old Liverpool friend, William Shepherd: 'I wish you might get a bishopric for my worthy friend – both for my own sake (first) and for his own,'[41] to which Shepherd replied, 'I wish I could clap a mitre on Mr. Cary's head.'[42] But bishoprics were not so easy to come by even in the early nineteenth century, and later Shepherd regretfully told Panizzi that, though he had 'ear-wigged the Lord Chancellor' in an effort to obtain even a modest living for Cary, he had been completely unsuccessful. 'In moving the mind of Lord Brougham I have done all I can in the business,'[43] he wrote and left it to Panizzi's own discretion, as to whether or not Cary himself should be told.

Whilst one must not doubt Panizzi's genuine kindness of heart, of which there are so many examples throughout the course of his life, one cannot help feeling, as indeed Panizzi himself implied, that the removal of the sick and ageing Cary from his path would indeed be more than welcome. The younger man, full of ambition and conscious of his great abilities, as yet not fully employed, would gladly see the kindly but, in his eyes, incompetent clergyman safely bestowed in a pleasant living, leaving the field free for Antonio Panizzi, his plans and his visions.

Cary, at length, returned to duty, though he never appears to have fully recovered from his breakdown. He continued to work quietly and steadily but, doubtless, not a little alarmed and apprehensive of the energy and powers of work of the fiery young Italian, some twenty-five years his junior and so obviously ready to supplant him.

Panizzi, however, had not fully made up his mind whether or not to stay on at the Museum. He was only an Extra Assistant Librarian, no more, at the best, than third in succession. Without counting Cary or the possibility of some outsider being appointed, Baber was still in excellent health and might remain as Keeper yet for many years. He had made inquiries about a job in the Record Office[44] and had also explored the possibility of becoming tutor in

Italian to the young Princess Victoria. Lady Dacre had kindly made inquiries of the Archbishop of Canterbury. His Grace, however, had been forced to tell her that he was unable to help her protégé. Such matters, he explained, were still entirely in the hands of the Duchess of Kent, the young lady's mother and with her Lady Dacre, unfortunately, had no influence.[45] So the future Queen had lost the opportunity of having Mr Panizzi as her tutor. It is interesting to speculate what might have happened had the two been thus brought together. Women were always enchanted by Panizzi and it is likely that the young Victoria would have been no exception. It is thus possible that Panizzi might have exerted his influence over the course of events by an entirely different means.

But it was not to be and Panizzi worked out his destiny within the walls of the Museum. He did indeed make one more effort. Somewhat surprisingly, he applied to the Duke of Sussex for the vacant post of librarian to the Royal Society.[46] As might have been expected, he did not succeed. The Royal Society had had quite enough of Panizzi for the moment. Very soon, however, all ideas of any change was put firmly behind him.

In addition to the three regular staff, Baber, Cary and Panizzi, there were now in the Department the three further officers who had come with the King's Library. They were employed on a part-time basis and though a most useful addition to their over-worked colleagues, were never fully integrated into the normal structure. There was also the Rev. Thomas Horne,[47] biblical scholar and bibliographer, who had been employed as a temporary assistant for a number of years on the compilation of a classed catalogue. In the neighbouring Department of Manuscripts, the Rev. Josiah Forshall,[48] for the time combining the duties of Keeper and of Secretary to the Trustees, already regarded Panizzi with a hostile eye, whilst his deputy and successor in the Keeper-ship, the fierce and implacable Sir Frederic Madden,[49] was more than ready to carry on the feud.

It will have been noted that many of these learned gentlemen were in Holy Orders, combining, in some cases, their Museum duties with the care of a parish or with a chaplaincy. They breathed, for the most part, the air of an earlier and more leisured day. Into this narrow, comfortable, amateurish little world strode

Antonio Panizzi, the turbulent revolutionary and devoted professional; the alleged Carbonari and the friend of cabinet ministers; a wind that would sweep away for ever the quiet, placid life of the old Museum.

NOTES TO CHAPTER 5

1 Joseph Planta, 1744–1827. Born in the Grisons, Switzerland. Came to London as a child. Succeeded his father in the Museum as Assistant Librarian in 1773.

2 Purchased for the nation in 1816 for £35,000. Lord Elgin had spent over £74,000 in acquiring them.

3 Sir Henry Ellis, 1777–1869.

4 Rev. Henry Hervey Baber, 1775–1869. Keeper of Printed Books, 1812–1837. Rector of Stretham, Cambs., 1827–1869.

5 J. S. Mill, *Spirit of the Age*, p. 6.

6 Speech by Brougham in House of Commons. 'There was another person abroad . . . the schoolmaster . . . and he trusted to the schoolmaster armed with his primer more than he did to the soldier . . . for upholding and extending the liberties of the country.' [*Hansard*, N.S. XVIII. 57, 58.]

7 The Museum was one of his pet aversions. He let no opportunity slip by to denounce it.

8 *Select Committee*, 1836, para. 4773.

9 *Select Committee*, 1836, para. 4774.

10 Robert Smirke, 1781–1867. Knighted 1832.

11 It would seem probable that the story first mentioned in the *Quarterly Review* in 1850 is untrue. This alleged that George had first offered it to the Tsar and had only with difficulty been restrained from selling this magnificent collection to the highest bidder. There is no contemporary evidence for it and those best qualified to know, such as Croker and Princess Lieven hotly denied it. The staff who came to the Museum with the Royal Library were Carlisle as under-librarian ('a rank equal with my own', Baber), Armstrong as assistant librarian and Glover with the same rank, plus two juniors. Carlisle worked two days a week at the Museum, Armstrong three and Glover four [*Select Committee*, 1836, *Minutes*, para. 4514].

12 J. W. Croker, 1780–1857. Politician and essayist.

13 The Principal Librarian, Ellis; five Keepers, Baber, Forshall, Hawkins, König and J. G. Children; and two Assistant Keepers, Cary and Madden had residences. [*Parliamentary Papers*, 1841, vol. XIII, pp. 240–245.]

14 Peter Mark Roget, 1779–1869. Physician and savant. Secretary of the Royal Society, 1827–1849.

15 *Letter to President of the Royal Society*, p. 6.

16 *Letter*, p. 6.

17 *Letter*, pp. 7–16.

18 *Letter*, p. 17.

19 Sir John William Lubbock, third baronet, 1803–1865. Astronomer and mathematician.

20 Fagan, I, p. 127.

21 Fagan, I, p. 127.

22 *Letter to President of the Royal Society*, p. 42.

23 Augustus Frederick, Duke of Sussex, 1773–1843. Sixth son of George III. President of the Society of Arts, 1816, and of the Royal Society, 1830–1839. Caroline Fox declared that he was 'steady, persevering and unchanging in his political principles'.

24 *The Athenaeum* in its review of Panizzi's '*Letter*' declared: 'Mr Panizzi writes English with a dreadful facility that makes one tremble to think of a correspondence with him.' [*Athenaeum*, 1837, p. 892.]

25 *Select Committee*, 1836, para. 4855.

26 *Catalogue of the Scientific Books in the Library of the Royal Society*. London, 1839.

27 *Catalogue of the Miscellaneous Literature in the Library of the Royal Society*. London, 1841. The society also published, in reply to Panizzi's letter, a *Defence of the Resolution for omitting Mr Panizzi's Bibliographical Notes*, ascribed by A.P. to S. P. Rigaud.

28 For example, John Lindley, botanist and horticulturist, 1799–1866, who wrote on November 21, 1839, to congratulate Panizzi that all was over. [Add. MS. 36, 715, f.72.]

29 The dislike was mutual. Both of Panizzi's attempts to become a member of the Athenaeum seem to have been frustrated largely through the opposition of the scientists. Hallam, who was his sponsor at the first attempt in December 1840, was convinced that his failure was due to this. 'It was not long after your dispute with the Royal Society which had prejudiced some of the people.' [Add. MS. 36, 715. f.92.]

30 Add. MS. 36, 714. f.300.

31 Add. MS. 36, 714. ff.364, 365.

32 Wicks, p. 271, gives the text.

33 George Eden, first Earl of Auckland, 1784–1849. Statesman and Governor-General of India, 1835–1841. Dudley Ryder, 2nd Earl of Harrowby, 1798–1882. Styled Viscount Sandon. Succeeded to title 1847.

34   Report by Baber to Special Committee of Trustees, April 26, 1834. *Royal Commission on British Museum, Appendix,* p. 104.

35   Fagan, I, p. 131. *Royal Commission, Appendix,* p. 115.

36   Fagan, I, p. 132.

37   Fagan, I, p. 133.

38   Grenville to A.P., August 3, 1835. Add. MS. 36, 714. f.398.

39   Henry Francis Cary, 1772–1844. Had first visited the Library to obtain materials for his annotations to his translation of Dante. Joined the staff on June 12, 1826. Had supported Rossetti for the post of Professor of Italian at London University.

40   H. Cary, *Memoir,* v.2, p. 198.

41   A.P. to W. Shepherd, March 23, 1832 (?). Shepherd Papers, Manchester College, Oxford. Quoted by Brooks, p. 204.

42   Shepherd to A.P., April 4, 1832. Add. MS. 36, 714. f.261.

43   Shepherd to A.P., July 25, 1832. Add. MS. 36, 714. f.271.

44   Add. MS. 36, 714. f.327.

45   Lady Dacre to A.P., undated. Add. MS. 36, 726. f.49.

46   A.P. to Duke of Sussex, undated. A fair copy not in A.P.'s handwriting. Add. MS. 41, 667. M

47   Thomas Hartwell Horne, 1780–1862.

48   Josiah Forshall, 1795–1863.

49   Sir Frederic Madden, K.H., 1801–1873. Knighted 1833. A fine scholar, despite his cantankerousness and inability to co-operate with other members of the staff.

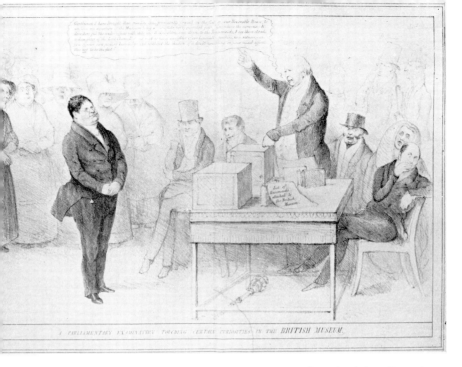

A PARLIAMENTARY EXAMINATION TOUCHING CERTAIN CURIOSITIES IN THE BRITISH MUSEUM.

Henry Ellis, Principal Librarian of the British Museum before the Select Committee
835. The reference is to Sir Henry's remark that his powers of patronage were limited
to the appointment of the housemaids

he cartoon above the speaker is saying: 'Gentlemen, I have brought these maidens thus
ninently forward on the floor of your Honourable House, to confirm my assertion of the
seum being a complete boy of parental patronage, where the Governors & directors
he under offices with their sons & daughters, even down to the housemaids, I say there
ds a daughter of the Lord Chancellor and next to her a daughter of our honourable
ker's, now witness, can you of your own positive knowledge and without the shadow of
ubt remaining on your mind affirm this *not* to be the fact?'

Thomas Grenville,
1755–1846, aged 80

Sir Frederic Madden,
K.H., 1801–1873,
Keeper of the Depart-
ment of Manuscripts,
British Museum

6

THE WORLD EXPANDS

PANIZZI was now beginning to enjoy life. He had a new and interesting position, even though, at times, the future might seem obscure. He was still young and in comparative good health and turned with renewed zest to the gay round he always so loved. From his earliest days at Brescello almost to the very end, Panizzi was very much a social animal. He delighted in good food and good wine, even when gout warned him to forego these pleasures. In the company of his many friends, this essentially lonely man sought a substitute for the family he was destined never to have.

After the first months of bitter poverty, Panizzi had enjoyed at Liverpool a wide circle of acquaintances. All his life, he was blessed with the great gift of making friends easily, in every rank of society. One could never be indifferent to Antonio Panizzi. All must either hate or love him and those who really knew him, both men and women, loved him devotedly. Beneath the grim, often forbidding exterior, there was a kindliness and a generosity few could equal. Old Roscoe, back in Liverpool, had loved him as a son and men as diverse as Brougham and Shepherd, even at this date, testified to his powers of friendship. When he left Liverpool, Panizzi continued to write to William Shepherd, who, particularly after his friend had joined the staff of the Museum, bombarded him with requests for books and for miscellaneous information on various subjects. With proper solicitude, he suggested that Panizzi might care to supplement his Museum salary by taking on pupils and put forward the names of suitable young ladies.[1]

4

Panizzi was far too tied up with his work for the Royal Society to undertake such tasks and, in any case, he had always hated teaching. Just before coming to the Museum and whilst still a Professor without pupils, Panizzi had started to bring out his editions of Boiardo's *Orlando Innamorato* and of Ariosto's *Orlando Furioso*. This scholarly work in nine volumes appeared between 1830 and 1834, prefaced by an *Essay on the Romantic Narrative Poetry of the Italians*.[2]

Panizzi dedicated this work, which had occupied his leisure for many years, to his friend and first patron William Roscoe, 'in testimony of respect from his obliged friend, Antonio Panizzi'. The old man was delighted with this tribute. On May 1, 1830, he wrote to thank Panizzi for his gift of the first volume and for dedicating it to him.[3] He was, alas, never to see it completed. The following year, to the other's deep sorrow, Roscoe died from a severe attack of influenza.[4]

Panizzi's edition of the *Orlando Innamorato* is held by responsible critics to be among the most authoritative of modern times. It has, of course, its defects, arising, for the most part, from his inability to consult the earliest editions. It is, though, in his introductory essay that Panizzi shows most clearly what a fine scholar was lost in a great administrator. The Essay is a formidable feat, especially for one writing in a language not his own.[5] The width of reading it displays, the parallels drawn from Celtic and other epic traditions, bear tribute to Panizzi's deep understanding of his subject. It was a great blow to him that, in a very short while, cares of office made it virtually impossible for him to pursue his academic studies and only in occasional articles could he reveal his powers.

During these years, Panizzi was becoming more and more of an Englishman and more and more regarded life from the point of view of his adopted country.[6] His sensitiveness on this point was undoubtedly one of the principal causes of his angry reaction to the review by Thomas Keightley[7] of his edition of Boiardo and Ariosto, which appeared in *The Foreign Quarterly Review* in 1835. Panizzi had known Keightley slightly for about two years. The latter had succeeded in securing an interview with Henry Baber, who had, in turn, passed the inquirer on to Panizzi. Subsequently the latter had assisted Keightley in the translation of certain obscure passages from Boiardo, on which Keightley himself was now working.

Like so many visitors, before and since, he had several times, whilst at the Museum, thrust himself upon Panizzi and had, at last, asked him for a copy of his Boiardo in order to review it. In exchange, he had presented an obviously reluctant Panizzi with three little volumes of his own work. Panizzi had then felt obliged to present Keightley with a copy of *his* book, and there, for the moment, the matter rested.

Keightley must have brooded over an imagined insult in Panizzi's reluctance to be reviewed by him and may well have been offended by the other's brusque manner. We know, all too well, that Panizzi had no time for fools and he was often plagued by foolish and importunate readers. Whatever the cause may have been, on February 9, 1835, Keightley sent Panizzi a letter, in which he accused him of an attack in an anonymous review. It was, he considered, 'a piece of the basest treachery . . . I bide my time and may yet repay you, but not by a stab in the dark.'[8] Panizzi, having no knowledge of having written any such review and being, at the time, completely prostrated by illness, brought on by over-work, answered this remarkable effusion by a short note, in which he merely expressed his regret 'that the writer of it should be afflicted by a touch of insanity'.[9]

Such a reply must have served only to increase Keightley's anger. In the following month, there appeared his review of Panizzi's work, filled with spite and malice against the man who, he considered, had so deeply offended him. He sneers at Panizzi as: 'one of those Italians who have been obliged to fly their country for their political opinions – a circumstance, by the way, as our readers must be aware, no ways conclusive in proof of the moral dignity of the exiled patriots' souls . . . In his own country . . . utterly unknown as a man of letters.'[10] The appointment of such a man first to London University and then to the Museum was ob-viously the result of the unworthy patronage of the 'Ex-Chancel-lor' Brougham. There were 'deserving Englishmen of letters . . . able to write out the titles of books as well as a foreigner'[11] and so on for the rest of the review.

It was this last remark, however, that really roused Panizzi's anger. *He* was no foreigner. He had been made an Englishman 'by an act of the Legislature'.[12] He loved his adoptive country as much as the one in which he had been born and had only contempt for such utterly unworthy native-born citizens as the wretched Keightley.

Such taunts, and the further ones in the review that Panizzi was 'the virulent assailant of the literary reputation of his illustrious compatriot Rossetti',[13] infuriated the victim beyond measure. He would not stand for such public slurs on his character and reputation. He wrote angrily to the proprietors of *The Foreign Quarterly*, complaining bitterly that such a slanderous attack on the integrity of a man of honour should be permitted to appear in the pages of their 'hitherto respectable journal'.

As to Keightley, he disdained to take any more notice of him. Nevertheless, he threatened that, if he should give further trouble, he would either take legal proceedings or would 'forcibly impress on him that I have partially recovered the use of my limbs'.[14]

These threats of legal action or of the use of brute force, fortunately for the irate Panizzi, never had to be carried out. His friends, greatly alarmed at the vehement expressions in the letter, which Panizzi had promptly published, calmed him down and warned him against the probable effects of too hasty action.[15]

The affair at last blew over and Panizzi again turned to further literary labours during his scanty hours of leisure. Old Grenville had greatly helped Panizzi in the preparation of his edition of Boiardo and Ariosto by lending him, as has been said, several of the early editions of these poets. He was now entrusting his friend with further treasures from his magnificent collection. To show his appreciation of the old man's great kindness, Panizzi had had produced for Grenville a special copy on vellum of the *Bibliographical Notices*. He now sent it to him, together with an ordinary copy of the limited edition of his essay, which he had had printed.

Grenville was delighted with his present and Panizzi proceeded to pay a further compliment to the old bibliophile. To crown his labours on Boiardo and to mark his delight in the poems of a writer, who came from the very same part of Italy as he did himself, whose work was full of allusions to the countryside he feared he might never see again, Panizzi had prepared an edition of the *Sonetti e Canzone* of this then unjustly neglected poet. It was to be a real labour of love; a tribute to one whose work he had admired from his youth. 'I fancy the volume,' he wrote. 'Do not laugh at my conceit. I never did anything so much *con amore*.'[16]

Grenville had already written emphasizing the necessity of including notes, of which Panizzi was dubious. 'They will much increase the value of the publication',[17] and would enhance Panizzi's own reputation. With his usual kindness he now gently asked Panizzi whether he might assist him in the venture. 'As an humble associate in so laudable an undertaking I trust you will have the goodness to accept me as such.' Grenville well knew that his friend was by no means a wealthy man and ever careless over money matters, and feared lest the expense of bringing out such an edition, solely for distribution among his own friends, was beyond his means. Grenville, therefore, included with his reply a draft for £100. He hoped that Panizzi would accept it, as an earnest of his own desire 'to assist in promoting your literary labours, so useful to all readers of taste and so creditable to the distinguished editor'.[18]

Panizzi, by return, equally gently and politely, firmly refused the proffered gift and sent back the draft. He begged Grenville to permit him to dedicate the work to him, without any condition as to helping in the venture. If, however, his old friend was unwilling, Panizzi would nevertheless bring out the work, whether it was dedicated to Grenville or not.

Grenville, in turn, replied that he would be 'highly honoured and gratified by your inscribing the book to me'.[19] Panizzi, touched by the old man's behaviour, thanked him for the 'fresh proof of that delicate kindness to me, which I have so often experienced . . . and which I shall never forget'.[20]

In a short while, the book appeared. It bore the inscription 'All' onorevolissimo signor Tomasso Grenville', with a short laudatory note addressed by Panizzi to his old patron and with the full critical apparatus, which Grenville had considered to be so useful.

From time to time, friends suggested that Panizzi should undertake further scholarly work, but he was unable to find the opportunity to do so. His Museum duties pressed ever more heavily upon him and all that he was able to manage were contributions to various periodicals. Eventually these too ceased, as all his time was taken up with his official duties. Of these articles by Panizzi, we shall speak in a later chapter. Here we will only note that in these, as, indeed, in his letters and in his daily life, Panizzi quickly and thoroughly acclimatized himself. Almost alone among his fellow-exiles, he, from the start, assumes an English personality. No one reading his reviews or his letters, after, say, 1830, would ever assume them to be by one not born an Englishman. His sentiments, his turns of expression, his very prejudices are those of a liberal Englishman of his age and class, interested deeply both in home and foreign affairs, as were most educated men of the day. Like them, he loves Italy, distrusts revolutionaries, whether at home or abroad, fears the power of the Church and is as critical as any Protestant Whig of the renewed pretensions of the Papacy. Only in his great affection for his native land, which never wavered, in any circumstances, and his undying hatred of her oppressors, does Antonio Panizzi show himself to be a true son of the Risorgimento, determined to help unite Italy by any means within his power.

His speedy adoption of English ways is nowhere better exemplified than by his love of London Society. He adored dining or indeed often breakfasting in the company of a select number of friends and acquaintances. His Liverpool circle has already been described, but on his arrival in London, he moved almost at once on to a loftier and more socially distinguished stage. The words Lord Campbell wrote of Henry Brougham might equally have been said of Antonio Panizzi: 'From his first introduction to men of the highest birth and the most distinguished position, [he felt] himself on entire equality with them and without any approach to vulgarity or impertinence he treated them with the utmost familiarity.'[21]

He had been briefly introduced into Whig society and to what one may call liberal intellectual circles during his short stay in London in 1824. But then he was a penniless fugitive, speaking little or no English, an undistinguished member of the flock of needy refugees who, for a short while, crowded the drawing-rooms of their English sympathizers.

He was now in a very different position: a professor at an English university; a distinguished author, and an official – and an increasingly important one – of the British Museum. Above all, he had, as he always had had, the gift for making friends and his friends now moved, for the most part, in the right circles. Brougham, Lord Chancellor or not, was still very friendly, writing to him long letters in Italian. Grenville, as we have seen, was regarded by Panizzi with deep and filial affection; the Ewarts, John and William, though a certain estrangement was growing between them and their old acquaintance, were still on amicable terms. In December 1836, Panizzi writes to Shepherd that he is continually 'in our friend Ewart's house'.[22] W. S. Rose from Brighton complains that he lacks 'the quick and nimble spirit which is in Anthony',[23] since the said Anthony was far too busy to come and see him. He was becoming acquainted with others, such as Gladstone and Clarendon, of whom we shall speak later and Anthony stood on the threshold of that world of the great Whig houses, which he was soon to know so well.

But perhaps the friend to whom he was closest in these early years in London was Barbarina, Lady Dacre. Though Panizzi never married, his relations with women, at least with one woman, usually, in his early days, one older than himself, were always very close. This position of confidante was now, and for some little time to come, filled by Lady Dacre.

Barbarina Brand was already sixty-one and a grandmother, when Panizzi first met her. One of the most talented women of her generation, she had married, as a widow, Lord Dacre, a middle-aged Whig, who had not long succeeded to his ancient title. Lady Dacre was already well known in literary circles for her plays and for her translations from Italian. She was, moreover, an accomplished artist. Foscolo had dedicated his *Essay on Petrarch* to her and had included therein many of her translations. Her husband suffered from chronic bad health and there are frequent references to his illnesses in his wife's letters to Panizzi. He had long given up active politics and remains rather a dim figure in the background.

Panizzi had first met this elderly blue-stocking in 1829. Introduced by the Broughams,[24] Lady Dacre and Panizzi soon became firm friends. He was a frequent guest at their country house, 'The Hoo', in Hertfordshire, though never as often as the old people would have liked. There he was treated as an intimate friend of the family, talking politics to Lord Dacre, Italian literature to his wife and playing games with their small grandchildren. Lady Dacre was now engaged on what she regarded as her life's work, her *Traduzione dall' Italiano*, which appeared, privately printed, in 1835. Panizzi had included some of her translations in his edition of Boiardo – 'You speak very flatteringly of the trifles you allowed me to furnish to your Boiardo,'[25] she wrote – and he was now busily engaged in helping her with translations of Dante and Petrarch, which she constantly sent to him for his comments and revision.

Another friend of these days and an even more indefatigable correspondent was William Rose, whom we have briefly mentioned before. Rose, who had married an Italian lady during his stay in Venice in 1817, was now living quietly in Brighton. Although only in his late forties, he was already a chronic invalid, 'a deaf and rheumatic man, who looks prematurely old',[26] as Crabb Robinson described him. He had met Panizzi during the latter's first months in England, probably at Digamma Cottage, but on Panizzi's return to London in 1828, a warm friendship sprang up between the two men. Rose, who almost always wrote to Panizzi in Italian, constantly asks for his friend's help and advice. During these years, he was slowly bringing out his translation of Ariosto[27] and lent heavily on the younger man's willing assistance. Rose writes to congratulate Panizzi on the publication of *his* Ariosto, which, 'will do you credit with the discerning, whatever may be its success with our literary rabble'.[28] He will, in turn, 'profit by your industry, & . . . finish *my* life of Ariosto'. He intends, however, to translate only the 'decent book', 'as it unfitting at my reverend age (he was only forty-nine) to read even philosophical bawdry.' One longs to hear Panizzi's comment on such a remark!

Another old friend, also living at Brighton, was his fellow-exile Giuseppe Pecchio. Like Panizzi, he had soon settled down in England and had become engaged to a Miss Philippa Brooksbank. Sydney Smith, who alludes to the forthcoming marriage in a letter to Lord Holland in 1828,[29] reassured the bride's parents as to the suitability of their prospective son-in-law. Shortly after their marriage, Pecchio and his wife settled at Brighton, more kindly to Pecchio's far from robust health than Yorkshire, where he had previously been living.

From his house at 4 Mills Terrace, Pecchio writes constantly to Panizzi on the state of Italy, on the Italian poets and on the doings of their fellow refugees. He praises his friend's *Essay* and congratulates him with unfeigned delight at his good fortune in getting into the Museum. Like Panizzi, he had little time for the plotting

and revolutionary activities of certain of the exiles. He deeply distrusted their 'invincible ignorance, the prejudice, the imbecility
and other misbegotten passions',[30] of which he had too often
seen the results at first hand. His influence may well have done
much to restrain the natural impetuosity of the still young and hot-
blooded Panizzi and to turn his energies into less dangerous
channels. Pecchio would rather live quietly at Brighton, with his
friends and neighbours, the Roses. Not far away was Panizzi's old
companion of his student days, Ambrogio Berchet, who, like
Panizzi before him, was trying to make ends meet by teaching
Italian. But Pecchio's health was not good and he died, to Panizzi's
grief, still comparatively young, at his house in Brighton in 1835.

Such were for now the friends and correspondents of Antonio
Panizzi during those early years in London. There were, of course,
others. Macaulay writes from Calcutta, thanking Panizzi for his
present of a copy of his Boiardo and hopes to write an essay or a
review based upon it.[31] Old Samuel Rogers was always pleased to
see the young Italian, whom Roscoe had recommended to him[32]
and Panizzi must have been often present at the poet's famous
literary breakfasts. They would have had much to talk about together. Rogers liked to think of himself as an authority on Italy
and would have also fascinated Panizzi with his recollections of the
literary and political figures of earlier generations. But for the
moment, Panizzi's real interest lay in his work at the Museum and
it is to his career there that we must once again now turn.

NOTES TO CHAPTER 6

1 W. Shepherd to A.P., n.d. [1833]. Add. MS. 36, 714. f.319.

2 *Orlando Innamorato di Bojardo: Orlando Furioso di Ariosto. With an essay on the romantic narrative poetry of the Italians; memoirs and notes by A.P.,* 8 vol., William Pickering; London, 1830–1834.

3 Roscoe to A.P., May 1, 1830. Add. MS. 36, 714. f.169.

4 H. Roscoe to A.P., June 30, 1831. Fagan, I, p. 50.

5 Rose writes: 'My dear Professor, for I cannot write in Italian to one who writes so well in English.' [Add. MS. 36, 714. f.199.] Panizzi's command of written English was, indeed, remarkable. There is little, if anything, in the later articles, reports or letters to suggest that it was not his native tongue he was writing in. His command of spoken English, however, seems to have been less sure and he never lost a most un-English accent.

6 Panizzi never forgot, though, that he had once been a penniless and friendless exile. All through his life he was most generous to those in need, especially foreigners who, unfortunately, often tried to put upon him. [Gallenga. *Episodes*, p. 22.] The Polish exiles made him an honorary member of their cultural society as a tribute to his efforts on their behalf. [Add. MS. 36, 714. f.333.]

7 Rev. Thomas Keightley, 1789–1872. Author and critic.

8 *To the Assignees of Messrs A. Richter*, p. 6.

9 *To the Assignees*, p. 7.

10 *To the Assignees*, p. 1.

11 *To the Assignees*, p. 2. Panizzi takes the opportunity of paying a tribute to Brougham, then very much out of favour with the general public, 'who during a period of more than ten years has uniformly treated me not as a patron (such airs are unknown to him), but as a friend'.

12 *To the Assignees*, p. 4.

13 *To the Assignees*, p. 2.

14 *To the Assignees*, p. 8.

15 Rose, in a poetical epistle of April 15, 1835, adjures his friend to take care, even though he had 'blown your enemy to bits':

But do not in your honest rage outrun
The rule the ghostly king enjoined his son;
Tho' you 'speak daggers – use none' – this I know
You'd scarcely do – I mean don't use your toe
Or break his head, or pull him by the nose
Always yours truly,

W. S. Rose.

[Fagan, I, p. 93.]

16 A.P. to Grenville, September 12, 1834. Add MS. 36, 714. f.345.

17 Grenville to A.P., September 10, 1834. Add. MS. 36, 714. f.343.

18 Grenville to A.P., September 15, 1834. Add. MS. 36, 714. f.347.

19 Grenville to A.P., September 19, 1834. Add. MS. 36, 714. f.356.

20 A.P. to Grenville, September 22, 1834. Add. MS. 36, 714. f.359.

21 Campbell, *Lives of the Lord Chancellors*, vol. VIII, pp. 251, 252.

22 A.P. to W. Shepherd, December 18, 1836. Ewart had been ill and Panizzi writes: 'I am delighted to be able to say he is better.' *Shepherd MSS.*, vol. VII, p. 87. Quoted by Brooks, p. 205.

23 Add. MS. 36, 714. f.329.

24 Brougham to Lady Dacre, March 3, 1829. Add. MS. 36, 714. f.127.

25 Lady Dacre to A.P., November 19, 1834. Add. MS. 36, 714. f.362.

26 H. Crabb Robinson, *Diary*, vol. 2, p. 144. Entry for January 6, 1834. 'Breakfasted with Rogers and his sister by invitation. With them was Stuart Rose, a deaf and rheumatic man who looks prematurely old. He talks low and I should not have guessed him to be a man of note.'

27 *The Orlando Furioso. Translated into English verse . . . with notes.* 8 vol., John Murray; London, 1823–31.

28 Add. MS. 36, 714. f. 336.

29 Holland, *Memoir of S. Smith*, vol. 2, p. 286. 'I cannot say how happy it makes me to see in port a man so clever, so honourable and so unfortunate.'

30 *Lettere ad A.P.*, p. 85

31 Fagan, I, p. 85.

32 Fagan, I, p. 73.

7

CATALOGUES AND COMMITTEES

T HERE was still widespread discussion within the Department of Printed Books and in literary circles on the merits or otherwise of the catalogues available to the public in the Reading Room. The readers were still using an interleaved copy, in twenty-three folio volumes, of the printed catalogue of the old library, which had been prepared between 1807 and 1810 by Ellis and Baber.[1] Into these interleaved copies had been transcribed the titles of a large proportion, but by no means all, of those books which had been received since the completion of the printed catalogue, amounting, in all, to some 30,000 additional titles.

There were also available for readers copies of the Catalogue of the King's Library, less some 10,000 tracts which had been omitted from the printed text and an additional catalogue of the maps, prints and drawings contained in that Library.

There were in existence two such interleaved copies of the catalogue, one, as has been said, for the use of readers, the other for the use of the staff. Both these copies, but particularly the Reading Room copy, were showing marked signs of the heavy use to which they were exposed. In addition, there was increasingly less space available on many of the pages to insert the accessions slips in their correct place within the alphabetical sequence. Many errors had also been found arising from the practice of employing some of the attendants, without proper supervision or instruction, on the highly intricate task of incorporation.

For some years past, Horne, with the occasional help of Madden, had been engaged on the preparation of a classed catalogue of the library. There were many, especially among scientific men, who considered that this form of catalogue was far superior in every way to an alphabetical one. The officers of the department, especially Panizzi, were by no means of this opinion. Panizzi's own views may well have been coloured by his unfortunate experiences with the Royal Society, but Baber, and, to a certain extent, Cary, were of the same opinion. Though Horne was both competent and industrious and was now solely engaged upon the preparation of this catalogue, the work proceeded very slowly. Between 1831 and 1834, six-sevenths of the titles of the books in the old Library had been collected and arranged, but there still remained some 20,000 titles to do. In addition, there were the 120,000 titles from the King's Library. Horne reckoned that it would take at least another ten years for him to complete his task, and that, of course, without taking into account the ever-growing volume of accessions.

Something, obviously, had to be done. The Trustees, in April 1834, appointed a Sub-Committee to consider the state of the present catalogues and the preparation of a new alphabetical one to cover the whole of the collections. They were to consider how long it would take to prepare such a work in manuscript and how long to have it printed. The Keeper of Printed Books was directed to prepare answers to those questions and, also, to report on the present duties of the officers of his department.

On April 26, 1834, Baber submitted his first report. It had been compiled with the active co-operation of Panizzi, who fully concurred, 'with one or two trifling exceptions, not worth mentioning',[2] with the proposals made in it.

The new catalogue should be strictly alphabetical, arranged under the surname of the author, followed by a complete description. Anonymous works should be catalogued under some principal word from the title; pseudonymous works under the pseudonym used. Other suggestions were put forward, suggestions which, developed and expanded, formed the basis of Panizzi's '91 Rules', the foundation of the present rules used by the Department.

Baber further recommended that, since the Trustees wished that the work should begin immediately and be completed with all possible speed, it could best be done by the appointment of a single officer to supervise the whole process, aided by three assistants.

Baber strongly urged that Panizzi should be given this task. 'Mr Panizzi's age,' he wrote, 'activity of mind and various literary acquirements eminently qualify him as the superintending officer of this work, which employment he would cheerfully accept and engage to accomplish in five or six years from its commencement.'[3] Three 'well-educated young men' should be engaged to assist him. Baber also considered that the work, when completed, could be printed off in three years.

But the Trustees were still hankering after a classed catalogue. On the 30th Baber gave it as his firm opinion that 'a classed catalogue . . . if completed, would not be extensively used nor frequently consulted'.[4] At all events, if ever the Trustees wished, the titles, prepared for the alphabetical catalogue, might always be rearranged. Yet worse was to come. The Sub-Committee, under the influence of Ellis, who could conceive of no method superior to that with which he had himself prepared the earlier catalogue, rejected completely Baber's eminently sensible plan. They recommended that Panizzi, Glover and Horne should all be employed on the new Catalogue. They would be relieved of their present duties and devote their time exclusively to the preparation of this work. No additional assistants would, therefore, be required and no one person, be it Panizzi or any other, would fully supervise either the preparation or the printing. Baber had, perforce, to acquiesce in this decision and on May 6 submitted a new plan to the Trustees. He now proposed to divide the work among these officers: Glover to take all the titles in the English language; Panizzi, Spanish, French, Italian and other southern European tongues; Horne, Greek and Latin. He further suggested that a suitably qualified foreigner be employed for German, Danish and other northern European languages. Cary and himself would co-ordinate the work, as far as their other duties would permit. The titles, when revised, would be put in order by one of the attendants and a senior official would supervise their final preparation for the printers.

Baber pointed out once more that the titles could be so marked as to facilitate their rearrangement in class order, if desired. The books in the King's Library would be the most suitable, in his opinion, on which to commence work.

At the meeting of the Special Committee on the same day, these new proposals were considered. Horne and Madden had stated that the titles already prepared for the classed catalogue, some 110,000 titles, were quite correct and would not need any further revision. Panizzi strongly disagreed and urged that *all* titles should be compared with the books they represented. He argued vehemently that Baber's first plan was far superior to the second, in that 'it would produce a more uniform catalogue and that in shorter time and with less expense'.[5]

But the Committee would not have it. Panizzi decided to make one last attempt to get them to change their minds. Two days later, he wrote to Forshall, elaborating his reasons for urging the acceptance of the first plan.[6] But it was no good. The main body of the Trustees endorsed the recommendations of their Special Committee. Baber was instructed to proceed with the alternative plan. Copies of the provisional rules were sent to the cataloguers and their great task began.

The first thing was to sort out the existing titles. Then, assisted by Carlisle, Panizzi proceeded to catalogue the works in the Romance languages in the King's Library. On July 12, Baber was able to report that he had succeeded in obtaining the services of another cataloguer. This was Dr Schier, previously employed in the Manuscripts Department and, at the moment, tutor to the family of Prince Lieven, the Russian Ambassador. Schier was entrusted with the cataloguing of books in the German, Scandinavian and Slavonic languages, of which latter, there were, at this time, very few.

By December, all the titles had been arranged in the respective classes and 13,000 titles already revised. Of this number, Panizzi had revised almost as many titles as all the others put together and naturally the Trustees wished to know how it was that he was at the 'head of the poll'[7]. Baber explained that only Panizzi and Schier were employed full time six days a week on the job. The others did not work more than five days, whilst Schier, who had not started till August, was dealing with particularly difficult languages. Notwithstanding these explanations, it was a formidable achievement for Panizzi and the Trustees were duly impressed.

In the meantime, the transcription of the old catalogue was making progress, though not very satisfactorily. The officer in charge was inefficient and frequently absent. The Trustees,

therefore, gave permission for four transcribers, a new and inter-
mediate grade, between assistants and attendants, to be recruited
specially for this task.

Panizzi had recently been ill. The immense amount of work he
had got through ever since leaving Italy and, in particular, during
the last few years, had damaged even his magnificent physique.
In addition, he now had the worries and vexation of his dispute
with the Royal Society to contend with. He had been forced to be
away for no less than six weeks and, even then, returned before he
was really fit. As a result he had only this time revised comparatively few titles, though, even so, nearly as many as his colleagues.
In 1835, the new transcribed copy of the Reading Room Catalogue
had got as far as the letter 'A' and 'B' was well on its way. Baber
himself, together with Panizzi, Cary and Schier, was busy correcting it and all seemed hopeful.

But the steady progress of the work on the catalogues was now
to be interrupted. By July all work on them had ceased, as the
officers of the department concentrated on preparing the evidence
to be given before a new menace, the 'Select Committee of the
House of Commons on the British Museum'.

It had long been evident that, in those days of reform when
every venerable institution, whether of Church or of State, was
being called into question and when eager members of the House
of Commons were looking busily for the slightest sign of a comfortable sinecure, inherited from the more tolerant days of the
eighteenth century, that the turn of the Museum would come.[8]

The immediate cause of the Inquiry was a certain Mr John
Millard. Millard, who had held a post as a supernumary in the
Department of Manuscripts, had been discharged for inefficiency.
He had, however, certain influence in Parliamentary circles, particularly with Benjamin Hawes,[9] the radical member for Lambeth.
It was felt that this was an opportunity for inquiring into the
affairs of the Museum, which, to an increasing number of the
learned world, seemed far from satisfactory. On Friday, March 27,
1835, the House of Commons resolved that a Select Committee be
appointed to inquire into the Condition, Management and Affairs
of the British Museum.

A large Committee was appointed with Hawes, and two of the
most active of the Trustees, Lord Stanley[10] and Sir Robert In-

glis,[11] among its members. Also upon it was Panizzi's old friend, J. William Ewart, whilst the Chairman was Southeron Estcourt,[12] the Conservative member for Devizes. The members of the Department of Printed Books were not summoned before this 1835 Committee, their turn was to come in the following year. Ellis, Forshall and Madden were, however, all prominent witnesses.

The main purpose of this first Committee, on which radical influence was strong, was to find evidence that the Museum, like so many other bodies, which they had already investigated, was decadent, moribund and the child of aristocratic patronage. The view of at least some members of the committee are well summarized in the words of Cobbett: 'Whatever in the wide world was this British Museum and to whom, to what class of persons was it useful . . . He would like to have a list of the salaried persons . . . whether or not they were dependents of government – some of the aristocratic fry . . . this British Museum job was one of the most scandalous that disgraced the present government . . . The management . . . as bad as bad could be. The officers . . . were . . . clergymen who employed poor curates to perform their duty . . . whilst they were living in indolence and affluence here in London.'[13]

With such sentiments in mind, the main attack of the Committee was first directed to the question of the composition of the Board of Trustees and to the whole system of the management of the Museum. From the first day, May 18, 1835, they harried and worried the calm and imperturbable Sir Henry Ellis as to the duties, status, rank and qualifications of the Trustees. After Ellis had duly informed them that his personal powers of patronage were limited to the housemaids and to the watchmen, the Committee went on hammering at their main contention, that professional men, and especially scientists, were rarely, if ever, elected to be Trustees. This exalted position, 'always considered' as Ellis admitted 'in the literary and scientific world as the blue ribbon of literature',[14] was, in fact, filled almost entirely by men of rank and fashion, who might, or might not be, amateurs of literature or, more rarely, of science.

Sir Henry remained unmoved. 'I never found, even among men of literature and science who have written books, so many men [as the Board of Trustees], who displayed more judgement upon every difficult case which came before them respecting the Museum.' In his opinion, as in Forshall's, it would be disastrous to have promiment scientists on the Board: 'A man who is merely a scientific man would not be a fitting Trustee.' 'I look to the benefit of the Museum, not to the general benefit of science.'[15]

Baffled for the moment, the Committee turned to other grievances. Could not the hours of opening be extended? Here again, in the opinion of the Principal Librarian, the present state of affairs could not be bettered. How otherwise could the Museum be kept clean? On being asked whether he did not consider that such deserving members of society as business men and lawyers would not find it more convenient if the Museum opened in the evening, the good Sir Henry loftily replied that he could not conceive it possible that they would not be able to come during the present hours.

The Committee showed some justifiable anxiety about the position of Forshall and of other officers who had outside appointments, in addition to their Museum duties. Panizzi was instanced, but Ellis loyally, and, no doubt, accurately replied: 'I believe he remains in the list of Professors at London University, but there is nothing that ever calls him away. There is no man more punctual in his attendance.'[16]

Other matters which now engaged the Committee's attention were the disposal of duplicates, finance and the appointment, salaries and promotion of the staff. These disposed of, at least to Ellis's satisfaction, the Committee turned to a favourite topic, the desirability of a classed Catalogue. Here Ellis was vague, referring them for details to Baber, who had not yet given evidence. He did, however, give his opinion, an opinion which was to be more vehemently echoed later by Baber and Panizzi: 'I do not know that a classed catalogue is indispensable, an alphabetical one is. An alphabetical one is referred to 500 times, where a classed catalogue is referred to once.'[17] But the Committee, now having learnt the words 'Classed Catalogue' were loth to forget them.

It was now Forshall's turn. Having explained, more or less satisfactorily, how he managed to combine the duties of Secretary to the Trustees, Keeper of Manuscripts and Chaplain to the Foundling Hospital, he was closely questioned, not only on general Museum matters but on the dismissal of John Millard, the ostensible reason for the whole inquiry. Here Forshall was on firmer ground. He had, he said, written a testimonial for Millard, when the latter had applied for the post of Secretary to the Wyndham Club, and had been as generous as possible. Sir Henry supported Forshall in a vague, surprised way, but it was the redoubtable Sir Frederic Madden, the fiery Assistant Keeper of Manuscripts, who finally disposed of the unfortunate man. He was short and brutal. Millard was, in his opinion, 'totally incompetent for the task to which he had been appointed'[18] and instanced examples of his numerous mistakes in cataloguing. Cross-examination could not shake him. Millard was incompetent and, moreover, lazy and neglectful of his duties. Forshall confirmed this and though Millard was called in to give his story, there was little doubt that the Committee were convinced that the Museum had acted rightly in dispensing with his services. The fact that he was Horne's brother-in-law made it somewhat embarrassing for other members of the staff, but the charge of improper dismissal had clearly collapsed.

After some discussion with the heads of the scientific departments, the Committee reported on August 6. They felt unable to report any resolutions to the House and suggested that a new Committee be appointed to continue the inquiry in the next session.

It was quite certain that the new Committee, unlike its predecessor, would inquire primarily into the administration and working of the Department of Printed Books and to contrast it with comparable libraries elsewhere. As early as 1833, it had seemed probable that, sooner or later, some sort of inquiry into the Department would be set up. Baber, therefore, in consultation with Panizzi, had considered that it was advisable that as much information as possible should be collected in advance on the management of the principal foreign libraries.[19] Panizzi, with the assistance of Baber, then drew up a questionnaire and circulated it, largely through his personal friends and acquaintances, to as many libraries as possible. Replies were, in due course, received from thirty-six institutions, but it was obvious that these would have to be supplemented by personal visits. Accordingly, in the winter of 1835, Panizzi went round the main libraries of Western Europe. Italy and the Austrian Empire was, of course, still forbidden and potentially dangerous territory and, in any case, the time at his disposal scarcely permitted him to venture further. Apart from a short visit to Rouen, this was Panizzi's first trip abroad since his arrival in England thirteen years before. How he now valued the feeling of being no longer a hunted fugitive, but an important official of a great national library and an Englishman into the bargain. Baber wrote to him at Paris, giving him all the news and thanking him for his 'slight report . . . on your bibliographical tour'. His Keeper goes on to say, 'I look with impatience to your return, as I am confident you will bring back with you much interesting information respecting the management of the libraries you may have visited.'[20]

During Panizzi's absence, Baber had suggested, unofficially, that the officers of his department should be given an opportunity of stating quite freely to the Trustees their own views on the new alphabetical catalogue. The Trustees agreed to his good-natured suggestion and so on January 19, 1836, two of their number, the Bishop of London and Sir Robert Inglis, saw first Baber and then such of his colleagues as were available. Baber again emphasized that he would much have preferred to have had his first plan adopted, the one he and Panizzi had drawn up together but, as the Trustees wished it, he would persevere with the alternative arrangements. He made further practical suggestions to the two Trustees and then Cary was sent for. He had but little to add and soon withdrew. The Trustees then asked to see Glover and Panizzi. Glover was not at the Museum, whilst Panizzi, of course, was still abroad. They therefore deferred further inquiry until the latter's return.

Early in February, Panizzi returned. On the 18th of the month the two Trustees interviewed him, at first alone and then with Baber. He was then asked to make a written report on the question. Panizzi jumped at the opportunity of laying before the Board his decided views, not only on the catalogue but also on the Library in general.

He starts, as usual, from first principles. 'The first and chief object of a catalogue . . . is to give an easy access to the works which form part of the collection' – a truism which is, all too often, overlooked – and went on to lay down bluntly that 'the library of the British Museum does not possess such an alphabetical catalogue as the public have a right to expect in such an institution'. It was high time that such a catalogue should be composed, 'without regard to cost or time'. He lays down, in outline, how such a catalogue should be compiled, the genesis of his later rules, and emphasizes, even more strongly than had Baber, the folly of the decision not to have one man, whether himself or another, in charge of the whole operation. At the same time, a subject index should be begun, to supplement the main catalogue. Some might still, he admitted, prefer a classed catalogue, 'such however is the magic of names', and if such were decided on, none could carry it out better than his colleague, Horne. He also strongly advocated the preparation of special catalogues, such as of rare books or of such collections as the Civil War or French Revolutionary tracts. All this would, of course, take both time and money, but 'no consideration of expense ought to weigh against doing what is absolutely necessary to render a great national institution worthy of this country'.[21] Proud words, but no man ever meant them more sincerely than did Antonio Panizzi. In a final appeal, he urges the Trustees to take the advice of their officers and to rely on their experience, honesty and zeal. Unfortunately for the Museum and for Panizzi himself, the Trustees, under the malign influence of Forshall, were increasingly unwilling to do as he so earnestly suggested.

The Board must have been impressed by such strong sentiments expressed with marked vehemence by a comparatively junior officer, but decided to defer consideration of his views until a later date. In the meantime, they asked the other officers for their ideas. They had few, apart from a decided preference, unlike Baber and Panizzi, for a classed catalogue. It was abundantly clear who was the dynamic personality in the department.

More urgent matters were now closely engaging the attention both of the Trustees and of their principal officers. The new Committee was a smaller and more able body than its predecessor. Several of the more belligerent and less intelligent members had departed and it might be fairly anticipated that the new Committee would spend less time smelling out imaginary scandals and abuses and would, instead, genuinely seek to discover what, if anything, was wrong with the Museum and would then do its best to recommend appropriate remedies.

In the middle of February appeared a pamphlet: *A Letter to Benjamin Hawes, Esq. MP, being strictures on the Minutes of Evidence taken before the Select Committee on the British Museum.* This was the work of Edward Edwards, a young man of working-class origins, who had been for some time a reader at the Museum. When the Minutes of Evidence of the 1835 Committee had been published the previous August, Edwards had read them with avidity and, within a few months, had produced his little book. In it, whilst gently deriding Sir Henry's Toryism, he makes numerous valuable suggestions for improving the service to readers and for the Museum in general.

This publication, the work of a member of the public quite outside Sir Henry's ken, was eagerly read by members of the staff and, not least, by Panizzi. Here, it would seem, was one who shared his belief in the future of the Museum, his desire to make it the greatest institution in the world and, of course, though they were destined to quarrel so bitterly, Panizzi and Edwards had much in common. For the moment, they did not meet, as Panizzi prepared for the moment when he would appear before the Committee. But that time was not yet. The men of science, both inside and outside the Museum, must first have their say and propound their frequently preposterous theories.

At last, on June 2, it was the turn of Printed Books. At once, one feels, the character of the evidence changes. Here, at last, were men who knew their own minds and who really knew what they were talking about. Baber, for all his old-fashioned, gentle ways, was a good librarian and knew his job and he had, undoubtedly, been well primed by Panizzi. Gone are the outmoded bumblings of Sir Henry and the equivocal answers of Forshall. Here, at last, is the plain truth, well and clearly spoken. After a little preliminary skirmishing, the Committee got down to a further study of that old favourite, the classed catalogue. Despite close questioning, Baber remained unshaken in his belief that with such a catalogue, however desirable it might be in theory, in practice a reader would always find an alphabetical one more useful. To compile both simultaneously would need very much more money and more staff than he was ever likely to get and, in his opinion, all their efforts should now be directed to the preparation and publication, as speedily as possible, of a revised alphabetical catalogue.

Still the Committee persevered. Was not such a catalogue now being undertaken for the Royal Society? Baber was quick to make the point that, despite Panizzi's remonstrances, the men of science had made a complete mess of it and that even a man of Panizzi's own undoubted competence could never produce such a catalogue without errors. After that, the Committee rapidly shied away from the subject. Baber went on to refute some of the allegations in Edwards's pamphlets as to certain gaps in the collections and then Edwards himself was called in. He reiterated his demands for various reforms, especially for a properly qualified Superintendent for the Reading Room, a change Panizzi himself was to introduce some twenty years later. His evidence, especially from one so young and in the presence of men, by the judgement of the day, by far his social superiors, was most impressive. As his latest biographer says: 'Edwards's recommendations were, in effect, a programme for development and reform. They compared more than favourably with those made by all members of the Museum staff, with the notable exception of Panizzi.'[22]

But now, one week later, on June 7, Panizzi himself was to give evidence, this brawny man of forty, with the face of a bandit, as Crabb Robinson said, about whom so many tales were already told.

The questioning began quietly, Lord Stanley, the future Prime Minister, being the principal interrogator. Panizzi briefly explained his present position at the Museum and then launched on to a detailed comparison between the British Museum and various continental libraries. 'As a national establishment for this nation' – the theme is stated straight away – 'it is very poor . . . far inferior to the king's library at Paris . . . the finest in the world.'[23] He spoke of his personal acquaintance with many foreign libraries and, his liberal sympathies suddenly showing, derided the Russians for building their library at St Petersburg from the Polish libraries they had carried off, and the French for withholding still books taken from Italy and elsewhere by the armies of Napoleon. Better far to be without a national library, than to increase it by such means. Yet in England, government support for the national library was ludicrous. From 1820 to 1824 no more than £200–£300 a year had been voted as a purchase grant for the Department. The tiny state of Parma had spent more than £4,000 on one collection alone.[24] Panizzi spoke too of his wish to have more public libraries, as had Edwards, at least two for educational purposes in London alone. Then comes the heart of his evidence, the principle he always had and always would maintain. 'I want a poor student to have the same means of indulging his learned curiosity, of following his rational pursuits, of consulting the same authorities, of fathoming the most intricate inquiry as the richest man in the kingdom, as far as books go, and I contend that the Government is bound to give him the most liberal and unlimited assistance in this respect.'[25] Here is the essential radicalism of the man, his proud assertion, in *laissez-faire* and caste-ridden England, of the fundamental rights of any student, however poor and humble, to have the very best available and the obligation, nay, the duty, of the state to provide it, whatever the cost. This sentiment, which we in the twentieth century take so much for granted, was new and revolutionary, when uttered in the middle years of the nineteenth century.

How was this aim to be achieved? The first thing was to have far more generous grants from Parliament for the purchase of books, at least, in his opinion, £10,000 per year. In addition, there should be additional grants for more modern books, particularly in fields not yet covered by the Museum. The Science departments should go, so as to make the Museum collections more homogeneous. Space would soon become a pressing consideration and one must start planning well ahead. Like Baber, he comes out strongly in favour of an alphabetical catalogue. To undertake both kinds at once would be very difficult and both would probably suffer. His vehemence and the wealth of his examples seems to have shaken the Committee. Panizzi poured scorn on the plan, adopted by the Trustees, 'for some reason, unknown to us, the officers of the library',[26] and showed how he had tried, without success, to make them change their minds. He complained bitterly of the lack of consultation between the Trustees and the heads of departments and the other, more junior, officers. Though the personal relations between Baber and himself could not be better, there was little or no opportunity for officers, such as he, to bring forward their views or to make constructive suggestions. All that was expected of the staff was 'blind obedience, passive obedience, and nothing else'.[27] All his life, Panizzi bitterly resented having to carry out orders and instructions he felt to be wrong. No man could be more loyal, no man, certainly, could work harder, even at a scheme he knew was largely worthless. Yet to a man of his strong passions and decided views, such a position could be, and often was, intolerable.

Like his superiors, Panizzi felt that the Museum had benefited greatly from having men of rank as Trustees. He disliked the idea of scientists or other specialists coming on to the Board, merely in virtue of their special knowledge. Such a course would be a disaster. 'An officer,' he bitterly exclaimed, 'would have no chance against a scientific man, who should take a crotchet into his head and they are all crotchety!'[28] He most certainly loathed scientists and wanted nothing more to do with them. Panizzi now turns to his ideal of what the Museum's future should be and of the place it should properly occupy in the life of the nation. The general public were only interested in the Museum as a show place. 'As to its most important and most noble purpose as an establishment for the furtherance of education for study and research, the public seem to be, almost, indifferent.'[29] It was to be Panizzi's life work to change, in so far as it lay within his power, this deplorable state of affairs. These facilities, too, must be open to all, however humble, whatever, he implies, some of the other officers might think.

It was very plain to every member of the Committee that here was a man of large and generous ideas, far-seeing, dedicated to the creation of a great and ever-increasing National Library. He would spare no one, least of all himself, to bring these schemes to a successful fruition. It is surely no exaggeration to say that with Panizzi's evidence completed, the rest of the proceedings were no more than an epilogue. After the Archbishop had briefly explained how this remarkable man had come to the Museum and a few further points had been ventilated, the Committee concluded its labours.

On July 14, 1836, it issued its report. It was quite short and consisted, essentially, of eighteen resolutions, which were considered to be necessary for the more efficient running of the Museum. The Trustees should remain pretty much as they were; there should be, if necessary, further departments created; there should be more frequent consultations between the Trustees and their Keepers; Parliament should be far more generous in its grants;

and there were a few other minor recommendations. It was, however, resolution eleven that was the most important, both for the Museum and for its effect on Panizzi's own future. This resolution urged that the officers should receive salaries more in line with their responsibilities and experience, but that, in return, they should be strictly forbidden 'to hold any other situation conferring emolument or entailing duties'.[30] Sir Frederic was furious,[31] but all the staff must have wondered what it would entail.

The Trustees lost no time in meeting to discuss these developments. They decided to approach the Chancellor of the Exchequer with regard to the financial proposals and to implement the others, wherever possible. On March 11, 1837, therefore, they resolved that the holding of any outside situation was incompatible with the retention of any position at the Museum.

This drastic decision immediately and adversely affected most, if not all, of the senior officers. The question now with each of them was whether to resign their outside appointments or to leave the service of the Trustees. Panizzi, of course, had no difficulty in making up his mind. His chair at the University had long been an empty honour, of which he was thankful to be rid.[32] Madden, too, though with obvious reluctance and much grumbling, acquiesced in the decision, as also did Forshall[33] and most of the younger men. But what about Baber? Would he, too, decide to stay or would he prefer, in these circumstances, to leave the Museum?

NOTES TO CHAPTER 7

1 'Librorum impressorum qui in Museo Britannico adservantur Catalogus', 7 vol., 1813–19.

2 Select Committee, 1836, para. 4851.

3 Report by Baber, April 26, 1834. Royal Commission, Appendix, p. 104.

4 Minutes of Special Committee, April 30, 1834. Royal Commission, Appendix, p. 107.

5 Minutes of Special Committee, May 6, 1834. Royal Commission, Appendix, p. 110.

6 Panizzi to Forshall, May 8, 1834. Royal Commission, Appendix, p. 110.

7 Report by Baber, February 14, 1835. Royal Commission, Minutes, para. 2763. Appendix, p. 115.

8 That acute observer, Toqueville, had noted the change in the climate of opinion. Writing in 1833, he remarked, 'It is easy to notice one alarming system in England: it is a spirit of innovation spread through all classes . . . a spirit of discontent with the present and hatred of the past . . . much more bent on correcting what is wrong than in preserving what is good.' Voyage en Angleterre. Collected Works, vol. 8, p. 331.

9 Sir Benjamin Hawes, 1797–1862. MP for Lambeth. Advocated many reforms, including the penny post and the electric telegraph.

10 Edward Stanley, fourteenth Earl of Derby, 1799–1869. Three times Prime Minister.

11 Sir Robert Harry Inglis, 1786–1855. A strong Tory who opposed all the principal reforms of his day.

12 Thomas Southeron Estcourt, 1801–1876. Home Secretary, 1859.

13 Hansard, 3.S., vol. 20. c. 617, etc.

14 Select Committee, 1835. Minutes, para. 138.

15 Select Committee, 1835. Minutes, para. 93, 146, 693.

16 Select Committee, 1835 Minutes 1835, para. 334.

17 Select Committee, 1835. Minutes, para. 1690.

18 Select Committee, 1835. Minutes, para. 2080.

19   *Select Committee on Public Libraries*, p. 51 [*Parliamentary Papers*. H of C, 1850, vol. XVIII].

20   Add. MS. 36,714. f.420. Panizzi had received special permission to add the Christmas holidays to the normal month's vacation. [*Select Committee*, 1836, para 4779].

21   Report of February 23, 1836. *Royal Commission, Appendix*, p. 130.

22   Munford, *Edwards*, p. 21.

23   *Select Committee*, 1836. *Minutes*, para. 4773, 4474.

24   *Minutes*, para. 4785. Panizzi presumably got his information from his old friend, Angelo Pezzana.

25   *Minutes*, para. 4795.

26   *Minutes*, para. 4860.

27   *Minutes*, para. 4886.

28   *Minutes*, para. 4930.

29   *Minutes*, para. 4936.

30   *Select Committee*, 1836. *Report*, para. 11.

31   According to Ellis, Madden at this time did not hold any other office but he was undoubtedly doing a great deal of outside work. [*Select Committee*, 1835, *Minutes*, para. 333.] In Madden's copy of Edwards' pamphlet, there are angry refutations of the author's insinuations that Madden was working at the Public Record Office in Museum time.

32   He actually resigned on December 6, 1837, on being appointed Keeper of Printed Books, 'a chair which I was always proud to hold in an Institution I always took and shall always continue to take the most lively interest'. [Wicks, p. 270.]

33   Forshall appears to have retained, at least nominally, his Chaplaincy at the Foundling Hospital until his death.

8

KEEPER OF PRINTED BOOKS

ALMOST at once, Baber gave formal notice of his intention to resign at the following midsummer. A quiet, peace-loving man, he realized that, at his age, he had not the energy to introduce the vast reforms that he saw, quite clearly, were necessary in his department. The Trustees' resolution of March 11 gave him the perfect excuse for retiring in good time. Already sixty-two, he was to live in his parish of Stretham in Cambridgeshire, of which he had held the living now for some ten years, until 1869, to die at last, only a few weeks after his old friend Sir Henry Ellis, at the ripe old age of ninety-six.

The question, now, was who would the Trustees appoint to succeed him? The obvious man was Cary, who had been Assistant Keeper, and, as such, Baber's deputy since 1826. Blessed with a wide circle of friends, amongst them Coleridge, Rogers, Wordsworth and, above all, Charles Lamb,[1] Cary was known preeminently for his celebrated translation of Dante. Widely read, a fine scholar and a man whose personal relationships with other members of the staff were always extremely harmonious, Cary would seem to be, at first sight, just the man to succeed Baber and to steer the department through the troubled waters ahead. This was the whole crux of the matter. Would this now prematurely aged scholar, whose health was more than dubious, be ever able to manage a rapidly expanding library, in an age which would no longer tolerate peaceful sinecures?

For Cary's health was indeed precarious. His wife's sudden death in 1832 had completely prostrated him.[2] He never seems to have ever fully recovered, and on his return to the Museum had been forced to take things easily. Doubts about Cary's state of health had reached the ears of the Trustees. They were by no means sure he would be fit enough to undertake such an arduous responsibility, even if he were suitable in every other respect.

Panizzi always liked and admired Cary. It is quite certain that he never, in any sense, intrigued against him, nor sought, by improper means, to have him passed over. Such conduct would be completely foreign to his nature. With all his obvious faults of irascibility and hasty temper, he would never stoop to further any plot against a sick and ailing colleague. He would move heaven and earth to get rid of someone he despised, but not such a man as Cary. Yet he felt certain that he could run the department more efficiently than Cary could ever hope to, and he now wished that his earlier efforts to secure a comfortable living for his colleague had met with some success. But Panizzi was never the man to waste time on vain regrets and all that he could now reasonably hope for, was to succeed Cary as Assistant Keeper, and, perhaps, if all went well, in a few years' time, as Keeper.

As soon as he had heard the news of Baber's approaching resignation Panizzi had written to the Archbishop, requesting that the Trustees should 'keep my humble services in view should any place become vacant for which I should be deemed qualified. I take the liberty of appealing to my past as an earnest of my future conduct, should the Principal Trustees deem it expedient to promote me to any higher situation than that which I now hold.'[3] He also addressed similar letters to the other two Principal Trustees, the Lord Chancellor and the Speaker. It would seem clear from this that Panizzi had, at the moment, no real expectation of obtaining the Keepership.

In the meantime, Cary had not been idle. He had contacted his old friend Rogers, who had, of course, considerable influence, and had asked him to approach the Principal Trustees on his behalf. Rogers consented to do so and thereupon wrote the necessary letters of recommendation. But Rogers was all too well acquainted with the state of Cary's health and, no sooner had he dispatched the letters, than he began to have serious doubts as to the suitability of his protégé. The more he thought, the more his doubts increased. He therefore felt obliged to write once more to the

Trustees, expressing his now considerable misgivings as to Cary's real fitness for the post.

Rogers also spoke to Abercromby,[4] the Speaker, on the subject. He was now very worried, indeed, about Cary. Abercromby agreed with him and revealed that such doubts were now held by many of the Trustees. 'I have heard of a Mr Panizzi who is next; what do you know of him?' Rogers promptly replied that Panizzi would serve them very well. 'Well, to tell you the truth we think he will be the right person to be appointed, if Mr Cary is not appointed.'[5]

Panizzi, too, was undoubtedly Baber's choice. A warm effection had sprung up between the old clergyman and the former revolutionary and, for the last few years, Baber had looked far more for assistance to Panizzi, than to Cary, his nominal deputy. Panizzi's reports to the Trustees on the catalogue, his restrained, but decisive evidence before the Select Committee, had made it plain that here was the man the Department needed.

On June 24, the post of Keeper of Printed Books was officially declared to be vacant. The same day Cary made a personal application for the position to the Archbishop. The latter then told Cary that in view of his indifferent health, objections to his obtaining it had been raised by certain of the Trustees.

On his return to the Department, Cary immediately told Baber and Panizzi, who were there together, what had happened. 'Then,' exlaimed Panizzi, 'this concerns me.' 'Yes,' replied Cary, 'certainly it does.'[6]

During the past three months, the possibility of Cary being unfit to succeed Baber had been widely discussed. The names of candidates from other departments, or even of complete outsiders, Ernest Hawkins[7] of the Bodleian or Richard Garnett,[8] were freely canvassed. It was only Panizzi's great sense of loyalty and his personal affection for Cary, which had, hitherto, prevented him from putting his own name forward.

Now that he had heard from Cary's own lips that there was a chance for him, Panizzi resolved to waste no more time. He at once asked Cary if he now had any objection to he himself applying for the post. 'Not at all,' replied Cary. Panizzi, thereupon, in the presence of both Cary and Baber, sat down and wrote to the Archbishop in the following terms: 'I hope your Grace will not deem it presumptuous in me to beg respectfully of your Grace and the other Principal Trustees to take my case into consideration, should they think it requisite to depart from the usual system of regular promotion on appointing [Baber's] successor. I venture to say this much having been informed by Mr Cary of the conversation he has had the honour to have . . . with your Grace.'[9]

Panizzi showed the letter to Cary, who read it and approved. Cary then went home. Ten minutes later, he sent one of his sons to Panizzi for the letter. About four o'clock, Cary himself returned it and repeated that he had no objection to it being sent to the Archbishop. Since by this time, it was late on the Saturday afternoon, Panizzi waited till Monday before personally taking the letter down to Lambeth. Before leaving the Museum, he called at Cary's residence there to tell him that he was just off to the Archbishop. Cary again raised no objection and so Panizzi, at last, handed in his request.

Far from being underhand in this business, Panizzi had taken every precaution to be scrupulously fair to Cary. Subsequently he did, indeed, talk the matter over with some of the Trustees and ask for their support. They made it abundantly clear to him that, in their opinion, Cary was now out of the race and was no longer considered as a serious candidate by a majority of the Board. The issue now lay entirely between Panizzi himself and some 'stranger'. Panizzi afterwards alleged that his appointment was largely due to the Trustees' wish to make amends for their failure to grant him a higher salary. This does not really seem to be likely. Once Cary's claims on the grounds of seniority had been dismissed, Panizzi was obviously the only possible candidate.

But this was not the opinion of many of his colleagues, nor, indeed, of the world at large. Feeling was already running high against the possibility of a 'foreigner' succeeding to the post of Keeper of Printed Books. 'Should the appointment of Mr Panizzi take place,' wrote one indignant journalist, 'it will be hailed by one burst of honest indignation.'[10] In vain, it was pointed out that Panizzi was by no means the first not of British birth to hold high office at the Museum. Leaving aside Maty and Planta, both of foreign extraction and both former Principal Librarians, there was Panizzi's present colleague, Charles König,[11] born in Brunswick and, since 1813, Keeper of the Natural History Department. But

König was a German and, therefore, in the eyes of many, almost an Englishman. He, too, had been at the Hanoverian University of Göttingen, where he had been a contemporary of the Duke of Sussex, the young Queen's uncle. Panizzi, on the other hand, was an Italian, a member of a despised and faintly ridiculous race. He was already becoming known as an intimate of prominent Whig noblemen and his appointment seemed to be, to disappointed Tories or to class-conscious petty tradesmen, a glaring example of the habit of the 'Melbourne-Rads' of finding comfortable sinecures for those whom they favoured.

Appeals were made to every kind of prejudice. Panizzi was a papist, whilst Cary, his far more worthy rival, was a Protestant clergyman. There was no comparison between their respective scholastic achievements. The one was 'a mere scissors-and-paste compiler of editions of Italian authors, without one particle of original genius'; the other, 'a scholar and a poet of European reputation'. To many, the most damning indictment was that the 'O'Connellized Melbourne cabinet' had promoted an Italian Carbonaro, 'unknown to this country and unhonoured in his own' over the head of the eminently deserving, but unfortunately somewhat elderly Tory, Mr Cary.[12]

All too many of these views were shared by certain of Panizzi's colleagues. Madden hated him, both for personal and for political reasons, and Madden's political prejudices were shared by Sir Henry Ellis.[13] When Sir Henry, therefore, was asked to give a formal testimonial as to Panizzi's suitability for the Keepership, he politely, but firmly, refused to do so. Hawkins, the Keeper of Antiquities, also expressed his dislike of Panizzi and his resentment at his new appointment. Cary was widely admired and respected, both as a scholar and as a man, whilst Panizzi, it must be admitted, often appeared to be harsh and overbearing, especially to those who did not know him well. To many, if not to most, it must have seemed that the better man had been unfairly treated. Panizzi made no reply to all these sneers and innuendoes, which deeply wounded his sensitive nature. Time and his own achievements would alone justify him.

But this is to look ahead. At the moment, Panizzi's appointment had not yet been confirmed. Cary, soon after Panizzi had sent his letter to the Archbishop, seems to have had second thoughts. He now knew that the principal objection to his succeeding Baber was on health grounds. He therefore consulted three medical men and obtained certificates as to his physical fitness for the post. These he forwarded to the Principal Trustees. The Archbishop, influenced by this and by a conversation he subsequently had had with Cary himself, told the latter that he would now support his candidature for the vacant post, but warned Cary that, if he obtained it and should his health deteriorate further, he must, at once, resign.

But the other two Principal Trustees, and a majority of their colleagues, were of a different opinion.[14] On July 17, the House of Commons was to be dissolved and subsequently there would be, for a time, no Speaker. Abercromby, therefore, two days before, asked for the certificate of Panizzi's appointment to be prepared immediately so that he might at once sign it. The Archbishop was out of town and could not, at the moment, be found. The blank appointment was, in consequence, taken by Forshall that evening to the Speaker's secretary, who filled in Panizzi's name. It was then signed by Abercromby and, immediately afterwards, by the Lord Chancellor, Cottenham.[15] Forshall then sent the certificate down to the Archbishop, who, in turn, signed it and returned it to the Museum.

The following Wednesday, July 19, 1837, Panizzi was officially informed of his appointment. He at once wrote to the Archbishop, as the senior of the three Principal Trustees, to thank him. 'Your Grace will allow me to add that it will be the height of my ambition to show myself not unworthy of the honourable trust reposed on me by a zealous discharge of the arduous duties of my office to the utmost of my humble powers.'[16]

The post had been seen quite otherwise by his disappointed rival. On the previous Monday, when the news of Panizzi's appointment had been broken to him by Forshall, Cary wrote the last of several letters he had sent to the Lord Chancellor, complaining of the treatment he had allegedly received at his hands. Cary writes, 'My age, between 64 and 65 years, it was plain, might rather ask for me that alleviation of labour which in this as in many other public offices is gained by promotion.' Poor Cary could not see that, for the Museum at any rate, the days of such sinecures were numbered. The Trustees, if they had the real interest of the Department at heart, could not do otherwise than appoint a man, eager for and capable of dealing with the volume of work which the post must now, of necessity, entail. To provide a quiet haven for an elderly clergyman, however deserving, was no longer either possible or justified.

Cary then called for a public inquiry into the reasons for Panizzi's appointment, particularly when, as he maintained, the Archbishop, 'the only one of the three nominators, who regularly inspects the minutes of the establishment and is at all likely to have an intimate and accurate knowledge of its concerns' had been opposed to it.[17]

In his anger, Cary made the mistake of sending a copy of this letter to *The Times*.[18] This was an unforgivable breach of etiquette for a serving officer of the Museum and Cary must have known it would do him no good.

Despite angry letters in support of Cary, advising him to petition the new Queen and insulting editorial comments about Panizzi himself, responsible public opinion, especially in government circles, was increasingly in favour of the appointment. At length, Cary felt there was no alternative for him but to resign. Accordingly, on October 12, he sent in his resignation to the Trustees and left the Museum at the end of the year. Despite his natural disappointment at not obtaining the Keepership, he was not really sorry to go. Cary was, above all, a scholar, and such have rarely made good administrators.

No sooner had Panizzi's appointment been announced than there was renewed controversy within the Museum. On July 19 Madden wrote to his friend Bliss:[19] 'Mr Panizzi's appointment was signed on the 15th. He is my senior and if the Trustees *on that plea* give him the preference over me in regard to Baber's house, it will put me to the great expense and inconvenience of residing out of the Museum . . . I begged the Archbishop to ante-date my appointment . . . and thus give me the position I am entitled to over Mr Panizzi.'[20]

But the Archbishop had not heeded Sir Frederic's pleas. Panizzi was now the senior and entitled to all the privileges of seniority. But this was to reckon without Sir Frederic. Despite Panizzi's protests, over the houses question Madden emerged victorious. Only July 27, Madden wrote with ill-concealed glee, 'The

Trustees . . . assigned to me the apartments lately occupied by Mr Baber.'[21] He is still indignant at the Archbishop's having filled up the blank date as July 18, 'with great injustice to me . . . thus confirming the accidental seniority of Mr P and of course with the advantages which result from that position.'[21] In vain did Panizzi point out that, since Baber had gone on June 24 and as appointments were normally dated from the time of the previous occupant's departure, he should, by rights, have been not three *days*, but three *weeks* senior to Sir Frederic. Madden still nursed his sense of grievance, one more score to be settled with the hated 'foreigner'.

Panizzi had, in the meantime, turned his attention to far more important things. The two main problems of the early years of his keepership – and there were, of course, a host of minor ones – were the safe and speedy transfer of the contents of the library from old Montagu House to the quarters that had been assigned to Printed Books in Sir Robert Smirke's new building at the north end of the Museum site, and the constantly reiterated demand of the Trustees for a new printed catalogue. The former, though a worry until it was safely completed and a constant drain on Panizzi's limited staff resources was at least straightforward, and the Keeper was left alone to manage it in his own way as best he could. On the second question, Panizzi was harried and badgered by the Trustees and by Forshall on every possible occasion. His advice on this subject was continually disregarded by men who would never have dreamed of interfering with the day-to-day running of any other department, yet presumed, for nearly ten years, to know better than the head of the library, on every minor point of cataloguing and general administration.

Panizzi's first and immediate problem was staff, staff to undertake and supervise the impending move; staff to catalogue the ever-increasing intake of new books; above all, staff to carry out both the very necessary revision of the manuscript catalogues and to prepare, at the Trustees' insistent commands, a new printed edition of the catalogue.

His resources were, at first and, indeed, for most of the time, very limited. It had been decided that as the supernumerary staff, who had joined the department in 1827 on the acquisition of the King's Library, left the service of the Trustees, they would not be replaced. The senior staff would henceforth, therefore, consist only of the Keeper, the Assistant Keeper and the Extra-Assistant Keeper. Glover had now gone and the other men who had come with the King's Library were elderly, not particularly efficient and gave only part-time service to the Museum. There was also Horne, a very hard-working, but again only part-time supernumerary, and the newly joined Winter Jones[22] and Yeates, a dim and sickly figure in the background, as the two assistants. Jones, who throughout his career was to be Panizzi's highly valued right-hand man and successor, had joined the Trustees' service on April 18, 1837. There were, in addition, the temporary specialists in the Germanic languages and Hebrew, Schier and, later, Bialloblotsky, and that was all.

The situation, at the moment, was particularly difficult. Cary was due to go at the end of the year and though still doing some cataloguing, cannot have been, in the circumstances, of much assistance. No one had, as yet, been appointed to succeed him and no extra-assistant keeper had come to fill the vacancy caused by Panizzi's own promotion. Jones was still too new and inexperienced, the others, too old or past caring and, for the moment, all rested on the broad shoulders of the Keeper. He at once decided that it was impossible for him that year to take his normal annual leave. There was so much to be done and Panizzi felt that only he could really tackle it. There were alterations, long overdue, to be made in the Reading Room service, preparations for the move to be put in hand and, above all, the ever-present demand for a new catalogue.

In a letter of October 12, 1837, Panizzi made an urgent appeal to the Trustees for more staff to cope with the crisis. He pointed out that, with so many of his nominal staff on a part-time basis, the department was losing from the senior officers no less than sixty-six working hours per week. He begged that at least two additional full-time assistants should at once be appointed. Such would have been no more than adequate for the efficient running of the Department in ordinary times. At the moment, with ever-increasing responsibilities, this was the very minimum needed to keep things on an even keel. The Catalogues must be brought up to date. 'The absolute necessity for new catalogues becomes every day more evident,' wrote Panizzi, in desperation.[23]

Help was soon to come, but never enough to cope with the

ever-growing pressure of work. On April 16, 1838, the Rev Richard Garnett suddenly appeared to fill the vacant post of Assistant Keeper, without Panizzi knowing a thing about it. Despite this unfortunate introduction, Garnett proved himself to be a loyal and hard-working second-in-command, and though Panizzi never seems to have felt for him the affection with which he undoubtedly regarded Jones, they got on well together and Garnett's comparatively early death was a bitter blow.

Another new arrival that year was Thomas Watts,[24] who proved himself to be one of the most accomplished members of the staff the Museum was ever to have. Put, almost immediately, on to the task of selecting and classifying the collections as they were transferred from the old building to the new, Watts laid the foundations of that phenomenal knowledge of the library for which afterwards he became so renowned. Others, later to hold high office in the Department or to become well known elsewhere, Rye, Parry, Bullen and Edwards,[25] were soon to come and, before long, Panizzi had gathered round himself a devoted and hard-working team, who, for the most part, respected and adored their often difficult chief, but who served both him and the Museum well, knowing as they did that Panizzi would, in turn, loyally support them and assist and help them, if he could, in every way possible.

The new Keeper's thoughts were mainly engaged at the moment, as indeed they must have been for some years past, on how to make his Library supreme, not only in Great Britain, but throughout the world. 'This emphatically *British* library,' he wrote, 'ought to be directed most particularly to British works and to works relating to the British Empire, its religious, political and literary as well as scientific history, its laws, institutions, commerce, arts, etc. The rarer and more expensive a work of this description is the more . . . efforts ought to be made to secure it for the library.'[26] Panizzi speaks with the very voice of High Victorian patriotism, the answer to those who sneered at the 'foreigner's' ignorance of and indifference to his adopted country.

The Reading Room first claimed his attention. Here great tact was needed. Both the Reading Room and its staff were under the direct control of Ellis, as Principal Librarian, and Ellis was very jealous of his rights. Panizzi, the Keeper of Printed Books, was responsible for the supply of books to readers and for the maintenance of the catalogues and it was often most difficult to define their respective spheres of influence. Many of the criticisms levelled at Panizzi by ill-informed readers were due to factors over which he, personally, had no control. He was always most sensitive to and not a little resentful of this undeserved injustice. In consequence, whenever a reader did complain, he took great pains to investigate thoroughly any justifiable grievance and, at all times, kept a close eye on the Reading Room and its activities.

In September 1837, Panizzi introduced the use of printed application forms for books. These tickets, with simple instructions to the readers on the back, were basically the same as those still in use today. This innovation, though obviously of great help, both to the staff and to readers, aroused resentment among the more conservative or more indolent habitués. Even more fuss was made over a second new regulation, that readers should return their books personally and receive their tickets back in exchange and that, until they had so claimed their tickets, they would be held responsible for the books issued to them. This simple practical reform aroused great anger among certain readers. A Mr James Thompson, a constant reader since 1826, wrote indignantly complaining of these new regulations and alleging that he had been treated by Panizzi 'in a tone, manner and language singularly free from anything approaching to courtesy' and that he seemed 'anxious to play the part of a drill-sergeant'. [27]

Panizzi's manner was, at times, to say the least, brusque and his temper all too easily aroused. But it would seem that in this case Mr Thompson had largely himself to blame. Panizzi himself found the book for the reader, who on being handed it became 'intemperate and noisy . . . bent on finding fault with whatever was done or said'.[28] The Keeper hotly denied that he had ever been anything but calm and polite and the incident was forgotten. But this occurrence, and others like it, built up an atmosphere of ill-feeling between the staff and many of the readers. All were blamed, deservedly or not, on the boorishness and vanity of the 'Italian Harlequin'.

Not all disapproved. The usually most critical Sir Nicholas Harris Nicolas wrote to Panizzi expressing warm approval of the innovation and that the new arrangements were 'not merely reasonable, but . . . indispensable . . . No better mode could possibly be devised for immediately obtaining any book than the printed tickets you have suggested.'[29] He congratulated Panizzi on the 'great improvements which have taken place since your last appointment; . . . you have done wonders in a few weeks', words he was afterwards to have regretted he had ever written. By October 1842, Panizzi was able to report that all works, with the exception of those in the Reading Room, had been given a third mark and could thus be quickly identified by the number alone.

In the following December, final arrangements were made for the move to the new Reading Room. This was situated in the North, or Library, wing, which Smirke had recently completed and which formed the northern side of the range of buildings erected round the old garden. The new reading rooms occupied the east end of the ground floor and were approached, not from the main entrance, but by a side passage, leading in from Montagu Place.

Panizzi must have been very relieved at getting the books out of the crumbling and dangerous old house. In 1836, Smirke had reported that it was in a very insecure state, most of the floors being supported by props behind the bookcases and the flues in such a bad condition that the danger of a disastrous fire was ever present.[30] In the new building, every possible precaution had been taken. A fire was always a terrible risk in the absence of any safe means of artificial light.

The move, which was carried out in the first week of January 1838, when the Museum was normally closed, and under Panizzi's constant supervision, went according to plan. The new Reading Room was opened on January 9, to the satisfaction of most, if not all, of the readers. There remained, however, the far greater task of moving the whole of the library itself from the rooms and passages of Montagu House to the newly built rooms in the northern wing waiting to receive it. The plan adopted was to classify the books before moving them, transfer them a class at a time to their new quarters, arrange them there on the shelves, press mark them and, finally, enter these press marks against the relevant entries in the catalogues. It was obviously a long and arduous undertaking. Apart from certain special collections, which were to remain intact, all the rest of the library was to be redistributed according to the new scheme. This was Watt's task and nobly he performed it.

All through 1838 and 1839 the move proceeded smoothly. As early as April 1838 Panizzi reported that all was going well and that 'no inconvenience of any consequence has hitherto arisen to the readers, from the removal of the collection'.[31] The work did, however, seem to be going more slowly than he had first hoped. In an effort to speed things, he had permitted the attendants to carry their leave over until the new year, since he had been forced to forbid all leave during the first months of the move. Ellis objected most strongly to this arrangement, which he regarded as an infringement of his own prerogative. The Trustees agreed, somewhat reluctantly, to confirm Panizzi's arrangements, but warned him not to do such a thing again.

Panizzi had always believed in seeing for himself and such ungentlemanly behaviour must have been particularly galling to the urbane and indolent Sir Henry. On March 22, 1839, Panizzi received a report, which fortunately proved to be false, of a chimney on fire in one of the rooms off the King's Library. He at once tried to climb out himself on to the roof to see exactly where the danger was. To his rage, however, no one was able to find a key to any of the skylights! An indignant letter to Sir Henry was sent off immediately. [This] Panizzi demanded, 'appears to me to require *immediate attention*'.[32] Life could, indeed, be very difficult for his colleagues with Panizzi around.

As the task of moving the library progressed Panizzi could not help remarking on a serious deficiency in Smirke's plans. The accommodation provided was barely sufficient to take the present holdings and allowed absolutely no room for future expansion. In addition, no proper working rooms had been designed for the staff. A plea for two small extra rooms belonging to another department was promptly rejected by the Trustees.

The Board was continually being, what to their harassed and overworked Keeper of Printed Books must have seemed, most unco-operative. Many of his proposals for the purchase of books, both antiquarian and modern, were summarily turned down, without a word of explanation and he himself was sternly rebuked for overspending his grant. Relations between Panizzi and the Trustees were strained over the vexed question of the printed catalogue, as we shall see later, and there were little tussles with Sir Henry over minor matters. But these differences were as

5*

nothing to the great row which suddenly blew up between Forshall and Panizzi over the attendant Kemp. The latter, an intelligent, hard-working young man in the Secretary's office, had been accused by Panizzi, in one of his more irascible moods, of not delivering a certain message to Forshall. An anonymous informer told the Secretary that Panizzi had spoken to the unfortunate Kemp 'in a very angry tone'. Forshall, at once up in arms, then wrote off to Panizzi, complaining of this and asking him to forward any future complaints of a like nature to the proper quarter, that is to himself. An angry and astonished reply came back, hotly denying the allegation and demanding that Kemp should bring the matter before the Trustees, if he had any cause of complaint.

An increasingly acrimonious correspondence followed. Both Panizzi and Forshall were now extremely irate and disinclined to accept any compromise. Forshall eventually told Panizzi that he had no alternative but to lay the whole matter before the Trustees, which, to Panizzi's fury, despite his view that the Trustees were not a fitting Tribunal for 'a case of personal discourtesy', he promptly did. The matter was referred back to Ellis, who managed, at length, to calm his angry colleagues, but, in the future, there was even less cordiality than before between the Secretary and the Keeper of Printed Books.[33]

Almost immediately afterwards, there was a further row between Panizzi and Madden. Relations between them had always been strained and Madden could never forgive or forget Panizzi's seniority by three days. There was constant bickering. Madden complained of the difficulties he and his staff allegedly experienced in getting books from the Library and of the injustice of *his* attendants being taken away from Manuscripts to serve in the Reading Room.

There was no direct communication between the two. Notes, as between two hostile powers, were delivered via Sir Henry or would suddenly appear on Panizzi's desk, without a word of explanation, 'aping all the forms of a diplomatic note, without any of its courtesy'. But these were as nothing over the bitter warfare which now broke out over the question of the manuscripts in the King's Library.

There were in that collection a certain number of manuscripts, which Madden had always considered as more properly belonging to his department. In February 1840, therefore, he advised the Trustees that he now proposed to remove them and that he had Panizzi's consent to do so. About a year later, suddenly and without any further notice, he had them taken away one morning to his own department.

Panizzi was furious at this outrageous behaviour. He hotly denied that he had ever, in any way, consented to the transfer. The removal of these manuscripts was a violation of the conditions under which the collection had been received, and, as far as he knew, done without the authority of the Trustees. 'The Manuscripts,' he exclaimed bitterly, 'should not have been removed after such a solemn pledge.' An angry letter to Madden followed: 'Being conscious of having shown you always every proper mark of courtesy, I confess I did not know what construction to put on an [action?] which seemed indicative of contrary feeling . . . As these MSS. were *taken* from the Department I cannot acquiesce in the statement that they were received from it.'[34] But there was little he could do. The Trustees supported Madden. It was a dangerous precedent and Panizzi was determined it should never be repeated.

But all these vexations, however annoying, must have seemed trifling beside the bitter and long-drawn-out controversy over the question of printing the catalogue.

Panizzi had never favoured a printed catalogue. His ideal was an alphabetical manuscript catalogue, which could be kept continuously up to date. In addition, he advocated a supplementary subject index and printed catalogues of special collections, designed primarily for scholars. In his report to the Trustees of February 23, 1836, he had gone into great detail on this question, but the Trustees were now firmly resolved to have a printed catalogue at all costs and as soon as possible and nothing Panizzi might do could shake their resolution. He tried hard. Shortly after becoming Keeper, he made a [first attempt. 'He ventures to think,' he reported, 'that the determination of printing such a catalogue might deserve further consideration,' and offers to lay before the Trustees his arguments against this policy.[35]

The Trustees asked him to do so, which he did at some length. But all was in vain. At a Sub-Committee on the following day it was resolved: 'That the Trustees still continue to be decidedly

of opinion that a general Aphabetical Catalogue should be
printed, and that at the earliest practicable period . . . that it is
desirable that Mr. Panizzi should be made acquainted with the
deliberate determination of the Trustees on this point.'[36] That,
then, was clearly that and Panizzi had no option but to obey. The
Trustees then asked their Keeper to lay before them a copy of
Baber's rules of 1834 and of any supplementary ones that he
might now consider to be necessary. No copy of the Rules could be
found in the Department, but Forshall kindly supplied the office
copy, which was, in due course, laid before the Trustees.

Panizzi again attempted to get the Trustees to reverse their
decision over the method of compiling the catalogue. He implored
them to adopt Baber's first plan of having a single responsible
editor and fears what may happen by persevering with a defective
plan. Whatever the outcome may be, he will carry out loyally the
Trustees' wishes to the best of his ability.

The Trustees, probably under Ellis's influence, would listen to
no suggestions. They were resolved to stick to their original plan,
but graciously permitted Panizzi 'to offer to the Trustees, from
time to time, such suggestions . . . as shall . . . most effectually
tend to accomplish the intention of the Trustees within the
shortest possible period.'[37]

By December, the Trustees, getting impatient, ordered Panizzi
to lay before them at once a plan for the immediate printing of the
Alphabetical catalogue. Panizzi forwarded his plans, which, together with a little note from Sir Henry[38] as the only serving officer
who had ever produced a printed catalogue, were laid before the
Trustees. A new source of trouble now arose. Panizzi had suggested verbally to Garnett some slight modifications in the rule for
cataloguing anonymous books. The Trustees for some reason took
strong exception to this and started a controversy which was to go
on at intervals for over ten years.

On Boxing Day, Panizzi produced his detailed plans for the
new catalogue.[39] He had had to revise them on hearing the unwelcome news that the Trustees, instead of waiting till the whole
catalogue was finished, as both Baber and he had suggested, now
proposed to start printing in the following year. It could be done,
declared Panizzi, if not well done and he would be willing to
undertake the task as best he might. To do so, however, would

require considerably more assistance than he had at present. The Trustees kept on interfering. No detail was too petty for them. Even through the formal tone of Panizzi's replies one may detect the increasing strain of keeping his temper with them and their foolish ways.

On February 7, 1839, Edward Edwards joined the service of the Trustees and started work at once on the new catalogue. He had written to his future Keeper some months before a long letter, criticizing the department on the lines of his evidence before the Select Committee, and asking Panizzi for a job. There was then no vacancy, as Watts had decided to stay and the eager reformer had to wait a further few months.[40]

Much of the revision was being done by Panizzi himself, in addition to all his other duties and, despite delays, the work went on. In March the Trustees ordered that new cataloguing rules, based on those of Baber, should be prepared and in the remarkably short space of a week Panizzi had them ready to lay before the Board. In his evidence before the Royal Commission on the British Museum, Humffreys Parry, then a newly joined assistant but by 1849 a rising barrister, told of the efforts which were made to achieve this. 'Each separate rule was the subject of long and anxious discussion . . . to later hours in the evening, in fact until dark; and on one or two occasions we came in on the Sunday and worked the greater portion of the day.'[41]

These rules were, in the main, Panizzi's own work, ably assisted by Jones and the others. In addition, Panizzi also submitted a specimen heading, catalogued according to them. After going through the rules with Panizzi for nearly three hours, the Sub-Committee accepted them, with some minor modifications and they were ordered to be printed.

Tenders had now been invited for the printing of the catalogue. Panizzi, however, was firmly of the opinion that nothing could be finally ready for the press for at least eighteen months. Two articles, *Academies* and *Aristotle*, could be ready at once, but Panizzi begged that these should be treated merely as specimens. The Trustees, however, ordered that these articles were to form part of the final printed catalogue. It would seem that, at the moment, Panizzi had only to make a suggestion, however reasonable, for the Trustees to come immediately to an opposite decision.

They now firmly laid it down 'that their object is to have the best catalogue, cross references included, which can be delivered to them complete from the press on the 31st December 1844', in Panizzi's view an impossible task.[42]

Whatever his private doubts as to the feasibility of the Trustees' instructions, in his orders to the staff, accompanying copies of the new rules, there is no note of defeatism or disaffection. Such is the Trustees' will and it must be carried out. 'All our efforts,' he wrote, 'must be directed to that end'[43] and the revision of titles cut to a minimum. 'No effort is spared in order that the catalogue may be printed before the end of 1844 . . . even at a sacrifice of much of its correctness and utility.'[44] He was determined to get the thing finished, if it was at all possible. He had to have more staff and those he had must work longer hours, at least in the summer. He would give up his annual vacation and continue working. The Trustees decided in their wisdom that such was by no means necessary and that overtime, too, could be avoided.

All through the early months of 1840 the cataloguing and printing of the first volume went on. By the middle of the year it was out, full of errors, as Panizzi had foreseen. Once again he warned his masters that what they had ordered was impossible. If the printing was to be carried out in the same hurried manner, 'the catalogue will be bad, it will cost more, and no time will be saved, but lost. And under any circumstances, no hope can be entertained that this catalogue can be completed by the end of 1844.'[45] By November, the interleaved copies of the first volume were available for the Reading Room and for staff use but full, already, of additions and corrections. The work was pressed on with all possible speed. Nevertheless, in January 1843 Panizzi had to tell the Trustees that were all the titles ready for printing, it would take four years to get them done. The titles, however, were by no means ready and could not be so for some considerable time. Already carping and ill-informed criticism was being heard on all sides, accusing Panizzi of being responsible for the delay. Panizzi resented unjust accusations very keenly. No man was less guilty than he. 'I . . . never took any step that could improve the catalogue if that tended to prolong its completion.'[46] The stupidity and ignorance of many of the criticisms angered him. 'Those who press them have never given the subject more than a passing thought and have neither the knowledge nor the data on which to ground any of the conclusions at which they arrive.'[47]

In all he had the firm support of his colleagues, especially of Jones. They agreed that there was no quicker way of working, and that nothing further could be done to speed things up. Watts demurred slightly, and thought, if absolutely no notice at all were taken of accuracy, it might be just possible to increase the rate, but with the certainty of producing a thoroughly bad catalogue. Watts, of course, was not so closely concerned with the new catalogue as were the others. He was still supervising the move into the new buildings. By September 1843, it was completed and all the books safely removed from Montagu House and installed in their new quarters.

But to return to the catalogue. By the summer of 1844, the Trustees were again getting impatient. They asked Panizzi for a progress report and any suggestions he might be able to offer for expediting its production. Within a few days Panizzi replied, reiterating once again that a proper catalogue would require 'years of unremitting and heavy labour'.[48] Nothing further could be done to hasten things. He begged the Trustees to defend him publicly against malicious accusations of undue delay, accusations they well knew to be completely unfounded.

With a slight softening of their hitherto inflexible attitude, the Trustees now asked Panizzi when it would be possible to finish the catalogue in manuscript. In Panizzi's considered opinion, it would take at least another ten years! This stumped the Sub-Committee, who reported back to the General Board. No more was heard for some time. The catalogue was hurried on as best it may, whilst the Trustees remained, at least, quiescent.

But on January 10, 1846, an ominous minute was transmitted to the Keeper of Printed Books.[49] Would Mr Panizzi kindly state the reasons which had induced him to suspend the printing of the new catalogue. Panizzi promptly replied that it was evident that no part of such a catalogue should be printed until the whole was ready for the press, to ensure completeness as well as correctness. He would moreover wish the Trustees to judge, when the whole manuscript was at last presented to them, whether such a work, in at least forty volumes, and likely to cost as many thousand pounds, was really worth printing.

Suitably altered, the Trustees submitted Panizzi's statement to Parliament.[50] However, in July, they again repeated their desire for a printed catalogue and, in desperation, ordered Ellis to make a report on the subject, which Sir Henry laid before them the following October.

Panizzi wrote to the Principal Librarian, going once again over the reasons why it was impossible to carry out the Trustees' wishes. Though they had not specifically said so, they had appeared to acquiesce with the ideas expressed in his last report and to have acknowledged the insuperable difficulties, which their plan of printing the catalogue entailed. 'It appears to me, in conclusion,' wrote Panizzi, 'that there cannot be any doubt as to whether it is better to have a GOOD catalogue in manuscript or a bad one in print. A bad catalogue, like other bad books, ought not to be printed at all . . . it does more harm the more it is propagated . . . You and I know many catalogues which are a deplorable illustration of this obvious truth.'[51]

On October 9, Panizzi himself reported to the Trustees. He begged them, that since they seemed to be dissatisfied with his conduct, to institute an inquiry, not only into the catalogue controversy, but also into the general management of the Department. This the Trustees declined to do. They intimated, merely, that if Mr Panizzi had any further suggestions to make, the Principal Librarian would, doubtless, be pleased to receive them. On November 14, Ellis made his report. The reasons for the delay were, in his opinion, the scope of the catalogue, the unnecessary number of cross-references, the multiplication of rules and so on. The only practical suggestion he was able to make was to relieve Panizzi of the task of the final revision of the manuscript and to divide this among three or four other members of his staff. The Keeper would merely supervise in general the whole proceedings. This was, in effect, a return to the second plan of Baber, which had long been rejected as unworkable.

Panizzi's reply to all this was delayed by his frequent bouts of illness, a sign of the great pressure under which he was now working. At last, on January 7 the following year, Panizzi answered Ellis. In a long, detailed and masterly report,[52] he gives the whole vexed story of all the catalogues since 1787 and, in particular, of the mischievous intervention of the Principal Librarian in the business ever since 1834. It was clearly his interference which had swayed the Trustees and had made them more obstinate than they would otherwise have been. It was to him that the unfortunate rejection of Baber's first plan was due, the initial mistake from which all subsequent ones had derived. Panizzi, once again, emphasizes how disastrous the Trustees' decision to print had been and how, almost throughout, the enterprise had been further handicapped by lack of staff. He welcomes an inquiry. Neither he nor his subordinates have anything to fear. The vacillating and contradictory orders of the Trustees are courteously, but clearly noted. The postponement of the printing had been consented to by them. The catalogue might still be finished in a further nine years, if the Trustees so desired.

Panizzi next proceeds to demolish Sir Henry's arguments. Not to have a single editor was to court disaster. Sir Henry's own catalogue of 1819 was by no means free from faults, and Panizzi lists the many mistakes to be found in it. He concludes by demanding that the Trustees should make up their minds: 'Whether a catalogue, which, when published, will be subject to the ridicule and indignation of all persons who understand what a catalogue of a splendid national library ought to be. Whether all the work hitherto done is to be thrown away, whether the Museum is ever to have a good catalogue . . . whether a sum amounting probably to £60,000 is to be spent on publishing a catalogue and a supplement to it . . . well calculated to mislead those who may have occasion to consult it.'[53] This was his case and he made it with all the fervour and skill of one trained in the law. It was now up to Sir Henry and the Trustees to answer it if they could.

On January 14, Ellis replied, in what he described as 'a triumphant refutation'.[54] He does indeed succeed in scoring more than once over the perhaps over-eager Panizzi, but the general impression is that he is trying to explain away too much, a small, plump fish wriggling on a very large hook. What particularly annoyed him was that Panizzi had got these charges copied out 'by one of the inferior agents of his department'. 'Nothing can be more surely calculated than this to sow the seed of insubordination broadcast.'[55] Poor Sir Henry! It was dangerous to tangle with the redoubtable Keeper of Printed Books.

Panizzi now replied with a second and far longer list of errors to be found in the old catalogue.[56] He did, however, soften the blow by agreeing to omit any passage found objectionable by either the Trustees or by the Principal Librarian. Panizzi's list is a masterpiece of bibliographical erudition and must have completely confounded his adversaries.

Sir Henry brushed off this devastating attack as best he might, stating bravely that he would glory in his defence before the world. Once more, he bitterly complained of his traducement by a subordinate officer, who had, moreover, added to his offence by getting his assistants to make a copy of the passages in question.

On February 20, 1847, the Sub-Committee met yet again. Panizzi was called before them. 'I had then a series of questionnaires put to me,' he recalled, 'they were to be four.' But before he had answered the whole of the third question, he was stopped by Lord Stanley and the Bishop of London, who were interrogating him, and permitted to withdraw. 'They saw at once the facts in their true light . . . the resolution . . . was not carried. But for that interview, it might have been carried and its effects would have been more injurious than even those of the minute of July 13 1839.'[57]

The resolution referred to by Panizzi was that proposed a few minutes later by Sir Robert Inglis.[58] Inglis, it was said, disliked Panizzi and certainly, was a man of rigid, conservative principles. He now proposed that the printing of the catalogue be immediately resumed and that the most stringent measures be laid down for achieving this end. Had such a motion been carried, it would have been tantamount to a vote of no confidence in Panizzi's administration of his department and, undoubtedly, would have entailed his immediate resignation.

The resolution was, however, negatived. Panizzi's influence was, at last, being felt. At the next Sub-Committee meeting, Panizzi told the Trustees that, in his opinion, it would take no less than thirty-five years to get the catalogue printed and, as it could not be ready before 1860, this meant 1895, a date by which most of those present would long have ceased to take any interest in the matter! Chastened by this thought, the Sub-Committee considered certain resolutions brought forward by W. R. Hamilton, a close friend of Panizzi, which amounted to a complete vindication of his whole policy and a condemnation of the Trustees' previous attitude. This, at the moment, seemed too much and the Trustees contented themselves with passing a resolution, regretting the fact of Panizzi's detailed criticisms of Ellis's catalogue but hoping that he and the Principal Librarian would 'unite in the cordial and harmonious discharge of their respective duties'.[59] The terms of this resolution were unaccountably not conveyed to Panizzi, and the whole summer passed in constant bickering between Forshall and the Keeper of Printed Books and complaints by the latter to the Trustees that he was not allowed to revise his reports, when printed, and, in consequence, that when laid before the Board, they were full of inaccuracies.

At last, on November 27, 1847, Panizzi's moment of triumph came. The Sub-Committee now learned that their resolution of March 6 had never been communicated to Panizzi, either by Forshall or by Ellis.[60] The Secretary was at once instructed to repair this telling omission and the Sub-Committee considered Hamilton's proposals. Sir Robert Inglis then moved another resolution, that a printed catalogue should be produced without delay and reaffirming the Trustees' previous minutes on this subject. Again, however, the motion was defeated. The Trustees had had enough. By a combination of skill, knowledge, resolution and experience, Panizzi had, at last, defeated them. Hamilton then proposed that Panizzi 'be directed to proceed with the utmost dispatch in the compilation of a full and complete catalogue, in manuscript, of the books in his custody, in such a manner as may appear to him most consistent with correctness and accuracy and adhering, as closely as circumstances will permit him, to the rules laid down and approved by the Trustees on the 13th July 1839.'[61] This, and a subsequent motion that Panizzi should inform the Trustees of any means by which the completion of the catalogue might be speeded up, were passed, a third motion that plans should be put into operation for printing special catalogues of the rare book collections was, after some discussion, withdrawn.

A fortnight later these two resolutions were put to a general meeting and carried. Panizzi had won.

Won, at least, as far as the Trustees were concerned, but another and even more trying ordeal now confronted him.

NOTES TO CHAPTER 8

1   Lamb had enjoyed a final dinner in Cary's rooms in old Montagu House a few days before his death in November, 1834. [H. Cary, *Memoir*, v. 2, pp. 277–279.]

2   His son wrote, 'There was but little outward show of grief, an awful stillness . . . a look of mere childishness, almost approaching to a suspension of vitality.' [H. Cary, *Memoir*, v. 2, p. 198.]

3   Add. MS. 36, 715 f.7.

4   James Abercromby, first Baron Dunfermline, 1776–1858. Speaker, 1835–1839.

5   *Royal Commission, Minutes*, para. 2764.

6   *Minutes*, para. 2764.

7   Rev. Ernest Hawkins, 1802–1865. He was, at this time, under-librarian at the Bodleian. Subsequently Secretary of the Society for the Propagation of the Gospel.

8   Richard Garnett, 1789–1850. Ancestor of a long line of distinguished literary figures.

9   Fagan, I, p. 136. *Royal Commission, Minutes*, para. 2764.

10   Letters to *The Times*, July 1, July 18, July 19, July 21, 1837.

11   Charles Dietrich Eberhardt König, 1774–1841, mineralogist.

12   *The Times*, July 26, 1837.

13   Ellis, a strong Tory, was a lifelong friend of Lord Aberdeen whom Panizzi tended to distrust. Edward Hawkins, 1780–1867. Numismatist. Keeper of the Department of Antiquities, 1826–1860.

14   Hallam, the historian, 1777–1859, for instance, strongly supported Panizzi. [Add. MS. 36, 715. f.18.]

15   Sir Charles Pepys, first Earl of Cottenham, 1781–1851. Lord Chancellor, 1836–1841.

16   Fagan, I, p. 140.

17   Fagan, I, p. 137. H. Cary, *Memoir*, v.2, p. 286.

18   *The Times*, July 18, 1837.

19 Rev. Philip Bliss, 1787–1857, University registrar and keeper of archives, Oxford, 1824–1857.

20 Madden to Bliss, July 19, 1837. Add. MS. 36, 715. f.20.

21 Madden to Bliss, July 27, 1837. Add. MS. 36, 715. f.21.

22 John Winter Jones, 1805–1881. Had been travelling secretary to the Charity Commissioners. Introduced to the Museum by Carlisle. A candidate for the vacant Assistant Keepership after Cary's departure. Turned down, though strongly backed by Panizzi, by the Trustees under the influence of persons to whom the Keeper of Printed Books was 'obnoxious' on the grounds of his 'connexion with the establishment is of recent date'. Jones bore no resentment against Garnett, 'but from that hour I determined that I would be Principal Librarian'. [R. Garnett, *John Winter Jones*, p. 6.] Keeper of Printed Books, 1856–1866; Principal Librarian, 1866–1878.

23 Panizzi first wrote and then crossed out 'Every day, every hour almost the evil increases and if not attended to immediately it will become irremediable.' Perhaps he thought this too strong, as yet, for the Trustees. [PP. 1837 f.11.]

24 Thomas Watts, 1811–1869. Superintendent of the Reading Room, 1857–1866, Keeper of Printed Books, 1866–1869. Watts was first employed on January 17, 1838, on a temporary basis and was not formally appointed till November 27.

25 William Brenchley Rye, 1818–1901, Keeper, 1869–1875. Rye was first employed as a transcriber in June 1838, becoming an assistant on 19th July 1844. Jones had introduced him to the Museum service.
George Bullen, 1816–1894. Keeper, 1875–1890. C.B., 1890. John Humffreys Parry, 1816–1880, barrister. Serjeant at law, 1866.
Edward Edwards, 1812–1886. Librarian and author. Of the principal figures in the department during this period, no less than four, Panizzi, Jones, Parry and Rye had had legal training. Panizzi and Parry were, of course, fully qualified lawyers, whilst Jones and Rye had both been employed in a lawyer's office. Hence Espinasse's gibes at the 'two ex-attorney's clerks'. *Espinasse*, p. 17.

26 PP. 1837. f.11.

27 Letter to Forshall from J. Thompson of Pickering Place, Bayswater. PP. 1837 f.23. See also a letter in *The Age*, September 30, 1838. The introduction of the rule was mainly due to a bad outbreak of book stealing.

28 PP. 1837. f.37.

29 PP. 1837. f.31.

30 *Select Committee*, 1836. *Minutes*, para. 5425.

31 PP. 1838. f.169.

32 PP. 1839. f.59.

33 PP. 1839. f.196 et seq.

Egerton MS. 284, 42, ff.320, 322. On the other hand, the two were not always at loggerheads, at least on Panizzi's side. The latter wrote in a most affable manner to Sir Frederic in April, 1844, to ask his advice on the question of some manuscripts and offering to do what he could to get some for him. [*Egerton MS.* 2843. f.287.]

35 *Royal Commission, Appendix*, p. 130. Report of November 9, 1837. [*Appendix*, p. 147.]

36 Sub-Committee Minute of November 18, 1837. [*Royal Commission, Appendix*, p. 151.]

37 Sub-Committee Minute of April 25, 1838. [*Royal Commission, Appendix*, p. 160.]

38 *Royal Commission, Appendix*, p. 155. It would seem highly probable that it was Sir Henry's intervention and that of his patron, Lord Aberdeen, together with Forshall's influence over the Archbishop, that finally determined the Trustees to pursue a policy contrary to the expressed wishes and advice of both Baber and Panizzi. [See also Fagan, I, pp. 142–145 and Esdaile, pp. 97, 98.]

39 Report of December 26, 1838. [*Royal Commission, Appendix*, p. 169.]

40 PP. 1838, ff.217; 265a. *Royal Commission, Appendix*, p. 178.

41 Royal Commission Minutes, para. 7311 et seq. Panizzi himself always spoke of them as the Trustees' rules. [*Royal Commission, Minutes*, para. 4109, 4111.]

42 General Meeting Minute of July 13, 1839. [*Royal Commission, Appendix*, p. 227.]

43 Circular Letter to staff of Dept. of Printed Books of August 8, 1839. [*Royal Commission, Appendix*, p. 228. PP. 1839, f.144.]

44 Report to Trustees of January 25, 1840. [*Royal Commission, Appendix*, p. 234.]

45 Report to Trustees of July 22, 1841. [*Royal Commission, Appendix*, p. 254.]

46 A.P. to W. Jones, January 20, 1841. [*Royal Commission, Appendix*, p. 265.]

47 Report to Trustees of January 26, 1843. [*Royal Commission, Appendix*, pp. 264, 265.]

48 Report to Trustees of June 27, 1844. [*Royal Commission, Appendix*, p. 275.]

49 Committee Minute of January 10, 1846. [*Royal Commission, Appendix*, p. 285.]

50 *Account of the Income, etc.*, 1845 [B.M. Annual Report] H. of C. *Sessional Papers*, no. 141, p. 6. [*Parliamentary Papers*, H. of C. 1846, vol. XXV, p. 217.] The report gives A.P.'s reasons for delaying the printing until everything is ready and adds: 'Upon these representations the Trustees have consented for the present to suspend the printing of the catalogue.'

51 A.P. to H. Ellis, October 2, 1846. [*Royal Commission, Appendix*, pp. 290, 291.]

52 *Observations on the Report of Sir H. Ellis*, January 7, 1847. [*Royal Commission, Appendix*, pp. 298–319.]

53 *Royal Commission, Appendix*, p. 308.

54 *Report of Sir H. Ellis*, January 14, 1847. [*Royal Commission, Appendix*, p. 334.]

55 *Royal Commission, Appendix*, p. 335. The 'inferior agents' were Rye and Major.

56 Report of February 11, 1847. [*Royal Commission, Appendix*, pp. 336–350.]

57 *Royal Commission, Minutes*, para. 4124.

58 Library Sub-Committee Minutes of February 20, 1847. [*Royal Commission, Appendix*, p. 351.]

59 Sub-Committee Minutes of March 6, 1847. [*Royal Commission, Appendix*, p. 353.]

60 Sub-Committee Minutes of November 27, 1847. [*Royal Commission, Appendix*, p. 445.]

61 *Royal Commission, Appendix*, p. 446.

9

FURTHER DIFFICULTIES OF
A LIBRARIAN

BUT, before dealing with this problem, we must retrace our steps
and see how Panizzi and his beloved library had fared in general
during these years of controversy and bitterness.

Panizzi had, all the time, two principal objects in view. The first,
to build up the library by every means in his power, so as to make
it the greatest and most representative collection on earth; the
second, to make the books so acquired speedily and readily available to all readers.[1]

To secure the first object, he needed greatly increased government grants and the proper enforcement of the Copyright Act,
together with active and zealous agents throughout Europe and
the United States. For the second, he must have more and better
staff, the best catalogues possible and, above all, adequate accommodation to house the books he was now, at last, getting.[2] Of his
constantly frustrated efforts during these years to prepare and
make available a catalogue worthy of the Department, we have
already spoken. It is now time to deal with his, if anything, even
greater efforts to improve the library in every other respect.

Staff, of course, was a constant problem. In the lower ranks,
not only were many of the attendants far from satisfactory, but, in
many cases, they were much too old for the heavy tasks the
Keeper now laid upon them, one, in fact, being no less than ninety.
The better men, despairing of promotion, were constantly leaving. At one point, things were so desperate that Panizzi was reduced to getting the books for the readers himself.[3] The same was

true of the transcribers and of the supernumerary assistants. Good men, such as Parry, were lost too soon to the Museum, others stayed on from a sense of vocation, in the hope of future promotion or for the want of anything better to do.

Panizzi constantly pleaded with the Trustees to improve conditions and prospects for his staff. In more than one case, he helped the desperately needy out of his own pocket. No man could be more kind or more generous to those sick or in want, nor more loyal to those who repaid his trust by a devotion to duty. No man, on the other hand, was more stern or more utterly ruthless in dealing with any cases of backsliding or incompetence.[4]

Even the industrious Watts and the gentle Horne felt, on occasions, the lash of his tongue. It was not such as these, whose occasional and venial faults he readily forgave, who really angered him. It was, rather, such weaker brethren, as Espinasse, and the unfortunate Edwards, who aroused his sustained enmity and disgust.

As early as December 20, 1841 Panizzi had written a stern letter to Edwards.[5] He has had to remonstrate with no other assistant as he has been forced to do with him. He is careless, his writing is largely illegible but, most serious of all, his relations with his colleagues were deplorable. No discussion was possible without long argument 'with so much bitterness'. The other assistants, Panizzi wrote, lose 'their tempers whenever they come into contact with you.' Edwards constantly breaks 'the good understanding' of the others. He must greatly alter his conduct, 'if you wish to continue among us and be treated by your colleagues as they treat each other'.

Harsh words indeed, but Edwards, for all his abilities, constantly seemed to put people's backs up. Whether it was the brashness of a self-made man or whether his treatment by the Select Committee of 1836 had gone to his head, one cannot tell. It is evident that he aroused an intense dislike among many of his colleagues and so, by his conduct and lack of discretion, laid himself open to constant censure.

He was soon again in trouble. In a report on Edwards's conduct made to the Trustees, Panizzi accuses the younger man of faking his diary, in order to 'humbug' his chief and suggests that his repeated misbehaviour does not merit for their leniency.[6] Within a short time, Edwards and Oliphant, another of Panizzi's aversions, were severely reprimanded for coming in late in the morning, but, early in 1846, the culprit was in real hot water.

Edwards, by this time, rightly or wrongly, seems to have felt himself to be a victim of unjust persecution. In a fit of temper, he had been rude to Jones in the presence of the Keeper, despite the former's constant efforts to cover up his mistakes. To make matters much worse, he had then immediately written a letter to the Trustees, giving vent to all his suspicions and dislikes, which he had already voiced to Sir Henry Ellis.[7]

The Trustees, at this, wished to dismiss Edwards immediately. Panizzi, however, represented to them that he did not, at the moment, think it necessary to proceed to this extremity.

Edwards was thereupon ordered to apologize in writing, both to his Keeper and to Jones, which, reluctantly, he then did.[8] Panizzi accepted his apology, but remarked that he could not now place any trust in Edwards's assurances of future good conduct. To mark their extreme displeasure, the Trustees suspended the culprit from his employment and consequently from receiving any salary for a month, no small punishment for one so placed as was Edwards.

Despite all these difficulties, the staff situation slowly improved. Additional assistants to deal with maps, with Hebrew and with Chinese books, as well as with the general run of accessions, had now been obtained. New transcribers had also been engaged and, given reasonable luck, Panizzi's staff was now probably sufficient for his immediate purposes. Not so, alas, with accommodation. The greatly increased volume of accessions had falsified all forecasts as to the future needs of the department. To make matters worse, in 1838 Forshall and Sir Robert Smirke, between them, had grossly misled the Select Committee on Plans and Estimates as to what was needed.[9] Neither Ellis nor Panizzi had been consulted and, in consequence, the amount of space required had been gravely underestimated. Instead of there being sufficient space in the department to last, at least, until 1865, Panizzi now estimated that if the intake continued at its present rate, there was barely room enough for three or four years.[10]

There was already the greatest difficulty in carrying on efficiently the work of the department. In an effort to gain a little

more space, Panizzi asked the Trustees for extra room in the basement beneath the King's Library. Only a portion of it, however,
was granted to him, the rest being assigned to the Departments of
Zoology and Geology. This was done, despite Panizzi's complaints about the offensive smells produced by the specimens belonging to the former department: 'The atmosphere of one of the
finest rooms in the world will be so polluted and become so nau-
seous as to be insupportable.'[11] Most of this year, 1846, Panizzi
had been far from well. In August Ellis had so far forgot their
differences as to commiserate with him on his 'severe illness',[12]
and perhaps this had made him more sensitive than usual to the
smells proceeding from beneath his room!

The space question was still unsolved. In a letter to Lord
Aberdeen, Chairman of the Buildings Sub-Committee, in 1848,[13]
Panizzi warmly advocated a complete redistribution of the rooms
in the East Wing. The collections of the Manuscripts Department
should be rearranged and the resulting empty rooms handed over
to Printed Books, who would then have also an entrance worthy
of the principal department of the Museum. Madden's reaction to
this proposal would have been, one presumes, unprintable, and
the whole question of adequate space for the library remained
unsolved, if indeed it can ever be said to have been solved to this
day!

It was mainly the greatly increased Parliamentary grants that
had brought about this situation. The enforcement of the Copyright Act, which was to be Panizzi's great task a decade later, was
still in the listless hands of the Secretary's department and little,
in that respect, could as yet be done. Panizzi now laid the
foundations of the Library's great supplementary collections of
music, maps, newspapers[14] and, by no means least, of English and
foreign official publications.[15] He insisted, moreover, in obtaining
while it was still possible to do so apparently trivial publications, of
infinite value to future historians, such as the pamphlets issued by
the socialist and Chartist movements of the day. But it was to the
fields of antiquarian and of foreign books that most of his efforts
during the last ten years had been directed. In his opinion, contemporary English books should be secured by a proper enforcement of the Copyright Act; in the field of antiquarian and foreign
purchasing, speed was everything.

To assist him in his task of obtaining foreign books, particularly those in the German and Scandinavian languages, Panizzi had secured the help of an industrious and intelligent Berlin agent Adolphus Asher,[16] whilst in the American field his discovery of the youthful Henry Stevens was a stroke of genius.[17] Stevens has described[18] how the Museum acquired what was, at that date, the largest and best collection in existence of works of American history and literature. It was almost entirely due, he modestly claimed, 'to the broad chest and broader mind of Panizzi'. The Museum was, as Stevens said, first in the field and so secured the best. Stevens had been here of invaluable assistance to Panizzi. He had shown to the Keeper the list of the Museum's American desiderata, which amounted to some ten thousand books not in the department. Panizzi was delighted at the young man's enterprise. He at once asked Stevens to 'sweep America for us, as you have done London for America'. No man could have obeyed this injunction better than did Stevens. By 1865, the year of Panizzi's formal resignation from the Museum, Stevens had secured for the department no less than 100,000 volumes! Panizzi got on very well with the young man from Vermont. Both knew their own mind and were not afraid to speak it, but, as Stevens gratefully acknowledged, 'No two men ever worked together in better harmony or less friction.'

In 1838, Smirke, advised by Forshall, had estimated an annual intake of some 8,000 volumes over the next twelve years. As it turned out, the annual increase was already over 12,000 or including parts, no less than 23,000 items per year!

Not unnaturally, Panizzi had become alarmed at this phenomenal rate of increase. In 1843, he had prepared the long and very detailed statement on the condition of the library, its origins and the deficiencies now to be found in it, class by class, and language by language.[19] Two years later, he presented this report to the Trustees. These were his plans for creating what was virtually a new department, to create for the nation a library at last worthy of it. The means, indeed the only sure means, of so doing were regular, unfettered Parliamentary grants, spread over a considerable number of years. Such grants were necessary both to purchase the books themselves and to ensure that, once bought, they were quickly and adequately catalogued, bound and made available to

FURTHER DIFFICULTIES OF A LIBRARIAN 157

the reader within the shortest possible time. The Trustees were, no doubt, impressed by this brilliantly argued plea and, indeed, they could hardly fail not to be. For the moment, however, little was done to implement it. At last, in the autumn of 1845, it was brought to the notice of the Chancellor of the Exchequer, an ex-officio Trustee and of the Secretary to the Treasury. The Trustees now warmly endorsed Panizzi's requests and asked for no less than £10,000 a year for the next ten years for the purchase of old books, £5,000 per annum for new books, and £2,500 for binding.[20] These were very large sums, indeed, for any government to grant in mid-Victorian England. However, the Treasury, somewhat surprisingly, agreed to recommend to Parliament an annual grant of £10,000 for the purchase of all books and this was, in due course, done. By no means everybody was pleased at Panizzi's success. Madden, for one, was furious. 'Are all the world mad about this gentleman?' he plaintively asks and wishes, not for the first time, he might leave the Museum 'never to return to it'.[21]

The grants, although generous, were never enough. Rare works had, on more than one occasion, to be turned down, since there were insufficient funds to purchase them. The loss of the precious volumes was, however, compensated to a certain extent for Panizzi by a knowledge that he alone at the Museum then possessed.

For many years, as we have seen, Panizzi had been on most friendly terms with the bibliophile, Thomas Grenville. Even before his arrival at the Museum, Grenville had regarded the young Italian scholar with warm affection. Latterly, Panizzi had acted as his literary adviser and never failed to return from abroad without some choice new rarities for his old friend. Grenville was always most grateful. 'I have always been truly sensible of the kindness with which you have satisfied the occasional literary inquiries with which you have allowed me to trouble you,' he wrote. 'You . . . have taken so friendly an interest in the details of my small collection of books and in its gradual improvement.'[22]

Panizzi was a constant visitor, either at Grenville's town house at Hamilton Place, Piccadilly, or at his country seat at Dropmore, near Maidenhead. The friendly old man delighted to entertain the foremost political and literary figures of the day. Gladstone, Rogers, Sydney Smith and others of Panizzi's acquaintances were frequently of the company, but Panizzi himself seems always to have occupied a special place. Grenville regarded him as a son and deeply valued his 'unceasing kindness to the wreck of an old man'.[23] By now, 1845, the great collector was visibly showing signs of breaking-up. His handwriting suddenly becomes very shaky and it must have been evident to all his friends that he had not long to live.

Panizzi was deeply concerned about the possible fate of Grenville's library. A magnificent collection, it had cost over £54,000 to acquire. In Panizzi's words it had been 'formed and preserved with the exquisite taste of an accomplished bibliographer, with the learning of a profound and elegant scholar and the splendid liberality of a gentleman in affluent circumstances, who employed in adding to his library whatever his generous heart allowed him to spare from silently relieving those whose wants he alone knew'.[24]

Was such a collection now to be sold up or to be left elsewhere than to the national library? Panizzi knew, all too well, what a low opinion Grenville had of the present Board of Trustees and his fears for the ultimate fate of the collection were very real.

On Sunday, November 2, 1845, Panizzi called, as usual, on his old friend. They were, by chance, alone. Grenville took the opportunity of telling Panizzi what he intended to do. Despite his anger at the way the Trustees had treated his protégé and incidentally himself, conduct which had at first determined him to leave the whole precious collection to his nephew, he had been so moved by Panizzi's loyalty to the Museum and zeal for its service that he had now changed his mind. 'Your generous conduct made me think that if you, who had been much more injured than I was, forgave them, I ought.'[25] He knew, too, how pleased Panizzi would be to have these valuable and lovely books and how well and how carefully he would look after them. Grenville was also moved by the consideration, so infrequent in a man of his generation, that, since he owed much of his ability to purchase such rarities to the government sinecure which he had so long enjoyed,[26] it would be only just to leave them to the nation and thus to pay back, to some extent, what he had been given. He had altered his will[27] so as to leave the entire collection to the Museum, expressing only the wish that all his books should be kept together and that a catalogue of them should be published. Panizzi, 'strongly moved almost to tears', thanked Grenville for this wonderful gift and for the 'affectionate manner in which he had spoken of me and of my conduct'.[28] It was agreed that it should remain a secret, known only to Panizzi, until Grenville's death. The next day, Panizzi prepared a long memorandum, giving his account of the meeting and deposited it, in a sealed envelope, with his friend Hamilton.

Grenville died on December 17, 1846, just over a year after his interview with Panizzi. The following day, the memorandum was opened. Panizzi, himself unwell, was deeply moved at his friend's death. 'I was very much affected and I hardly knew what I was saying,'[29] he wrote. He had lost 'one of the best friends I have had, whose kindness was uniform as it was excessive . . . a man alone in the world, a foreigner, without any other ties of affection or blood concentrates all his feelings in his friends and to lose one of them is a greater loss to him than it is to others, whose heart is filled by other objects.'[30]

Panizzi was determined to honour Grenville's memory by caring for his beloved collection in every possible way. But to do so was not so easy. The Trustees duly accepted the magnificent donation, but were uncertain where to put it. On January 9, 1847, they conferred with Panizzi on the question of the library's removal from Hamilton Place. Panizzi saw no difficulty over the actual move, but told the Board that there was absolutely no room to receive it in his own department.

For the moment, it was decided, therefore, to put it on its arrival in the Western Manuscript Room, the first to be entered on leaving the Front Hall. This room was empty, except for a few manuscripts at one end. Panizzi agreed with the Trustees' suggestion and informed them that it might well be possible to house the Grenville library eventually in one of the new rooms being built at the east end of the King's Library. A furious Madden was ordered to make available to Panizzi the empty presses and instructions given for the bequest to be transferred to the Museum forthwith.[31]

Elaborate plans were made by Panizzi for the safe transportation of this priceless collection. Young Rye was detailed by his Keeper to supervise the actual move. But even before that could take place, there was trouble. Panizzi denied that he had ever told the Trustees that the *unoccupied* presses in the Western Saloon would be sufficient. *All* the room would undoubtedly be required.[32] As it was, Sir Frederic was hastily filling all the presses there that he could with more and more manuscripts, so as to make even less space available. He was quite obviously going to be as awkward and as difficult as only he knew how.

Panizzi now asked Ellis for the keys to the glazed presses in the Saloon and for a specific order from the Trustees for the books to be collected. He would act, he said, only when he had received such authority and when an adequate and secure place was allotted to them for their reception.[33] Tempers were already rising, but a flustered Sir Henry sent Panizzi both the keys and the necessary authority and at last the move was on.

Rye was instructed to collect the books from Hamilton Place, shelf by shelf, in correct order, starting at the top of the house and working downwards. First the contents of each shelf were to be carefully recorded, then the books, wrapped in blankets, carried downstairs and placed in special vans waiting to receive them. Each van had been itself shelved, so that the books could be fitted on to them with the utmost care. As the van carried its precious cargo from Piccadilly to Bloomsbury, an attendant walked behind all the way. Nothing must be left to chance.

Rye, writing nearly forty years later, vividly recalled the scene, that January 28, 1847. It was snowing and bitterly cold and he would have dearly liked something warming, which, to his disgust, none of Grenville's old servants troubled to offer him. The young man was full of admiration for the meticulous arrangements made by his chief, the detailed planning thought out by that 'methodical mind, which in common with his many other natural gifts, this Prince of Librarians possessed'.[34]

As Rye returned to the Museum at the end of each long day, he found 'Mr Panizzi full of animation & delight at the inspection of so many bibliographical gems – many being familiar acquaintances of his and expatiating on their beauty & rarity to . . . a group of his assistants'[35] – a charming glimpse of Panizzi, the dedicated librarian, happy and exalted, surrounded by the young men, who, for the most part, so greatly admired and respected him.

But troubles were only just beginning. As Panizzi had foreseen, the available shelving was now entirely inadequate. To his rage and chagrin, his old friend's most valuable books now had to be laid out on trestle tables, those only scarcely less precious, on planks on the floor. Madden was being difficult in every way possible. He refused to let Panizzi have a set of keys for all the cases. He demanded that any manuscripts be transferred to him, despite Grenville's wish that the collection should be maintained intact. Though his ally Forshall, he managed, at length, to secure an order from the Trustees to this effect, which Panizzi completely ignored, as long as he could. Madden's final blow was to get hold of the precious volume of plates by the artist Julio Clovio, which Rye had himself brought back in a cab to the Museum, on the specious excuse that he must show it to the Duchess of Cambridge, then visiting his department. To all Madden's little tricks, Panizzi displayed a steady and, in the end, triumphant opposition. Conscious of his own rectitude, he was certain that he would win in the long run, but the strain was beginning to tell.

For not only had he to cope with Sir Frederic and his ways, but he was having even more trouble than usual, both with staff and with readers. He was preparing the vital evidence which he would soon have to present before a Royal Commission, his cataloguing difficulties were still great and he was harassed and badgered on every side. There were difficulties over his new residence and on his return from leave, found, with disgust, that his old study had been pulled down in his absence, whilst his new one was not yet ready.

Panizzi complained bitterly. He had nowhere to sit, nowhere to write, nowhere to receive his constant stream of visitors. 'Consider,' he wrote angrily to Sidney Smirke, the new architect to the Trustees, 'how I am situated and just think for a moment how you would feel in my circumstances'.[36] Smirke speedily put things right and on November 11, 1847, Panizzi moved in to his new study, a study still occupied by his successors to this day.

His difficulties with the staff were many and varied. One attendant had been transported for writing a threatening letter to a lady reader; others had been rebuked for playing chess in the King's Library. Transcribers got continually drunk and had to go and Edwards was, as usual, in trouble.

Though others might fall foul of Panizzi and either hastily leave or, in some cases, be received back into favour, with Edwards it seems to be different. He seems to have aroused such bitter hostility among almost all his colleagues, even the kindly and urbane

6

Winter Jones, that each seemed to be set on finding fault with the poor man on every possible occasion.

Panizzi now frankly loathed him and made no secret of his determination to be rid of him at the earliest opportunity, and obviously was determined, in the meantime, to make life as difficult as possible for his unfortunate subordinate.[37]

It must be freely admitted that there is something self-righteous and even repellent in Panizzi's reports, as he gleefully tells the Trustees of Edwards's latest fall from grace. He pursued his victim with all the energy and determination of one to whom a vendetta was second nature and whose legal training gave him the power and forensic skill of a stern and uncompromising public prosecutor.

Compared with the genial Sir Henry, short and dumpy, so fat that he waddled rather than walked, chatting to everyone, regaling the assistants with improper stories, the tall, stern figure of Antonio Panizzi must have struck terror into the hearts of many. To his intimates, he could be delightful, full of fun and adoring practical jokes. To those whom he disliked or scarcely knew, he could appear morose, proud and distant, hiding his essential shyness and simplicity under a grim and forbidding exterior. He was, as that hostile critic Espinasse acknowledged, a dangerous foe, with strong likes and dislikes and to Edwards he had most certainly taken an intensely strong dislike.

As early as December 1846, Panizzi had taken up a chance remark of Sir Henry's, that he had been informed confidentially by W. Lumley, the bookseller, that a certain party, employed by the Trustees, had used both Museum time and Museum paper in compiling a work for him. Panizzi at once wrote to Lumley,[38] asking to see the manuscript so that its paper might be compared with that used by the Museum. Lumley, however, does not seem to have complied with his request. For a year or more, nothing was done. Complaints were made about Edwards's lack of punctuality or of his taking leave without obtaining permission but secretly and in silence the attack was being prepared. Perhaps the worries of the Royal Commission had driven this comparatively trifling business to the back of Panizzi's mind, but when the blow at last fell, it was with a shattering effect on the head of the wretched culprit.

On November 22, 1848, Edwards received a letter[39] headed 'Wednesday morning, 10 o'clock' and beginning:

'Sir, I have seen some thousand titles of a catalogue which you undertook to compile in or about 1845 written on slips in every respect like those used in this house' and ordering Edwards '*without any delay whatever*'[40] to furnish his Keeper 'with the name and address of the Stationer . . . from whom you bought . . . the paper . . . I am waiting in my study for your answer that no unnecessary delay may take place in my receiving it.'[41]

Edwards's consternation at receiving this awful summons may well be imagined. He replied immediately (not on Museum paper, but on his own, black-edged for his recently dead father), that he needed time 'for reflection, for reference . . . and for advice. Were I to offer to you any observation at this moment . . . I fear I could not express myself in those terms of respect which befit a subordinate in addressing his superior officer.'[42] Panizzi was beside himself with rage at this reply. He can hardly put pen to paper. His usual scrawl is almost unreadable and heavily scored out. He thunders:

'An hour has elapsed and you were silent . . . You must either answer me AT ONCE by bearer or take the consequences.'[43] No answer was received. Edwards could be just as stubborn as Panizzi himself. The matter was thereupon reported to the Trustees. Edwards had already rushed round to see Ellis, who told him that the complaint would presumably come before the Trustees the following Saturday. The fat was now properly in the fire.

Panizzi now revealed that Jones had been asked by Lumley to revise the catalogue left unfinished by Edwards. He had thought it proper, however, to notify his superior officer before refusing or accepting the task. Panizzi promptly asked Jones to let him see the original slips prepared by Edwards some two years before, and it was on this evidence that he had issued his challenge. Panizzi makes no attempt to hide from the Trustees his dislike and distrust of Edwards. 'A person like Mr Edwards who had had repeatedly to be warned & reprimanded for neglecting his duty, who has been twice convicted of making false entries in his diary, who has been suspended for misbehaviour and who . . . has appropriated to his own use the money belonging to the Union of which he was secretary . . . ought no longer to be allowed to remain in the Museum.'[44] This is strong stuff, but Panizzi always hated inefficiency and deviousness, what he called 'humbug',[45] and Edwards, for all his sterling qualities, seems, as with many self-educated men, a bit of a queer fish. As Fortescue said long afterwards, 'With Panizzi, you either got on very well indeed or not at all and if not at all, I do not think he was over particular as to how he got rid of you.'[46]

Edwards had now sent in to the Trustees a long explanation of his conduct.[47] Despite Panizzi's offer to be 'ready with more proofs of Mr Edwards' dishonesty',[48] and his discovery that, not only had Museum titles been used but Mrs Edwards had used some of them herself at home, the Trustees, doubtless under the influence of Forshall, who would do anything to spite Panizzi, decided by a majority to give the culprit one more chance. They stated categorically that 'they were unable to divest themselves of suspicion'[49] as to his probable misconduct, but gave him the benefit of the doubt. His suspension from duty was raised and Edwards, too rashly, at once returned to his department, before either the Principal Librarian or his Keeper had been officially told of the Trustees' decision. On the Monday, the genial Bullen advised him to make his peace with Panizzi and formally tell him of his return to the fold.

Panizzi had, perforce, to accept the Trustees' ruling, though with bitter complaints. He knew his time would come. Edwards was sure to trip up again and, next time, there would be no mercy.[50]

1848 had indeed been a difficult year. Of the upheavals abroad and of Panizzi's connection with them, more will be said later. We shall hear, too, of the Royal Commission and of Panizzi's evidence before it. In April, domestic troubles had reached a climax with the Chartist demonstrations and their plans for the presentation of a monster petition to Parliament. The authorities feared widespread disturbances and damage to public buildings, such as had occurred during the Gordon riots, some sixty years before. The Museum seemed to be an obvious target for outbreaks of mob violence, if such should arise and their apprehensions were fully shared by Sir Henry. So, if for different reasons, were they by Panizzi. Undoubtedly swayed by his old radical instincts, he sympathized with many of the demands put forward by the Chartists, but a threat to his beloved Museum, from any quarter, must be stoutly resisted.

On April 8, Antonio Panizzi, like so many others, including the future Napoleon III, had been appointed a special constable for the preservation of the public peace and for the protection of the inhabitants of the parishes of St Giles in the Fields and St George, Bloomsbury,[51] and proceeded to carry out his new office with his accustomed vigour. His contempt for Edwards was certainly not lessened when the latter indignantly refused his Keeper's request that he too should be sworn in as a special constable, along with the rest of the staff. 'What! Not defend the place from which you get your living!'[52] he snapped. He would probably have been even more indignant had he known that Edwards, that very morning, had signed the petition for the Charter in Tottenham Court Road on his way to the Museum.[53]

In all some 250 of the staff, including the men working on the site, were sworn in under Panizzi's enthusiastic direction.[54] The 'Western Division' of the Chartist forces had been appointed to assemble in Russell Square and it was feared that the mob would take the opportunity to sack the Museum on their way to Kennington Common, from whence the march on Parliament was to start.

An officer of the Royal Engineers was sent to advise on putting the place into a state of defence by the erection of barricades and, the previous evening, Panizzi had himself toured the building, looking for weak places through which the mob might burst in. He noted 'that the Museum can be well defended by a well-directed fire of musketry from the roof which commands not only every side of the building but every approach to it as well as some most important points of the interior'.[55] Firearms should be provided for such of the staff able and willing to use them, doubtless including himself, and the fire engines standing by to deal with any conflagrations. Stones were ordered to be taken up to the roof, to be cast down on to the heads of the mob, should they succeed in getting through the outer defences and stretchers and medical supplies to be handy in case of need.[56]

The old revolutionary was certainly thoroughly enjoying himself. The garrison of the Museum was now increased to two officers and fifty-seven other ranks, together with twenty Chelsea pensioners. Fifty muskets and the necessary ammunition had been sent from the Board of Ordnance, together with cutlasses and between two and three hundred pikes.

On the 10th, provisions for a three days' siege having been laid in, the staff assembled ready, under their valiant leader, to defend the Museum to the last man. Cowtan boldly notes: 'Fergus O'Connor or any of his confederates would have found rather a warm reception if they had ventured to force their way into the Museum.'[57] There were doubtless many of the staff only too eager for them to try.

The fatal day wore on. Panizzi was everywhere, encouraging his forces with the injunction, 'England expects that every man this day will do his duty.'[58] This Nelsonian phrase, uttered in a distinctly un-English accent, must have struck the more irreverent members of the staff as decidedly comic. Panizzi was constantly sending out scouts to find out what was happening. Nothing so far had been seen or heard of the enemy, save a murmur of voices from the direction of Russell Square. At midday, the troops, both amateur and professional, were heartened by the sight of tables laden with beef, bread and beer, though smoking was forbidden, even in this emergency. Nothing was seen of the Chartists and by evening it was realized that the great demonstration had been a complete fiasco, foundering 'not in blood but in ridicule'.[59] There was no need to fear any longer what Thiers had called 'la violence des montagnards'.[60] London was not Paris and the demonstrators dispersed quietly to their homes. At the Museum, the married men were allowed to return to their wives and families and life gradually returned to normal. By common consent, Panizzi had been the commander of the garrison of the threatened institution and the hero of the hour. A few days later, the Trustees gratefully acknowledged 'the intelligence, energy, zeal and union which had been displayed by their Principal Librarian, the heads of departments and by the gentlemen engaged under them'.[61]

But, alas, this 'union' was all too short-lived, and soon the public were to be regaled by the spectacle of the most acrimonious controversy and washing of dirty linen by members of the Museum staff as the Royal Commission proceeded on its stately way.

NOTES TO CHAPTER 9

1 The memorandum, *Origin, Progress and Present State of the Library of the Printed Books*, drawn up by Panizzi in 1843, presented to the Trustees on January 1, 1845, and by them submitted to Parliament on December 16, 1845, gives a detailed account of his aims and achievements. [*Parliamentary Papers*, H. of C., 1846, vol. XXV, p. 229.]

2 The increase is striking. The purchase grant for Printed Books in 1779 was £102; in 1831 £1,084; in 1837 £2,944; in 1842 £3,192; in 1843 £5,091; in 1844, £7,738; in 1845 £5,672; in 1846 £8,904.

3 PP. 1839. f.193.

4 He had, for instance, managed to secure for the junior staff an official lunch break of half an hour. This was granted only on the condition that they remained a quarter of an hour after closing time. [PP. 1838. ff.242, 264.]

5 PP. 1841. f.115.

6 PP. 1843. f.40c; 1846 f.199.

7 PP. 1846. f.322. See also entries in Edward's *Diary* for July 27, 28, and August 1, 1846.

8 PP. 1846. f.339.

9 *Select Committee on Plans and Estimates for the Completion of the Buildings of the British Museum*, July 30, 1838. [*Parliamentary Papers*, H. of C., 1837–38, vol. XXIII.]

10 PP. 1846. f.436.

11 PP. 1846. f.423a. Panizzi complained bitterly of the 'putrified animal matter' the zoologists kept in the basement beneath his study.

12 PP. 1846. f.336.

13 PP. 1848. f.111.

14 *Royal Commission, Minutes*, para. 3972, 3978, 4029, 4040. Panizzi had got hold of such items as the numerous maps and plans produced during the railway boom in the 1840s.

15 Henry Stevens had succeeded in persuading the United States Government to present to the Museum all its official publications, the beginning of the present enormous holdings in this field. Stevens wrote, 'I hope you will be able to find room for they are very numerous,' sentiments certainly echoed today. He continues, 'I have little doubt I shall prevail upon all the states to imitate the liberality of the general government,' an aim he was, very largely, to succeed in carrying out. [Add. MS. 36, 715. f.339.]

16 Adolphus (Adolf) Asher, 1800–1853. Asher also served as a political informant for Panizzi as to what was happening in Austria, Prussia and in central Europe generally.

17 Henry Stevens, 1819–1886. Described himself as 'bibliographer and lover of books'. Garnett called him 'genial, expansive, sanguine, both crafty and candid'.

18 *Library Association, Transactions*, 1884, p. 117.

19 *Parliamentary Papers*, H. of C., 1846, vol. XXV, p. 229.

20 Letter from Rev. J. Forshall to C. E. Trevelyan, December 16, 1845. [*Parliamentary Papers*, H. of C., 1846, vol. XXV, p. 229.]

21 Madden to Bliss, February 18, 1846, March 15, 1846. Add. MS. 36, 715. f.346.

22 Grenville to A.P., September 15, 1834. Add. MS. 36, 714. f.347.

23 Grenville to A.P., December 2, 1845. Add. MS. 36, 715. f.242.

24 *Account of the Income and Expenditure of the British Museum for the year 1847*, p. 9. [*Parliamentary Papers*, H. of C., 1847–48, vol. XXXIX, p. 273.]

25 Fagan, I, p. 271.

26 Grenville's sinecure was that of Chief Justice in Eyre, south of the Trent. Worth over £2,000 per annum, he was the last holder of this office, it being abolished at his death.

27 Grenville had intended to leave the collection to his nephew, the Duke of Buckingham and Chandos (1797–1861). It was fortunate that he did not do so, since in a few years that nobleman was forced by his creditors to disperse his own extensive collections. The sale of these treasures lasted forty days, but brought in only £75,562.

28 Fagan, I, p. 273.

29 *Royal Commission, Minutes*, para. 2553.

30 A.P. to Mrs Rutherfurd, December 22, 1847. Quoted in Wicks, p. 147.

31 PP. 1847. f.14. The Grenville Library is still housed in this room.

32 PP. 1847. ff.28, 31.

33 PP. 1847. f.28.

34 PP. 1847. f.57b.

35 PP. 1847. f.57b.

36 PP. 1847. f.683. Sydney Smirke, 1798–1877, had succeeded his elder brother in 1846.

37 Espinasse, p. 18, tells a probably apocryphal story of Edwards being ordered by Panizzi to shave off his moustache as being incompatible with the status of an assistant in the Museum.

38 PP. 1846. f.456.

39 A.P. to Edwards, November 22, 1848. PP. 1848. f.556.

40 Panizzi was almost as fond of underlining as his Sovereign, Queen Victoria.

41 PP. 1848. f.556. Edwards, *Diary*. Entry for November 22, 1848.

42 PP. 1848. f. 553. *Diary*, 1848, November 22.

43 PP. 1848. f.555. Headed '¼ past 11'.

44 PP. 1848. f.557. Panizzi encloses a specimen of the disputed paper. The reference to the 'Union', is to the Art Union of London of which Edwards had been Honorary Secretary. His mismanagement of its funds appears to have been due rather to carelessness than to criminal intent.

45 PP. 1848. f.565b.

46 George K. Fortescue, 1847–1912. Keeper, 1899–1912.

47 PP. 1848. f.565b. *Diary*, November 25, 1848.

48 PP. 1848. f.565b.

49 PP. 1848. f.620. Hamilton, who voted against the motion to give Edwards a chance, gave as his reasons the impossible position the Trustees' decision put Panizzi in. [*Royal Commission, Minutes*, para. 10922.] *Diary*, December 9, 1848.

50 PP. 1848. f.630b. For a different point of view, see Espinasse and *Diary*, 1848.

51 PP. 1848. f.203.

52 Fagan, I, p. 281. Fagan merely says 'an objector', but there can be little doubt Edwards is meant. *Diary*, April 4.

53 *Diary*, April 8.

54 A distinction they shared with half the members of the House of Lords and a considerable number of enthusiastic volunteers from the 'dock rabble'. Halévy, *History of England, 1841–1852*, p. 211.

55 Fagan, I, p. 282.

56 *Diary*, April 10, 1848.

57 Cowtan, p. 150. Feargus O'Connor, 1794–1855. The Chartist leader.

58 Cowtan, p. 150.

59 Halévy, p. 213.

60 Fagan, I, p. 242.

61 Fagan, I, p. 283. Add. MS. 36, 716, f.26.

10

THE ROYAL COMMISSION AND ITS AFTERMATH

ALL through the 1840s, public discontent with and criticism of the Museum, and of the Reading Room and the Department of Printed Books in particular, was growing. Regular readers grumbled at, to them, irksome and unwelcome new regulations; the literary world, or at least the most vocal part of it, demanded to know what had happened to the printed catalogue, which they had so long been promised, and voiced dark suspicions of the library and of its foreign head, whose excessive familiarity with so many members of the governing classes provoked much envious comment.

Many of these grievances were to be ventilated in the correspondence between Panizzi and Sir Nicholas Harris Nicolas. It seems to have started with a personal letter[1] to the Keeper complaining of delays in obtaining books and threatening to call the attention of the government to the difficulties arising from the new regulations and from the state of the catalogue. A sharp exchange of letters followed, with Nicolas insisting that, though he was not bringing charges against Panizzi personally and some of the faults were clearly due to the mistakes of higher authority, the former was certainly answerable, in his opinion, 'for much of what seems to be improper in your department'.[2] Panizzi was deeply annoyed at what he called 'the vague and serious charges which you have volunteered against me', and asked the Trustees to institute an inquiry, 'submitting the whole system to a searching investigation'.[3]

Panizzi, as Lady Dacre had once said,[4] was only too ready to rush into print and now got in first with a pamphlet entitled: *On the Supply of Printed Books from the Library to the Reading Room of the British Museum*.[5] Sir Nicholas's long-forgotten tribute to the newly introduced system of press-marks was prominently displayed on the title-page. Basically a defence, and a most able one, of his nine-year rule of the Department, Panizzi pulled no punches in attacking his critics and in demolishing their arguments. He ends, 'I shall not defend myself, except before a competent judge. Wherever an inquiry which I have courted . . . and still court . . . shall take place . . . I will prove . . . that no reliance can be placed on his [Nicolas's] opinions.'[6]

Nicolas replied in a further pamphlet. He accused Panizzi, 'an Italian notary . . . undistinguished even in the literature of his own country', of deceit, of undue influence over the Trustees, 'as unbounded as it is prejudicial' (Panizzi must have smiled wryly at this), of sheer incompetence in failing to issue a printed catalogue and whose ninety-one rules, 'eternal cross-references', and suchlike 'frivolities', redounded neither to his credit nor to that of an institution ruled by a body of amateurs and dilettanti.[7]

Prejudiced, to a great extent based on ignorance and misrepresentation as Nicolas's criticisms were, they contained enough semblance of truth to make many persons, not at all ill-disposed, distinctly unhappy at the state of the Museum. To the outsider, and particularly to the increasingly important scientific world, the Museum seemed to be old-fashioned, incompetent and riddled with corruption.

Questions were asked in the House. Members demanded to know whether the Government intended to institute any inquiry into the constitution of the Board of Trustees. This 'self-elected' body refused to add any further scientists to its numbers and the spending of large sums of public money on such an unrepresentative institution was to be deplored. Lord John Russell, the new Prime Minister, made soothing noises, admitted that 'certain improvements' might well be made, but considered that whether or not a commission should be appointed was a matter for mature consideration.[8]

Letters to *The Times* complained of the Reading Room and of the catalogues. It was also remarked that the previous Boxing Day large crowds had been turned away from the gates of the Museum, since it 'never opened on Saturday'.[9]

Rumours, and doubtless much more than rumours, were widespread of the constant quarrels and ill-feeling amongst members of the staff. The almost open warfare between Madden and Panizzi was notorious. There can have been little doubt in the public mind that it was indeed high time that some light was thrown on to these turgid waters.

It would also seem not improbable that Panizzi himself may have used his already considerable influence in political circles to urge the setting up of some sort of public inquiry. As we have seen, he had constantly implored the Trustees to do this. The victim for so many years of malicious and ignorant criticism, proud of his great achievements against heavy odds, even though none realized more than he how much yet remained to be done, determined to have his name cleared in the most public manner possible, he undoubtedly would have done his utmost to further the setting up of that 'higher authority', to which alone he might appeal.

His friends were now in power. John Russell was Premier; Clarendon, Foreign Secretary; Andrew Rutherfurd, Lord Advocate; all of them men with whom he was on the best of terms. If, by the setting up of a Royal Commission, they could not only satisfy a genuine public demand, but also be of assistance to Panizzi personally, they would not have hesitated for a moment.

On March 10, 1847, a memorial[10] was addressed to the Prime Minister, expressing dissatisfaction at the undue weighting given to non-scientific men in appointments to the Board of Trustees.[10] On June 17, a Royal Commission was duly appointed to inquire into 'in what manner that National Institution may be made most effective for the advance of Literature, Science and the Arts'.[11] The Royal Commission was a powerful one and on it were several of Panizzi's friends and acquaintances. The Chairman, Lord Ellesmere,[12] was a distinguished scholar as well as a great nobleman and on friendly terms with the Keeper of Printed Books. Rutherfurd and Langdale were also members and with them on the Commission, Panizzi could be sure that his interests would never be neglected. Indeed of all its members, only one or at the most, two, Monckton Milnes[13] and, perhaps, Hume,[14] were likely to be at all hostile. He could scarcely have wished for a better tribunal before which to appear. This is not to cast any doubt on the Commission's integrity. Had Panizzi been, indeed, the fool and the impostor his enemies claimed him to be, he would have received short shrift. All he needed, and this he was to receive, was a chance to plead his case and to vindicate his policy before an impartial and discerning court.

The Secretary to the Commission was John Payne Collier,[15] the Shakespearian scholar and Librarian to the Duke of Devonshire, and a lifelong habitué of the Reading Room. Though his appointment was warmly welcomed by *The Times*,[16] events were to show that as Secretary Collier was far from satisfactory. He lacked the necessary impartiality, and was too easily swayed by his own feelings. Had the majority of the Royal Commission not been so able and so highly placed, his influence might well have been disastrous, both for Panizzi and for the British Museum itself.

On July 10, the Royal Commission began its labours. It was, unfortunately, only able to hold that year three meetings. Already numerous returns and copies of the Trustees' minutes had been forwarded by Forshall to the Commissioners, and these were to be made freely available both to the members and to the witnesses. Panizzi had already written to Ellesmere, asking permission to be present during the whole of the inquiry. The permission was readily granted, not only to Panizzi but also to Ellis, Forshall and each head of a department.[17]

Things began quietly. Sir Henry was the first witness. To that benign and genial soul, all was well. When asked if there were any 'disputes or difficulties' among the members of his staff, he solemnly replied: 'They are all upon very fair terms. I do not know of any absolute disputes among them.'[18] He was, he assured the Commission, unaware of any 'dissensions or private disputes', surely the understatement of the year, when one thinks of the faction fights which had for so long raged throughout the Museum. He had no complaints or suggestions to make to the Commissioners, except that he would like a room of his own. No change seemed to him, he told the Commissioners, to be either desirable or necessary.

Forshall, by now a very sick man, was next examined. It was quickly clear that here was one source, at least, of the confusion, inefficiency and bad feeling which had for so long plagued the administration of the Museum. It was plain that the Secretary's department had grown out of all proportion and its efficiency was by no means commensurate with its size. Forshall, in virtue of his office, had exercised a disproportionate, and, at times, malign, influence over the Trustees. Ellis had been pushed, for the most part, well into the background and many of the duties more properly performed by the Principal Librarian had been usurped by the over-ambitious Secretary. For all practical purposes, he was an insuperable barrier between the Trustees and the heads of the Departments, a source of frustration and annoyance to all the other officers. On July 13, after only three days' examination of these witnesses, the Commission was forced, temporarily, to a close, leaving the star witness, Antonio Panizzi, still unexamined.

During the early months of 1848 it became clear that the original Commission was too small, and the quorum, as laid down in their instructions, too large, to ensure regular attendances. As a result, on May 5 a new Commission was issued, increasing the number of members from eleven to fourteen, whilst their quorum was reduced to three.[19]

Meanwhile, the previous February, the questioning had been resumed. Sir Henry was again the first witness, giving a short account of his duties and of his relations with Forshall. After a brief discourse by Hawkins, the Keeper of Antiquities, Forshall himself was again called in to undergo a vigorous cross-examination.

To Forshall succeeded Madden, full of grievances and loudly-voiced complaints. *His* department *never* had enough money; *his* staff were never at his disposal; there had been four distinct orders of the Trustees to hand over the Grenville manuscripts, yet he had not received them; it was impossible for his staff to obtain any book from the library and so on. He once again raised the old story of the gross injustice of his receiving his appointment after Mr Panizzi. He grumbled about the Julio Clovio manuscript and about the smallness and inconvenience of his new residence. Everything, he implied, was explicitly or implicitly the fault of that 'damned foreigner'.

The moans of the distinguished Keeper of Manuscripts at length came to an end and at last, on May 17, Panizzi first rose to answer the charges brought against him for so long by 'a herd of small and some of them contemptible men'.[20] He was a striking figure, standing there, tall and handsome, his hair now greying, but still thick and curly. Gone were the plump, Pickwickian Sir Henry and the skinny Sir Frederic. In their place was Antonio Panizzi, proud, calm and dignified and very much the master of himself and of the situation.

Quietly he dealt with Madden's complaints about the residences, determined to be generous, yet contemptuous of the pettiness of his adversary, 'I would not lose my rights of seniority . . . I chose on purpose and deliberately, and on the ground that I was senior to Sir Frederic Madden . . . If he will ask me for it now, I will give it up to him . . . I have said before that he shall have whichever house he chooses, but he must not have it as a matter of right.'[21] As always, it was the principle that mattered. Careless, as ever, of his own comfort or material advantage, he was absolutely inflexible whenever a fundamental question of right or wrong was involved. He had always the lawyer's respect for abstract justice.

Madden's specious claims on the Grenville manuscripts were speedily disposed of and a warm tribute to the staff of Printed Books followed. Their Keeper could but regret, however, that conditions and prospects for the vast majority of them were so appalling. 'Mine is a fair remuneration,' he remarked, 'I believe the Assistant Librarian and everybody else are badly paid.'[22]

An important disclosure was now made. Panizzi had, it would seem, been grossly misled. It will be remembered that on July 13, 1839, the Trustees had committed themselves to the printing of the catalogue. Yet the manuscript minutes communicated to Panizzi by Forshall contained important omissions which he had never seen until the printed version was issued. The minute itself had been passed at a general meeting, at which only one member, and he a most sporadic attender, of the preparatory committee had been present. More than this, in the minute, as received by him, he had been ordered to have the catalogue ready *in* press by December 1844. In the minute as published Panizzi was merely instructed to have it *ready for* the press by that date, an important and vital distinction, which, in his opinion, had cost the country thousands of pounds, as well as endless distraction and anxiety to his staff and to himself. The omission of the final paragraph, too, that the General Committee would not regard their order as final, if the members of the preparatory Sub-Committee, not then present, should object, was a flagrant injustice to Panizzi. Had he known of this possibility of an appeal, he would undoubtedly have taken steps. Knowing nothing, he had been bound hand and foot to an impossible task for nearly ten years.

Whether this failure to keep him fully informed of this grave decision was by mischance or by design, was not for him to say. Although he had been at all the meetings of the preparatory Sub-Committee which examined the question, at the final meeting he was not permitted to be present, although any decision reached at it was clearly of vital importance to him, especially when the one which was reached was quite inconsistent with what the Sub-Committee had already agreed. It was quite clear that the Trustees had not played fair with him. There were other things, too, of less importance. Panizzi may well have been over-suspicious, particularly of Forshall and some of his minor criticisms do, indeed, savour of hair-splitting, but the fundamental thing was this: all these long years he had not only been frustrated and maligned, he had been deceived into the bargain.[23]

Forshall, a tired and ailing man, complained bitterly of the aspersions which, it seemed to him, Panizzi's evidence had now cast upon his character. Under the close questioning, however, of the Lord Advocate, he was forced to admit some of the deficiencies of his department. The rest of the time before the summer adjournment was spent by Panizzi in enlightening the Commissioners on every aspect of his duties. Thanks to his own efforts and to the generosity of the Government, he had at last succeeded in building up his collections. Now, money was desperately needed for new buildings and for more staff. If nothing was done, in two or three years it would be impossible any longer to find the books or to keep up the catalogues, a state in which all too many continental libraries now found themselves. As to the complaints of the readers and others, many were merely frivolous. Panizzi challenged all his critics to lay their grievances before the Commission. 'I should like very much that the Commissioners would have the goodness to examine some gentlemen who I know have complained in order that they should state especially what they have to complain of.'[24] He then handed to Ellesmere a list of those who had publicly criticized his administration and of those who could give information as to those who had preferred to remain anonymous.

He strongly defended the innovations he had introduced. Even though, like everything else, they were subject to human error, 'whenever I have found that we were in the wrong, I have never found that it was the system which was wrong.'[25] His final plea was for closer contact between the Trustees and their officers. Though they had done wrong and made mistakes, it was, in his opinion, not through wilfulness, but through a lack of knowledge. If only the heads of the departments had had a close and continuous relationship with the Trustees, then the mistakes and misunderstandings of the last few years might easily have been avoided.

On July 21, the Commission adjourned for the second time. By now they had a clear idea of how very different the popular version of Panizzi's régime was to the reality. All the blame which he had so freely incurred for the delay in preparing and printing the catalogue was to be laid on the misguided and contradictory orders issued by the Trustees or in their name. Opinions might still be divided as to the advisability or not of printing the catalogue. There could now be little doubt as to the reasons for the delay.

It was, however, in the next and final session, which began the following February, that Panizzi completely and finally disposed of the carping criticism to which he had been exposed for so long. The previous year he had challenged his detractors to voice their criticisms plainly and openly before the Royal Commission. Now they were about to do so and he was ready for them.

He once more drew the attention of the Commissioners to the overwhelming need for more and more space. He suggested that new buildings should be erected on the north-east corner of the Museum site. There he would house the Department of Manuscripts, while the Printed Books would take over the rooms at present occupied by Manuscripts. 'Build another Manuscript Department,' he boldly exclaimed, 'and I promise to make use of space now thrown away for printed books.'[26] The scientific departments should be moved to another site, a reform Panizzi himself was not destined to live to see, despite his vigorous attempts to get rid of them when, later, he became Principal

Librarian. Such sentiments were not likely to endear him to his colleagues in the Natural History departments, but this would never trouble him. Panizzi would, as Macaulay said, 'at any time give three mammoths for an Aldus'.[27] He revealed, too, that it was already being discussed what use could be made of the central quadrangle. Already the germ of an inner reading-room was in his mind.

Not everyone was critical of the Reading Room, though Panizzi himself would be the first to admit that there was much room for improvement. Little as yet could be done in the present cramped and overcrowded accommodation. Many greatly needed reforms needs must wait. Henry Stevens had, however, induced two distinguished Americans, Professor George Sumner and Charles Jewett, Librarian of the Smithsonian,[28] to send warm tributes, praising in the most handsome terms not only the reading-room service but also Panizzi himself. These testimonials he now produced before the Commission. Sumner wrote: 'I do not hesitate to declare that in none of the large libraries of Europe have I found the readers in the public room enjoying so great facilities as do those of the British Museum.'[29] His compatriot Jewett was also enthusiastic. The British Museum 'is by far the best regulated library in the world . . . The public are more promptly served than in any other library with which I am acquainted.'[30]

Both warmly praised the press-mark system and Panizzi's other innovations and the increase in the number of reference books on the open shelves available to the readers.

Fortified by this support from the New World, Panizzi once again issued his challenge to his detractors. 'Now I have a request to make of the Commissioners which is that they will examine the complainers . . . I want those gentlemen who make complaints . . . to come to this table and state the facts they have to complain of, and I pledge myself to answer their complaints; I shall be very sorry if they do not make their complaints here.'[31]

The first of his critics to be examined and one of the most formidable was Thomas Carlyle, then almost at the height of his fame. The Reading Room was far too noisy and far too crowded and gave him what he described as a 'Museum Headache'. The present catalogue was worse than useless and the new one promised to be no better. The lack of an up-to-date printed catalogue was 'an immense evil'. Carlyle then enlarged upon the difficulties he had experienced in obtaining what he required from the collections of French Revolutionary tracts. Only after he had failed to find them in the catalogue was he allowed by the 'person in charge of these books' freely to examine them. 'For all practical purposes,' he complained, 'this collection of ours might as well have been locked up in water-tight chests and sunk on the Dogger Bank as put in the British Museum.'[32]

Monckton Milnes then questioned Carlyle about his subsequent experiences with the Thomason Collection of Civil War tracts. With these, it appeared, Carlyle had been luckier. 'In spite of every obstacle, I succeeded in getting great benefit from them.'[33]

Special consideration should be given to important readers, like himself, who were doing serious research and time not wasted on readers 'who blow their noses in an insane state'. All his evidence was wild, self-centred and without any real understanding or any attempt to understand the difficulties and complexities of running a large library or of compiling a large catalogue. He, Carlyle, was 'no catalogue-maker', but, of course, he was quite certain he could easily produce what was needed. 'Elaborate catalogues,' he pontificated, 'are not what we require but legible catalogues accessible to everybody.'[34] Admirable sentiments, no doubt, but expressed without any realization that it was precisely this that Panizzi and his team of highly skilled cataloguers were, in fact, trying to do.

Carlyle's more outrageous and insubstantial statements got short shrift from the Commissioners, but at least one sensible and constructive suggestion he did make, as Panizzi, somewhat grudgingly, acknowledged. This was that there should be members of the staff specially detailed to whom readers might go for information and assistance, a reform that had to wait for nearly a century before it was fully implemented.

Others of Panizzi's critics were now examined. One complained, in the course of his remarks, that: 'Mr Panizzi as usual was not there,' to be sharply rebuked by Sir Henry: 'I beg officially to say that from the moment of Mr Panizzi's entrance into this institution, no officer was ever more regular in his attendance upon his duties and frequently, especially in the evenings, has given much more attendance than was required of him by our rules.'[35]

Some were naturally less hostile. 'Mr Panizzi's catalogue was infinitely better than its predecessors'; 'The principle of Mr Panizzi is a capital one but it will take so much time to complete it.'[36] What readers wanted, even the most patient, was something to be done immediately.

But a new and potentially more dangerous critic now appeared: John Payne Collier, the Secretary to the Royal Commission itself. Panizzi had addressed an open letter to Lord Ellesmere.[37] In it he had set out in greater detail than was possible in his evidence before the Commission exactly what his methods and rules of cataloguing implied. It is, in fact, a masterly summing-up of his position in the controversy.

Collier now took the extremely dubious step of refuting Panizzi's arguments in a second open letter to Ellesmere.[38] The propriety of such action on the part of the Secretary to the Commissioners may well be questioned. He not only had the advantage of his official position and the opportunity to study at leisure all the documents submitted to the Royal Commission, but the sight of its Secretary engaging in public controversy with the principal witness was scarcely an edifying one. There were, naturally, doubts as to his impartiality or even integrity. Langdale, possibly prompted by his friend Panizzi, wrote to Ellesmere to make certain that all the papers submitted were being circulated to every member of the Commission. He complained, too, of unauthorized disclosures to the Press. Ellesmere assured Langdale that no papers, other than those he had seen, had, in fact, been circulated and all was in order.[39]

Collier himself appeared to be conscious of the equivocal nature of his position, but declared himself to be ready, in the public interest, to go through the ordeal which Panizzi had required that persons who were adverse to his views should go through.

His oral evidence before the Royal Commission was to the same effect, that Panizzi's plan was 'useless', and was only persevered with so as to add to his own reputation. In Collier's opinion what was needed was a 'brief, intelligible catalogue', which could easily be prepared in four years and printed off in one. He had catalogued a few books from his own library, to show what could be done. These entries had been written 'with the utmost ease', at the rate of some twenty-five or thirty an hour, 'at perfect leisure' and he had then corrected them.[40] Collier gave the titles to the Commissioners, who passed them on to Panizzi for his comments. These were not to be long delayed.

Another of Panizzi's critics who had burst into print was John Gray,[41] Keeper of the Zoological Collections since 1840. He, too, had written an open letter to Lord Ellesmere, bitterly attacking his colleague.[42] Collier, at least, had tempered his criticism with faint praise, though even he had sneered at Panizzi's foreign origin. Gray, on the other hand, was sweeping in his wholesale condemnation of the administration of his distinguished contemporary and of Panizzi's theories of cataloguing. This was even more noticeable in a second letter, which Gray addressed to Ellesmere on April 4, 1849. His own ideas on the subject were distinctly peculiar, and fully deserved the scorn with which Panizzi treated them. The Keeper of Printed Books had appealed to the Trustees against these vicious attacks upon him by a fellow officer. The Board advised him not to reply to them. They themselves would openly support him and themselves rebut any attacks, from whatever source, upon his honour and integrity. With this statement, Panizzi, perforce, had to be content.[43]

A powerful voice was now raised in support of Printed Books and of its chief. This was Augustus de Morgan,[44] mathematician and bibliographer and a professor at London University. He was utterly opposed to the abbreviated form of catalogue proposed by Carlyle, Collier and their like. Any such production would be useless and inaccurate. It would take as long to be got ready as a full catalogue and, in any case, Collier's estimate of a year for printing was hopelessly inadequate. He had little time for other catalogues praised by some of the witnesses. That of the Bodleian was no credit to the University, whilst that of the London Library was worse than those produced by dealers. He warmly approved both of Panizzi's 'rules' and of the general administration of the Department. 'I believe,' he concluded, 'that Mr Panizzi does everything he possibly can for the library and for the comfort and convenience of those who read here.'[45]

Another friendly witness was Asher, the Museum's German agent. He gave striking testimony to the knowledge, care and skill with which Panizzi pursued his accessions policy. Books were now procured in a very large number of different languages, few if any of which were obtained before Panizzi's day.

Edwards too supported his chief, if somewhat half-heartedly. He would have still preferred a classed catalogue and differed from Panizzi's own views in a number of ways.

Perhaps the most telling witness yet to appear on Panizzi's behalf was his former assistant, John Humffreys Parry. Now a coming man at the Bar, Parry vividly describes how the rules were framed, the 'long and anxious discussion',[46] which each entailed. Though always a great stickler for punctuality and discipline, no man was fairer or more easily accessible to his staff than was Panizzi. Far from refusing advice or constructive criticism, he was always most anxious for suggestions, both from his staff and from the public and all such suggestions were carefully and sympathetically considered. Panizzi had made every effort, despite difficulties and obstacles that would have daunted a lesser man, to expedite the completion of the catalogue. He had constantly urged on his staff to achieve this end. His assistants had nobly responded and, as Parry remembered, would try to outbid each other in the number of titles completed each day. All was in vain. It was an impossible task they had been set. The printing of the first volume, forced on the department 'by ignorant pressure from without', had materially delayed the chances of completing the catalogue. Parry concludes with the words: 'I wish, not as a personal friend, but as an Englishman, to express my thanks to him for the services I know he has rendered to our national library. I would rather have done it in his absence, but I cannot avoid it in his presence . . . Since his appointment to the head of the Printed Book Department, the library has increased by nearly 200,000 volumes . . . It was mainly to his exertions and owing to his exposure of the deficiencies and wants of the library, that the increase of the annual grant to 10,000 *l* took place. I know that he was instrumental in obtaining one munificent bequest of books to the Museum, and in all respects I believe he has rendered invaluable services to the department over which he presides.'[47]

Panizzi was feeling very depressed.[48] The long struggle, the personal attacks were at last having their effect. This warm and generous tribute greatly moved him and did much to comfort him.

Cureton, the Assistant Keeper of Manuscripts, also contributed by telling how, contrary to the general opinion, Panizzi had always sought to be on good terms with his colleagues and most desirous to meet the just wishes of his brother officers. Both Panizzi and his subordinates were always helpful to any who required their assistance. A very different picture now started to emerge from that so assiduously and so maliciously put about by Madden and Gray.

At last Panizzi was ready to answer his critics in detail and to make the final assessment of all he had tried to do for his department during these last ten years. On May 1, 1849, he faced the Commissioners again. First he showed once more how he had built up the library, despite a weak and inadequately operated Copyright Act. He replied to his critics, showing how paltry and misinformed their objections mostly were. He had done as much as lay in his power to remedy the defects of the Reading Room and to meet reasoned criticism, but with such readers as Thomas Carlyle he had no patience. That historian's 'misconduct', in forcing an attendant to get him a book personally, was unforgivable. 'I will have the servant obey my orders and nobody else's if I am to be responsible,'[49] he thundered, and he was furious with Carlyle, as with Madden, for constantly wasting the time of members of his staff. All readers, however eminent they might consider themselves to be, must obey the rules laid down for the conduct of the room. 'All,' he declared, 'are equal there.' In a rare humorous aside, Panizzi referred to Carlyle's remark that most readers were thicker skinned than he as a justification for his receiving preferential treatment. 'I have never,' he observed, 'felt the skin of any reader and they are all treated alike.'[50]

He defended the innovations he had made. The careful benefited; only the careless, the awkward or the inconsiderate complained. Panizzi would not deny that reforms were needed. More room was badly wanted, both for readers and for additional reference books. A better educated superintendent was highly desirable and more money for the hard working and grossly underpaid staff.

Though, through his own efforts, the library had so greatly expanded, the staff was still far too small. Indeed, he had fewer officers than had had Baber, his predecessor. He considered that Jones and Watts, at least, should be promoted as speedily as possible.

As to the critics of the catalogue and of its rules, he contemptuously dismisses them. Collier, especially, is held up to ridicule and his specimen cataloguing proved by the invaluable Jones to be full of every possible error. Panizzi, at the last, turns once again to Forshall and refutes that gentleman's various allegations. With his usual fairness, Panizzi concluded: 'If Mr Forshall had been in good health, he would not have given this evidence.' He replies to the taunts on his being a foreigner. 'As to the management of the library, I do not think I have done less than my predecessors who were Englishmen or less than my present colleagues who are Englishmen have done for their departments.'[51] Thus proudly, Panizzi leaves it to the Royal Commission to justify both him and his works.

Their task was virtually over. Panizzi's old opponent Inglis told the Commissioners that, in his opinion, the Trustees should have taken a firmer line and have insisted that Panizzi completed the printing of the catalogue when ordered to do so. His fellow Trustee Hamilton, on the other hand, paid Panizzi the highest compliments —the Keeper of Printed Books was one 'whose equal certainly there is not in England'[52]—and testified that Panizzi was: 'One of the best public servants I ever knew.'[53] As usual, the final word was with Madden. He was the very last witness to appear before the Commissioners, still complaining about his hated rival.

The long investigation into the Museum was at last over and the Commission's report was eagerly awaited. On March 28, 1850, it appeared and proved to be a triumphant vindication, both of Panizzi and of his policy. 'It is obvious,' commented *The Times*, 'that great changes must take place in this national establishment',[54] and it was equally obvious to all, save to those blinded by prejudice, that one man, and one man alone, was fit to initiate and to direct these changes.

In the Report the Trustees and in particular their Secretary were gently but firmly rebuked. Over the years Forshall had usurped many, if not most, of the functions more properly belonging to the Principal Librarian. The very size of the Board 'by dividing or rather extinguishing individual duty or responsibility has . . . interfered with the superintendence and control which might have been usefully exercised by any smaller, selected number specially charged with the duty'.[55] Thus, by folly and neglect, the administration of the Museum had fallen into hands 'to which it was never intended to be entrusted'.[56] To the over-powerful Secretary and to the consequent feelings of frustration and suspicion which he aroused among the members of the staff, the Commission roundly attributed 'the unfortunate and unseemly jealousies which the evidence shows to have long existed among the principal officers'.[57] Madden and Gray were rebuked for 'the manifestation of similar feelings . . . of ill judged criticism',[58] as had been shown by other critics of the Reading Room and of the Department of Printed Books and, for the most part, such critics had revealed themselves to be entirely ignorant of foreign libraries and to be completely lacking in effective standards of comparison.

The decision to publish the first volume of the new catalogue was ill advised, arousing, as it did, expectations that could never be fulfilled. The Trustees should never have interfered, as they constantly had done, with the preparation of the catalogue. 'The fact of their constant supervision and frequent authoritative interference is not unimportant as bearing on a question of justice to an individual officer of the Museum.'[59] With what satisfaction Panizzi must have read that passage but more was to come.

In every respect, the Commission upheld and approved of Panizzi's suggestions: on cataloguing shelf by shelf; the rule for the cataloguing of anonymous books; his wish to delay printing until all was ready; his reading-room reforms, even his conduct over the disputed residences, all those things which he had striven and argued for ever since 1837 now had the full and public approval of some of the most distinguished men in England.

Despite Panizzi's 'exaggerated sensibility', what Nicolas had more unkindly called his 'morbid irritation', due to 'some peculiarities of his position',[60] a foreigner at the head of a great national institution, he had shown, again and again, 'pregnant proofs of the acquirements and abilities, the manifestation of which in subordinate office led to Mr Panizzi's promotion . . . under circumstances which in our opinion . . . did credit to the Principal Trustees of that day.'

A clear and unambiguous answer, indeed, to all the sneers and malevolent criticism under which Panizzi had, for so long, suffered. His 'habits of order'[61] and practice of useful record of facts and transactions, so clearly manifested in all his evidence, was singled out for favourable comment, habits already well known within the Museum and soon to be displayed to a wider public. Panizzi's accessions policy was judged to be excellent, his refusal to buy English books due under the copyright regulations being upheld as fully justifiable in the circumstances.

As has been said, Madden and Gray were quietly reproved. It was indeed allowed, in the case of Madden, that even such follies as his objections to the plans for the disposal of the Grenville library sprang from 'a zeal for what he considered the just interests of his own department',[62] a generous interpretation that the conduct of Sir Frederic scarcely merited.

It was the failure of the Trustees and of their Principal Librarian, the lack of a 'more prompt and vigorous system of management',[63] which had so gravely exacerbated the situation and which had led to that 'want of harmony and good understanding between the heads of departments to which . . . the epithet rival would be grossly misapplied.'[64]

Final and complete triumph for Panizzi. The Julio Clovio and the other manuscripts taken or claimed by Sir Frederic were ordered to be transferred again forthwith to the Grenville Library.

The Commissioners' principal proposal to rectify the alleged deficiencies of the Board of Trustees, as then constituted, was the abolition of the offices of both Principal Librarian and of the Secretary and the creation of a responsible Executive Committee. This was the unanimous view of the Commissioners, but they differed as to the details. The majority favoured a Chairman, chosen by the Crown, five other persons chosen by the Trustees from among their own members and two additional appointments, also by the Crown, of one officer to supervise the scientific departments, and of another to be in charge of the non-scientific. These last two members of the Committee and, possibly, the Chairman, were to receive adequate salaries. The minority favoured a smaller Executive Committee, and considered that to have, in addition, two such officers as were favoured by the majority would be to reinstate the Principal Librarian, though under another name and to create a parallel appointment for the natural history departments. They also feared lest the creation of these posts would make it more difficult for the Keepers to approach the Trustees directly, a state of affairs the evidence before the Commission had made it quite clear was to be deplored.

But little else remained. A brief mention of the question of an adequate remuneration for the staff; an endorsement of Panizzi's suggestion that Watts and Jones should be made Assistant Librarians, a brief survey of the other matters touched upon and the report drew to a close.

The reception given to the Report was, on the whole, favourable. *The Times* commented that it offered 'ample proof, of the diligence, care, and impartiality with which they have investigated the large and intricate subject'.[65] In the opinion of *The Athenaeum*: Panizzi, Jones and Watts were 'a race of bibliographical giants and the first of these commanded our admiration by the manly spirit in which he faced all difficulties and grappled with all opponents'.[66] Nevertheless, it considered, a printed catalogue would have to be produced.

The majority of his colleagues, and especially his own staff, were delighted at Panizzi's triumphant vindication and warmly congratulated him. Edwards, however, took a different view. He remarked that the report was substantially the same as Ellesmere's draft of the previous autumn, 'with a few additional Panizzean modifications'. He welcomed the idea of an Executive Committee, as sound in principle, but considered that 'that part of the report . . . which deals with the management of the library & especially with the catalogues', to be 'a mass of rubbish'.[67]

The Trustees themselves, in a minute of May 4, 1850, commented unfavourably on the suggestion for an Executive Committee. They then appointed a Sub-Committee to consider in detail the Royal Commission's proposals. Their report, largely the work of Sir Robert Peel,[68] stressed the comments in which the Commission had praised the Board and denied that any drastic changes were either due or necessary.

The Government, for the moment, did little to implement the Commission's recommendations. Panizzi, the most affected of all, seems to have left no record of the feelings of relief and satisfaction with which indeed he must have regarded the Report. His thoughts and energies were now preoccupied with another Parliamentary inquiry, in which he took the greatest interest. This was the Select Committee on Public Libraries, which owed its main inspiration to Panizzi's old acquaintance, William Ewart. The Ewart family had for long distrusted the Italian's 'cloak and dagger' method of conducting his affairs, and William, in particular, seems to have developed a marked dislike both to the

British Museum as a whole and to its Keeper of Printed Books in particular. Edwards had, of course, enthusiastically embraced the chance to help his friend Ewart. Not only was he genuinely desirous of promoting the public library movement, appealing alike to his radical instincts and to his distrust of privileged monopolies, but the Select Committee seemed to be a heaven-sent opportunity of getting his own back on Panizzi and the department he now so much hated. The Royal Commission had been too indulgent, too over-eager to justify the Museum and its chief officers. The Select Committee must serve as a means of redressing the balance of opinion.

The Committee had first been set up on March 15, 1849, to investigate 'the best means of extending the establishment of libraries freely open to the public, especially in large towns', and reported the following July.[69] The report was distinctly critical of the British Museum and of the other principal libraries and compared them, to their disadvantage, with similar institutions abroad. Edwards was their star witness and was warmly commended for his services.

Panizzi was furious. This ignorant rascal had dared to behave as if he were an official representative of the Museum and had then, in Panizzi's eyes, done nothing but traduce his own department. He had preferred foreign libraries, of which he knew little, to his own and to others in Great Britain. But Edwards's greatest crime, in the opinion of his angry chief, was the following. When asked by Ewart:

'Are you aware that complaints have been made that the readers of the British Museum do not find there books which have been recently published?' Edwards complacently and misguidedly replied: 'Yes, and I believe they are very well grounded.'[70]

To Panizzi, that such a statement should be made about his beloved Library by a man whom he regarded as little better than a criminal, was insupportable. The wretch must be openly and publicly discredited.

Already he had warned the Trustees as to the harmful effect the activities of the Select Committee might well have on the reputation of the Museum. In his letter of June 8 to the Trustees, he wrote: 'Mr Panizzi has reason to think that incorrect statements respecting the Library of the British Museum have been made

. . . which from the character assumed by one of the witnesses may receive the attention to which they are not otherwise entitled.'[71]

In a subsequent letter to Hallam, Panizzi plainly indicated his mistrust of Edwards, pointing out the culprit's previous lapses, such as the false returns and the 'stolen paper', and that he was 'guilty of embezzlement elsewhere and . . . was not therefore to be trusted.'[72]

But the counterblow was being prepared. The Report of the Select Committee had been well received and it was urgently necessary to discredit both it and the Committee's principal witness.

On November 17, 1849, the columns of *The Athenaeum* were enlivened by a spirited attack on Edwards and his evidence by an anonymous writer, calling himself 'Verificator'. He alleged that the statements and statistics given by Edwards, and to which the Committee had given such wide currency, were largely false, the product of ignorance and carelessness. Though some of the examples quoted by 'Verificator' were trifling, the whole effect of the article was to throw great doubt both on the reliability and on the veracity of Edwards's testimony. Attention was drawn to the fact that the Committee had largely ignored the evidence of Henry Stevens, despite his far greater knowledge and experience of foreign libraries. As far as was possible without committing a breach of privilege, the writer implies strongly that the Committee were ignorant and prejudiced and had been gulled by the evidence of a plausible rogue.

Edwards's fury at the attack was increased by his subsequent discovery that it had been produced by a number of his departmental colleagues, under the editorship of Watts. The letters, which had been compiled with the eager assistance of Panizzi, Jones and several others, bear marked evidence of Watts's somewhat waspish humour and Panizzi's love of a detailed and overwhelming brief for the prosecution.

A second letter then appeared, attacking this time not only the wretched Edwards, but also his ally Weld, Librarian of the Royal Society. Both, it was alleged, had got their facts wrong and had committed every possible error. The evidence of two such nincompoops, it implied, was valueless and any plain man could see it. On December 8, there appeared a third letter. This dealt in greater detail with Edwards's evidence, carefully demolishing many of his arguments and referring sarcastically to his advocacy of an international exchange with France, in 'several manifest Panizzi passages'.[73]

Three weeks later Edwards replied, but not in a very convincing manner. He proudly announced he was preparing a new edition of his statistical evidence and was not discouraged from attempting this by his 'own occasional mistakes or by the pertinacious misrepresentations of opponents, whether avowed or anonymous'.[74] 'Verificator' promptly replied. He deplored the advent of a new edition of such a work as Edwards's. There were, he thought, far too many editions of that publication already and sneered at the writer's 'fatal facility for committing new errors, when endeavouring to amend the old'.[75]

Panizzi, meanwhile, had not been idle. These light-hearted attacks were merely the beginning. Edwards and his accomplices must be shown to the whole world, as the ignorant cheats they were. Asher had been instructed to get evidence against Edwards and his informants, to show, beyond all possible doubt, that the testimony they had given about continental libraries was not only inaccurate, but had been obtained by false pretences, by fraud or, in some cases, merely concocted.

On February 14, 1850, the Select Committee was reappointed. The membership was largely as before, with a strong radical flavour, except that Lord Seymour and Cornewall Lewis replaced Lord Ebrington and the Lord Advocate. In the opinion of Edwards, both these two new members had been introduced on to the Committee as the result of a successful manœuvre by his arch-enemy Panizzi. Rutherfurd, the Lord Advocate, was, of course, a close intimate of that gentleman. He had unfortunately been only able to attend the previous Committee on one single occasion. He willingly now withdrew to give place to two more active champions.

When the new Committee met on March 7, 1850, Edwards was again the first witness. This time, however, he met with a very different reception. Seymour and Lewis, 'prompted and drilled' by Panizzi, were determined to show him no mercy. On the whole, Edwards stood up well to their 'very illiberal and paltry questions',[76] but the general effect of their sustained cross-examination was to completely discredit his standing as an expert witness. Edwards, despite the efforts of Ewart and Monckton Milnes to help, was badly shaken, but worse was to come.

His ally, Weld, now made an attack on the resources of the Museum and the impossibility of getting current material there, as did other witnesses and then it was Edwards's turn again. Thanks to new evidence, enthusiastically gathered by Asher and relayed by Panizzi to Lord Seymour and Cornewall Lewis, Edwards's case for the superior merits of foreign libraries was shown to be largely based on false or inaccurate evidence and his ignorance of the workings of such collections to be abysmal. Asher's researches in Munich and elsewhere had shown conclusively that Weld's visits there, on which Edwards had relied, had almost certainly never taken place and that, in his opinion, both 'these fellows' fully deserved the public chastisement which, he trusted, was shortly to be administered to 'this noble pair'. It was indeed dangerous to quarrel with the great 'Pan'.[77]

On the following Tuesday, Panizzi himself gave evidence. He at once disposes of the carping criticism of lesser opponents and then proceeds to the main burden of his testimony, the superiority or otherwise of foreign libraries over those of this country and, in particular, the National Library, the British Museum.[78] He quickly demonstrated his familiarity with the majority of these and his personal knowledge of their contents. 'Of the 383 public libraries mentioned by Mr Edwards ... I have visited at least 95 ... English and foreign . . . I beg to add that I have visited them professionally as it were; that inasmuch as an admiral seeing a fleet or a printer seeing a printing office knows what to observe and how to observe better than I should, so I think I observed and tried to find out, better perhaps than one who is not a librarian would have done, how those libraries were managed . . . As a general result I have no hesitation in saying that I never learnt a single thing that I could apply to the British Museum.'[79] A proud statement indeed, but Panizzi was never one to be too modest when speaking in a good cause.

The Library of the British Museum was much more liberal, with longer hours than foreign institutions. In particular, in 'the security and preservation of the books and the great expedition in supplying readers with them . . . the library of the

British Museum, as far as I know, has no rival'.[80] These bold words of Henry Stevens he proceeded to justify in ample detail.

Panizzi told the Committee he was by no means opposed to public libraries. On the contrary, he had long ago proposed the establishment of such 'educational libraries' to the Select Committee of 1836. He, in fact, was all for such, 'and having plenty of the right kind'.[81] He would never, however, approve of the policy of lending books from the Museum collections or of opening late in the evening. He pours scorn on the schemes for international exchange as advocated by Edwards. On the whole, he far prefers to buy foreign works, since with an international exchange 'you never know even whether they send you a complete set'.[82] As to the activities of M. Vattemore, Edwards's particular protégé, Stevens had revealed that they existed almost entirely in the fertile imagination of their promoter. 'In Paris,' Stevens went on, Vattemore was 'considered a charlatan and his system of International Exchange . . . only a substitute for his worn-out voice for ventriloquism,'[83] another blow to his enemy's veracity.

Panizzi upbraided his subordinate's temerity in dating his letters to foreign libraries from the Museum. 'He had no business,' he exclaimed, 'to date from the British Museum, because he does not reside there,'[84] and the practice had led foreign libraries to consider these communications as official. He confessed that he had never thought, however, that the information so obtained would ever have been used for the disparagement of the great institution to which Edwards himself belonged, and had raised no immediate objections, therefore, when the matter had been brought to his notice some months before. Since Edwards had made what could only be regarded as improper use of that information, Panizzi had now written to both Berlin and Munich, the principal libraries approached by Edwards, to acquaint them with the true facts of the situation.

Panizzi had done his best, by fair means or foul, to uphold the honour and reputation of his beloved Museum. Edwards, naturally, poured scorn on his efforts. 'The whole is thoroughly characteristic, but much of it must tell rather against than for him both with the Committee & the public.'[85] Panizzi's intervention, nevertheless, does seem to have been effective. The Committee produced a short, non-committal report to which no one could object. On August 14, Ewart's modest little bill received the Royal Assent, enabling municipal libraries to be established, if so desired, in individual towns.

But the long struggle between Panizzi and his troublesome subordinate was almost over. Edwards's comments in his diary on the Royal Commission's report and, still more, on Panizzi's evidence before the Select Committee, show how far he had now drifted away from the views, not only of his chief, but those of the majority of his colleagues. He had never really fitted in at the Museum. Had not Panizzi been the domineering and masterful figure that he was, it would seem to be probable that Edwards would always have been considered somewhat of an outsider. He had long been on bad terms with many of the other assistants, who considered his manner offensive. His own subordinates, it would seem, disliked him intensely. Only the amiable Bullen and the kind-hearted Parry, whose radical views Edwards shared, seemed able to put up with his tears and his tantrums.

At all events, Panizzi now, at length, the virtual master of the Museum, was resolved to have done, once and for all, with a man whom he now openly regarded as a treacherous trouble-maker.

On May 4, 1850, Panizzi firmly refused to sign Edwards's pay voucher. The wretched man wrote in his diary: 'At $\frac{1}{4}$ before 3 Sir H. Ellis sent for me to Bd. Room and told me Mr Panizzi refused to sign my voucher and that the Trustees would take the matter into consideration on Saturday next.' Sir Henry then offered Edwards an advance of six guineas out of the twelve owed to him which the latter 'somewhat too indignantly perhaps' declined.[86]

Panizzi, in his official report to the Trustees on the matter, stated that 'he has no confidence in [Edwards's] statements as to either attendance or work done and because his rude and insolent manner deters Mr Panizzi from inquiring as he might into the value of his services'.[87] Though these statements were true, they were merely the excuse. Panizzi was determined to rid the Museum of this, to him, unprincipled subordinate.

The following Saturday, May 11, Edwards was summoned before the Board and told the reasons for his Keeper's refusal to sign the voucher. Edwards hotly denied the charges, particularly that of insolence. He then withdrew and waited, as patiently as he was able, till four o'clock, some hour and a half later. Ellis then

7

informed him that a letter would be sent to him early on Monday morning. The inference was plain. Panizzi had triumphed.

According to Espinasse, a hostile witness, Macaulay had said during the subsequent discussion among the Trustees: 'One or the other of them must go.'[88] There could be little doubt as to who that one would be. Panizzi, by now, *was* the Museum, the friend and boon companion of Cabinet ministers and of other Whig grandees. Edwards, despite his ability and tireless energy, was the radical, self-educated son of a bricklayer. To Victorian eyes, at least, there was not, nor could be, any real comparison. The Trustees' decision was soon made. 'It appears,' they minuted, 'from the continued disagreement between Mr Edwards and the Head of the Department in which he is serving that the business of the particular department is seriously interrupted: the Trustees are of the opinion that the services of Mr Edwards cannot be continued with advantage to the Museum.'[89]

On Monday morning, Edwards, on returning from a visit to the Royal Academy, found waiting for him a letter from the Principal Librarian. In it Sir Henry said it was his painful duty to announce the Trustees' resolution. Edwards was dismissed, but a cheque was enclosed for £15 15s and an additional one for £25, 'in consideration of length of service'.[90]

The long fight was over; Panizzi had beaten him. It is fruitless now to speculate as to the reason for the enmity between them, and a bitter one it was on both sides, despite Edwards's friendly references to his old chief in published works. Fundamentally, it seems from the start to have been a temperamental antipathy, inflamed by mutual faults. Both men were hot-tempered and immoderate in their language when roused and Panizzi had, in addition, the vendetta instincts of his race. Once Edwards was marked down for destruction, no holds were barred. Possibly, Edwards was jealous of his opponent's social successes, though he never says so, whilst Panizzi may have despised and distrusted in Edwards those radical tendencies, which he, by now, had so largely lost. At all events, what might have proved to have been, in different circumstances, a fruitful partnership was destined never to be and the two greatest figures in the library world of nineteenth-century England went their separate ways.

NOTES TO CHAPTER 10

1 PP. 1846. f.263.

2 PP. 1846. ff.266, 269.

3 PP. 1846. ff.286, 271.

4 Add. MS. 36, 714. ff.416, 417.

5 *On the Supply of Printed Books from the Library to the Reading Room of the British Museum.* London, 1846.

6 *On the Supply,* p. 17.

7 Nicolas, *Animadversions.* Parry, asked for his opinion by Jones, categorically stated that Nicolas had often expressed opinions directly contrary to those he now put forward. 'Had minutes of his conversation been taken down it would be found to contradict his present professed opinions almost as flatly as his letter of 1837.' [PP. 1846. f.290.]

8 *Hansard,* 3S., vol. 90, col. 250.

9 *The Globe,* December 26, 1847.

10 Memorial to the First Lord of the Treasury presented March 10, 1847, by members of the British Association for the Advancement of Science and other Scientific Societies respecting the management of the British Museum. [*Parliamentary Papers,* H. of C., 1847, vol. XXXIV, p. 253.] '... no effective provision . . . for the proper guidance of the Natural History Department'.

11 *Parliamentary Papers,* H. of C., 1850, vol. XXIV.

12 Francis Leveson-Gower, 1800–1857. Youngest son of first Duke of Sutherland. Changed his name to Egerton. On being created Lord Ellesmere always signed his name Egerton Ellesmere. A 'liberal conservative' in politics. 'He gave me the impression of being a shy man. There was about him an air of pensive gravity which was peculiar.'

13 Richard Monckton Milnes, 1809–1885. Created Baron Houghton 1863. Always bitterly opposed Panizzi. No known reason for this antipathy, unless it sprung from the fact that Milnes was very pro-German and pro-Austrian.

14 Joseph Hume, 1777–1855. Radical politician.

15   John Payne Collier, 1789–1883. Critic. Worked in the Bridgewater library under Ellesmere. Was subsequently widely considered to be guilty of numerous literary forgeries.

16   *The Times*, July 6, 1847. '. . . has the habits of application and business which peculiarly fit him for his new office.'

17   PP. 1847. ff.563, 581.

18   *Royal Commission, Minutes*, para. 371.

19   The first Commission, consisting of eleven members, was set up on June 17, 1847. The second, of fourteen members, on May 5, 1848. The three members added were Viscount Canning, Lord Seymour and Shaw Le fevre all personally acquainted with Panizzi.

20   Cowtan, *Biographical Sketch*, p. 40.

21   *Royal Commission*, Minutes, para. 2544.

22   *Minutes*, para. 2866.

23   *Minutes*, paras. 2953–2983.

24   *Minutes*, para. 4075.

25   *Minutes*, para. 4192.

26   *Minutes*, para. 4271.

27   Macaulay to Lansdowne, February 1856 [Fagan, II, p. 15.]

28   Charles Coffin Jewett, 1816–1868, bibliographer. George Sumner, 1793–1855. Jewett later wrote to Stevens, 'I hope Mr Panizzi is triumphing over his enemies. I consider his cause . . . identified with the interests of learning throughout the world.' [PP. 1849. f.285.]

29   *Minutes*, para. 4285.

30   *Minutes*, para. 4293.

31   *Minutes*, para. 4293.

32   *Minutes*, para. 4373.

33   *Minutes*, para. 4374.

34   *Minutes*, para. 4385.

35   *Minutes*, para. 4696.

36   *Minutes*, para. 4806.

37   *Royal Commission, Appendix*, pp. 378–395.

38   *A Letter to the Earl of Ellesmere on the Subject of a New Alphabetical Catalogue*, etc. Privately printed, 1849.

39   Add. MS. 36, 716. ff.47, 50.

40   *Minutes*, para. 6261.

41 John Edward Gray, 1800–1875. Keeper of the Zoological Collections, 1840–1874. He was, as far as is known, the first stamp collector, having bought blocks of 1d black, 2d blue postage stamps on May 6, 1840, the very day they were first issued.

42 *A letter to the Earl of Ellesmere, on the management of the Library of Printed Books in the British Museum.* Privately printed, London, 1849.
    A Second Letter. London, 1849.

43 Gray had also written a third pamphlet. On the intervention of the Marquess of Northampton, Chairman of the Sub-Committee of the Trustees dealing with P's complaint, he agreed to suspend the distribution of this after only a few copies had been circulated. [PP. 1849, f.234.] The Trustees subsequently passed a resolution approving of Panizzi's conduct in not answering Gray in print and recommending him to maintain his silence. They did not consider it necessary to 'call upon Mr Panizzi for any vindication of his conduct as impugned by Mr Gray'. This resolution was sent to all heads of departments. [PP. 1849, f.238.] [*Royal Commission, Minutes,* para. 9592.] 'I am quite satisfied with the approbation of Trustees, who are the only persons I have to look to.'

44 Augustus de Morgan, 1806–1871. Mathematician.

45 *Minutes,* para. 5757.

46 *Minutes,* para. 7313.

47 *Minutes,* para. 7430.

48 A.P. to Mrs Rutherfurd. Nov. 11 [1849.] 'I hate books, and writing and reading; above all things I am disgusted with the Library and my place.' [*Rutherfurd Papers.*]

49 *Minutes,* para. 9367.

50 *Minutes,* para. 9378.

51 *Minutes,* para. 9985.

52 *Minutes,* para. 10491. Hamilton goes on to say: 'I consider Mr Panizzi to have been very hardly used and unjustly arraigned for his general management of his department and specially for the manner in which he is drawing up the catalogue and in which he exerts himself for the supply of books.' Inglis' dislike of Panizzi may have been due both to religious and political prejudice. He was extremely anti-Catholic, as well as a die-hard Tory, having captured the University of Oxford seat from Peel on these grounds.

53 *Minutes,* para. 10586.

54 *The Times,* March 29, 1850.

55 *Royal Commission, Report,* p. 4.

56 *Report,* p. 6.

57 *Report,* p. 7.

58 *Report,* p. 13.

59 *Report*, p. 16.

60 *Report*, p. 25. Panizzi, undoubtedly, was always extremely sensitive on this point. He valued all the more the friendship of those who would accept him on his own terms. 'I never could have believed that a foreigner was so hated in England – a reason for feeling deep gratitude for those who, like you, are superior to such base prejudices.' [A.P. to Lord Holland, February 24, 1849.] [*Holland House Papers*.]

61 *Report*, p. 25.

62 *Report*, p. 31.

63 *Report*, p. 31.

64 *Report*, p. 31.

65 *The Times*, March 29, 1850.

66 *The Athenaeum*, May 11, 1850.

67 Edwards took strong objection to certain of Panizzi's answers which were critical of himself. He wrote to Ellesmere demanding an inquiry. The offending minutes were omitted in the published version, but the demand for an inquiry was ignored. [*Diary*, February 22, 1850; March 27, 28, 1850.] Panizzi wrote to Hallam on the subject, saying that Edwards was 'not . . . to be trusted' and objecting to being portrayed as a tyrant eager to crush a subordinate of unblemished character. [PP. 1849. f.322.]

68 The draft of the report, in Peel's handwriting, was found in his pocket after his fatal accident on Constitution Hill on June 29, 1850. The report is contained in *Parliamentary Papers*, H. of C., 1850, vol. XXXIII, p. 249.

69 *Parliamentary Papers*, H. of C., 1849, vol. XVII, p. 1.

70 *Select Committee on Public Libraries*, 1849, *Minutes*, para. 3296. Edwards furthermore stated among other criticisms of his department that, at times, it took three years for a book to get into the catalogue and that a printed catalogue was an absolute necessity. [*Minutes*, paras. 3323, 3307.]

71 PP. 1849. f.274. In a further letter of October 25, 1849, Panizzi again draws the attention of the Trustees to Edwards's activities. 'Evidence pervaded with an unfair spirit teeming with gross & absurd statements mostly from a pseudo-official source . . . in a form well calculated to throw discredit on this department and consequently on Mr Panizzi.' [PP. 1848. f.443.]

72 See note 67 above.

73 Edwards, *Diary*, December 8, 1849.

74 *The Athenaeum*, December 29, 1849, p. 1336.

75 *The Athenaeum*, January 5, 1850, p. 19.

76 *Diary*, March 7, 1850.

77 The Panizzi Papers are full of the evidence gathered concerning the goings-on of the two 'culprits'. Smirke brought over the information zealously collected in Germany by Asher. Panizzi also requested permission to make use of official papers to rebut this hostile evidence. [PP. 1849. ff.461, 462, 491 et seq.]

78 *Select Committee*, 1850, *Minutes*, para. 685 et seq. He had said a few words the previous Monday, but this is the main body of his evidence.

79 *Select Committee*, *Minutes*, para. 719. Panizzi goes on to say: 'although I believe that in many of them, if I had been librarian there I would have done just what they did.'

80 *Select Committee*, *Minutes*, para. 734.

81 *Select Committee*, *Minutes*, paras. 758, 759.

82 *Select Committee*, *Minutes*, para. 788.

83 *Select Committee*, *Minutes*, para. 788.

84 *Select Committee*, *Minutes*, para. 790.

85 Edwards, *Diary*, March 20, 1850.

86 *Diary*, May 4, 1850.

87 PP. 1850. f.250.

88 Espinasse, p. 18.

89 PP. 1850. f.269.

90 *Diary*, May 13, 1850.

II

PANIZZI IN POWER
Copyright and Reading Room

EDWARDS had gone and Forshall, now completely out of his mind, pensioned off, and with their departure, much of the anger and bitterness want out of Panizzi's life. At last he had arrived. Despite occasional sneers in *Punch* and in less reputable journals, Panizzi was now, on the whole, justly regarded as the man who had created a new national library, almost entirely by his own efforts, one worthy of the new age. Madden, for the time, had little to say. The rebukes administered by the Royal Commission seem to have silenced him, at least in public. He could still, when the occasion demanded, be as awkward and as unco-operative as ever, but it was a rearguard action.

Ellis, now rapidly ageing, leant more and more on Panizzi. He esteemed his advice and regarded the younger man with growing affection. During his frequent absences, the Principal Librarian left the Museum in Panizzi's care, though the latter was by no means the senior Keeper. When Panizzi was ill, the old man writes pathetically. The Library does not look like itself without you,'[1] a far cry, indeed, from the bad feeling and misunderstandings of earlier years.

Panizzi, of course, still had his troubles. Unsuitable members of the staff are dismissed and one, the argumentative and troublesome von Bach, forced to resign. Even Watts, once more, is rebuked for neglecting his duties. Watts thereupon replied to Panizzi in a long and pained letter. He was most upset, he wrote, to think that his chief considered him to be 'idle and inefficient'. He talks to no one, other than to readers and distinguished strangers. Though he may sometimes arrive late, he will never acknowledge that he is a bad servant of the Museum. All these years he has supported his Keeper to the utmost and feels most hurt now at these accusations. Panizzi quietly accepted his explanation and all was well once more.[2]

In September 1850, Garnett, his Assistant Keeper, had died after a short illness and, at long last, Panizzi succeeded in obtaining the post for Winter Jones. As we have seen, Jones had been Panizzi's choice the last time and though Garnett had been thrust upon him, he had never borne that worthy man any ill-will. Over the years, Panizzi had grown to like and respect Garnett, of a nature so very different from his own. His loss now was a sad blow. As a tribute to the self-effacing scholar, Panizzi managed to persuade the Trustees to appoint his son, Richard Garnett, the younger, although only sixteen, to an assistantship in the department. This typical act of kindness drew a warm letter of thanks from the lad's widowed mother.[3] It was a wise move. Richard Garnett was to dominate, in his own way, the next generation at the Museum, as Panizzi had done his and was always grateful to his old Keeper for giving him his first chance.

With Jones at his side and the Trustees, at last, his willing supporters, Panizzi, now at the height of his powers, felt able to face anything, even those two questions which were to dominate his official life for the next few years, the administration of the Copyright Act and the ever-growing problem of insufficient space in which to house the collections.

The enforcement of the Copyright Act was undoubtedly the problem which caused him the most trouble and which was to expose him, once again, to the most violent and unmerited abuse. As Panizzi had explained to the Royal Commission, it was idle to blame the Department of Printed Books for not having current English works, when the administration of the Act, by means of which they should be obtained, had been taken away and given to the Secretary. Panizzi would not, as a matter of principle, buy with public funds books which the Museum was, by law, entitled to receive without payment.

Forshall had admitted to the Commissioners that the enforcement of the Act by his staff was, indeed, dilatory and that a high

7*

proportion of the books which should have come to the Museum had never been sent. As early as 1836, Baber had complained of the ineffectuality of the then Act. Not more than two-fifths of the books to which the Museum was entitled, were actually received. 'Every dirty trick' was, he declared, resorted to on the part of the publishers, 'to impose on us and to evade the Act'.[4]

It was this deplorable state of affairs which Panizzi was determined to end. On January 8, 1850, he had addressed a memorandum on this subject to the Trustees. He understood that the Board intended to transfer to the Keeper of Printed Books the duty of enforcing the Act of 1842. He must, however, be given adequate powers. Half-measures would be worse than useless. 'The power of receiving what is brought to the Museum, without that of enforcing the delivery of what ought to be brought . . . will produce no benefit . . . the Trustees will continue to be defrauded as they have hitherto been.'[5] Vigorous enforcement with the means to deal firmly with offenders, was the key to the whole situation.

A few months later, Panizzi again reported. The Act was still being widely evaded, even in London. Elsewhere, things were far worse. 'As to those printed in other parts of England,' he declared, 'or in either Ireland or Scotland, the Trustees receive hardly any.'[6] Panizzi was now determined to enforce the law and to make the system itself simpler and more effective. On May 11, 1850, the Trustees ordered him to draw up a scheme. Ten days later, Panizzi submitted to the Board a long and detailed report, dealing not only with the Copyright Act itself, but also with the related question of International Copyright, into the intricacies of which he had gone with the assistance of Dundas, the Judge Advocate-General.

It was, though, the enforcement of the Act within the United Kingdom which seemed to him at the moment, to be of paramount importance. Some of the defects were undoubtedly due to the terms of the Act itself, as Panizzi had foreseen at the time. Such were clauses which permitted the identity of the publisher to be disputed and the period of grace allowed before books need be deposited. Much could be done, though, by having agents in all the principal cities and towns. In London, itself, steps should be taken to prosecute persistent offenders, though Panizzi advocated a policy of leniency, once conviction had been secured. 'The object being,' he wrote, 'to let it be generally known that the intention is to proceed strictly and vigorously for the future.'[7]

On the May 15, Panizzi was given power of attorney and full responsibility for the enforcement of the Act. By October, he had prepared a circular letter, which was to be sent to recalcitrant publishers and a month later, he informed the Trustees that the Museum solicitors were considering prosecuting certain persistent offenders. Many publishers still, he told the Board, 'seemed more than ever disposed to avoid complying with [the law]'.[8] In those cases in which a solicitor's letter had proved to be ineffective, he now proposed, with the sanction of the Trustees, to make full use of the powers given him. Somewhat reluctantly, permission was given, the Trustees reserving the right to be kept fully informed.

The first prosecutions were not long in coming. Some fifty warning letters had already been sent. It was decided to proceed further with thirteen of these publishers, who had proved to be obdurate. In five cases, the summons were withdrawn, as the culprits had at last agreed to send in their books. The remainder were dealt with by the courts. The amazed and indignant publishers were convicted and fined.

In Panizzi's opinion, in deference to the wishes of the Trustees, he had been far too lenient. Himself a lawyer by training and by instinct, the law was the law. He saw no reason why 'respectable publishers' and the readers who had every right to expect to find a book in the Museum should be penalized by the actions of an unco-operative few. Nevertheless, the results were remarkable. By the end of 1852, over three thousand more copyright books had been received than in the previous year and the number steadily rose.

It was hard and thankless work. Panizzi was subjected to a 'violent and indiscriminate storm of abuse' and this was only the beginning. The country publishers and those in Wales, Scotland and Ireland had, for the most part, still escaped his net. Despite his reluctance to draw upon his own head even more insult, Panizzi now determined to remedy this state of affairs. No man was more resolved to do his duty, cost what it might. 'When I entered upon the Keepership of Printed Books,' he wrote towards the end of his life, 'the Library was very defective. When I gave up that office, thanks to increased outlay & the enforcement of the

copyright act, the Library was rich.'[9] Thus, with his wonted terse-
ness, he justifies all the hard work, the misunderstandings and the
heartache of those weary years. To serve his beloved library was
all the reward he could hope for. At times he was bitter. 'Letter or
no letter, right or wrong,' he wrote to Haywood, 'the fact of my
being a foreigner will not allow justice to be rendered to me.'[10]

Few public servants, even in those days of sustained polemics,
have ever been so frequently, so spitefully and so unjustly abused
as was Panizzi. It is scarcely to be wondered at that he often felt
despondent and was hypersensitive to criticism. No wonder, too,
that his magnificent physique was breaking up under the strain. He
was now frequently ill. Visits to Aix and to other spas had proved
fruitless and still so much of his life's work lay yet before him.
Only his faith in himself and his indomitable will kept him going.

Now there were further controversies. Chapman, the publisher,
accused Panizzi of treating him with un-English vindictiveness, in
revenge for an article which had appeared in the *Quarterly Review*.
Panizzi indignantly denied the charge and pointed out to the
Trustees that it was himself who had succeeded in reducing
Chapman's fine to a nominal shilling.

It was now time to extend his activities further afield. In July
1852 Panizzi went to Scotland to deal with the publishers there.
Edinburgh and Glasgow were visited and information also obtained as to what was published elsewhere. He obtained local
advice on the complexities of the legal position in Scotland,
should any prosecutions be deemed necessary, and arranged for a
quarterly list of all books published in the country to be delivered
regularly to him. Panizzi was determined to be as firm with de-
faulting publishers in the northern kingdom, as he had been south
of the border.

In the September, it was the turn of Ireland.[11] Accompanied
this time by Henry Stevens, Panizzi set off for Dublin. The indefatigable pair went first to Oxford and next to Bangor. At the latter
town, Panizzi, on the spur of the moment, decided to visit nearby
Carnarvon, the main centre, at that date, for books published in
Welsh. There, he made the necessary arrangements for these, 'a
class of books . . . not generally known to exist', to be sent to the
Museum, where, either Jones or Watts, both of whom knew
Welsh, would be able to deal with them.

The travellers now embarked for Ireland. Panizzi had hoped that, by travelling strictly incognito, he would be able to arrive undiscovered, but, to his intense annoyance, the news of his visit soon spread and he was speedily recognized. In Dublin he found on sale many books of which he was unaware, and he again strongly urged the Trustees to authorize the sending of the usual letter to such publishers as refused to comply with the law and, where necessary, to prosecute them.

Panizzi was convinced that these journeys, exhausting as he found them to be, were abundantly worth while and that the results obtained more than justified the trouble he had taken. In Ireland, as elsewhere, his firm determination to stand no nonsense and to see that the law was strictly obeyed brought about a most welcome increase in the numbers of copyright books deposited at the Museum.

On returning to London, more troubles awaited him. Amongst the publishers recently summoned for non-compliance with the Copyright Act was a Mr Bohn. In him, Panizzi had found a worthy antagonist, every whit as obstinate as the great man himself. In court Bohn vigorously counter-attacked. The books he had sent to the Museum could not be found when he himself had subsequently asked to see them. He never, he declared, got receipts for more than half the books deposited and other charges of a similar nature were freely made. All these accusations Panizzi indignantly denied. He was now utterly weary of the whole business. He had, he felt, been most unjustly subjected to violent abuse on every side, merely for doing his duty, as the law demanded. He could not nor would not do more. He poured out his heart to Haywood, for so long his closest friend and confidant. Ellis was now receiving an extra £200 a year in view of his scarcely exacting duties as Secretary. 'To me nothing has been given and I will not go on . . . They will soon see the difference in the number of books which they will receive between my *fearless and honest* conduct and that of anybody else whom they may appoint.' Panizzi begged of the Trustees to rid him of this onerous and invidious duty. It seemed to him that he no longer enjoyed their confidence. Would they not therefore transfer his unwelcome powers 'to a hand better fitted for such an office'?[12]

The Trustees were horrified. In their opinion no one was better fitted than the Keeper of Printed Books to carry out the task and, with all their might, endeavoured to persuade Panizzi to continue.

Reluctantly and wearily he agreed to do so. On January 27, 1853, Bohn had again appeared in court. His counsel denounced Panizzi's proceedings against his client as harsh, vexatious and tyrannical. Englishmen, he thundered, knew how to treat each other and no Englishman would ever have exposed Mr Bohn to the annoyance and trouble which he had had to undergo. Panizzi, sitting in court with the Museum solicitor, must needs listen to this unjustified and wounding attack. To make matters worse, the presiding magistrate seemed to agree with counsel. After a few words of praise bestowed somewhat perfunctorily on both parties to the dispute, he fined Bohn a shilling!

This was too much! On February 2, there appeared in *The Times* a strongly-worded letter from Panizzi, stating in plain terms what the Act was, why it had to be enforced and how he had endeavoured 'both from my own inclination and in compliance with the instructions of the Trustees', to enforce the law as leniently as was possible. Such leniency had not paid. Publishers had continued to default and further prosecutions had had to be initiated. He had never been tyrannical. It was his plain duty to enforce the Act and by doing his duty he had obtained books which otherwise would have had to be purchased at the public expense. Experience had shown that only such firmness paid. 'It justifies my determination to continue to act as I have done hitherto, so long as the law and my duty remain unaltered.'[13]

The Times, in its leading article, praised Panizzi, but thought that he should not waste either his time or that of others in these 'ridiculous squabbles' with Bohn. It was merely silly, it thought, to be 'perpetually engaged in a guerrilla warfare against each other ... for ... the gratification of a foolish pique' and took both Bohn and Panizzi to task for engaging in 'so paltry and discreditable a warfare', which could only harm the reputations of both.

Though somewhat unfair, this criticism does contain an element of truth. Panizzi, as we know, was a good hater and however much he might protest as to his own disinterestedness and probity, was always determined to get his man. Bohn had certainly annoyed him by what *The Times* had called 'a series of petty affronts' and Panizzi was set on obtaining his revenge.

The following day, Panizzi again wrote explaining further why Bohn had had to be prosecuted. Bohn in turn replied, justifying his conduct and readers of *The Times* must indeed have wearied of their mutual recriminations.

Again Panizzi asked to be relieved of this burdensome duty which should have been, by rights, part of the Secretary's but in vain. As some compensation he had been granted an extra £100 a year. Thanking the Trustees for this gratuity, he informed them that he had now installed a new and younger collector of copyright and from henceforth things would go well. His hopes were justified. Cowtan, the new collector, was both zealous and able. Summons were less frequent as publishers bowed to the inevitable, and gradually this particular nightmare passed.

Panizzi was now deeply concerned at a far graver question, that of adequate and sufficient space, for books, for staff and for readers. The Museum was filling up and filling up fast! His successful efforts to secure greatly increased Parliamentary grants had naturally made matters worse, as indeed, he himself had foreseen, and now the drive for copyright works threatened to make the situation desperate.

A few years previously, Panizzi had suggested to the Royal Commission that a new Manuscript Department might be built in Russell Square to the east of the then reading-room and the rooms vacated by them given to Printed Books.

Such new buildings would, however, take a number of years to build. The rooms, to be taken over by Printed Books, would in themselves afford relief for only a comparatively short time and time was the one thing the library did not possess. They were already overcrowded. The reading-rooms were quite inadequate to the demands now being put upon them. There was little room for readers and even less for the catalogues and the necessary reference books. The approach to the rooms was unworthy of so great a library, through 'a mere cart gate' from Montagu Street and then along a dark and narrow passage and stairway. The whole arrangement was obviously inconvenient and out of date.

As long ago as January 1849, Panizzi had reported to the Trustees that there was little or no room to place the vast additions which the increased grants had secured for the library. The resulting confusion and delay in making such books available to readers was already apparent and readers were already finding fault with the Keeper 'as if he were responsible for not entering titles, not marking books and not placing them whilst he had neither transcribers, markers nor room'.[14]

Very soon he was forced to double-bank to cope with the accessions. By the end of 1850, the huge bulk of the ever-growing manuscript catalogue was causing chaos in the reading-room and was a further cause of annoyance to the long-suffering public. Panizzi, again and again, urged on the Trustees 'the absolute necessity of providing more space both for readers and for catalogues'. The number of the former was now rapidly increasing, while very soon there would be no room at all for the catalogues. He begged them, perhaps over sanguinely, to devise a remedy for this situation and urged them to visit both Library and Reading Room to see for themselves how desperate the situation had now become. 'It will be impossible to add to the collection if room be not first provided' and the public, already disgusted with both reading-room and catalogues, 'will become more dissatisfied than ever with the management of the Museum'.[15]

During the following year, the problem became ever more acute. It was, Panizzi said, 'daily, hourly, more pressing'. He had had, much against his will, to ask for a reduction of the annual purchase grant to a nominal £2,000. The time was rapidly approaching when even this sum would be too great. At last, the Trustees became alarmed and, at their request, on July 25, 1851, Ellis sent an urgent letter to the Treasury.[15] It was imperative that a considerable enlargement of the present buildings should be authorized immediately, since the Department of Printed Books was now growing at a rate of 1,600 square feet a year. Ellis recommended that twelve houses in Montagu Street and fifteen in Russell Square should be purchased to provide a site for the new buildings, which should include a new and enlarged Reading Room. These proposals were duly considered, but the cost, about £300,000, was thought, at the moment, to be too great.

A solution of all the difficulties was at hand. It had long been obvious that better use could be made of the inner courtyard, 'cold, lean and wretched' as it was, with its 'sad-looking grass plots' seen by few and on which only Madden's children played. As early as March 1837, Thomas Watts had contributed an article to the *Mechanics Magazine*, in which he suggested the building of a reading-room in the central quadrangle.[16] Twelve years later, William Hosking,[17] Professor of Architecture in the University of London, had put forward certain proposals to the Royal Commission. These were subsequently incorporated in a plan which he submitted to the Trustees. Hosking suggested turning the northern half of the King's Library into a reading-room, whilst, in the quadrangle, should be erected a domed rotunda for the display of sculpture and other antiquities. Another architect, James Fergusson,[18] issued his *Observations on the British Museum*, in which he advocated the dispersal of all scientific and antiquities collections. At Bloomsbury would be gathered all public records and similar archives, which, with the library, would be adequately housed in the now empty galleries. In the central courtyard would be built a reading-room, surrounded by broad terraces.

These ideas and others similar were well known to the Museum officials, but no firm decision had, as yet, been taken. On the evening of April 18, 1852, Panizzi drew a rough pencil sketch of what he thought was needed and on the back of the sheet scribbled down the dimensions. These were a square of 197 feet, a square within it of 170 feet. Within this second square, a circle of 100 feet diameter. Within this again, a circle of 40 feet diameter.[19] Such was the genesis of the great Reading Room.

The following morning, Panizzi showed the drawing to Jones, who gave it his warm approval. After a few more days spent in preparing finished architectural drawings, the proposal was submitted to the Trustees. In his accompanying report,[20] Panizzi made the point that in any alternative scheme involving the demolition of existing buildings, delays up to several years might be expected. His scheme would provide instant relief for his department, at a comparatively small cost. Apart from the outside retaining walls, all the inner walls of the stack area would consist of the stacks themselves. This would result in a great saving of space. The lighting and ventilation of the present buildings would not be interfered with. The central area would provide a reading-room capable of holding some five hundred readers, 'at one and the same time, all comfortably seated'. Such a building, in his opinion, promised to be 'striking as well as elegant'.[21]

Sydney Smirke,[22] the Museum architect, warmly approved of

the 'ingenious suggestions of Mr Panizzi' and was enthusiastically in favour of their speedy adoption. On June 1,[22] Panizzi made a second appeal to the Trustees, stressing the advantages of his plan over any possible other. Its main virtue, in his eyes, was the speed with which it could be ready for the reception of both books and readers.

The Trustees still hesitated. A few days later, Panizzi told them that he had heard privately that the Government were about to reject the Trustees' previous request for new accommodation for books and readers and urged them, before it was too late, to stress the absolute necessity for this.

But it was all in vain. The Treasury decided to reject all the Trustees' proposals, at least for the current session. Panizzi must again get to work, using all the influence he possessed and pulling every string, as only he knew how.

In November, he warned the Trustees against adopting his own former proposals. Whatever their merits may have been at the time, they were no longer practicable. The Board, however, was still not convinced of the value of Panizzi's new suggestions, even though Smirke and now Sir Henry were strongly behind him.

In December 1852, a long article appeared in the *Quarterly Review*, a journal, on the whole, friendly to Panizzi. This poured scorn on his proposed 'birdcage' in the quadrangle and suggested, instead, roofing over the whole inner courtyard with glass, in order to make a large sculpture gallery and then to move into it all the Museum collections of statues. In the vacant galleries would be housed the Printed Books, whilst the readers would be accommodated in the North Library, with perhaps additional rooms on either side.[23]

To add to Panizzi's troubles there had now been a change of government, with all the delays that that involved. Still he kept urging the absolute necessity of doing something immediately. Very soon it would be too late, if, indeed, it was not too late already. The staff copy of the catalogue had, even now, to be laid on planks in the King's Library, there being nowhere else to put it.

At last, early in 1853, things started to move. Panizzi, probably through his friend Gladstone, had got the ear of the new Prime Minister, Lord Aberdeen, who, moreover, had himself been an active and conscientious Trustee for many years. The Prime Minister agreed to receive a deputation from the Trustees to put before him the case for the Museum. The position there was now desperate. In March 1853, all purchase of books had been indefinitely suspended, 'owing to the actual want of room to place books and the utter failure of all applications to have some provided'.[24] Shortly afterwards, Panizzi himself had an interview with Aberdeen and with Sir William Molesworth, the First Commissioner of Works. On June 9, Panizzi addressed a long memorandum to Molesworth, reiterating the advantages of his plan over that 'suggested by an amateur in the *Quarterly Review*'.[25]

Unfortunately, this now gained a powerful and highly professional supporter. This was Sir Charles Barry,[26] architect of the newly erected Houses of Parliament and it was said that both government and the Trustees were very seriously considering it. Panizzi was greatly alarmed. In a series of letters to Molesworth, backed by expert witnesses, he attempts to demolish Barry's 'preposterous' scheme. Molesworth, however, was slow in making up his mind. Barry had now prepared detailed plans of the alternative proposals, which Panizzi and Smirke were permitted to see. The whole future seemed to be very uncertain. As always, when danger threatened, Panizzi was indefatigable. Backed wholeheartedly by Smirke, he prepared paper after paper to refute Sir Charles's theories. He, a practical museum man, knew exactly what he wanted and was determined to get it. Barry's plan would be more costly; he had underestimated both the time and the labour necessary to complete the scheme, but, above all, the time.

On November 5, 1853, Panizzi submitted to the Trustees a detailed criticism of Sir Charles's proposals, in which he heavily stressed this factor.[27] It was, in his opinion, for the Trustees and for them alone, to decide whether any proposals for the reconstruction of the Museum should or should not be adopted. They must now and finally make up their minds 'whether it is of greater public advantage to postpone providing room for readers and for books until after a general and comprehensive scheme has been adopted for the rest of the Museum', or to proceed at once with plans for a new reading-room. To Panizzi, there was no doubt as to what should be the Trustees' answer.

For two anxious months Panizzi waited, while first the Trustees and then the Government came to a decision. At last, on January 26, 1854, Ellis jubilantly wrote to tell him: 'I have this moment received the Treasury letter approving the plans and proposed the expenditure of 86,000.'[28]

Authority having been received, things moved quickly. By early February, Smirke was able to show to Panizzi the model for the new Reading Room; by March he was getting in the tenders and, though a month later Smirke was complaining of the delay in obtaining the Office of Works' final approval of the scheme, and was fearful of missing the fine weather, he was very soon able to inform Panizzi that he had received permission to accept the lowest tender and that work on the site was to start immediately.

For the next four years Panizzi watched his reading-room grow. No detail was too small for his personal attention. Jones wrote, 'It is well, however, that the secret of this great success should not be overlooked. It will be found in the daily communications between the constructor and the librarian, in the patient and careful consultation upon every point of detail however small in the fact that Mr Panizzi understood thoroughly his own plan and that Mr Smirke and Mr Fielder, as architect and builder, cordially exerted themselves in carrying it out.'[29]

The first brick was laid in September 1853, the first iron standard was erected in January 1855. Panizzi and his two associates, Smirke and Fielder, the managing partner of the contractors, worked together in the utmost harmony, freely adopting each other's suggestions. There were naturally difficulties. Panizzi succeeded, against Treasury opposition, in obtaining consent for raising the height of the library buildings to accommodate the vastly increased number of books now expected. His subsequent suggestions for having a painted ceiling and for placing statues between the windows in the cupola were fortunately not adopted.[30] All problems were triumphantly overcome and by May 1857 the building was at last completed. On the 2nd, the Reading Room was formally opened. A grand breakfast was given to celebrate the great event in the room itself, the catalogue desks being temporarily converted into tables.

This was indeed Panizzi's hour. Ellis wrote to him, 'Without lessening the merits of Mr Smirke & Mr Fielder in carrying out its plans, the contriver and the real architect throughout has been

Antonio Panizzi.'[31] No longer merely Keeper of Printed Books, but Principal Librarian of the British Museum, he received the rank and fashion of London under the great dome which he had created. The fools, the envious and the prejudiced, were at last silenced. Panizzi, the despised Italian mountebank, had had constructed, almost entirely by his own efforts, one of the wonders of the age. Ellis, who had seen the growth of the Museum now for over half of a century, was delighted with this latest achievement of the man whose greatness he now fully recognized.

Madden, alone, was irreconcilable. It was he who wrote 'perfectly unsuited to its purpose and an example of reckless extravagance occasioned through the undue influence of a foreigner. Had Mr P been an Englishman, the Treasury would not have granted £20,000 for the purpose.' On the day of the party he walked out of the Museum to avoid having anything to do with it. 'I wish the Trustees and Mr P in a hot place fifty times a day.'[32]

There were, naturally, a few other malcontents. Hosking now alleged that Panizzi had filched the idea of a central reading-room from the pamphlet which he, Hosking, had submitted to the Trustees in 1849 and had pirated the very design. Panizzi denied the charges. Until this moment, he had had absolutely no knowledge of Hosking's proposals, and, anyhow, they bore no real resemblance to the plans actually carried out. Nevertheless, a bitter controversy in the newspapers followed between the advocates of Hosking and those of Panizzi. To many, it was one more chance to vent their spleen at the hated, yet, it would seem, uniformly successful Panizzi, regardless of the merits or demerits of the particular case. To such papers as *The Athenaeum*, whatever Panizzi did was wrong and if it turned out to be right, then it obviously could not have been his work.

One who would have heartily subscribed to this sentiment was Thomas Carlyle. He had had, as we know, more than one brush with Panizzi and he also could be as obstinate and even more vindictive than his illustrious antagonist. It was abundantly clear that Panizzi's main worry throughout these years, until the opening of the Reading Room and of the new library for a time solved the problem, was space and decent accommodation for the readers. No one would have been more ready to agree than he that the accommodation available was very poor and grossly overcrowded, what with the dictionary makers, the novel readers and the mere idiots, of all of whom Carlyle so bitterly complained.

To Carlyle, it seemed only just that he, a distinguished historian, should receive special consideration. On April 11, 1853, he addressed a curt note to Panizzi, 'whom I do not love and who returns the feeling',[33] in which he requested permission to have a private room in which to study. The following day, Panizzi replied, 'I do not recollect ever having stated that either you or anyone else could have a private room to study in at this institution . . . All readers should be . . . treated alike . . . our reading-rooms are not, of course, as quiet and as snug as a *private* study. Ours is a *public* place.' Only if the Trustees specifically ordered it would Panizzi make an exception in Carlyle's favour. 'I do not see how I can of my own account make any exception in favour of any reader however high his literary claims and great my wish to serve him.'[34] This, one would have thought, was a fair and friendly reply, but Carlyle thought otherwise. A few days later Panizzi laid the whole correspondence before the Trustees, with the comment that the historian 'claims in fact the right to have the library to himself and the clerks he brings with him to the exclusion of the majority of readers. If such privileges were granted, it would be grossly unfair to all other readers.'[35] The Trustees agreed and approved, without further comment, Panizzi's reply to Carlyle.

Despite the efforts of mutual friends, such as Lord Clarendon, Panizzi would not budge. Public duty united with private pleasure to resist the demands of the acrimonious and overbearing Scot and Carlyle must needs later take his revenge by successfully defeating the candidature of James Lacaita,[36] the protégé of Panizzi and Gladstone, for the post of librarian to the London Library.

But to return to Panizzi. By at least 1854, it was abundantly clear that the long reign of Sir Henry Ellis was, at last, drawing to a close. For the past year or so his health had been failing. The waters of Tunbridge Wells had not succeeded in restoring him to his accustomed vigour and the deaths of his brother and of his wife had shaken the old man severely. He had long come to look upon Panizzi as his destined successor and was more than content to leave the running of the Museum in his capable hands during his now frequent absences. The negotiations for the erection of the reading-room had tried him considerably, even though Panizzi had borne, by far, the greater share of the burden. It was plain that the Principal Librarian was now too old to face all the complex problems which would have to be settled in the near future. Throughout the year 1855, he carried on, reluctant to leave the post he had held so long, but, by the following year, it was evident that he must go, as much for his own good as for that of the Museum. He was now in his seventy-ninth year and must, at last, give way to a younger man. Early in 1856, it was put to him discreetly that if he should voluntarily agree to resign, he would be given the full amount of his salary and other emoluments in lieu of pension. To this tempting offer, Ellis at once agreed and handed to the Trustees his long-awaited resignation. The Board unanimously passed a resolution[37] expressing their sense of the uniform fidelity, zeal and activity, as well as courtesy, with which he had, during so many years, devoted himself to their service. Thus Sir Henry, full of geniality and urbanity to the last, prepared to leave the stage.

The question now was who was to succeed him?[38] Informed opinion had long favoured Panizzi, but, as always, there existed a factious and loudly-voiced opposition to such a solution. Hawkins and Madden were both senior to him by length of service, and Hawkins had been a keeper far longer. The papers now made much of the Royal Commission's proposal for the abolition of the office of Principal Librarian and the substitution of the Executive Committee, and its two 'directors', but the Government, for the moment, refused to be committed.

The anti-Panizzi journals, of whom there were all too many, raised their usual cry and protested lest an 'extraordinary influence' might still succeed in getting a foreigner appointed to such a post of dignity and honour. In their opinion, such action would be an 'affront to British genius and character'. *The Saturday Review*, in particular, strongly attacked Panizzi for his 'discourtesy and unpopularity', as well, naturally, for being a foreigner and for his social successes. *The Literary Gazette* thundered: 'To raise to the supreme direction of the Museum the chief of that department which has been conducted of all others with the least satisfaction to the public, whilst the appointment is not supported by the claims of experience, seniority or competency, would be an example of patronage at once corrupt and detrimental to the interests of this great national institution.' Others, *The Times* and even *The Athenaeum*, were less severe in their strictures, more resigned, it seemed, to the apparent inevitability of an appointment of which they could not wholly approve.[39]

But to one man, at least, the appointment seemed to be anything but inevitable. Panizzi was now full of doubts and fears, but with his usual thoroughness, was determined to do whatever he could to help his own cause.

He seems to have got wind of Sir Henry's probable intentions very early, long before that master of irresolution had finally made up his mind. At once he started to employ his considerable talents for backstairs intrigue and general wire-pulling. This is not to decry him. In that age of patronage, no other course existed for a man determined to succeed and Panizzi knew he could still run the Museum far better than anyone else.

Important and influential people were contacted. Despite Panizzi's lack of sympathy for the usually pro-Austrian court, the Prince Consort was sounded, through General Grey, his private Secretary. Albert was non-committal, but not hostile.[40] Of more real importance was Grey's nephew, the Home Secretary, and the man who would, in fact, make the actual choice. Panizzi got his dear friend, Lady Langdale, widow of the late Master of the Rolls, to write to the Home Secretary, extolling Panizzi's virtues and emphasizing what a high opinion her poor late husband had of the Keeper of Printed Books. Lord Langdale, she said, had indeed considered that Panizzi ought to have been made Principal Librarian years before.[41] Her daughter Jane, in a letter to her 'dear Master Pan', reassured him. 'I think you are quite right not to leave anything to chance.'[42]

Ellis also told him not to worry. No one, he remarked, certainly no 'stranger' was more suitable than Panizzi. 'I myself felt all which you now feel,' he went on, 'in 1827 at the time my predecessor [Planta] was approaching his end . . . I cannot help thinking your fears groundless. I cannot believe that any stranger, did he know the toil of mind to be encountered before experience can be obtained, would wish for such an appointment.'[43]

On February, 18 Panizzi, thus encouraged, addressed a formal application to the Archbishop, requesting that his case might be taken into consideration. In this, he expressed the 'hope that I may not be deemed unworthy of having my name . . . submitted as being a fit person to succeed Sir Henry', and called His Grace's attention to the high opinion of his services already recorded both by the Trustees themselves and by the Royal Commission.[44] In reply, he received a somewhat frigid note from the Lord Chancellor,[45] who, it seemed, at the moment had other views.

Panizzi, a few days before, had gone to see Lord Lansdowne. To his consternation, Lansdowne showed 'less interest in my success than his former conduct had led me to expect'.[46] On the 13th, he learnt the reason. Dundas,[47] one of the Trustees themselves, was putting forward his own name. Lansdowne, Panizzi feared, had half promised his support and so, it would seem, had at least one other Trustee, Somerset.[48] 'Why a man who has never succeeded in anything should be deemed good enough for us and rob those who have served faithfully the Trustees (of which he is one!) for many years of their legitimate rewards, it is not for me to say,' wrote Panizzi, bitterly, to Lord Holland. He begged his old friend to write to Lansdowne, to ask him to use his influence with Grey and the Lord Chancellor; he would judge from the answer whether Lansdowne was for him, against him or merely neutral.[49]

Panizzi was greatly alarmed at this development, not only on his own account, but for the Museum. Dundas was an odd character. 'Many think he is not quite, quite right and at times I think so too.'[50] Holland at once complied with the request and, a few days later, was able to tell the anxious Panizzi that all was well. Lansdowne was *for* him.[51]

In a previous letter, Panizzi wrote emphasizing that it was only with Lansdowne himself that he wanted Holland to intervene. 'Do not take the slightest trouble about any one else. I will not beg or allow my friends to beg for what I consider myself entitled to as deserving it. I wish to have justice and to be treated as I deserve and no more . . . As to canvassing or begging, I never shall, coûte que coûte.'[52]

But nevertheless the necessary influence was being brought to bear on Panizzi's behalf. Sir George Grey, the Home Secretary, was receiving almost daily letters from highly placed personages, extolling the virtues of the Keeper of Printed Books. Ellesmere, the Chairman of the Royal Commission, wrote in the warmest terms, both to the Home Secretary and to the Archbishop, supporting Panizzi's claims. He stressed a feature of his friend's character, almost unknown to the general public, his very great kindness and consideration towards the humbler members of his own staff. The appointment of Panizzi would be, in Ellesmere's opinion, 'the best that could be made'.[53]

Romilly, now Master of the Rolls, added his quota and informed Sir George of 'the strong opinion I have formed of his [Panizzi's] fitness'. Romilly, coached it would seem in this by Panizzi himself, also emphasized the fact that other foreigners, Maty, a Dutchman and Planta, a Swiss, had already held the position of Principal Librarian. He, moreover, reported to Grey that one of the Trustees 'intended to offer himself . . . for this office', a fact of which the Home Secretary was probably already well aware.[54] In a subsequent letter to Panizzi, Romilly emphasized the great impropriety of such an action,[55] a notion that may, by this time, have occurred also to Dundas himself, as little further is heard of his candidature.

Panizzi's old colleague, Cureton, now a Canon of Westminster and soon to be himself a Trustee, was an ardent advocate of the former's cause, actively lobbying the Principal Trustees on his friend's behalf.[56] Lord Panmure,[57] the former Secretary for War, was endeavouring to sway the Lord Chancellor, as yet not quite convinced of Panizzi's suitability for the post, apparently on the grounds that he was still not on speaking terms with some of the other officers. Lady Grey reported that her husband expected to have three names – actually two – submitted to him and that he did not think that 'there will be any who have brighter chances than Mr Panizzi'.[58]

Against all this pressure, and there was probably much more which has left no trace, the Trustees could do little, even had they so wished. Panizzi was clearly on his own merits by far the strongest candidate. Others, besides Dundas, had been under consideration. The claims of Madden, Hawkins and even Gray were widely canvassed, especially in the popular press, but it does not seem likely that they were ever considered seriously by the Board. Panizzi's hopes rose. 'It seems, even to me,' he wrote to Haywood, 'that the thing is as safe as it can be . . . but the thing is not done and there is, therefore, the *possibility* of a miscarriage.'[59]

There were sudden rumours of outside candidates; a Mr Kemble[60] was said to have offered himself, and, at the last moment, some of the Trustees, such as Macaulay, still were uncertain as to whether or not Panizzi would be the right choice.[61]

On February 19, Cureton wrote joyfully: 'I have just seen the Archbishop and . . . all is right in that quarter.'[62] Ten days later, he was able to tell Panizzi that his was definitely one of the names.[63] Sir George Grey now formally submitted them to the consideration of the Cabinet and on the Sunday, Lord Lansdowne told the anxious Panizzi: 'It is now certain and [I] cannot refrain from wishing you joy.'[64]

A few more days of mingled hopes and fears and then, on Wednesday, March 4, the Home Secretary sent Panizzi two letters, the first an unofficial one confirming the good news, the second the official intimation that Her Majesty had been pleased to appoint Antonio Panizzi to execute the office of Principal Librarian of the British Museum.[65] The following day, Madden noted: 'Mr Bond informed me that Mr P had told him this morning that he was sure of his appointment as P.L. The devil choke him with it, say I.'[66]

One little cloud of disquiet yet remained. The official letter had laid down that the appointment was 'subject to any changes in the duties of the office which Parliament may think fit to make'[67] and referred to the alterations proposed by the Royal Commission. Panizzi therefore, in his formal letter of thanks, hastened to point out that the majority of the Commissioners had recommended, not merely certain changes, but the total abolition of his new office, a point that had been eagerly seized on by the more hostile newspapers. He wished for an assurance that he should not be deprived of the post, without due notice or without regard to his present position or past services nor placed in a worse position than that which he now occupied. Grey readily gave these assurances, and Panizzi could at last enter into his inheritance.

Now the congratulations started to pour in. Even before their Keeper had opened the fatal envelope, his devoted staff, who had seen Grey's superscription on the outside and guessed its contents, had crowded round to congratulate their chief. Cureton, on hearing the news, burst into tears, so great was his joy and relief. As Panizzi had said, writing to Haywood a few days before: 'What

pleases me is that in this house all – excepting of course Madden
and Hawkins, who looked to the promotion themselves, are
strongly for me'[68] and now all grades hastened to wish him well.

Garnett, till then unaware that his colleagues had already waited
upon their Keeper, writes hurriedly: 'No one in the department
can feel more indebted to you than I do, alike for the kindly
warmth with which you promoted my appointment, and for the
extreme courtesy and forbearance I have invariably experienced
at your hands.'[69] Old Grabham, still superintending the Reading
Room, offered his congratulations, as did many others of his colleagues of every rank. Hawkins, according to Madden, remarked
icily that a loyal English gentleman was much better than an Italian
traitor and Sir Frederic himself, nursing his rage and spite, wrote
in the safety of his journal, 'It is hard to think that if this cursed
fellow had never come to England with a rope round his neck . . . I
should now have had the fairest chance of a good house and £1,000
per annum. And what has he done for the Museum and the Public
that I have not done, ay and ten times more? My bitter ban on
him!'[70]

But despite Madden's curses, congratulations still came in from
all quarters. His Italian compatriots, delighted at the honour done
to Italy in the person of one of her greatest sons, were warm in
their praise.[71] Sir James Hudson, his old friend the British minister at Turin, sent his heartiest good wishes.[72] Nearer home, prominent literary figures and great noblemen, such dear friends as
Haywood and Jane Bickersteth, joined in the chorus. Jane light-
heartedly wished him 'a comfortable instalment in your honours
(even tho' Sir F. Madden do chance to die of it).'[73]

The Times and *The Athenaeum* received the news unenthusias-
tically, but with resignation. The latter journal remarked: 'On the
whole, the selection of Mr Panizzi is probably the best that could
have been made,'[74] a sentiment that was echoed by most of the
other papers. Some voices were still raised in protest, notably that
of Milnes in the Commons debate on April 21, only to be
completely overborne by the combined onslaught of the Speaker,
the Prime Minister, Russell, and Disraeli, the leader of the Opposition.[75] Criticism of Panizzi's appointment quickly faded to half-
hearted sniping in obscure periodicals. The world at large now, at
last, recognized Panizzi, as he had long been by those who knew

him well, as the only possible man for this honourable but trying position.

One task yet remained to be done. Two of his friends, Haywood and James Booth,[76] put up the necessary money for Panizzi's bond of £5,000, and on Saturday, March 15, the Keeper of Printed Books wrote his last official letter to Sir Henry, begging him to lay before the Trustees his appointment as Principal Librarian and enclosing the essential securities and bonds. The same day, the Trustees formally put Antonio Panizzi in possession of his new office. Despite the long years of ridicule, of animosity and of contempt, the early privations and frustrations, his handicaps, both of race and religion, Panizzi, the penniless political refugee, was, at last, at the head of the great institution he had done so much to drag, however unwilling it was, into the modern world.

NOTES TO CHAPTER 11

1   PP. 1854. f.205.

2   Add. MS. 36, 716. f.460.

3   PP. 1851. f.79.

4   *Select Committee*, 1836, para. 4630.

5   PP. 1850. f.73.

6   PP. 1850. f.248.

7   PP. 1850. f.281.

8   PP. 1850. f.550.

9   PP. 1852. f.322d.

10   PP. 1853. f.20b.

11   PP. 1852. f.456. This was apparently not Panizzi's first visit to Ireland. He seems to have gone there in the early thirties in connection with a court case. [*Library Association, 7th Annual Meeting, Transactions*. p. 141.] When served a second time with a subpoena, 'the big fellow got up on his hind legs and roared like a bull'.

12   PP. 1852 ff.534, 539; 1853 f.20b. [A.P. to Haywood, February 3, 1853.]

13   *The Times*, February, 2, 1853.

14   Report to Trustees, January 24, 1849. PP. 1849. f.65.

15   *Communications relating to the Enlargement of the British Museum. Parliamentary Papers*, H. of C., 1852, vol. XXVIII, p. 206.

16   *Mechanics' Magazine*, vol. 26, pp. 454–459. *The New Buildings at the British Museum*, signed PPCR, 'Peerless Pool, City Road', as Watts told Garnett, the open-air swimming pool in Islington owned by his family.

17   William Hosking, 1800–1861. Architect and civil engineer.

18   James Fergusson, 1808–1886. Writer on architecture. His views were regarded as somewhat extreme.

19   A reproduction of Panizzi's sketch is in Preface by Jones to *A List of Books of Reference*, p. xvi.

20   PP. 1852. f.326b.

21 PP. 1852. f.326b.

22 PP. 1852. f.349.

23 *Quarterly Review*, vol. XVII, p. 157.

24 PP. 1853. f.149.

25 PP. 1853. f.270.

26 Sir Charles Barry, 1795–1860. Architect also of the Reform Club and of Bridgewater House which he designed for Lord Ellesmere. Smirke thought little of his plan for the Reading Room. 'The more I consider it in detail, the more preposterous it seems.' [PP. 1853. f.113.]

27 PP. *Miscellaneous*.

28 PP. 1854. f.81.

29 Jones, *Introduction*, p. xxv.

30 PP. 1854. f.418.

31 Fagan, I, p. 366.

32 Madden, *Journal*, quoted in Barwick, pp. 110, 111.

33 Carlyle, *Journal*, quoted in S. Nowell Smith, *Carlyle and the London Library*, p. 65.

34 PP. *Miscellaneous*. [April 12, 1853.]

35 PP. *Miscellaneous*. [April 16, 1853.]

36 Lacaita also strongly disliked Carlyle whom he described as 'coarse, vulgar, paradoxical both in his thoughts and in the way in which he gives them utterance'. *Diary*. Quoted in C. Lacaita, p. 86.

37 Committee Minute, February 9, 1856. [PP. *Miscellaneous*.]

38 Panizzi wrote to Lord Holland. 'The Government have determined to get rid of Sir Henry Ellis and, of course, a successor is to be appointed . . . I think I have a right to that appointment. [A.P. to Lord Holland, February 14, 1856. *Holland House Papers*.]

39 Madden Collection. Fagan, II, p. 4.

40 Fagan, II, p. 12.

41 Add. MS. 36,717, f. 311. In *Passages*, p. 33 Panizzi says that all letters to Grey were written 'without my knowledge' but it is quite clear from Jane Bickersteth's letters that Panizzi had asked her mother, Lady Langdale, to write to Grey and there may well have been other cases.

42 Add. MS. 36,717. f.313.

43 February 14, 1856. *Passages*, p. 31.

44 February 18, 1856. *Passages*, p. 30.

45 February 18, 1856. *Passages*, p. 31. 'I can say no more than that I shall feel it my bounden duty to consult exclusively the interests of the Museum.'

46 A.P. to Lord Holland, February 14, 1856. *Holland House Papers*.

47 Sir David Dundas, 1799–1877. Solicitor-General under Russell, Judge Advocate General, 1849–1852.

48 Somerset to A.P., February 7, 1856. Add. MS. 36, 717. f.291.

49 A.P. to Lord Holland, February 14, 1856. *Holland House Papers*.

50 A.P. to Lord Holland, February 14, 1856. *Holland House Papers*.

51 Lord Holland to A.P., February 20, 1856. *Holland House Papers*.

52 A.P. to Lord Holland, February 16, 1856. *Holland House Papers*. Strangely enough it was Lansdowne who many years before had intervened decisively to secure Sir Henry's appointment. [Fagan, II, p. 6.]

53 Ellesmere to Grey, February 18, 1856. *Passages*, p. 32. Add. MS. 36, 717. f.308.

54 Add. MS. 36, 717. f.304. Panizzi cut out all reference to this in the published text.

55 Add. MS. 36, 717. f.319. Romilly to A.P., February 20, 1856.

56 *Hansard*, 3 Series, vol. 141, col. 1354. *Passages*, p. 34 gives Ellesmere's letters to Cureton. The latter had asked Ellesmere to write also to the Archbishop. William Cureton, 1808–1864. Syriac scholar. Canon of Westminster, 1849–1864. Assistant Keeper, Department of Manuscripts, 1837–1850. Royal Trustee, 1859–1864.

57 Fox Maule, 2nd Baron Panmure, 1801–1874. 11th Earl of Dalhousie, 1860.

58 Add. MS. 46, 717. f.321.

59 Fagan, II, p. 14.

60 John Kemble, 1807–1857, philologist and historian. Eldest son of Charles Kemble, the actor. Rutherfurd wrote, 'I do not think that even one of the name of Kemble will play a *principal* part in the drama.' [Add. MS. 36, 717. f.335.]

61 Fagan, II, p. 16.

62 Cureton to A.P., February 19, 1856. *Passages*, p. 35. Add. MS. 36, 717. f.315.

63 Add. MS. 36, 717. f.328. *Holland House Papers*. A.P. to Lord Holland, February 29, 1856. 'I have just heard that two names have been submitted to the Queen today . . . to fill Ellis' place, my own and John Kemble's. I must be a very worthless fellow if Sir G. Grey advises the Queen to prefer him to me. I now think the result cannot be doubtful.' See also Panmure to A.P. [Add. MS. 36, 717. f.327.] 'A Mr Kemble is your opponent.'

64 Lansdowne to A.P., Add. MS. 36, 717 f.341.

65 Add. MS. 36, 717. ff.343, 349.

66 Madden, *Journal*, March 5. Quoted in Barwick, *Reading Room*, p. 108.

67 Add. MS. 36, 717. f.349. 'A condition was attached to my appointment rendering it so insecure that I would rather remain where I am than accept it on such terms. Everybody says I am so manifestly right that it will be altered and made on the terms which I have a right to. Vedramo . . . Nothing can exceed the kindness of Lord and Lady Palm.[erston] towards me in all this affair.' [A.P. to Lord Holland, March 8, 1856.] [*Holland House Papers.*]

68 Fagan, II, p. 14.

69 Add. MS. 36, 717. f.356.

70 Madden, *Journal*, February 19, 1856. Quoted in *Barwick*, p. 108.

71 *Lettere ad A.P.*, p. 260.

72 Add. MS. 36, 717. f.415. Hudson to A.P., March 19, 1856.

73 Add. MS. 36, 717. f.359.

74 *The Athenaeum*, no. 1479, March 1, 1856, p. 265.

75 *Hansard*, 3S., vol. 141, col. 1344–1367. Panizzi had provided Gladstone with the necessary information to rebut Milnes though Gladstone in fact took little part in the debate. In a letter to Lord Holland Panizzi spoke of the 'great attack on me, poor foreigner . . . but I shall want no support against so base and cowardly a fellow.' [April 19, 1856. *Holland House Papers.*]

76 James Booth, 1796–1880, writer on legal subjects. Secretary to the Board of Trade, 1850–1865.

12

POLITICIAN AND PATRIOT

WE MUST now turn back a few years, leaving, for the moment, Antonio Panizzi on the threshold of his new life as Principal Librarian. It must never be forgotten that during this time of constant anxiety and unceasing effort at the Museum, Panizzi was not only busily engaged in a whirl of social activities, but also fully occupied in various political enterprises, many of a semi-clandestine nature.

With the passage of time, a number of his friends of the early years had either died or Panizzi had long ceased to be intimate with them. Francis Haywood, whom he had known since the far-off days in Liverpool, had remained, perhaps, the closest of all, but Haywood, alas, was also very soon to die. With certain of his fellow exiles, notably Arrivabene[1] and Giovanni Berchet,[2] he had maintained fairly close relations, but, on the whole, as with many men of middle age, it was an entirely new set of friendships that he had now formed.

During the 1840s, Panizzi, to an increasing extent, had become familiar with the highest circles of the Whig party. The widowed Lady Holland[3] had taken him up in the last two years of her life and he had become a frequent diner at Holland House. With her son, the fourth Lord Holland[4] and his wife, Panizzi was on terms of the closest friendship. The younger Lady Holland, in particular, was his good friend for the rest of his life, despite their often dramatic differences. The Clarendons,[5] too, were now very friendly and were always delighted to see him, either for dinner or for weekends in the country. Others were the Rutherfurds, the

Lord Advocate and his charming wife, with whom Panizzi had conducted a lively correspondence for many years and stayed, whenever he could, at their house near Edinburgh. Panizzi adored Scotland and felt more at home there than anywhere else outside his beloved Museum. Either at the Rutherfurds or at the house of his other great Scottish friends, the Ellices, both father and son, Panizzi passed many pleasant holidays, drinking whisky, eating venison and, in his younger days at least, walking and shooting on the moors.

A lawyer by training and one might even say by nature, Panizzi had many friends among members of that profession. Rutherfurd, Langdale, James Booth and others delighted him with their conversation and knowledge. But perhaps the most important friendship now formed was that with the rising young hope of the Tory party, William Ewart Gladstone. Though the latter was godson of Panizzi's old Liverpool acquaintance, William Ewart senior, Panizzi does not seem to have met Gladstone until much later and it was through Thomas Grenville that they now became acquainted. Mrs Gladstone was a great-niece of the old man, and he had been much struck by the character and abilities of her husband. Grenville realized that his great friend Panizzi and young Gladstone had much in common and he quickly introduced them. A mutual liking for the great Italian authors ripened into a deep and abiding friendship. These two very dissimilar men remained warmly attached to each other until the day when Gladstone, now Prime Minister, took a final farewell of the sick and weary old man, 'this very true and trusty hearty friend',[6] whom he had known and respected for so many years.

This was, indeed, a friendship the result of which was felt far outside the narrow world of libraries and scholarship. It may fairly be claimed that it was the influence of Panizzi over the younger man which first turned the thoughts of Gladstone towards the redress of Italy's wrongs and, as John Morley long ago pointed out,[7] it was Italy and his hatred of the tyranny and oppression which he found there, that was so largely instrumental in turning the rigid Tory of the early days into the great Liberal leader and eager democrat.

It was, perhaps, strange that two men of such very different, but equally forceful characters, should, for so long, remain such close friends. For as Cardinal Manning said, 'Mr Gladstone is a substantive and likes to be attended by adjectives and I am not exactly an adjective,'[8] and, nor indeed, was Panizzi. Yet despite a certain formality on Gladstone's part, of which the warm-hearted Italian complained more than once, they remained good friends and true allies in the cause of Italian unity. It may be that both felt that they were strangers in the closed circle of the great Whig families in which they both now moved.[9] Panizzi was a foreigner, Gladstone the son of a north-country merchant, who owed perhaps more to the manifold connections of his wife's family than to his father's wealth as a means of entry into the houses of the Whig nobility. For, if there was all the difference in the world between the redoubtable Sir John Gladstone, that old 'negro driver',[10] and poor Luigi Panizzi, still running his little shop back in Brescello, yet both had, it was said, in their youth served behind the counter, and the thought of this, even if never expressed, may well have served as an unacknowledged link between the eminent statesman and the Principal Librarian of the British Museum.

Panizzi had now been away from Modena and its neighbouring states for more than twenty years and though he had travelled widely on the continent, he had not, as yet, dared enter the confines of the Austrian Empire nor had ventured south into those territories under her direct influence. In 1839, he had got as far as Genoa, still in Piedmontese territory, but the experience had not been encouraging.

He now began to make inquiries, through Gladstone, as to whether permission might not now be secured from the Austrian authorities and from their puppet administrations in northern Italy as to whether he, a British subject, might go there with safety and remain a free man.

On June 14, 1842, he received a reply from the Foreign Office to his letter of the previous April. The Modenese authorities had assured the British Government that, in the event of Panizzi visiting Austria, they would not ask for his extradition and, in a further letter, the former Carbonaro was informed that Metternich himself had told HM Ambassador in Vienna that, should Panizzi so wish, he was free to travel within the confines of that Empire, without any danger of being handed over to his former countrymen, as a wanted criminal.[11]

However, his freedom to travel was not to be unconditional and despite Panizzi's further representations, the Foreign Office declined to press Vienna for any further relaxation of the restrictions.[12] So, for the moment, the matter rested. Panizzi proudly refused to go, unless completely unrestricted and though Gladstone wrote on June 12, 1844: 'I have spoken to Lord Aberdeen on the subject of your note. He has the subject in hand . . . and by no means despairs of success,'[13] no permission ever came. Gladstone went on trying on his friend's behalf and badgered Lord Aberdeen, the Foreign Secretary, who was not oversympathetic to the cause of Italian unity. On April 3, Gladstone wrote: 'I earnestly hope that these accounts of movements in Italy, may not prove an insuperable impediment. I am sure every one who knows you will say they ought not.'[14] At last, however, on June 1, Gladstone was forced to tell Panizzi that, for the moment, it was hopeless.[15] For one thing, conditions in Italy were again in a ferment, and, secondly, in the suspicious eyes of the Austrian and Modenese governments, Panizzi's own reliability seemed to be less assured. For he had suddenly appeared as the champion of Giuseppe Mazzini;[16] the man most hated and feared by the Austrians and by all the reactionary governments of Italy. This alone was more than sufficient to rearouse their latent suspicions.

Mazzini had reached England in 1837 and though he soon made Panizzi's acquaintance, they had never been close friends. Mazzini, for instance, had preferred to get his Reading Room ticket, not through his distinguished compatriot, but through the good offices of a Scottish lady admirer. Panizzi was as suspicious of Mazzini's republicanism and secret plotting as the latter must have been of the other's grand friends and English ways. 'Panizzi,' he grumbled, 'by making himself English, in opinions, manners and in everything else, has become librarian of the public library.'[17] For the two men moved in very different circles. Not for the *Profeta* were dinners at Holland House or weekend parties with the Clarendons or with other members of the Whig nobility. His English friends were, to a very large extent, men of the extreme left, such as Holyoake[18] and though he quickly became friendly with the Carlyles, this would scarcely have endeared him to Panizzi.

Nevertheless, both men shared a deep and genuine love of Italy and for Italian literature and during these early years there was undoubtedly a certain intimacy between them. On his visit in 1839 to Piedmont, Panizzi had promised to visit Mazzini's aged parents at Genoa, but had been unable to do so owing to the obstructive and insulting behaviour of the local authorities, which had forced him to return to England without either seeing the elder Mazzinis or visiting Lucca, as he had also intended. In 1844, however, Panizzi's hatred of injustice was deeply stirred and perhaps for the last time, he exerted himself on the other's behalf.

The Foreign Secretary, Lord Aberdeen, was a well-intentioned man of strict integrity and of high moral principles.[19] He was, however, very much a politician of the old school, whose opinions and outlook had been moulded by the need to uphold the settlement of Europe, devised by the Congress of Vienna. He had little or no sympathy, therefore, with the turbulent forces of the new nationalism. Persuaded by Metternich, he considered that it was his duty to assist in suppressing the revolutionary activities of Mazzini and his like, at all times and in all places.

This was, of course, at the moment, more the duty of the Home, than of the Foreign Office. Aberdeen, therefore, passed on to Metternich's request to his colleague, Sir James Graham,[20] the Home Secretary.

Graham agreed to have Mazzini's letters opened and their contents passed on to the Austrian Embassy. From this source, the Ambassador managed to communicate to Metternich much vital information on the activities of the Italian revolutionaries. This was said to include the news of the plans of the insurrection headed by the Bandiera brothers, which, forwarded to the Neapolitan authorities, led to their speedy arrest and execution.[21]

Mazzini's suspicions had now become aroused. He succeeded in persuading a sympathetic MP, Thomas Duncombe,[22] to raise the matter in the House. The ensuing public outcry led to the appointment of Secret Committees of Inquiry in both Houses and it was the publication of their respective reports which was the occasion of an article by Panizzi, *Post Office Espionage*, in the *North British Review* of November 1844.[23]

Panizzi's private opinions on the activities of Mazzini were probably not far removed from those expressed by his friend Shepherd: 'Mazzini seems by his own showing to be a habitual intriguer taking good care of his own carcase, whilst watching and in some degree controling, if not directing, the efforts of men bolder than his prudence will allow him to be,'[24] but he hated injustice anywhere and to anyone and, above all, he hated Austria and all she stood for, political and spiritual despotism.

In his article, Panizzi trounced Graham and the majority of the members of both Committees. He does not spare, either, those members of the government whom he believes to be guilty of collusion with the hereditary enemy.

Mazzini had committed no offence against English law, nor had premeditated 'any wicked design against England'.[25] Aberdeen had sunk to becoming an informer for the Austrian and Neapolitan governments and through that action alone, gallant patriots had been caught and executed.

All Panizzi's strongest feelings, his hatred of tyranny and his passionate love of liberty, rose to the surface, as he roundly condemned a British government which, to its everlasting shame, had 'volunteered its services as a spy to the King of Naples'.[26] It was this fact that really, above all else, disgusted Panizzi. England, the cradle of liberty, the refuge of the oppressed, had lent its aid to the police of foreign despots.

Though Panizzi, like many of his countrymen, came in after years more and more to doubt the wisdom of such methods as those advocated by Mazzini and disliked and distrusted his revolutionary activities, yet he could never help retaining a certain respect for a man who had given so much for the cause of Italian unity.[27]

Despite these efforts in support of Mazzinian activities, within a few months he at last succeeded in obtaining permission to visit the Austrian Empire. In July 1845 he arrived in Vienna, having previously spent a few days in Munich. Thanks to the kind offices of Lady Holland,[28] he was warmly received by the British Ambassador, Sir Robert Gordon,[29] a friendly and charming Scot. Gordon quickly obtained for Panizzi the necessary authority to go anywhere in the imperial states, without fear of molestation.

By a strange coincidence, there was in Vienna another visitor from Modena, his former sovereign, Duke Francis IV. Panizzi was already on comparatively friendly terms with one of the petty princes of northern Italy, Charles, Duke of Lucca,[30] whose capital he had tried, in vain, to visit six years previously. He now thought that here was an opportunity to make his peace with Francis and to receive from him the necessary permission to return to Modena and to see once again his friends and relatives.

Sir Robert Gordon, therefore, paid Duke Francis a visit 'and informed him of my arrival, plans of travel, etc. His Royal Highness assured *him* that I might go safely to his dominions.'[31] Francis then told Gordon that he would be pleased to receive Panizzi, if the latter so wished. Panizzi accordingly waited on the old Hapsburg the same day and met again the man who had sentenced him to death so many years before. 'We talked,' Panizzi wrote, 'over old times as well as future prospects for half an hour exactly. He received me with great courtesy, but very coolly at first: but we went on much better as the conversation grew warmer & we parted much better friends than we were at first. He renewed the assurance given to Sir Robert as to my being allowed to go safely to his states and so on Saturday next the 26th inst I shall start off for Innsbruck & Venice.' Panizzi was delighted at the prospect of an early reunion with his family, but, alas, he was quickly doomed to disappointment.

Even before he had closed the letter announcing his good news to Lady Holland, he discovered, to his mingled alarm and indignation, that he had been deceived. In a hurried postscript, written the next morning, he exclaims, 'To my great surprise I learn this moment that the D of M who never hinted this to me will not allow me to go to his capital!! I therefore give up going to his dominions at all!'

Panizzi was full of anger at this treacherous behaviour of his old sovereign. Not only was permission not now granted. It had never been intended that it should be. No less than eleven days before their meeting, steps had been taken to watch the unwelcome visitor and to send a full account of his doings and associates to Modena.

Bitterly, Panizzi now wrote to his cousin, Prospero Cugini: 'In the honour of your government I have no faith. I will not go to Modena where I have heard a week ago there are orders against me and which have been issued by the Duke himself.'[32] A courteous note to the Modenese authorities asking for an explanation was met by a short and uncivil reply. Thus did this petty state treat her greatest son.

His friends back in England were relieved at his decision not to go to Modena. Lord Ponsonby, to whom Lady Holland had passed on Panizzi's note, wrote, 'I think he is right not to trust Modena. It might be easy for an enemy there to make up a story of his meddling with politics & I suspect the Duke might not be over nice in the keeping of his word.'[33]

In the meantime, Panizzi had gone to more liberal Parma, the scene of his happy university days and of his first acquaintance with the secret societies and the heady waters of Italian nationalism. There, at last, he met some of his relatives and friends, who were overjoyed to see him. The names of all Brescellese, however, were noted by the authorities and duly reported to the Modenese police. Fortunately, no harm seems to have come to anyone for meeting their now distinguished fellow-citizen.[34]

Soon he was back in London, to the unfeigned delight of all his acquaintances. Old Shepherd expressed his relief that Panizzi had returned, 'having kept your neck out of the noose',[35] whilst Clarendon rejoiced to hear that he was 'well and prosperous & had returned more *devotedly attached* than ever to the Duke of Modena'.[36] The Embassy at Vienna wrote that they had conveyed Panizzi's thanks to Metternich for the facilities he had received in Lombardy and that the great man had seemed pleased. There was little doubt that he might return, at least to Austria, whenever he so wished.[37]

But for the moment, Panizzi was once more the gay socialite, the inveterate diner-out, cheering, in company with Thackeray, the ageing and lonely Melbourne, desolate at the sudden death of Lady Holland.[38] Even though Holland House was, for the moment, empty, Panizzi still went the rounds of the fashionable establishments, still spent his weekends at the great Whig country mansions, so that, as Grenville wrote mockingly: 'You are so much in vogue' that he had little time for anything else.[39]

But these social occasions were not without purpose. As much as Panizzi loved good food, good wine and congenial company all his life, he loved politics still more, and they were never far apart in the intensely political society in which he moved. He did not restrict his friendships to English politicians and had many acquaintances among European statesmen of a more or less liberal outlook.

8*

Amongst these was Adolphe Thiers,[40] then leader of the opposition in the parliaments of King Louis Philippe. Panizzi seems to have made Thiers's acquaintance about 1840 and the two men became, for a time, fast friends. They were much together whenever Thiers was in England. It was Panizzi who first introduced the Frenchman into English political circles and, in particular, to Palmerston[41] and he, henceforth, was himself to be the link with that statesman and the French opposition.

To what extent Thiers himself benefited by these English contacts is more doubtful. As Clarendon wrote to Panizzi: '[Thiers] really flits round Europe like a flash of lightning & if he means to know anything about this country and its inhabitants he ought not to come only for a week.'[42]

Though the Frenchman's knowledge of England and English ways might be scanty and though, in turn, Panizzi had no illusions as to Thiers's vanity and undeniable vulgarity, it was Panizzi who was destined to be the means of conveying to him English opinion, and, in particular, Lord Palmerston's opinion and to provide him with the ammunition to attack the policies of his rival, Guizot.

The occasion was the affair of the Spanish Marriages, one which aroused such feelings of bitterness at the time that they are still reflected in the sober pages of Fagan some forty years later. In brief, it was the attempt of the King of the French, or, more probably of his minister, Guizot, to reassert French influence at the Spanish court by marrying the young Queen, Isabella and her sister to princes agreeable to France. After lengthy and complicated intrigues, involving most of the courts of Europe, during the course of which the sudden appearance of a Coburg candidate, allegedly sponsored by Britain, led to Guizot suspecting that upright Presbyterian, Aberdeen, of double dealing. Queen Isabella was wedded to the supposedly impotent Duke of Cadiz and her younger sister, at the same time, to King Louis' son, Montpensier.

The simultaneous marriage was regarded by Palmerston, since the midsummer of 1846 Aberdeen's successor at the Foreign Office, as a violation of the pledges given personally by the King to Queen Victoria, an opinion fully shared by his royal mistress, who considered Guizot's conduct 'beyond *all* belief, shameful and so shabbily dishonest'.[43] The Foreign Secretary now turned upon the erring Guizot and his master the full fire of his wrath.

On January 12, 1847, Thiers wrote to Panizzi a letter condemning Guizot's conduct, both with regard to the Spanish Marriages and in general. He suggested that if only the King knew what the Whigs now thought of his unworthy minister, he would dismiss him: 'Quand il croira les Whigs solides et la question serieuse, il se décidera à une changement de personnes',[44] and so restore Anglo-French amity.

Panizzi, already, the previous November, in a long and detailed letter, which he had undoubtedly first shown to Palmerston, had clearly expounded the British point of view. He had sent this note to Thiers secretly, by the hand of a friend, enjoining his correspondent not to trust to the French postal services, but to send his replies back to Panizzi, through the British Ambassador.

On January 14, Panizzi, having received no reply, wrote again with some urgency, enclosing details of Aberdeen's correspondence with the Spanish minister in London and other confidential papers for Thiers to make use of in the French Chamber. Thiers, at last, replied in the letter mentioned above and used the material supplied by Panizzi in his attacks on his rival Guizot, and on the Queen Regent of Spain.

No further letters from Panizzi to Thiers have survived, but the two men seem to have corresponded, rather fitfully, for a number of years. Gradually their friendship cooled. Thiers was less enthusiastic, than Panizzi would have wished, for the cause of Italian unity. The latter's subsequent friendship with Prosper Mérimée and with Louis Napoleon and his Empress would have been sufficient to damn him in the eyes of Thiers, a determined anti-Bonapartist. The affair of the Spanish Marriages, trivial in itself, clearly reveals the growing influence of Panizzi in the inner circles of the Whig party and the use that could be made by them of his wide contacts throughout Europe.

Panizzi, after the fall of the Orléans dynasty, became very friendly with the exiled royal family. Aumale,[45] perhaps the ablest of the brilliant sons of Louis Phillippe, was a particularly close friend, who shared his love of books and good company. He was also on intimate terms with other members of the family, especially the widowed Queen, despite the fact that she was a Neapolitan princess and an aunt of King Ferdinand.

During this time, moreover, Panizzi had been considering

visiting Naples to see for himself the state of affairs in that king-dom, which had long been anathema to all right-thinking Italian nationalists. With the election of the 'liberal' Pope, Pius IX,[46] and the grant of constitutional reforms in Tuscany, events in Italy seemed, once more, to be on the move. Panizzi, doubtless, wanted to be informed, at first hand, as to what was happening. Inquiries were made, through the Foreign Office, as to whether it would be possible for him to visit Naples. Sir William Temple,[47] the British Minister, emphasized to the Neapolitan government the high esteem in which Panizzi was held 'by distinguished men of all parties', and requested that the former Carbonaro might be allowed to enter 'without hindrances & be free from molestation'.[48]

In November a reply was received that, despite objections raised by the Minister of Police, King Ferdinand had assured Temple: 'that he had granted the permission & given orders that Mr Panizzi may be allowed freely to enter the Neapolitan states.'[49]

At that particular moment, Panizzi was unable to take advantage of the royal benevolence. Too many problems now faced him at the British Museum. The Royal Commission was still sitting and absence abroad was, for the moment, completely out of the question.

Before this was again possible, Europe had experienced the mingled hopes and disappointments of 1848, the year of revolu-tions. Panizzi had little direct contact with the events of these stirring times, save, as we have seen, by his organization of the defence of the Museum against the possible attacks of the Char-tists. He followed, however, the course of events abroad with the keenest interest. Several of his friends played important roles in the various uprisings throughout Italy and Panizzi was used by them as the channel through which their views and aspirations might be made plain to sympathizers in England and to the British government itself. Emerico Amari,[50] whom Panizzi had assisted during the former's poverty-stricken exile in Paris, became a member of the revolutionary government of Sicily and, for a time, Minister of Finance. He was then sent as a special envoy to the French and British governments to plead for their assistance. It may be safely assumed that in England, it was through the Keeper of Printed Books that he was able to contact such friends of free Italy as Lords Minto and Palmerston.

But it was to northern Italy, rather than to the far south, that Panizzi's thoughts, as always, turned. Himself a northerner, it had long seemed to him that it was around the nucleus of the independent state of Piedmont that a united Italy might grow. In this view, he, of course, differed from the republican Mazzini and other extremists, but Panizzi, for long now himself a citizen of a constitutional monarchy and an instinctive lover of order, was ever predisposed to such a solution of the problem.

In the north, too, the fight was directly against the hated Austrian and Panizzi, throughout the whole of his long life, never abandoned his dislike of and contempt for the government which had enslaved so much of his native land and which, through its puppet Duke, had driven him into exile.

In the years 1848 and 1849, the gallant city of Milan and the armies of Charles Albert of Piedmont were the main objects of his hopes and fears and he watched, with enthusiasm and with growing anxiety, the fortunes of the struggle in the north. In a long letter to Pompeo Litta,[51] Minister of War in the provisional Milanese government, Panizzi outlined the state of English public opinion on the events in Italy and proffered suggestions on the line of action which, in his opinion, the government at Milan should now take. Above all, he urged, never negotiate or treat with the Austrians; they surely can no longer have any faith in fine words. Such were merely a device for gaining time. Already Panizzi had urged on the British government the necessity of a speedy recognition of the north Italian kingdom, to forestall the threatened intervention of republican France. Now he implored his Italian friends to take every advantage of English sympathy for their cause. To gain the active support of Britain would be of an inestimable advantage, since only she was in a position to make advances to the Austrian authorities on their behalf.

This letter and others similar which Panizzi wrote to his friend Berchet,[52] now secretary of Public Instruction at Milan, were at once laid before the heads of the provisional government. They, in turn, begged Panizzi to use all the influence he possessed to gain for them British intervention and, as the régime crumbled, to mediate with Austria on their behalf.

But it was not to be. The Court and many leading politicians were distinctly pro-Austrian. Peel, for instance, had but little sympathy with the revolutionary and often bellicose programmes of the various movements of national liberty. In this, as in so many other things, he was representative of much of public opinion. The Italian risings of 1848 were never so popular in England as the earlier Greek and Spanish revolts had been. It needed the colourful figure of Garibaldi to make English public opinion once more favourable to the Italian cause.

Panizzi's efforts were thus in vain. Piedmont was defeated, Milan and Venice overcome. Everywhere, throughout Europe, reaction triumphed. Throughout these anxious months Asher had constantly reported to Panizzi how things were going in Prussia, in Austria and in Italy, but now, all was over.

Panizzi was bitterly disappointed at the failure of all his hopes and his consequent dejection is reflected in a series of letters which he wrote at this time to Gladstone. The latter had requested Panizzi's assistance in connection with an article he was writing on the Italian poet, Leopardi. In his replies to his friend's queries, Panizzi's gloom and bitterness are very apparent. To him the Western powers had betrayed the cause of liberty, by failing to stand up to the Eastern despotisms. Had they done so, 'Venice would not be desolated, the Italians in the Romagna and Tuscany would not be shot and bastinadoed like dogs and now there would be no danger of the peace of the world depending on the will of a madman!'[53]

In a further letter to Gladstone, Panizzi speaks with bitterness of those in England who had helped to bring about the downfall of Italian hopes, and the victory of those forces of reaction to which he was so deeply opposed.

'The Conservative party in Italy – that party which has the support of the *friends* of *order* here – as they call themselves, of Lord Aberdeen for instance, is made up of persons exactly as Leopardi's father. And we who thought and think otherwise are considered robbers, cutthroats, vagabonds, &, &. The Government of the Pope is, or seems to be, made on purpose to produce atheists and republicans, and it is to such governments that the wildness of continental Liberals is to be ascribed.'[54] There spoke out the true Panizzi, who for all his hobnobbing with the great ones of this world, remained all his life, in his heart of hearts, a man of the deepest and most generous liberal sympathies.

NOTES TO CHAPTER 12

1 Giovanni Arrivabene, 1787–1881.

2 Giovanni Berchet, 1783–1851. Not to be confused with Panizzi's other friend, Ambrogio Berchet, the soldier, 1784–1864.

3 Elizabeth Holland, divorced wife of Sir Godfrey Webster, Bart., 1765–1845.

4 Henry Edward Fox, second and eldest legitimate son of 3rd Lord and Lady Holland, 1802–1859. Married in 1833 Mary Augusta, daughter of the 8th Earl of Coventry, 1812–1889.

5 George Villiers, 4th Earl of Clarendon, 1800–1870. An admirable talker and most patient listener. His wife was a daughter of the first Earl of Verulam.

6 Morley, vol. 2, p. 196.

7 Morley, vol. I, p. 389.

8 Manning, quoted in Battiscombe, *Mrs Gladstone*, p. 42. Panizzi does not seem to have dined all that frequently with the Gladstones. He would probably have agreed with Mérimée, 'I see you dined with Mr Gladstone the other night. Plenty of plate and lamb, I suppose. I prefer our tête à tête dinners at the Museum.' [Mérimée, I, p. 38.]

9 Gladstone, it was said, was 'Oxford on the surface but Liverpool below'. [Morley, vol. I, p. 192.]

10 Shepherd to A.P., Add. MS. 36, 715. f.217.

11 Add. MS. 36, 715. ff.125, 126, 129.

12 Add. MS. 36, 715. f.130.

13 Add. MS. 36, 715. f.164.

14 Add. MS. 36, 715. f.183.

15 Add. MS. 36, 715. f.194.

16 Guiseppe Mazzini, 1805–1872.

17 Brooks, p. 63.

18 George Jacob Holyoake, Radical reformer.

19 Gladstone praised his 'dignity so tempered by a peculiar purity and gentleness'. [Morley, vol. I, p. 124.]

20 Sir James Graham, 1792–1861, politician. Home Secretary, 1841–1846.

21 Attilio and Emilio Bandiera, 1810–1844, 1819–1844. It seems probable that the information which led to their arrest and execution did not, in fact, come from the British government, but Panizzi and his contemporaries firmly believed that it did.

22 Thomas Duncombe, radical MP for Finsbury, 1834. Worked on behalf of the Italian and Hungarian refugees.

23 *North British Review*, vol. 2, 1844, p. 257.

24 Add. MS. 36, 715. f.217.

25 *Post Office Espionage*, p. 269.

26 *Post Office Espionage*, p. 295.

27 For the relations between Mazzini and Panizzi, see Fagan, I, p. 182.

28 A.P. to Elizabeth, Lady Holland, July 22, 1845. [*Holland House Papers.*]

29 Sir Robert Gordon, 1791–1847. Diplomatist, Envoy at Vienna, 1841–1846.

30 Charles, Duke of Lucca, 1799–1883, succeeded his mother in the Duchy of Lucca, 1824; for one year, 1847, Duke of Parma. [*Lettere ad A.P.*, pp. 130–139.]

31 A.P. to Elizabeth, Lady Holland, July 22, 1845. [*Holland House Papers.*]

32 Fagan, I, p. 192.

33 Lord Ponsonby to Elizabeth, Lady Holland, August 7, 1845. William Ponsonby, Baron Ponsonby, 1816–1861. [*Holland House Papers.*]

34 Among the friends he met both at Parma and Modena was Filippo Cocchi, his cousin Erminio Panizzi and his brother-in-law, Giuseppe Venturini.

35 Shepherd to A.P., October 20, 1845. Fagan, I, p. 194.

36 Add. MS. 36, 715. f.234.

37 Add. MS. 36, 715. f.239.

38 Caroline Norton to A.P., November 1845. 'Poor Lady Holland's death had deprived him of every near neighbour where he could be (without fatigue or form) in pleasant society and with all her faults she had certainly a very real regard for him.' [Add. MS. 36, 715. f. 252.] Lady Holland had died suddenly in November 1845.

39 Add. MS. 36, 715. f.264.

40 Louis Adolphe Thiers, 1797–1877. Panizzi was not alone in being suspicious of Thiers. Hudson considered him to be 'the most mischievous man in Europe', wrong-headed, narrow-minded, perverse and vain. [Add. MS. 36, 725. f.412.] Another French statesman who was on friendly terms was the Duc de Broglie, 1785–1870. They accompanied each other on a trip to Edinburgh to visit the Rutherfurds. [Add. MS. 36, 715. f.422.]

41 A.P. to Rutherfurd, October 30, 1845. Quoted in Fagan, I, p. 199.

42 Add. MS. 36, 715. f.234.

43 Queen Victoria to the King of the Belgians, October 6, 1846. *Letters*, vol. 2, p. 108.

44 Fagan, I, p. 225. See also Add. MS. 36, 715. ff.364, 370, 375.

45 Duc d'Aumale, 1822–1897. Fourth son of Louis Philippe.

46 Giovanni Mastai Ferretti, 1792–1878.

47 Sir William Temple, 1788–1856, younger brother of Lord Palmerston.

48 Add. MS. 36, 715. f.344.

49 Add. MS. 36, 715. f.351.

50 Emerico Amari, 1810–1889.

51 Pompeo Litta, 1781–1852.

52 Giovanni Berchet. Ambrogio Berchet had also returned to Italy to command the National Guard at Parma. [Add. MS. 36, 715. f.462.]

53 *Gladstone Papers*, vol. 189. Add. MS. 44274. f.12. The 'madman' is presumably Nicolas I of Russia.

54 Add. MS. 44274. f.21.

13

THE NEAPOLITAN PRISONERS

VERY soon he was to be in a position to help more actively those now suffering from the victory of reaction in Italy. In the autumn of 1850, Mr and Mrs Gladstone had travelled to southern Italy in search of a more favourable climate for their little daughter, Mary, whose health was precarious. This journey was to have momentous results, both for Italy and for Gladstone himself. Though Panizzi had probably spoken to his friend of what was said to be happening in Naples, he had not, as yet, been able to shake the younger man's innate conservatism. Gladstone's pre-possessions were still, in Morley's words 'pretty strongly in favour of established governments, either at Naples or anywhere else'.[1]

Gladstone, therefore, came to Naples purely on his private affairs, 'with no purpose of political propaganda'.[2] Whilst there, he considered it his duty to investigate the conditions under which political prisoners were confined and to look into the whole circumstances of their arrest and trial. What he discovered appalled him and very soon, through him, all civilized Europe. Gladstone was shocked and horrified. Everywhere before his eyes was the living proof of the cruelty, incompetence and corruption of the Neapolitan government. Men of unblemished character and reputation were seized on the flimsiest of pretexts, condemned on false evidence and imprisoned under barbaric conditions. We of the twentieth century who have experienced so much more of human cruelty and of human agony than ever the Victorians could have dreamed of, may think the sufferings of the Neapolitan prisoners to be mild compared with those endured by the victims of the Gestapo and of similar organizations. Gladstone may have exaggerated; the imprisoned liberals may not have been such paragons of virtue as he claimed, but neither Gladstone nor, later, Panizzi, were ignorant fools and, granted they were prejudiced, neither man was at all likely to be deceived nor to misjudge the situation so radically.

Human suffering is always human suffering and cruelty is still cruelty, to whatever degree it may or may not be inflicted. Panizzi, Gladstone and their contemporaries were all too right to be angered at and disgusted with what they saw and heard of the Neapolitan prisons, 'the extreme of filth and horror',[3] even if we know all too well that such an extreme may easily be surpassed and the 'charnel house' of the Vicaria prison at Naples, a mere nothing besides the later charnel houses of Auschwitz and Belsen.

On Gladstone's return to London, he determined to make more widely known the details of the fate of such prominent Neapolitan liberals as Baron Poerio,[4] Luigi Settembrini[5] and many others.

Having failed to get any satisfaction from an unofficial approach to the Prime Minister, Lord Aberdeen, Gladstone decided to address an open letter to that statesman. With the eager co-operation of Panizzi,[6] he therefore with great care and taking considerable pains not to overstate his case prepared the letter. Even while he was writing, he learnt that the conditions under which the prisoners laboured had been changed for the worse. His pamphlet, *A Letter to the Earl of Aberdeen on the State Prosecutions of the Neapolitan Government* created a sensation. Palmerston, still Foreign Secretary, was so pleased with it that he had an edition printed at government expense and circulated to every court in Europe. Gladstone had written the letter early in April 1851, but had delayed the publication, hoping that Aberdeen might use his considerable influence to alleviate the lot of the prisoners. As the months went by and nothing was done, Gladstone grew desperate. 'I must absolutely print next week, unless I learn that something good has been done,' he wrote to Panizzi.[7] On July 11, 1851, he at last published his letter, to be followed up three days later by a second letter, amplifying the first and giving the reasons for the delay.

The following year Gladstone issued a third pamphlet, *Examination of the official reply of the Neapolitan Government*, in which, with the assistance of Panizzi, he dealt with the objections raised against his pamphlets, both by the Neapolitan government itself and by various French and English apologists for the régime.

Gladstone, like Panizzi, was certain he had been right to draw attention to the treatment meted out to political prisoners in Naples, even though it implied criticism of an ostensibly friendly power. 'The people of England,' he wrote, '[were] not aware of the facts and I believe it to be in every sense better to give them the facts and let them judge.'[8] Panizzi's attitude was, in addition, one of whole-hearted gratitude to the man who had laid before the British public, in so powerful a fashion, an account of the sufferings, which so many of his countrymen still endured.

'I ought to have began,' he tells his friend, 'by thanking you in the name of humanity, of justice & of truth for your generous interference on behalf of the Neapolitan victims.'[9] 'What you say is all true & true not at Naples only. It was and I suppose it is so at Rome and was so at Modena.'[10]

But it was by no means only in letters that Panizzi demonstrated his sincere gratitude for all that Gladstone had tried to do. He employed his great critical ability, his trained, legal mind, his massive intelligence to defend his friend and to discomfort the efforts of those who would in turn discredit him.

In an article in the *Edinburgh Review* of October 1851, he deals with the two letters and with the various replies to them. He roundly denounces both the Neapolitan government itself and the efforts of its apologists to defend 'iniquities perpetrated in the name of legitimate government and of religion by a set of persons, who having crouched before the popular enthusiasm when triumphant, now abuse their, we trust temporary, success, without respect for either divine or human laws'.[11] Panizzi ends with a stirring call: 'We implore men of all parties, of all nations, of all creeds to raise a unanimous and unmistakeable cry of abhorrence in the name of outraged humanity against deeds to which pagan tyranny, oriental despotism and African ferocity can hardly find a parallel' – a decided exaggeration, but, doubtless, a creditable one in the circumstances.

It was lucky for Panizzi that his review was anonymous[12] and that the Neapolitan government had, at least officially, no knowledge of his authorship of it. Panizzi was now determined to go to

Naples himself and see what conditions there were really like. As he had already told Gladstone, he was profoundly sceptical of the ability, or, indeed, of the desire of the Neapolitan government to achieve any lasting reforms. Panizzi was, however, still of the opinion that King Ferdinand[13] himself, a genial, if ruffianly character, might somehow be unaware of the evil deeds that were perpetrated in his name. He determined, therefore, if he could, to see the King and to enlighten him as to what was going on. At all events, he was eager to exploit any possibility, however slight, of alleviating the lot of the wretched prisoners.

Gladstone warmly approved of his friend's idea. To obtain a second opinion on the state of the prisons would do much to counter the arguments of the defenders of the règime, but, in view of Panizzi's past record, how was he going to be able to obtain admission to the royal presence and the necessary authority to visit the prisoners?

Panizzi had for some time been in correspondence with Lord Shrewsbury,[14] a semi-invalid and prematurely aged peer, who spent most of his time in southern Italy. Shrewsbury was a very mild Whig and a very devout Catholic and was *persona grata* with the Neapolitan royal family. Panizzi had first written to him to solicit his aid in procuring some documents from the Vatican archives, in connection with a biography of Cardinal Alberoni, the eighteenth-century statesman, which he at this time was considering writing and which was, in the cunning Panizzi's opinion, an excellent excuse, in any case, to get into the good graces of that pious nobleman. The project fell through, as the Vatican authorities refused to grant the necessary permission, but Panizzi and Shrewsbury continued to correspond.

Both Panizzi and Gladstone were of the opinion that Shrewsbury might now be induced to accompany Panizzi on his proposed visit to King Ferdinand and, subsequently, to the prisons. Gladstone, indeed, was convinced that it would be far better for Shrewsbury himself to inspect the jails, whilst Panizzi remained quietly in the background, an 'unobserved and therefore independent companion'.[15]

To an English nobleman, whose devout Catholicism and more or less reactionary opinions were well known, doors would be opened which would remain for ever closed to an ex-Carbonaro

and a reputed friend of the dreaded Mazzini. Shrewsbury, unfortunately, after much wriggling and prevarication and despite
the most urgent pleas by Panizzi, begging him to accompany him
to Naples, would not undertake to be present there at the vital
time. Despairingly, Panizzi wrote to Gladstone: 'With him
[Shrewsbury] I might [do some good]. Shall I alone?'[16]

He now endeavoured to get letters of introduction to the Neapolitan authorities from other powerful friends, from Louis Napoleon, from the widowed Queen of the French, King Ferdinand's
aunt, and from her son, the Duc d'Aumale. He cannot make up his
mind. 'Tell me *at once* . . . shall I go?'[17] he implores Gladstone. In
his agony of indecision, Panizzi writes to his friend almost daily
and considers alternative ways of helping the prisoners. Dining
with Guizot, in England for old King Louis Philippe's funeral,
Panizzi presented the Frenchman with copies of Gladstone's
letters. Guizot, that stubborn reactionary, was not much help.
He considered the best plan was to approach the King of Naples
through the Emperor of Russia and through the aged Metternich
and promised Panizzi he would see what he could do.[18] Panizzi
must have felt little confidence in such intermediaries, and now
did his best to interest Aumale and other members of the Orleans
family. He breakfasted with the Queen of the French and her sons
and during the meal courteously but firmly urged that she should
remonstrate with her nephew. 'She answered . . . she never interfered, but I told her that a woman like her is bound to interfere
on the side of truth, justice and humanity.'[19] The Queen, doubtless
impressed by Panizzi's plain speaking, promised to do what she
could to help.

All these royal personages however proved to be of little real
assistance. Panizzi at last decided that he must himself go to Italy
and somehow or other, with or without a sponsor, reach Naples,
see the King and do something, however little, on behalf of the
prisoners.

On Saturday, September 25, 1851, he left England, bound for
Genoa. By some oversight, part of his baggage got left behind at
Calais and he had to wait three days at Paris, before he managed to
retrieve it. Panizzi used his enforced delay to urge his opinions on
the French government. He dined with the French Foreign Minister and discussed with him Gladstone's letters and Neapolitan

affairs in general. Before leaving England, Panizzi had been assured that he had every right to enter Neapolitan territory and that, as a British subject, he was fully entitled to the protection there of the British authorities.[20]

Gladstone had advised him on reaching Naples to contact at once two reliable men there, George Fagan,[21] the British attaché and Giacomo Lacaita,[22] the Legation's legal adviser. They, together with the Minister himself, Sir William Temple, were to prove invaluable allies, both now and in the not-too-distant future.

At last, on October 26, Panizzi arrived at Genoa. There he was given letters, telling him of the death of his sister, Margherita, since the death of his father six years before his only close relative. Panizzi was deeply grieved. He had been looking forward to seeing her in a few days' time and now it was too late. He was sorely tempted to give up and to return at once to England. His sense of duty urged him on and, cheered by a letter from Winter Jones,[23] he continued on his way. On reaching Rome, he was overjoyed to meet there, once again, his boyhood friend, Dr Minzi, who, so long ago, had helped him to escape from Modena. There, too, was Lord Shrewsbury, who presented Panizzi to the Pope, Pius IX. Despite his own position and the exalted circles in which he now moved, Panizzi's footsteps were dogged by spies throughout his stay at Rome and he thought it only prudent to make special arrangements as to what was to happen should he be kidnapped by secret agents.[24] On November 14, he left Rome and after considerable difficulties and delays, he was at last permitted to cross into Neapolitan territory. At Naples, Panizzi took up his residence at the Palazzo Roccella with his good friends Lord and Lady Holland. Despite the recent difference between Panizzi and Lord Holland, of which we shall speak later, both were delighted to see him and made him warmly welcome.

The British mission and its staff were at his full disposal and did everything in their power to assist him. George Fagan, the attaché and father of Louis Fagan, Panizzi's first biographer, was of the greatest help in putting him in touch with relatives of the imprisoned men and in accompanying him at his interview with King Ferdinand, which Lord Shrewsbury had, after all, managed to arrange.

Panizzi was still convinced, or, at least, regarded it as the one possible chance of alleviating the prisoners' wretched lot, that Ferdinand II knew nothing of the conditions within his own prisons. Panizzi had written the previous August to Shrewsbury, 'I start from this as a fact in my plans & *dreams*'[25] and now at last he was about to confront King Bomba himself, face to face. Hurriedly dashing into the church opposite the palace for a couple of minutes, so as to be able to answer truthfully the monarch's invariable first question, 'Have you been to Church?', Panizzi and Fagan were ushered into the royal presence.

Ferdinand was in a good mood and after the expected first question, listened with courteous patience while Panizzi lectured him on the sufferings of Poerio and the other political prisoners and on the abuses to be found throughout his kingdom. After some twenty minutes of listening to the great Pan in full spate, the King closed the interview with the words, '*Addio, terribile Panazzi*', and all was over. Ferdinand, who was by no means a fool, was quite aware of what was going on, but considered, with some justification, that his Neapolitans could be governed in no other way.[26]

Despite the continual presence of police spies, Panizzi seems to have enjoyed himself in Naples, playing practical jokes on the agents detailed to shadow his movements and astounding the local nobility by his fondness for horseplay. He was never unmindful, though, of the real object of his 'secret diplomatic mission', as Shrewsbury had called it.

On November 19, accompanied by Lord Feilding,[27] a recent convert to Catholicism and so regarded by Panizzi as a stand-in for Shrewsbury, he visited the Vicaria prison. With his usual painstaking thoroughness, he had prepared a detailed schedule of the particular points to be observed during his inspection, so as to miss nothing. Panizzi was deeply moved by the experience, as may be seen even in his purposely dispassionate account, both of what he saw that day and on his second visit three days later.

Gladstone had not exaggerated. Conditions there were even more terrible than he had feared. He left determined to do his utmost both to save his friends by any means within his power and to overthrow a government that permitted such atrocities to continue. Even Shrewsbury wrote to hope that the visit of Panizzi and Feilding might have done some good and to assure his friend that Sicilian prisons were much better governed than those of Naples, 'both for prisons and police'.[28]

Panizzi's stay was now drawing to a close. Lacaita, with whom he had struck up a warm friendship, decided that he too must at once leave Naples, rather than risk a second and more prolonged term of imprisonment, such as he had already undergone for assisting Gladstone the year before. A few days later, Panizzi himself left, the police spies shadowing him to the very end, but glad to see the last of '*quel pezzo grosso*', 'that big fellow'.[29] Safe at Genoa in Piedmontese territory he wrote to Gladstone to tell him of all that had happened: 'The trouble of my journey has been rewarded beyond what I could hope . . . I bring with me *proofs* that you have not said half what you could have justly said of that detestable government.'[30]

Panizzi decided to break his journey at Paris and succeeded in obtaining an interview with the Prince President. Louis Napoleon promised Panizzi to use his influence with the Neapolitan government to obtain some amelioration in the prisoners' condition and anything else that was at all possible.

Panizzi, with whom liking for this strange character was always mingled with a certain distrust, thought him to be 'too friendly by far'. He was now amazed and annoyed when Louis Napoleon, after dinner, 'suddenly took it in to his head to give me a decoration'. Panizzi, who detested all outward pomp, continued: 'It has made me miserable and I tremble to see it in the newspapers.'[31] To some extent, he managed to extricate himself from the embarrassing situation by telling the Prince President that, as an Englishman, he could not accept a foreign decoration without the permission of his own government, and subsequently took good care to ensure that despite the efforts of the French authorities to award him the unwelcome honour, no such permission was forthcoming. So much for what Gladstone described as the 'homage from vice to virtue'.[32]

By the second week in December, he was safely back in the Museum and trying to get in touch with Gladstone to tell him everything. Shrewsbury wrote, congratulating Panizzi on having safely returned from his journey through France, 'in the midst of those robbers & assassins the socialists & Rouges',[33] amongst whom he plainly considered should be included Lord Palmerston.

Gladstone was now considering whether or not he should write a further pamphlet on the subject of Naples. Panizzi begged him not to bring out such a 'fresh bill of indictment' for the moment. Somewhat reluctantly, Gladstone agreed, expressing the hope that Panizzi himself would publish an account of his experiences and on the state of affairs in Rome.[34] Panizzi, on the other hand, thought that fresh attacks on the Neapolitan authorities would only increase the severity of the conditions under which the prisoners were held and that alternative measures must now be considered.

In his earnest desire to do something, however little, for the prisoners, Panizzi made up his mind to try and bring Settembrini's young son, Raffaele, back to England. Whilst in Naples, he had become acquainted with the wife of the prisoner and with his two children, a boy and a girl. The Neapolitan authorities were inflicting upon the family all sorts of petty humiliations. No school would take the boy and he was becoming wild and unmanageable. To help the parents, Panizzi decided that the only thing to do was to have Raffaele educated in England.

It was not, however, easy to get him out of the country. Temple wrote in January: 'Your protégé is still here for want of any means of conveyance to Malta.'[35] Lord Holland had agreed to cope with the financial arrangements and deal with the money contributed by Gladstone and others for the lad's journey. Though there were many difficulties and disappointments, all were at last surmounted. In March 1852 young Raffaele arrived in England. Panizzi treated him like a son and the very first day, whisked him round to 11 Downing Street to see Gladstone, who, unfortunately, proved to be out. Panizzi wrote to the Chancellor, begging him to look after young Settembrini, should he himself suddenly die, 'so that he is not left friendless in the world'[36] and Gladstone freely promised to do so. Soon the boy was packed off to school and Panizzi had to admit: 'I confess I am weak enough to feel parting with him.'[37]

Unfortunately, all did not go well. Young Settembrini, a high-spirited active lad, was soon in trouble. Panizzi was deeply hurt and upset. He wrote off to Lady Holland in Naples to tell her the bad news. He had received a letter from the headmaster of the school at Richmond, Yorkshire, to which the boy had been sent.

'I have reason to think,' he wrote, 'that detestable boy has again been guilty of the same conduct of which he was guilty here.'[38] This was apparently pilfering, not really surprising in a young Neapolitan, deprived for some years of a father's influence, but deeply shocking to Panizzi, with his high moral standards. No words were now too bad for the 'unprincipled wretch', but Panizzi would still do what he could for young Louison, as he called him, for his poor father's sake. In a similar strain, he writes also to Rutherfurd: 'The fact that young Louison has behaved so ill at Richmond . . . that nothing remained for me to do but to send him to Italy . . . to see what can be done for him there.'[39] Panizzi now, therefore, made up his mind to send Louison to his old friend, Ambrogio Berchet, who was running a military academy at Turin.[40] There he would get the strict discipline and firm handling which, in Panizzi's opinion, he so clearly needed.

So that the whole responsibility should be his alone, Panizzi now sent back to the donors all the money subscribed for the boy's education and decided to pay for his education and keep entirely out of his own pocket. Panizzi was chiefly concerned at the effect all this upset might have on Raffaele's unfortunate parents and was grieved to hear from Temple that the poor mother 'was very much affected by the conduct of her son and feels deeply the bad return you have met with'.[41]

Panizzi's worries were by no means over. On December 16, young Settembrini left Liverpool, bound for Genoa, generously provided with pocket money by his stern yet kindly foster-father. Everything was paid for by Panizzi and arrangements were made for the lad to be met at Genoa and taken to school at Turin.[42] 'I promised to support him if he behaved well,' wrote Panizzi, 'if not, I wrote to him I would give him up altogether.'[43]

But Louison did not settle down at Turin under Berchet, an old soldier of Napoleon and doubtless overstrict with the wild young lad. The end came soon. The following July, Panizzi wrote to Lacaita: 'I believe he [Louison] has now left for Brazil as apprentice on board a merchant ship.'[44] The young man had, at last, found in the sea his true vocation. Hardened and disciplined by the rough life of a merchant seaman, and by service in the Crimean War, he was to reappear dramatically in a few years' time.

There remained, however, his father. Separated now from his friend Poerio, Settembrini was confined with other political prisoners on the island prison of San Stefano, but managed to continue to conduct a clandestine correspondence with Panizzi. Letters were smuggled in and out of prison in shoes, in the hemp supplied to the prisoners, or in other hiding places. All the letters passed through the hands of Signora Settembrini, a devoted and capable woman, who had also the full and unstinting assistance of Temple and Fagan. Temple, in particular, was tireless in his efforts to help Settembrini and the other prisoners, even though there was little he could do openly. He had sent back to his brother, Palmerston, a mass of documentary evidence on the various political trials, which the latter passed on to Panizzi to see what use he could make of them.

Temple continued to shelter and protect Signora Settembrini in so far as he was able, and saw to it that Panizzi received the prisoners' letters as quickly as possible, together with the latest information on the general situation at Naples. Meanwhile, in London, Panizzi was using what influence he possessed with the newly proclaimed Emperor, Napoleon III, to do something about the prisoners and even tried to get Vienna to persuade Bomba to be more merciful. Gladstone was trying to do what he could through Clarendon for the 'poor Neapolitans' and asked Panizzi if he could think of anything further he could do. But all was in vain. As Temple wrote, in a covering note to a letter of Settembrini's of March 1855: 'Things here are either stationary or getting worse.'[45]

In desperation, Panizzi decided on drastic action. Whether Settembrini himself first suggested a possible escape or whether Panizzi conceived the idea is now impossible to say with any certainty, but the planning of this wild venture was wholly Panizzi's. On July 26, 1855, he wrote to Lacaita[46] that he was able to arrange the escape of six of the prisoners and with his usual thoroughness, set about making the necessary arrangements. He had decided to direct the escape in person and, with all the ardour of his revolutionary youth, carefully planned the great break-out.

He approached selected friends to raise the necessary funds and although some merely wished him good luck and offered no money, others responded nobly. Within a very short time, he had collected between £1,000 and £1,500. Lord Holland subscribed heavily. Mrs Gladstone, by no means a wealthy woman, gave him £100 of her own and collected £200 more from among her friends. Panizzi borrowed £100 to give himself, a sum he could ill afford. Naturally, all had to be done hurriedly and in the greatest secrecy, lest the Neapolitan authorities get wind of what was afoot. The first need was for a fast steamer, but the demands on the available shipping of the Crimean War, which had just broken out, made this a matter of the greatest difficulty.[47]

Haywood, with his influence in Liverpool shipping circles, was eager to help and set about looking for suitable vessels.

Panizzi now applied for an extra month's leave of absence. This was duly granted by the Trustees, with permission to go to northern Italy and also to Tuscany and Perugia to examine the books from the library of a Mr Philip Senesi. Little did the Trustees dream of what their fiery Keeper of Printed Books was really up to, planning to raid the coasts of a friendly power, with the active connivance of at least two of Her Majesty's representatives abroad.[48]

For Panizzi had now set off to meet his great friend, Sir James Hudson,[49] his 'caro Giacomo', the British Minister at Turin, who, like his colleague Temple at Naples, was privy to the whole plot. Early in August, Panizzi arrived at Genoa. There Hudson introduced him to Agostino Bertani.[50] Bertani, a veteran conspirator and adherent of Mazzini, now put Panizzi in touch with that other famous revolutionary, Garibaldi.[51] The hero of the Roman Republic, now once more a merchant seaman, was delighted with so bold a plot, one most likely to appeal to his gallant and romantic nature. He assured Panizzi that it was quite feasible and, indeed, given luck, had every chance of success. Garibaldi also plotted a course for the rescue ship, which was to arrive at a lonely beach near the prison on a dark and moonless night.

Most unfortunately, Garibaldi was himself unable to take command of the vessel, as Panizzi had hoped. Had he been able to do so and had Panizzi's frantic efforts to get hold of a suitable ship been more successful, there can be but little doubt that, with Garibaldi's courage, skill and seamanship, and Panizzi's drive and energy, the hazardous enterprise would have been crowned with success.

But, in the meantime, things were going very wrong. Haywood wrote to Panizzi that he had heard of a 'beautiful little steamer',[52] just launched on the Clyde. Panizzi, delighted, telegraphed for more details, but, somehow, the deal fell through. Bertani had now sent an agent of his own to England to get hold of a vessel, but the man was slow and incompetent. Panizzi chafed at the constant delays, and drew up the details of the plans for the escape. Panizzi, who would have made an excellent staff officer, had worked the whole thing out and had managed, through Temple,[53] to get the plan smuggled in to Settembrini.

The vessel, with Panizzi on board, was to approach the island and pass to eastward of the 'convent', that is to say, the prison, one day in October. She would be flying a white pennant at one or more of her mastheads. On reaching the nearest point to the 'convent', the pennants were to be hauled down for a few minutes and then run up again immediately afterwards. The ship would then carry on her way. At midnight, she was to stand in as near as possible. A boat or boats would then approach the shore, but would not actually run right in until a light was shown from the land. The prisoners, having made their way down to the beach and signalled to the boats, would then be asked for the password. This was the name of Louison's friend, that is, 'Panizzi', the boat then giving the answer, Louison's father's name, 'Luigi'. The boats were to wait off-shore until four in the morning and, if no signal was given and no prisoners arrived, would then return to the ship. She herself would put out to sea and come back again the following night, when the operation would be repeated. If there was still no news from the shore, the plan would have to be considered a failure. A shortened version of these instructions was sent to Fagan at Naples to give to Signora Settembrini. The thoroughness of Panizzi's planning was again in evidence. Should she not be able to memorize the letter, she was to enclose it in a wax pill, covered with gutta percha, 'a piece of which is enclosed'[54] and swallow it if in danger of arrest and discovery. Fagan approved of the plan, but warned Panizzi to be very careful, as spies and police were everywhere and all members of the mission were now under constant surveillance.

Temple, too, had been making arrangements to facilitate the prisoners' escape,[55] and wrote to Panizzi giving details. Settembrini had managed to smuggle out of prison a further letter, giving what particulars he was able of the general layout of the prison and at what spot the ship's boats might best meet them. Temple duly forwarded this note to Panizzi at Genoa.[56]

All these hopes, however, were doomed to disappointment, Panizzi's forethought and careful planning was to go for nought and the unfortunate prisoners were condemned to further years of suffering. Luck, throughout, had been against the conspirators. The war had made it almost impossible to charter a suitable vessel and Panizzi was overjoyed when he, at last, heard that a small paddle steamer, *The Isle of Thanet*, had been purchased. She appeared to be just what they needed for the rescue operation. But disappointment followed. First, *The Isle of Thanet* was damaged in a sudden squall, due, it was said, to having too much coal on board.[57] She was forced to put back to Hull to carry out repairs. Put right at a cost of a further £300, towards the end of October, she set sail once more, only to be a total loss in a second storm off Yarmouth.

Panizzi was broken-hearted, but refused to give up hope. Together with Bertani and Garibaldi, further plans were made. Panizzi had had to return to the Museum and Garibaldi paid a lightning visit to him there, in February 1856, to discuss future arrangements. Things still continued to go wrong. Fagan had now been transferred to La Plata. 'If he leaves Naples,' wrote Panizzi, in despair, to Gladstone, 'I am paralysed'[58] and in June, Temple himself, now a sick man, came home.

Hudson strongly advised Panizzi to give up all idea of a rescue, at least for the moment. England had broken off diplomatic relations with Naples[59] and a successful attempt, even more an unsuccessful one, might well cause a major diplomatic crisis. The association with their plans of Bertani and other extremists was likely to cause acute embarrassment to Cavour and prejudice his schemes to unite Italy under the aegis of Piedmont. Bertani was, indeed, being very difficult and wished to use the money already raised to finance an armed attack on San Stefano in order to liberate all the prisoners by force, not only the political prisoners, but also the common felons confined there and for stirring up revolutionary movements at Naples and within the Papal States. Panizzi refused to have anything to do with such desperate schemes and strongly urged that the money should be used, either to help the families of the prisoners or else left for a more favourable opportunity. He wrote to Gladstone that he would be able to return 'every farthing' to the subscribers to the 'Genoese venture', and continued: 'I mean to issue an habeas corpus and pledge my honour to pay one thousand pounds to whomsoever brings me the body of S.[ettembrini]. I can do no more.'[60]

Completely downcast at the ruin of all his hopes, he was comforted by kindly and encouraging letters from Gladstone and from Temple, and, above all, one from Settembrini himself: 'Do not, however, think of me. I am inured to suffering and am not worth so much trouble. I grieve on your account the more as my own ill-luck seems to pursue those who interest themselves on my behalf.'[61]

The majority of the subscribers to the rescue fund declined to take advantage of Panizzi's offer to return their money, and the total sum, now amounting to about £1,000, was entrusted to Gladstone to be used as he thought fit, to relieve the dependants of the prisoners. The unfortunate Signora Settembrini was being persecuted by the Neapolitan police and took refuge in the Palazzo Roccella, where Lord and Lady Holland were living. The latter were somewhat alarmed, and not a little annoyed at this, since Signora Settembrini's action might cause extreme embarrassment and even danger, not necessarily only to themselves, but also to their host. To his disgust, they returned to Panizzi the money which he had forwarded to them to give to the Settembrini family, and, for the moment, refused to take any further part in his plans.

The prisoners' sufferings were, however, almost over. In December 1856, the Neapolitan government, in an effort to regain the good will of the western powers, made an offer. The political prisoners might either sue publicly for pardon or else be exiled to the Argentine. Settembrini and others of his companions favoured rather the second choice. Panizzi was emphatically against it, as he feared that, if transported to South America, they would there be enslaved, whereas, if they sued for pardon, they would, at least, be safe in life and limb.

Matters dragged on until December 1858, when the government issued a decree offering the prisoners merely a choice between emigration to the Argentine or indefinitely continued im-

Photograph of the construction of the Reading Room, c. 1855

Mary Augusta, 1812–1889,
wife of Henry Edward,
fourth Lord Holland.

Sir James Hudson, 1810–
1885.

prisonment. All the prisoners, save for Poerio, were willing to accept the offer to go to the Argentine, but his continued refusal led to the abandonment of the whole scheme. On January 6, 1859, however, a second decree was issued, permitting sixty-six of the prisoners, including both Poerio and Settembrini, to go to New York.[62]

This offer was joyfully accepted by all. In any case, as Palmerston had already said to Panizzi, they were not bound to stay there and would soon recover their full liberty 'by two voyages across the Atlantic'.[63] Everything was now fixed for the prisoners' departure. They were still officially 'galley slaves', and were still subject to prison discipline. From the Neapolitan vessel, *Stromboli*, Settembrini managed to write to Panizzi, hoping to be able to see him soon in England and asking for any news of his son, Raffaele. The poor man was to see them both far sooner than he had ever dared to hope.

Meanwhile, back in England, Panizzi was making what arrangements he could for their eventual reception and welfare on the other side of the Atlantic. As it was feared that the United States government might prove unco-operative, Panizzi had consulted Stevens and had also made approaches through the United States minister in London. Stevens had taken steps to forward all necessary information and money to the appropriate authorities in New York but, happily, there was to be no need.

On his arrival at Cadiz, Settembrini was informed that an English officer wished to see him. Somewhat puzzled, he consented, but to his delighted surprise, he now found that the 'English officer' was his own son, Raffaele, in disguise. At the moment, speech was impossible. All the young man was able to tell his father was: 'You shall not go to America.' Once on the high seas, Raffaele had planned to seize the ship, if need be by force, and induce the captain to return to Lisbon. The prisoners had now been transferred to an American ship the *David Stewart* and with young Settembrini on board, now further disguised as a steward, they set sail for New York. The plot was now disclosed to all the prisoners, who received the news joyfully. Only his father, Luigi, absolutely forbade any violence in order to effect their escape, or the use of the arms which his enterprising son had smuggled on board.

9

Within a few days, however, the exiles, led by Raffaele, had made the captain, under the threat of their seizing the ship and navigating her themselves, change course and put in to the nearest British port.

Ashore at Cork, they were given a tumultuous reception to be followed by even more enthusiastic welcomes at Bristol and in London. A fund was set up for the benefit of the prisoners, of which Panizzi became the secretary. The administration of this and the constant worry and frustration which it entailed caused Panizzi many a headache and he displayed an uncharacteristic patience and tact in dealing with some of the more troublesome claimants. To him, any annoyance and inconvenience he may have been caused was more than repaid by the thought that he was doing it for his beloved Italy. It was a fitting climax to his unsparing efforts on the prisoners' behalf for more than nine years. Throughout this period, Panizzi, working in close collaboration with James Hudson at Turin, was acting as the unofficial ambassador of Cavour.[64] The two men had first met in 1852, and the Piedmontese had immediately begun to make use of Panizzi as a channel by means of which his views could be circulated throughout English political circles and a steady influence brought to bear on such important figures as Palmerston, Russell and Clarendon. Panizzi undertook this task with the utmost willingness. By doing so, he felt that, in no inconsiderable way, he was helping the cause of Italian freedom which he had long held so dear. His close friendship with Hudson was now of great value. A constant stream of entreaties, memoranda and advice poured out from Turin, on every aspect of the struggle to defeat Austria and to achieve the unity of Italy.

Panizzi's growing friendship with Prosper Mérimée[65] enabled him to obtain the ear of Napoleon III and to tender valuable advice to that erratic monarch. Although, until the final triumph of Lord Palmerston in 1859, he was not able to exert so powerful an influence behind the scenes on the course of foreign policy, Panizzi did his utmost to bring to the notice of his many friends in high places the facts of the Italian struggle and to sustain the vacillating interest of the English public. Cavour, at any rate, had no doubt of the great value of Panizzi's services. 'Panizzi,' he said, 'has kept a truly Italian soul.'[66] Panizzi himself was often less sanguine. In

1858, just before the final risings, he had again travelled throughout Lombardy, Tuscany and the Romagna. He wrote despairingly to Gladstone. 'Poor Italy is going to ruin faster than ever . . . The Papal States are in a worse condition than ever . . . There is nothing else for that poor country than the destruction of the temporal power of the Pope.'[67]

The previous year, he had at last succeeded in visiting his birthplace, Brescello. The old Duke was now dead and his successor had more serious worries to contend with than the arrival in his Duchy of the distinguished man, who had, so many years before, been a conspirator against the régime.

Panizzi was full of joy to see the little town once more. 'The church of Brescello! The theatre of Brescello . . . the very house where I was born,' he wrote on his return to his old friend Minzi.[68] But joy was mingled with sorrow. Many of those he had known and loved were dead, his parents and his only sister amongst them. Though he spent the whole day going from house to house, renewing old acquaintanceships, he felt he was a stranger. He had been gone too long. As far as we know, he never saw it again, even when staying with his cousins nearby. The memories it aroused were too painful, and, like many another great man, he had outgrown the narrow circles in which he had been raised.

Two years later, after the overthrow of the Duke of Modena and the other monarchs of northern Italy, Panizzi spent a holiday with his cousin Prospero Cugini at the latter's villa at San Maurizio, near Reggio. He took the opportunity to search the archives for any documents which might further discredit the fallen régime. The great powers were considering enforcing the restoration of the princely rulers and Panizzi was determined to do what he could to influence public opinion against any such attempt. In a happy mood, despite his recurrent bad health, he basked in the warm Italian sun and enjoyed the hospitality of the Cugini family. He attended the assembly at Bologna, where the independence of the Romagna was proclaimed and then went to Parma, to be present at the opening of their national assembly. Everywhere, he wrote to Gladstone, was calm and orderly, but the whole people were determined never again to submit to their former masters. Even his Cugini cousins, who had faithfully served the Ducal authorities all their lives, now were strongly of the opinion that it would be a disaster for the Duke to return.[69] The universal wish, in Modena, as in Parma and throughout the Romagna, was to be united, as speedily as possible, to the Piedmontese kingdom. Panizzi, with the aid of Palmerston, the new Prime Minister and of Lord John Russell, the new Foreign Secretary, was determined to do what he could to achieve this end.

Although we know that all their efforts were to be crowned with success, Panizzi himself had many anxious moments. He had visited Cavour, for a short while out of office, and had discussed with him the whole situation. On his way back to England, he had vainly tried to secure a personal interview with Napoleon. He had, however, succeeded in obtaining, through Fould,[70] the Minister of Finance, a summary of the Emperor's views, which he then had passed on back to Cavour.[71]

All through this vital period, Panizzi was the channel through which the ideas and intentions of Russell, Cavour and Louis Napoleon circulated from one to another in a way impossible to have achieved through the official representatives of the countries concerned. In addition, Panizzi was himself acting as an unofficial ambassador for the provisional governments of Tuscany and Modena and through his hands passed all the threads which were to unite these ancient states to the new kingdom of Italy. In April 1856 Cavour had come to England. Panizzi was more impressed than ever by the great statesman. 'Cavour's . . . perseverance, courage and patience are above all praise,' he wrote to Lord Holland. 'Cavour in person [has just] come to see me. He has the greatest confidence in the Emperor,'[72] a confidence which his English friends, including Panizzi, did not always share. Panizzi took Cavour, together with d'Azeglio the Sardinian minister, to see Lord John Russell at his house, Pembroke Lodge, in Richmond Park and did all he could to help and assist Cavour during his stay in this country.

Within a few months, the dream was fulfilled, thanks to the skill and energy of Garibaldi and to Cavour's masterly diplomacy. Panizzi had been one of the first to know of Garibaldi's plans for the invasion of Sicily and had raised the money to buy a ship to join the expedition. Although he admired Garibaldi himself intensely, Panizzi had little time for some of the men who surrounded him and was deeply concerned lest the intention of some of the more radical of Garibaldi's followers to attack the Papal States might bring about an intervention by the French, an unmitigated disaster to the Italian cause. Palmerston, of late, had grown very suspicious of the intentions of Louis Napoleon and fear and suspicion of the French was, indeed, general throughout England. It was a mistrust that Panizzi, as in so many other ways, more English than the English, on the whole, shared, despite his personal acquaintance with the Emperor and with his family. More will be said in a later chapter as to his friendship with them, a friendship that, notwithstanding Panizzi's grave doubts as to the wisdom of much of the Imperial policy, was to survive the catastrophe of 1870.

An unfortunate incident now nearly marred that friendship. In July 1857, Panizzi had been introduced to Felice Orsini,[73] the Italian patriot, who had recently achieved fame by a spectacular escape from an Austrian prison, in which he lay condemned to death. Although somewhat suspicious of his new acquaintance's republican leanings and, despite Orsini's assurances to the contrary, of his secret connections with Mazzini, Panizzi was struck with the gallant soldier.[74] A warm liking sprang up between the two men. Panizzi always seems to have been captivated by men of action, such as Garibaldi and Orsini, men such as he might dream of being, and men, too, whose self-sacrifices in the cause of Italy appealed to his ardent patriotism. The two men became warmly attached to each other and it was a terrible shock for Panizzi, when he learnt, on Saturday, January 16, 1858, that his friend had been arrested for an attempted assassination of the Emperor Napoleon, an outrage which had caused the death of many people. To inquirers, that afternoon, at Brooks' Panizzi roundly denied that the suspected assassin could possibly be the Orsini he knew, since the two of them had an appointment to call on Palmerston the following day. Panizzi was greatly shaken and distressed by this event. He had been completely deceived by Orsini and seems to have been quite unaware of the plot which was being secretly prepared against the Emperor.

At all events, Louis Napoleon seems to have borne Panizzi no grudge and, in the summer of 1860, invited the Principal Librarian to spend a holiday with the Empress and himself at their villa at Biarritz. Panizzi was then able to tell the Emperor of Cavour's plans for the final unification of Italy and of the hostile reaction in England to the latest moves of the French. On his return to England, Panizzi at once made known to 'a very influential personage', presumably Russell, the result of his conversations with Napoleon and to remove, at least to a certain extent, the prejudices which were endangering the relations between the two countries at this critical juncture. Despite Panizzi's own doubts, he undoubtedly did much to bring about an improvement in Anglo-French affairs and to clear away many of the misunderstandings which had grown up between the two allies.

Louis Napoleon himself thought so and greatly valued all that Panizzi was doing to preserve the entente. As early as October 23, 1860, Mérimée told his friend that he had breakfasted with the Emperor and that the latter 'desired to be remembered to you . . . and to thank you for all you are saying and doing'.[75] Panizzi's task was to make known the French and Italian points of view in English political circles and, in particular, to Palmerston and Russell, who with Gladstone, were those members of the Cabinet determined to bring about Italian unity, with or without the assistance of France. He had to combat all the time the pro-Austrian and anti-French and anti-Italian sentiments of the Queen, of the Prince Consort and of the bulk of the Tory party. 'Believe me, my dear Sir,' wrote Dr Conneau, Napoleon's intimate friend and adviser, 'that by making known the character and opinions of the Emperor to your friends, you will help the cause of Italy.'[76] This was what Panizzi never forgot. He might be suspicious of the equivocal conduct of this strange man. He could never fail to remember that it was through him that much of Italy had been rescued from the Austrians and then safely united.

Throughout the sixties, Panizzi constantly laboured to present the French point of view to his English friends and to calm their doubts. 'You have seen,' wrote Mérimée, 'what few foreigners have seen, *their domestic life*, and you know more about their dispositions than all the Ministers of Europe. You can do much good I think, by giving utterance to your impressions.'[77]

The Roman question, which bedevilled Anglo-French relations until 1870 was now Panizzi's special care. With the help of Mérimée, he put both the English and Italian case to the not unsympathetic Emperor. Even the Empress, then considered both at home and abroad the mainstay of Napoleon's pro-papal policy, could sign herself, in a letter to the old Italian rebel, 'Your political ally, Eugénie'[78] and would listen to his wise advice.

Panizzi's reputation as a great Italian patriot rests securely on his work, during these difficult years, for the liberation and unification of his country. Other men, Victor Emmanuel, Cavour, Garibaldi, may have dared more for Italy; none, not even Cavour, was in the position to render her such unique services as was Panizzi. An Italian by birth, an Englishman by choice and by adoption, only he, with his intimate knowledge of both countries, was able to provide the necessary link between England and Italy in this vital decade. Only he was on terms of friendship with Palmerston and Russell, with Gladstone and Clarendon and with a host of minor figures. Only he enjoyed close relations with Cavour, with Victor Emmanuel, with Louis Napoleon and with the new ruling men of Italy and could make plain their most secret intentions to the leaders of his adopted country. It was, of course, a matter of the greatest good fortune that, during these months, Palmerston and Russell and not the pro-Austrian Derby, were in power, since Panizzi never enjoyed the same close connections with the Tory leaders as he did with the Whigs. His political judgement might, at times, be unreliable, coloured maybe too much by his unquenchable hatred of Austria, yet in his love for Italy and in his determination to serve, both her and his equally cherished adopted country, he never faltered for a moment.

NOTES TO CHAPTER 13

1 Morley, I, p. 389.

2 Morley, I, p. 389. He continues, 'The case had doubtless been opened to him by Panizzi . . . a man of warm, large and free nature, an accomplished man of letters, and a victim of political persecution who came to this country a nearly starving refugee.'

3 *Letter*, p. 15.

4 Carlo Poerio, 1803–1867.

5 Luigi Settembrini, 1813–1876.

6 Panizzi assisted Gladstone in reading the proofs. [Add. MS. 36, 716. f.177.]

7 Add. MS. 36, 716. f.272.

8 Add. MS. 36, 716. f.242.

9 Add. MS. 44, 274, f.24.

10 Add. MS. 44, 274. f.27.

11 *Edinburgh Review*, July/October, 1851.

12 A.P. to Haywood, March 20, 1852. '. . . my article in the *Edinburgh Review*'. Quoted Fagan, II, p. 127.

13 Ferdinand II of Naples, 1810–1849. Earned for himself the nickname of 'King Bomba' by his ferocious repression of the Sicilian revolt in 1848.

14 John Talbot, Earl of Shrewsbury, 1791–1852. 'A person of singularly mild and gentle disposition and of refined and elegant tastes.' Died of malaria at Naples.

15 Add. MS. 36, 716. f.289.

16 Add. MS. 44, 274. f.51 [August 4, 1851.]

17 Add. M.S. 44, 274. f.51.

18 Add. MS. 44, 274. ff.66, 71.

19 Add. MS. 44, 274. f.75. Subsequently Panizzi wrote on hearing that the Queen was dying, 'I grieve for her. I never thought I should for any of her family.' [A.P. to Lord Holland, November 24, 1855.] [*Holland House Papers*.]

20 Add. MS. 36, 716. f.307.

21 Add. MS. 36, 716. f.316.

22 Sir James Lacaita, 1813–1895.

23 PP. 1851. ff.153, 160. Jones writes hoping 'that the great object you have in view may be accomplished' and in his subsequent letter: 'I do hope you will reach Naples. Having done so much it would be much to be regretted if you should be obliged to stop short.'

24 *Daily News*, November 18, 1851. Add. MS. 36, 716. f.359

25 Add. MS. 36, 716. f.303.

26 As did Shrewbury. 'I do not believe,' he wrote to Panizzi, 'in the possibility of the constitutional system in these countries in these times.' [Shrewsbury to A.P., May 21, 1851. Add. MS. 36, 716. f.214.]

27 Rudolph Feilding, 1823–1892. Styled Viscount Feilding until succeeded as Earl of Denbigh in 1865.

28 Add. MS. 36, 716. f.352.

29 Fagan, II, p. 110.

30 Add. MS. 44, 274. f.84.

31 Add. MS. 44, 274. f.97. See also letters to Haywood and Rutherfurd in Fagan, II, p. 113. To Holland Panizzi wrote, 'Nothing could be more cordial than his reception nor more friendly than his reproaches that I had never called on him when at Paris before . . . If faith is to be put on words I have every reason to hope that I have not taken so much trouble uselessly . . . Great politicians laugh at my innocence for placing the slightest reliance on his word.' [A.P. to Lord Holland, December 24, 1851.] [*Holland House Papers.*]

32 Add. MS. 36, 716. f.384.

33 Add. MS. 36, 716. f.375.

34 Add. MS. 36, 716. f.386.

35 Add. MS. 36, 716. f.388.

36 Add. MS. 44, 274. f.107.

37 A.P. to Rutherfurd, n.d. [1852] *Rutherfurd Papers*. Panizzi also wrote to Holland: 'Nothing shall be omitted to reclaim him . . . his comfort, health and happiness shall be attended to as if he were my own son.' [A.P. to Lord Holland, December 24, 1852.] [*Holland House Papers.*]

38 A.P. to Lady Holland, November 20, [1852.] *Holland House Papers.*

39 A.P. to Rutherfurd, December 21, [1852.] *Rutherfurd Papers.*

A.P. to Lady Holland, February 8, 1853. *Holland House Papers.*

41 Add. MS. 36, 716. f. 472.
9*

42 See also *Rutherfurd Papers*.

43 A.P. to Lady Holland, December 15, 1852. *Holland House Papers*.

44 Quoted in Brooks, p. 105.

45 Add. MS. 36, 717. f.104.

46 Add. MS. 36, 717. f.139.

47 'It has been impossible to hire a steamer [in Italy owing to the risk of discovery by the Neapolitan authorities]. I have got my own captain and sailors and have sent to England to purchase a steamer.' [A.P. to Lord Holland, September 5, 1855.] [*Holland House Papers*.]

48 *Trustees' Minute* of July 28, 1855. Panizzi eventually excused himself for not reaching Florence by informing the Trustees that he had been prevented from doing so by an outbreak of cholera in that city. He offered, however, to return the money had had received for his journey. [Add. MS. 36, 717. f.226.]

49 Sir James Hudson, 1810–1885. As private secretary to William IV, it was he who was sent to Rome to summon Peel to return to form a government on the downfall of Melbourne in 1834. British envoy at Turin, 1851–1863.

50 Agostini Bertani, 1812–1886. Physician and revolutionary.

51 Giuseppe Garibaldi, 1807–1882.

52 Add. MS. 36, 717. f.146.

53 Add. MS. 36, 717. f.155.

54 Fagan, II, p. 140.

55 By bribing the guards and also the proprietor of the small trattoria through which the escapers must pass. This man had to be induced to chain up his dogs. [Add. MS. 36, 717. f.177.]

56 Add. MS. 36, 717. ff.160, 161.

57 One of the paddle wheels gave way and was smashed to pieces before the vessel could be stopped.

58 Add. MS. 44, 274. f.154.

59 Over an alleged insult to George Fagan in the San Carlo Opera House.

60 Add. MS. 44, 274. f.157.

61 Fagan, II, p. 142.

62 'An act attributed more to fear than to clemency,' wrote Odo Russell from Rome.

63 Fagan II, p. 149.

64 Camillo Benso, Count of Cavour, 1810–1861. Panizzi had an extremely high opinion of Cavour. 'Tell Cavour I have always admired his patriotism but never did I think him capable of so great a sacrifice as he is now making.' [i.e. surrendering Nice and Savoy to Louis Napoleon.] [A.P. to Lord Holland February 19, 1856.] [*Holland House Papers.*]

65 Prosper Mérimée, 1803–1870. Writer and politician.

66 Add. MS. 36, 719. f.322.

67 Add. MS. 44, 274. f.178.

68 Fagan, II, p. 35.

69 Add. MS. 44, 274, f.185.

70 Achille Fould, 1800–1867.

71 Panizzi was very despondent at the English reaction to all these events, of the 'sort of patronizing feeling in this country in favour of Sardinia, but the nation at large is still essentially Austrian. The "Protestants" cheer the Sardinian government in the foolish hope that Piedmont is becoming Protestant [as had the Duke of Lucca for a few years]. And the cheering will cease when it is observed that it is tolerant, not Protestant.' [A.P. to Lord Holland, April 14, 1856.] [*Holland House Papers.*]

72 A.P. to Lord Holland, April 19, 1856. *Holland House Papers.*

73 Felice Orsini, 1819–1858.

74 'He had given up Mazzini and all his wicked absurdities that he was quite a convert to the opinion that Italy had nothing to hope from anyone but Piedmont . . . so that I can hardly believe he is the same man.' [A.P. to Lord Holland, July 19, 1857.] [*Holland House Papers.*]

75 Mérimée to A.P., *Mérimée*, I, p. 145.

76 Add. MS. 36, 721. f.119.

77 Mérimée to A.P., *Mérimée*, I, p. 281.

78 *Mérimée*, I, p. 346.

14

PRINCIPAL LIBRARIAN

I T I S now time to leave the courts and chancelleries of Europe and to return to the smaller world of the British Museum, for it must never be forgotten that this determined plotter and patriot, this frequenter of the company of Emperors and their would-be assassins, was at the same time fulfilling the role of a hard-working public servant. We left Panizzi safely, at last, at the summit of his official career, head of that great institution which he had entered, a young refugee, nearly thirty years before. But as the Duke of Somerset wrote to the newly appointed Principal Librarian, there were a great many improvements to be made in the system and conduct[1] of the British Museum and Panizzi was the man to tackle them.

Two outstanding problems faced Panizzi during the ten years during which he held the Principal Librarianship: to ensure that his staff of all ranks would receive such salaries as would enable the Museum to obtain and to keep the best men available at every level and the perennial question of space. Once again, the buildings were inadequate for the proper accommodation and display of the greatly increased collections now committed to his charge.

Panizzi's first act as Principal Librarian was to send a letter to the Heads of Departments, formally telling them of his appointment and asking for their full co-operation in the tasks which lay ahead, 'that efficient assistance which is absolutely necessary for the good of the service'.[2] In turn, the Keepers replied, assuring their new chief of their loyal and willing support. All, that is, except Sir Frederic! Still bitter and disgruntled, he utterly refused to answer, leaving the task to his Assistant Keeper, Bond. Panizzi was not having any more of Sir Frederic's nonsense. He at once wrote to the Archbishop, as the senior of the Principal Trustees, to complain of Madden's lack of courtesy.[3]

'It is,' he wrote, 'unhappily too true that Sir F. Madden will not speak to me,' nor would the enraged Keeper of Manuscripts even write. Somewhat ingenuously, Panizzi goes on, 'I never intentionally by airs or words gave offence to Sir F. Madden and I am at loss to conceive the ground of his conduct . . . Such personal antipathies should cease,' and it was now up to the Archbishop to make Madden see reason and to realize that a new reign had begun. 'I mean to do my duty conscientiously,' he declared, 'with all due regard to other people's feelings but firmly,' and firm was the one thing he would always be.

What the Archbishop said, we do not know, but on April 3 a short note from Madden at last arrived and honour was satisfied. But on the whole, relations with his Keepers was not to be one of Panizzi's difficulties. Madden, perhaps less aggressive with age or more resigned to a hostile fate, remained comparatively quiescent, leaving more and more the conduct of affairs in the hands of Bond, who had always got on well with Panizzi. And, elsewhere, further changes and developments made Panizzi's task, in this respect, comparatively easy.

It had long been evident that the Department of Antiquities, presided over for so many years by Edward Hawkins, was too large and too all-embracing, both for efficient administration and for the growing specialization in the field of archaeology. On June 22, 1860, Hawkins at last sent in his resignation, and Panizzi took the opportunity of bringing about the necessary reorganization. He proposed to the Trustees that the existing, unwieldy department should be split into four: Oriental Antiquities, that is Egyptian and Assyrian; Greek and Roman; Coins and Medals and lastly, British and Medieval and Ethnography. These latter collections ought not, in Panizzi's opinion, to have been in the Museum at all, and he was by no means sorry when the Trustees, reversing an earlier decision of their Sub-Committee, added British and Medieval and Ethnography as a Sub-Department to Oriental Antiquities. It was, indeed, not until very shortly before Panizzi's retirement that this Sub-Department was created a Department in its own right.

It was now necessary to find three new keepers. For Oriental Antiquities, Birch,[4] a distinguished Egyptologist and for long Hawkins's right-hand man, was the obvious choice and as for Coins and Medals, William Vaux,[5] who had looked after the collections for some years and was a good friend of Panizzi's, was clearly destined to be Keeper of that Department. It was Greek and Roman Antiquities, to contemporary eyes, by far the most important of the three, which was the difficulty. The Assistant in charge of these antiquities under Hawkins was Edmund Oldfield, an able man, who had supervised successfully the safe dispatch to the Museum of the collection of antiquities bequeathed to it by Temple, Panizzi's old collaborator in the affair of the Neapolitan prisoners, who had died in 1856. Unfortunately for him, Oldfield seems to have been one of those whom Panizzi did not like. Somewhat self-opinionated, he had already annoyed his Principal Librarian by declaring that much of the Temple bequest was worthless, had, moreover, preferred suggestions as to the display of the antiquities without being asked, and, crowning offence, had given somewhat critical evidence before a Parliamentary Committee. Here, clearly, was another Edwards and one, too, who also must go. In addition, Panizzi had his own candidate for the post, his close friend and assiduous correspondent, Charles Newton.[6]

Newton had already served in the Department of Antiquities from 1840 to 1852, and had then joined the Foreign Service, as Vice-Consul at Mytilene. During his subsequent years in the Near East, he had conducted, with great vigour, a number of excavations which had resulted in the acquisition by the Museum of a whole series of masterpieces of classical art. In long and racy letters to Panizzi, he had described, in vivid language, the course of his excavations at Halicarnassus and elsewhere. In 1860, he had been appointed British Consul at Rome and though Newton himself was unhappy there, and his scope for archaeological excavations sadly restricted, he was invaluable to Panizzi, as a ready informant of all the news and gossip at the Papal capital.

So, despite the fact that Oldfield was Hawkins's choice as his successor, Panizzi was determined to make Newton Keeper of the new department. Although undoubtedly a sound choice, for Newton was a brilliant scholar, as well as an outstandingly successful excavator, Panizzi pursued his object with his usual not over-scrupulous thoroughness.

The Speaker, Dennison,[7] now the most active of the Principal Trustees, on whom the ultimate choice would fall, was, although a good friend of Panizzi's, somewhat annoyed at the latter's blandly telling him that there were only two suitable candidates now in the Trustees' service, that is, Birch and Vaux, and acidly reminded the Principal Librarian that Oldfield also had his claims, pointedly inquiring what Hawkins thought of the respective merits of the candidates and whether the latter's opinion of Newton coincided with that of Panizzi.[8] But the claims of Newton were overwhelming, every possible string had been adroitly pulled by Panizzi and poor Oldfield, after a brief struggle to avert his fate, resigned from the service of the Trustees.

Thus all the antiquities departments were run by men with whom Panizzi was on friendly terms and Printed Books was in the faithful hands of Winter Jones. Prints were under Carpenter,[9] who had always got on well with Panizzi, and in Manuscripts, Bond kept Madden quiet. There remained, however, the scientific departments and these, since the time of the Royal Commission, if not long before, had always been one of Panizzi's bugbears. Gray had been at least as difficult as Madden if at times, indeed, not more so and he, likewise, had seen himself as a possible successor to old Sir Henry.

But here luck was on Panizzi's side. Partly to implement the recommendations of the Royal Commission and partly to allay the still widespread criticism that science was unjustly neglected, the Trustees had decided to appoint a Superintendent of Natural History, to act as a sort of deputy director over the three scientific departments and to co-ordinate their activities.

Panizzi had, of course, known of this proposal, even before becoming Principal Librarian and was suspicious and, naturally, a little apprehensive that this new post would entail some curtailment of his own powers. Some of the Trustees, at least, regarded it in this light but Panizzi's mind was set at rest, a few days after his appointment, by a letter from the Home Secretary that the new office of Superintendent of the Natural History departments was definitely to be subordinate to that of the Principal Librarian, on whom would rest, as always, the ultimate responsibility for the whole Museum.[10]

On March 13, 1856, the new Superintendent, Professor Owen,[11] was appointed. On the whole, this arrangement worked well. There were occasional quarrels and difficulties, but on the main question of the hour, the separation of the scientific collections from the rest of the Museum, Owen's ultimate view was the same as that of Panizzi and on most minor matters, the two men, whenever necessary, seem to have agreed to differ.

Thus, internally, these ten years were a period of comparative calm after the feuds and bitter rivalries of the previous decades and Panizzi was, above all, glad to be rid of the millstone of the general catalogue. 'Thank God,' he wrote to Lady Holland, 'I shall have no more to do with that job for the future.'[12] But in the world at large, the controversy still raged around the Museum and further Parliamentary inquiries were to be enlivened by displays both of Panizzi's wit and of the idealism which was so prominent an element in his make-up.

By the early eighteen-fifties, it was abundantly clear that the Museum, as then constituted, was no longer adequate to contain the ever-rising flood of acquisitions now pouring in from all over the globe. Panizzi had long foreseen this situation and, as early as 1836, in his evidence before the Select Committee, had strongly urged the removal of the scientific collections.[13] He had then pointed out that the British Museum was forced to house objects which, in Paris, were already dispersed among a number of separate institutions. The question of space to display everything was now paramount.

The Department of Printed Books, once the most desperately in need of room of all the departments, was now, thanks to the new iron library, in a far better position than several of the others. Manuscripts, with their comparatively slow rate of growth, could just about manage, despite Madden's perennial grumbles. The remaining departments were in a desperate state. Already the precious sculptures unearthed by Newton at Halicarnassus and other places within the moribund Turkish empire had had to be housed on the colonnade, as well as was possible, behind glass screens. The magnificent Assyrian discoveries of Layard[14] were hidden, unseen by all, deep in a basement. Neither coins nor prints could be shown to the public, whilst the rapidly expanding medieval and ethnographical collections were all in one small room.

Various stop-gap plans were discussed by Panizzi and the respective keepers and, wherever possible, put into practice, but these were mere palliatives. It was evident that only drastic action could now prevent a disaster.

In a report to the Trustees on November 10, 1857,[15] Panizzi first enunciated publicly his solution of the problem. It was one which he had long considered. It was that not only should the scientific departments go elsewhere, but also the collections of prehistoric and post-classical antiquities. Panizzi had no love for or understanding of the Middle Ages. In this, as in so many other things, he was a true son of the Enlightenment and now strongly urged that the Museum should revert to its former practice of being only concerned with classical antiquities. The establishment of a new Museum, first at Marlborough House and then at South Kensington, as a specialist institution for arts and crafts, seemed to him to be an ideal opportunity for getting rid of an unwanted section of his own collections and to avoid what seemed to him to be the illogical position of having two national collections of post-classical antiquities. As to the Ethnographical collections – and by this term he meant not only the arts and crafts of primitive peoples, but also the treasures of the civilizations of China, India and the New World – all that could go anywhere, as long as he was no longer responsible for it.

Bloomsbury was quite unsuitable, also, for the scientific collections. There was, as Panizzi pointed out, no room at all to exhibit the larger zoological specimens and precious little room to exhibit anything else. One suggestion now advanced was that the botanical collections should go to Kew, but though this proposal received some support in scientific circles, more were opposed to it and the idea was dropped.

The scientists, who had for so long loudly voiced their disapproval of the Museum, were now in full cry. In July 1858 a petition was organized by the 'Promoters and Cultivators of Science' to protest at any attempt to remove the Natural History collections from Bloomsbury.[16] To Panizzi's disgust, the signatories included Owen and all three keepers of the Natural History departments. A counter-petition was hurriedly got up by the archaeologists, demanding adequate room at the Museum for their subjects, even if it did mean displacing the scientific collections, and the battle between the two cultures was once more joined.

Owen, meanwhile, had come round to Panizzi's way of thinking that a distinct and separate Natural History Museum, with adequate space for the proper display of all the collections, was the only practicable solution of the problem. In November 1859, the Trustees gave provisional approval to the following plan: that the Library Departments, antiquities and works of art were to remain at Bloomsbury, whilst five or six acres of ground were to be purchased at South Kensington for the erection of a new Natural History Museum. In the following January, the Trustees finally agreed, but by a majority of only one vote, that the scientific collections must go.

Now the fat *was* in the fire. The scientists used their not inconsiderable powers of lobbying and very shortly a Select Committee of the House of Commons was set up to study the whole question of accommodation.[17] On June 5, 1860, Panizzi himself gave evidence and left the Committee in no doubt as to what *his* views were. It was absolutely necessary to think in large terms, 'not to consider our life only, but the life of the country'.[18] He personally could not conceive of a library that would contain five or six million books, but adequate room must be left at Bloomsbury for the eventual accommodation of a collection of that size or even greater. Thus, some of the other collections must go. It was not, he emphasized, that he was opposed to or thought less of the scientific departments or, indeed, of the medieval and other antiquities, which he also considered should now be moved elsewhere.

'It is because I value [them] very much that I want them to be separate from the classical collections at the British Museum ... It is because I want a splendid collection of natural history that I wish it were removed.'[19] It does seem that he was here expressing his genuine opinions and not merely trying to curry favour with the Committee. He utters similar sentiments in a letter to Gladstone: 'The British Museum should contain all that is the work of Man, all nature ought to be transferred to a splendid separate establishment for the collection of natural objects.'[20]

Before this Committee, too, Panizzi gives the final summing up of one aspect of his life's work for his beloved library: 'The Museum is the library of the English nation and there ought to be in that library every book that was printed either by Englishmen or in English or relating to England.'[21]

But though Panizzi, and subsequently Owen, gave detailed evidence as to the desirability and, indeed, the extreme urgency of separating the collections, the Committee were not to be moved, at least as far as the scientific departments were concerned. In their report, they stated firmly and categorically that they attached 'the greatest importance to the retention of the Natural History collections'.[22]

Pictures, drawings, foreign post-classical antiquities and all the ethnographical specimens might go. Everything else must remain.

Both the Government and the Trustees, not to mention Panizzi himself, strongly demurred at these suggestions and plans went ahead for the acquisition of a site at South Kensington and the eventual removal there of the Natural History departments. A Bill to authorize these changes was, however, rejected by the House in 1862[23] and though plans for the move went on and Panizzi continued, in report after report, to draw attention to the ever-deteriorating situation, it was not till 1883, long after Panizzi's retirement and death, that the change was at last made.

The other major question which now occupied much of Panizzi's time was his determination to have his staff adequately paid and to be able to obtain the men he and his keepers wanted. For many years, he had bitterly complained of the miserable pittance on which most of his colleagues had to subsist, with little hope of promotion or of any improvement in their situation.

Now, as Principal Librarian, he was determined to do something to alleviate their lot and to make a Museum career more attractive.

The first problem was to tackle the subject of pensions for those members of the staff too old to work and yet unable, through poverty, to retire. At Panizzi's insistence, an investigation by two Treasury experts was carried out into the 'nature of the duties performed by different classes of officers and servants at the British Museum'.[24] Their conclusions were that the ordinary Civil Service regulations, with some modifications, should apply to that institution and that, in regard to superannuation, the staff should be on the same footing as in other public offices. Among the first beneficiaries of this ruling were Hawkins and old Horne, who, after more than thirty-six years in the Department of Printed Books, now, at last, felt able to retire, only to die a few months later.

It was this sort of thing which Panizzi was determined to avoid. Too many men in the past had hung on, often to extreme old age, which, in the nature of things, reduced efficiency and blocked the appointment of abler and younger men.

But equally Panizzi was resolved to make the Museum service a more attractive prospect for men of outstanding qualifications, who would not be tempted to leave later for more lucrative appointments elsewhere. They would not need, as had so many in the past, to supplement their slender incomes by additional part-time activities and, hence, divert from the service of the Trustees, energy and enthusiasm which Panizzi felt, very strongly, belonged more properly to the Museum.

Although Panizzi did not succeed entirely in his aims, if, indeed, it were possible to do so, he had done far more than any of his predecessors to improve the conditions of his staff at all levels. A hard man, demanding much and impatient of comparatively trivial faults he might indeed be; no man could be kinder or more sympathetic towards a truly deserving case.

Thus when the Assistants in 1860 sent a memorandum to the Government on the question of their salaries, comparing themselves, alas, not for the last time, with their more fortunate brethren in Whitehall,[25] Panizzi warmly supported their plea. He extracted from an invariably reluctant Treasury considerable increases in salary and the creation of a new upper division to the grade of Assistant First Class, to which promotion would be by merit. New departments, too, meant a higher proportion of senior posts than had formally existed.

But these gains were not secured without some attendant difficulties. The Treasury pointed out that the principle of extending the Superannuation Regulations to cover the Museum implied the need for appointment by examination, as was now the rule throughout the greater part of the Civil Service. Examinations of various degrees were, therefore, instituted for all prospective candidates for employment at the Museum.

This step soon led to considerable difficulties and to Panizzi's last fling against bureaucracy. A certain Mr Gemmer had been nominated for appointment to a vacancy as an Assistant in the Department of Manuscripts and, in due course, satisfied the Civil Service Commissioners as to his fitness for the post. Unfortunately for him, his Keeper, Madden, thought otherwise and complained bitterly of his lack of the most elementary knowledge of Latin and French, subjects he was supposed to have been examined in. For once, Panizzi and Madden were in full agreement and the wretched Gemmer was forced to resign to avoid instant dismissal. He then made the mistake of issuing a pamphlet,[26] complaining of his treatment by the Museum authorities and seeking to justify his appointment.

Panizzi very soon demolished the poor man's case, exposing with glee his complete lack of both knowledge and common sense. The Principal Librarian then went on to complain of the folly of the Civil Service Commissioners in accepting such an ignoramus, whilst, on the other hand, good, suitable men, highly recommended by their superior officers, and whose experience was likely to be of inestimable value to the Museum, were rejected over technicalities.

'The present system of examination by the Civil Service Commissioners,' he wrote, 'does not work well for the Museum, however excellent it may be for other departments of the public service.'[27] A better way, in his opinion, would be for a suitable officer of the Museum to assist in setting the papers and to be present whenever candidates were interviewed.

At this, the Civil Service Commissioners took umbrage and a long and increasingly acrimonious correspondence ensued between them and the Principal Librarian. As usual, Panizzi had the best of the exchange. He demolished all his opponents' arguments with his old fire and wit in a final broadside, which he jocularly described as his 'Christmas Box for the Commissioners'. Though Speaker Dennison congratulated Panizzi on this masterly communication,[28] the Commissioners had the last word after all. They merely rejected for a time all candidates, however highly qualified, who presented themselves for a Museum appointment.

But Panizzi had now little cause to worry about their vagaries. His health, which had for long been troubling him, now showed unmistakable signs of breaking down. In December 1862, by special permission of the Trustees, he had taken a long vacation in an effort to restore his failing powers. During his absence from the Museum, which lasted till the following May, Winter Jones, although by no means the senior Keeper, was appointed Deputy Principal Librarian and seems to have acquitted himself well.[29]

On May 9, 1863, refreshed by five months in the sun of Italy, Panizzi took up the reins once again, but rheumatism and gout still troubled him and he feared the onset of paralysis. Public life was becoming an increasing burden and his thoughts were turning more and more to retirement, before it was too late. He had opened his heart to James Hudson, now himself living near Pistoia. His friend strongly advised him to buy a villa, not too far from Florence, 'so that you might be *in* and *out* of society at your own good pleasure'. He must not think of resigning until he had 'seen and tasted Tuscany as at present ordered'.[30] But Panizzi was longing to have done.

On May 15, 1865, the weary Principal Librarian wrote to Gladstone to tell his old friend of 'my intentions of retiring from an office which I cannot any longer fill with advantage to the public . . . how deeply I should feel to separate myself from an institution to which I owe so much and in which I take and shall ever take more interest than in anything else in the world'.[31]

Gladstone promptly advised Panizzi to see the Prime Minister, Palmerston, before 'finally resolving on a step which may probably be followed by such important consequences',[32] a reference to the proposal, again revived, of abolishing the post of Principal Librarian or of severely curtailing its powers.

Gladstone, too, was alarmed lest Panizzi was resigning in a fit of pique at something which he himself had said to Lacaita. The latter, disturbed at the evident deterioration in Panizzi's health, had recently spoken to Gladstone on that subject. Gladstone had then said to James Lacaita that he could no longer, with propriety, as he had done on a previous occasion, urge Panizzi on public grounds to continue in harness. Panizzi, always hypersensitive over supposed reflections upon himself, had thereupon taken offence. 'My conspiracy,' wrote Gladstone, full of apologies, 'extends no further.'[33]

Panizzi, whether in a huff or not, formally tendered his resignation on June 24, 1865. In a letter to the Home Secretary, he explained that he was 'reluctantly compelled to take this step, not feeling myself now equal to the duties of so important an office'.[34] At the same time, he notified the Trustees of his decision, indicating, however, his willingness to continue to serve for a limited period, until 'his successor can enter on his duties and become familiar with them'. He also prays the Trustees to recommend that he be awarded a just superannuation allowance and, to make quite sure his merits were not overlooked, laid before the Board a statement of his services both as Principal Librarian and as Keeper of Printed Books.[35] The Trustees at once passed a series of resolutions, regretting his resignation, recording their deep sense of the ability, zeal and unwearied assiduity' with which he had discharged 'the very arduous and responsible duties' he had undertaken for so many years. They expressed, too, their particular regret that he should have to resign 'at a period when great changes are contemplated in the administration of the British Museum' and, finally, in view of the 'special services . . . above his ordinary duties' which he had so constantly carried out, that a special reward was due to him, a pension equal to his present salary and emoluments and this final resolution was at once communicated to the Treasury.[36] That department replied on July 9, that the Principal Librarian was, strictly speaking, only entitled to an annual pension of £933 6s 8d, but, in view of his extraordinary services and the financial savings which had been effected at the Museum by his efficient administration, they agreed to raise it to a total of £1,400. So all was well![37]

Two days previously, Sir George Grey had replied accepting Panizzi's resignation, 'with sincere regret'. He begged him, however, in the name of the Government, to 'continue your valuable services to the Museum, at least until early in the next year', if it were possible to do so without detriment to his health.[38] Panizzi was pleased and touched at this request. The Government, he wrote to Mrs Haywood, had behaved 'most handsomely', and he readily agreed to stay on, when requested to do 'in such flattering terms'. To the very end, Panizzi was always a little unsure of himself and was as delighted as a schoolboy to receive a pat on the head. 'I think,' he continued, 'the request I should remain is the handsomest testimonial I could wish.' If only his dear friend 'who cheered me when lonely and unknown' had lived to share his joy. [39]

So the old man, flattered and comforted, soldiered on through another winter. Although no longer, officially, Principal Librarian and so, at least on paper, doing the work for nothing, Panizzi once more gave all his mind to the problems of the Museum. Again, he worried over the ever-increasing menace of the lack of space, urging on the Government that a speedy decision on this question was more than ever necessary. [40] At last, an architect was appointed to draw up plans for a new building at South Kensington and Panizzi could hope that, perhaps, a solution to the problem was now in sight.

In the March, on his recommendation, it had been decided to create a new department of British and Medieval Antiquities and of Ethnography and the brilliant Franks was appointed as its first Keeper. [41] But what occasioned the greatest excitement and to Panizzi the deepest concern during the last months of his reign, was a bad fire which, on July 13, broke out in the binders' shop. Although some manuscripts, there for repair work, were destroyed, it might well have been far worse and might possibly have spread to the main buildings, had not a fireman succeeded in entering the blazing building and in closing an intervening door.

Panizzi was furious at the thought of this threat to his beloved Museum, always dreaded there since the disastrous fire some one hundred and thirty years before, which had so badly damaged the Cottonian collection. [42] An inquiry showed that the outbreak had been caused by culpable negligence on the part of the binding staff and a failure to adhere to the regulations. Praise and blame were soon bestowed on his subordinates. The binders had their contract revoked; an erring messenger, who had failed to answer the fire alarm, was summarily dismissed; the gallant fireman, and those who had assisted him, were suitably rewarded.

But to Panizzi, the inconvenience and annoyance were not ended. The rebuilding of the binders' shop meant the taking over of a considerable portion of his own garden, and the noise and the dust forced him to quit his residence. So, in the October, after nearly thirty years, he moved out of the Museum and took a house in nearby Bloomsbury Square, which was to be his home for the rest of his life.

Panizzi was now very weary and longed only for repose. He

had been pained and grieved by the attacks made on him in the Lords by his old enemy Monckton Milnes, now Lord Houghton,[43] and by scurrilous abuse in certain sections of the popular press. This had been so outrageous that the Assistants in Printed Books had spontaneously addressed a memorandum to their old Keeper, expressing 'their surprise and indignation at the virulent criticisms which had lately appeared in print upon the administration of the British Museum and upon its Chief Officer', and a similar statement had been drawn up by the Assistants in the Principal Librarian's office.[44] But pleased as ever by the loyal support of those who knew him best, Panizzi felt it was time for him to go.

Neither Government nor Trustees showed any sign of appointing a successor, and the 'short while', the few months, had already lengthened into a year. Tired and now feeling that he was being imposed on, Panizzi wrote once more to Grey. He had remarked a few days before to his old friend, Lord Dalhousie, that he had been confined to bed for a week with rheumatism and yet could get no respite from his labours. 'I am still in harness and see no prospect of being released.'[45]

On June 5, 1866, exactly a year after his resignation had been accepted, the last letter to Grey was sent off. 'I must not trifle with my health any longer.'[46] A few days later, the Home Secretary replied. Steps were at last being taken to appoint his successor, but would Panizzi please carry on until that successor was actually appointed.[47] Patiently the old man waited. He, at least, had always known whom he wanted, the man who, for so many years now, had been at his right hand in the bitter controversies over the catalogue, who had succeeded him as Keeper of Printed Books and who had acted for him in the winter of 1862, John Winter Jones. On June 22 he wrote to Jones, asking him whether, if he were to be appointed Principal Librarian, and Panizzi was careful to emphasize that it was only mere supposition, he would be prepared to accept any possible alteration in the status of that office. Jones promptly replied that he would.[48]

The two names submitted for Royal approval were those of Jones and Newton, both old friends of Panizzi and both efficient and able officers of the Museum.[49] There can be little doubt, however, which of the two would have been Panizzi's own choice and which of the two names, in the customary fashion, was placed first. A few days later, on June 26, Jones was formally appointed his successor and on July 14, 1866, Panizzi laid the appointment of the new Principal Librarian before the Board. His official life was over. Characteristically his very last act was to call the attention of the Trustees to the low salaries paid to the Assistants in the Principal Librarian's office, despite their heavy responsibilities and, in particular, to Butler, his Assistant Secretary, who had faithfully served him and before him, Ellis, for many years. By a touch of irony, also before the Board was Sir Frederic Madden's letter of resignation, timed to the very day on which his rival at last went. Madden, no doubt still envious of Panizzi, asked the Trustees for his full salary as pension. The Trustees accepted his resignation, but granted him a pension of no more than £600 per annum. To the very end, Panizzi had beaten him.[50]

Russell, the Prime Minister, offered Panizzi a CB, 'as a step to the higher class of KCB'. Panizzi had already, in July 1861, declined the offer of a knighthood, on the grounds that he, a foreigner by birth, had already received such great honours as to make many envious and, moreover, that 'I feel an instinctive shrinking for public distinctions of this nature'. In his reply to Russell, Panizzi now drew attention to his previous refusal and the grounds for it and went on to say: 'Next to that of the Queen's, your Lordship's approbation is all that I ever desired and wished.' So for the moment, in England at least, he was still plain Mr Panizzi.[51]

Now came the final farewells. On July 16, in a letter to all heads of departments, Panizzi took leave of those who had been his friends and rivals, his colleagues and helpmates for so long, giving them 'my warmest thanks for the efficient help which I have received . . . in the discharge of my duties'. This essentially kind and modest man went on: 'Although conscious of having at all times acted to the best of my ability and only for the advantage of the Museum and of those connected with it, I wish to add that if I have ever given unnecessary pain to anyone I regret it most sincerely and trust that credit will be given to me for having been uniformly influenced solely by a sense of duty.'[52] No man who knew Panizzi well would ever doubt the absolute truth and sincerity of what he wrote.

Beneath the formal language of the replies, one can feel the warmth of the affection with which the often stern old man was regarded by almost all. As Jones, his successor wrote: 'On this event there is but one feeling throughout the department, that of deep regret that we are about to lose one who has the strongest claims upon us, not only for acts of personal kindness, but for substantial benefits.'[53] Major, the assistant in charge of the maps, was so moved that he felt he must write personally to his old chief. 'You have made the grand institution with which we have the honour to be connected unspeakably grander' and rendering his most sincere thanks for all the many improvements in pay, holidays and general conditions for the staff, which Panizzi had brought about 'by your most kind and generous advocacy'.[54] Only Madden, bitter and hostile to the very end, felt unwilling to reply on behalf of his department and it was left to Bond, in his turn to be Winter Jones's successor, to thank Panizzi for all his kindness, which would be 'a lasting remembrance with us'.[55]

So all was over. The young Italian refugee, 'a man who came to this country without quite a sovereign in his pocket, knowing not one word of the language'[56] left, at long last, the institution which, in James Hudson's words, he had 'raised from the dust',[57] honoured, beloved and respected by all that knew him.

But, alas, not even now, by all. Though *The Times*, *The Telegraph* and even *The Athenaeum*, now sang his praises, many of the more scurrilous papers, cuttings from which were lovingly collected by Sir Frederic, were less friendly. *The Civil Service Gazette* already, the previous June, had printed a long and highly mendacious account of Panizzi's life and services, in particular attacking 'his imperious manner, arbitrary enactments' and his treatment of his subordinate staff. Further attacks were subsequently made, not only on the 'foreign Whig favourite', but also on Jones, as his destined successor.[58]

It would seem, as was perhaps inevitable in those days of rigid class distinctions, that the Principal Librarian's passion for order and discipline and for the vigorous enforcement of the Museum statutes pressed most heavily on the attendants and the other lower staff, whilst they too, on the whole, had the least opportunity of knowing the real kindness and generosity behind his stern, and often terrifying exterior. It must be remembered that the standards of discipline and of staff welfare were not those of a hundred years later, but, in the world of Mr Gradgrind and his fellows, Panizzi would have appeared as a foolishly over-indulgent employer, pandering needlessly to the whims of his subordinates.

The man depicted in these vicious attacks, as perpetrating a veritable reign of terror within the Museum would never, even then, have lasted as Principal Librarian ten weeks, let alone ten years. Irascible Panizzi may often have been, especially during these last years, sorely tried by gout and by failing health, at times, undoubtedly, unfair to individuals to whom he took a dislike, but such a monster, as described in the columns of *The Civil Service Gazette*, would never have received the spontaneous tributes, the unfailing proofs of loyalty and affection, which he had always received from those who knew him best.

NOTES TO CHAPTER 14

1 Add. MS. 36, 717. f.392.

2 Add. MS. 36, 717. f.425.

3 Add. MS. 36, 717. f.445.

4 Samuel Birch, 1813–1885. Egyptologist, Keeper of Oriental Antiquities, 1861–1885.

5 William Vaux, 1818–1885. Keeper of Coins and Medals, 1861–1870.

6 Sir Charles Newton, 1816–1894. Keeper of Greek and Roman Antiquities, 1861–1885.

7 John Evelyn Denison, first Viscount Ossington, 1800–1873. Speaker, 1857–1872.

8 Add. MS. 36, 721. ff.146, 151, 163.

9 William Hokham Carpenter, 1792–1866. Keeper of Prints and Drawings, 1845–1866.

10 See also Add. MS. 36, 717. f.478.

11 Sir Richard Owen, 1804–1892. Naturalist. Superintendent of the Natural History Departments, 1856–1883. It was he who finally achieved the separation of these departments from the rest of the library when, in 1881, they were at last transferred to South Kensington.

12 A.P. to Mary, Lady Holland, March 29, 1856. *Holland House Papers*.

13 *Select Committee*, 1836. para. 4800.

14 Sir Austen Layard, 1817–1894. Archaeologist and politician. Excavator of Nineveh.

15 *Papers relating to the enlargement of the British Museum*, p. 38. *Parliamentary Papers*, H. of C., 1857–58, vol. XXXIII, p. 373.

16 *Parliamentary Papers*, H. of C., 1857–58, vol. XXXIII, p. 499.

17 *Select Committee on the British Museum. Parliamentary Papers*, H. of C., 1860, vol. XVI, p. 173.

18 *Select Committee, Minutes*, para. 131, 133.

19 *Select Committee, Minutes*, para. 280. Panizzi also advocated separate students' rooms for the various departments. *Minutes*, para. 158.

20 Add. MS. 44, 274. ff.204, 224. Minutes, para. 3658.

21 *Select Committee, Minutes,* para. 409.

22 *Select Committee on Accommodation. Report,* 224, p. xxi.

23 *Bill to enable the Trustees of the British Museum to remove portions of their Collections.* First reading May 10, 1862. On second reading, the amendment to postpone consideration of the bill for three months, that is to reject it, was carried by 163 votes to 71. *Commons Journals,* 1862, p. 210.

24 Add. MS. 36, 728. f.316. The two experts were Sir Charles Trevelyan and George Arbuthnot; June 20, 1857.

25 *Parliamentary Papers,* H. of C., 1866, vol. XXXIX, p. 199.

26 *Memorial addressed to the Trustees of the British Museum,* 1864.

27 *Parliamentary Papers,* H. of C., 1866, vol. XXXIX, p. 251.

28 Add. MS. 36, 723, f.3.

29 *Trustees' Minutes,* vol. 30, f.10240.

30 Add. MS. 36, 722. f.566.

31 Add. MS. 44, 274. f.248.

32 Add. MS. 36, 723. f.122.

33 Add. MS. 36, 723. f.97.

34 Add. MS. 36, 723. f.125. A.P. to Grey, June 24, 1865.

35 Add. MS. 36, 723. f.134. *Statement of Mr Panizzi's Services.*

36 *Committee Minutes,* vol. 31, ff.10821, 10822, 10833.

37 *Treasury Minute* of July 6, 1865. Add. MS. 36, 723. f.145.

38 Add. MS. 36, 723. f.147.

39 Add. MS. 36, 723. f.152.

40 *Committee Minutes,* vol. 31, f.10823.

41 Sir Augustus Wollaston Franks, 1826–1897. Antiquary.

42 October 23, 1731, in which no less than 114 out of 958 manuscripts were completely destroyed and 98 very badly damaged. The library was then at Ashburnham House, Westminster.

43 *Hansard,* 3.S., vol. 181, col. 339–342. See also Add. MS. 36, 723 f.329.

44 *Committee Minutes,* vol. 31, f.10883.

45 Add. MS. 36, 723. f.425. What particularly annoyed Panizzi was the fact that since his full salary had already been granted to him as pension, he was working at the Museum for nothing. In a note (Add. MS. 36, 723. f.472) he compares, with some bitterness, the much more favourable treatment others had received in similar circumstances.

46 Add. MS. 36, 723. f.436.

47 Add. MS. 36, 723. f.451. *Committee Minutes,* vol. 31, f.11022.

48 Add. MSS. 36, 723. ff.459, 460. In December 1865 Panizzi had written to Gladstone that the cabinet must come to some decision in the proposed scheme for the *temporary* government of the Museum and had enclosed a memorandum. In this he urged the abolition of the trust as then constituted as an executive body of fifty members was too large and irresponsible, and hampered and embarrassed the Principal Librarian. They should be replaced by 'a gentleman of high standing', who should be in charge of all the national museums and responsible to Parliament for the appointment of their officers and for their general direction. There should be a principal officer in charge of each museum, whilst the chief officer should inspect all the museums and co-ordinate their policies in consultation with the individual directors, 'so as to ensure . . . an uniform system'. For the moment Panizzi suggested that the British Museum should have a new Principal Librarian, but on condition that he might have to vacate the post, should the system be altered. The Principal Librarian 'must be one conversant with the service of the Museum and its traditions; it would never do to intrude a stranger in what is meant as a temporary measure to last only as long as expedient'. [Add. MS. 44, 273. ff.299, 301.]

49 Add. MS. 36, 723. f.485. Newton wrote, 'I should not have accepted the office . . . Best where I am.' [Newton to A.P., July 10, 1866.]

50 *Committee Minutes,* vol. 31, ff.11035, 11038, 11039.

51 Add. MS. 36, 723. f.468.

52 Add. MS. 36, 723. f.494. The text of the various letters is given in *Passages* pp. 65–70.

53 Add. MS. 36, 723. f.515.

54 Add. MS. 36, 723. f.510. Richard Major, 1818–1891, became subsequently the first and only Keeper of an independent Map Department, 1867–1880.

55 Add. MS. 36, 723. f.500.

56 Add. MS. 36, 723. f.321.

57 Add. MS. 36, 724. f.552.

58 *Civil Service Gazette,* June 17, June 24, July 8, 1865, *etc.*

15

FRIENDS AND ACQUAINTANCES

BUT Panizzi was not only a distinguished librarian, in the opinion of one well qualified to judge, the greatest library administrator ever known;[1] not only a man whose advice and opinions were sought and valued both by his own government and those of foreign powers; not only a devoted patriot, ready in youth and in middle age to risk his life in the service of his beloved Italy, but a man, who perhaps above all else, treasured the company of his chosen friends, both men and women.

Panizzi had an unfailing genius for friendship. All types and conditions of men were proud to be numbered among his acquaintances and many could bear witness to his great personal kindness and generosity. Until advancing age and the continual pain of his gout made him increasingly cantankerous, no man could be more charming, more full of fun, and a better host to those who were privileged to enjoy his generous hospitality at the Museum. His table and his cellar were the delight of all his friends and no man appreciated more, as long as he was able to, the charm of good conversation. Women and children adored him. Said Mérimée, 'There never was anybody so spoiled by the women as you are, except old Ellice.'[2] and the young, especially, were quick to notice the warm, affectionate nature behind his gruff exterior. The Gladstone children, the little Prince Imperial, Jane Bickersteth, Marie Fox, Louis Fagan and many another child delighted in old Panizzi and in the tricks and games with which he would amuse them and continued to be his friends and admirers when grown men and women.

John Winter Jones,
1805–1881; Keeper of
Printed Books, 1856–
1866; Principal Libra-
rian of the British Mu-
seum, 1866–1878. From
the portrait by W. S.
Herrick

Richard Monckton
Milnes, Baron Hough-
ton, 1809–1885, aged
30. From the sketch by
Count D'Orsay

Sir Anthony Panizzi, aged 77. From the sketch by 'Ape' (Carlo Pellegrini)

As the years went by and as the young Modenese exile changed gradually into the great 'Pan', the presiding genius of the British Museum, so his circle of friends widened. By now, Panizzi moved freely in the company of the great Whig leaders; Russell, Clarendon, Palmerston and Devonshire were all close and personal friends, anxious for him to dine with them or to spend weekends, whenever he could be so persuaded, at their country houses. As we have seen, his friendship with Gladstone did much to turn the future leader of the Liberal party from his early Toryism and to give him an understanding of the powerful forces of the new nationalism.

Panizzi had little time for the Tories. Far too many were, in his opinion, pro-Austrians and, at the best, half-hearted in the cause of Italian unity. He mistrusted both the Peelite Lord Aberdeen and the Tory Lord Derby and his relations with Disraeli were never close. He suspected all romanticism and was uniformly hostile to any attempt to restore medievalism, whether in Church or State. He could be prejudiced and grossly unfair, but to those to whom he gave his friendship, he was ever loyal and true.

Even where the object of his friendship was perhaps unworthy of it, Panizzi was loyal. The case of Guglielmo Libri[3] is a case in point. Libri, a Tuscan by birth, had settled in Paris and had become a successful journalist, professor of mathematics and a collector of rare and costly books and of precious manuscripts. Closely associated with Guizot, he was accused, shortly after the revolution of 1848, of stealing a considerable number of items from the national collections. Even though it was to a considerable extent a political gesture, it was a serious accusation for anyone to face.

Panizzi had obtained through Libri certain books for the Museum and had formed an attachment for his fellow exile. On the scandal at Paris becoming known, Panizzi was extremely anxious, not only on account of his friend, but even more about the ugly rumours that he himself had been privy to the purchase of books known to be stolen or had in some way acted as a receiver of stolen goods. To a man of Panizzi's scrupulous integrity, such accusations, however unfounded, were intolerable. He strenuously defended Libri's reputation, whom he regarded, as did such distinguished French bibliophiles as Mignet, as largely the victim of

10

political prejudice and chicanery and strongly denied, then and later, that he had assisted, in any way, in any underhand transactions.[4]

Libri, coming to England, was befriended by Panizzi, who interested Gladstone in him and assisted him in many ways. Any reflection on Libri's reputation was, however, regarded as a slur on his own and an angry exchange of letters took place with the great collector, Lord Ashburnham,[5] who had purchased many books and manuscripts from Libri, which were then alleged to be stolen property. The latter was a difficult man, according to Mérimée, pestering friends and enemies alike and who, all too easily, took offence.[6] Panizzi, throughout the years, remained unexpectedly patient and loyal, ready to put up with the whims of one for whom he felt a great pity, even though, in his opinion, many of his misfortunes were due to Libri's own folly.

But what to Panizzi was a far more serious misunderstanding darkened, for a while, his friendship with one of his most valued friends and correspondents, Lord Holland.

The papers of his father, the late Lord Holland, had been passed to Lord John Russell for the purpose of writing a life of the elder Holland's uncle, the Whig Charles James Fox. Being unable to finish the work, Russell had returned the papers and such of the manuscript as he had been able to complete to Holland House. Using this as a basis, Henry, Lord Holland, decided to compile two books from the various papers and memoirs, calling them *Foreign Reminiscences* and *Memoirs of the Whig Party* and so, in a list of forthcoming publications, Longman's included *Lord Holland's Foreign Reminiscences*.[7]

At this, certain of the writer's surviving friends, and especially Lord John Russell, his brother, Bedford,[8] Lord Lansdowne and old Sir Robert Adair,[9] took alarm, in view of the late Lord Holland's often outspoken frankness and expressed concern lest an unexpurgated edition might adversely affect Holland's posthumous reputation. The times were no longer those of the uninhibited Regency era of which that peer had been so brilliant an ornament. The manners and modes of mid-Victorian England were very different and Lord John, in particular, feared the worst. He urged Henry Holland to sift every word with care and ended his letter with the somewhat tactless reminder that the papers had been first left to him and that he had assisted in their original compilation.

Russell now made the suggestion that Panizzi and he, together with the economist Nassau Senior, might have leave to go through the manuscript and to cut out any passages which they considered might give offence. In a letter to Panizzi, Russell expressed his fears lest the 'imprudent publication of . . . private matters' might harm Holland's reputation and regretted that his son had not consulted his father's old friends before deciding on publication.[10]

Holland, not a little nettled at all this tiresome, if well-meaning, advice, gave the necessary consent and replied that he was ready to expunge any passage which might, in Lord John's opinion, injure the memory of his late father. Russell, whose duties as Prime Minister left him little time, now deputed Panizzi and Macaulay to act entirely as they thought fit on his behalf and, in practice, Panizzi was left to be more or less sole arbiter.[11]

At this Holland really flared up. A stranger, a foreigner, and one who had, in fact, never known the late peer, was to be the judge as to the suitability of what he had included concerning his own father and promptly withdrew his permission. He was not annoyed with Panizzi himself and spoke of 'the kindness, good nature and consideration you have exhibited in the whole matter'.[12] On the other hand, he was very angry indeed with Lord John for making such a mountain out of a very inconsiderable molehill.

Panizzi's loyal attempts to defend Russell's actions led to further trouble. Holland wrote in reply, 'I cannot truckle to Lord John . . . You forget, my dear Pan, that Lord John interfered in a most overbearing and imperious manner . . . If they go on asserting their interference much longer I shall publish the whole of the correspondence.'[13]

Panizzi now bridled in his turn and again rebukes Holland for misunderstanding Russell's intentions and motives. Neither the Premier nor Macaulay 'go about the town lamenting and regretting passages . . . they had the power of suppressing'[14] and many of their objections had been grossly exaggerated. An acrimonious exchange of letters followed. Panizzi was no respecter of persons and roundly abjured Lord Holland to come off his high horse and asked what had come over him.

Holland, however, does not seem to have minded overmuch

Panizzi's hostile tone. A warm-hearted, generous man, he quickly begged the still irate Panizzi not to be so angry with him. 'Knowing how easily you take fire, I should have been more guarded in writing to you, but I also know that hot as you are you easily cool and that your indignation never really interferes with your kind feelings for old friends. In the meantime, write a letter to convince me that the storm has blown over.'[15]

Good relations were not at once restored. In August, Panizzi indignantly denied that he was still 'huffy' and would rather not call at Holland House, 'better to be missed than to find oneself *de trop*', and ends, somewhat self-righteously, 'I have not been angry, altho' I have been much tempted.'[16]

By Christmas, however, the two friends were once more on good terms. Panizzi speaks feelingly of Holland's 'great kindness' and 'I was never so happy in any house as in yours'.[17] Only Lord Holland's untimely death in 1858 was now to interrupt their friendship.

Strangely enough, almost at the same time, Panizzi was caught up in another very similar imbroglio. For a number of years, he had been very friendly with the distinguished lawyer, Henry Bickersteth, afterwards Lord Langdale, and his family. Langdale had been Master of the Rolls since 1836 and, as we have seen, had been most useful to Panizzi during the time of the Royal Commission, on which he had served. Panizzi was very fond of both Lord and Lady Langdale[18] and adored their little girl, Jane. He was a frequent visitor to their house in Richmond, dining there at least once a week and Lady Langdale and her daughter were to remain his close friends for many years.

In 1851, Lord Langdale had died and his widow entrusted the materials for a commemorative biography to T. D. Hardy,[19] an archivist and subsequently Deputy Keeper of the Record Office. Just as Russell and his elderly friends had been alarmed at the thought of possible indiscretions in Lord Holland's *Memoirs*, so now another old acquaintance of Panizzi was put out by certain passages in the *Memoirs of the Right Honourable Lord Langdale*.[20] Brougham, by now a cantankerous, disappointed man, who had quarrelled with most of his contemporaries, had still kept in touch with his former protégé, Panizzi, dining with him at Holland House and elsewhere. Brougham now became convinced that

Panizzi had had something to do with the production of Hardy's book and was therefore, to some extent, responsible for the mistakes and inaccuracies which the ex-Lord Chancellor claimed to have discovered in it. He wrote to Panizzi, begging him to use his influence over Lady Langdale to 'prevent more harm being done'.[21]

In a subsequent letter, Brougham was forced to admit that he had 'never supposed you had interfered with the book',[22] but still seems to regard Panizzi as, in some way, responsible for its contents. Like most of his circle, Panizzi was used to Brougham's peculiar ways and took little notice of all this. He remained always grateful to the old man for giving him his first real chance and the two continued to meet and to correspond for many years yet. Nearly twenty years later, Prosper Mérimée wrote to tell Panizzi that he had, once more, come across the old lawyer now nearly ninety, but as sprightly as ever. At long last, after a lifetime of scepticism, Brougham, it would seem, had taken to religion. There was, therefore, hope for Mérimée and Panizzi, if they too should ever achieve so great an age.[23]

Other friends of these years were the Scottish families of the Rutherfurds and the Ellices. Panizzi seems to have become acquainted with the Rutherfurds comparatively early in his career and was soon on close terms with them. Andrew Rutherfurd, a distinguished lawyer, had been Lord Advocate in various Whig governments and had taken an active part in the political life of the day. Panizzi frequently stayed with him and his wife in Edinburgh, and Rutherfurd, like so many of the former's friends, was the willing recipient of Panizzi's political views and confidences. Like Langdale, he had been of great help to Panizzi in the trying days of the Royal Commission, on which he, too, had served and, briefed by his friend, had done much to discredit hostile witnesses. When, in 1851, Rutherfurd was raised to the Scottish bench, none rejoiced more than did Panizzi. Lacaita, too, became a close acquaintance of the genial Scottish lawyer and both continued to enjoy his warm hospitality. It was with great sorrow that, in December 1854, Panizzi received the news that his old friend was gravely ill.[24] Within a few days, Lord Rutherfurd was dead. He was only six years older than Panizzi and this sudden death seems to have badly shaken the younger man.

The Ellices, father and son, and both confusingly named Edward, were other boon companions. The elder Ellice, nicknamed 'Bear', from his activities in the North American fur trade, and a brother-in-law of the Lord Grey of the Reform Bill, had been an intimate of Panizzi's for many years.

It was he, who, seconded by Clarendon, had secured in 1845 Panizzi's election to Brook's, the famous Whig Club, and which was for the next thirty years a second home to that lover of good company. Many pleasant holidays were spent at the Ellices' country seat at Glenquoich, near Aberdeen. Panizzi loved Scotland[25] and was perhaps happiest and most relaxed, when amongst its people and beautiful countryside. From the early 1840s onwards, he enjoyed above all to be there with the Rutherfurds, with the Ellices or with other Scottish friends. In 1844, Panizzi writes to old Lady Holland, to tell her of his jaunts to Scotland and of his experiences on making his first trip through a long railway tunnel.[26] In later years, when the journey tired him, he would spend a few days with other friends in the North of England, such as Lord Zetland[27] and talk over old times and old faces now gone.

To Ellice, more possibly than to any one else, Panizzi confided his thoughts, whether on Italy or on the general political situation. Letter after letter is filled with shrewd comments and accounts of what was happening in the world of politics and public affairs, especially during the critical year 1860. The death of old Ellice in 1863 was another bitter blow. 'The greatest friend,' Panizzi wrote to Mrs Haywood, 'I had lost since I lost one still more dear to me and to whom I owed more.'[28]

To such men as Ellice, Grenville and Sidney Smith, who befriended him when young and unknown, he owed his introduction to Whig society and it was by being fully accepted in such society that Panizzi had been able to do so much for his beloved native land. Panizzi never valued his friendship with such men as Russell, Palmerston, Gladstone and others just because they were distinguished figures, leaders of their party and members of the charmed circle of Grand Whiggery. No man was less of a snob than he. He would stand up to a Royal Duke or speak his mind to the greatest in the land. Not for nothing did King Bomba call him 'terribile Panizzi'. He esteemed the friendship of the great, as he did that of far humbler men and women, for its own sake and because he liked them and secondly, by being an intimate and welcome guest at their dinners and at weekends, he could advance the cause of Italy, quietly and discreetly, in a way no one else could. As we have seen, he was the intermediary through which the news of Cavour's latest policy or of the latest about-turn of Louis Napoleon could reach those ears, for which, secretly and unofficially, it was intended.

Panizzi's friendship with the younger Ellice was also close. One of the last holidays, if not the very last, that the old man took was at the Ellices' and braces of grouse and haunches of venison were a welcome present at 31 Bloomsbury Square, almost to the day of his death. Hudson might tease Panizzi about preferring Scottish mists and Scotch whisky to the sun and wine of his native land, but he never wavered in his frank enjoyment of the hospitality of the northern kingdom.

Like Panizzi, Ellice loved good food and wine. Both delighted in each other's dinners and adored politics and political gossip. Their letters to each other are full of the latest news, often with a racy commentary. Both Ellices were staunch Italophils and this naturally endeared them to Panizzi. Italy was ever foremost in his thoughts and even friendship could be, and was, sacrificed in the cause of patriotism. Whenever Ellice was in town, Panizzi and he would dine together, either at the Museum or at Brooks' and news of the feast would be sent off to Mérimée in Paris or Cannes or to Hudson in distant Italy. Whenever London grew too cold or too crowded, the friends would all meet in the South of France or in Florence to pass the time in happy companionship.

In their company, in later years, was very often to be found that other anglicized Italian, James Lacaita. As we have seen, after assisting both Gladstone and Panizzi in the case of the Neapolitan prisoners, Lacaita had fled to London to avoid a closer acquaintance with the inside of a Neapolitan jail. On arriving in England, he had at once married, his bride being a Scottish lady whom he had met whilst still in Naples. Like Panizzi, Lacaita was quickly accepted into the best society. The Hollands he had known in Italy and now he became friendly with Lord and Lady John Russell and with old Lord Aberdeen. A man of far less revolutionary fervour than was Panizzi, a natural supporter of law and order, he quietly merged into an English background, becoming, in due course, a member of the Established Church. Panizzi, for all his hatred of the temporal power of the Papacy and his distrust of Vatican politics, always remained, at least nominally, a Roman Catholic, whilst Lacaita, having embraced Protestantism in England, on becoming, in later years, an Italian landowner and business man, returned to the faith of his fathers.

The death of his young wife in childbirth was a terrible blow to Lacaita, and his friends, including Panizzi, did much to help him during those difficult days. On Panizzi's advice, he accepted the post of lecturer at Queen's College, Dublin, but it was Gladstone who really put him on his feet. Gladstone had been appointed High Commissioner to the Ionian Islands and chose Lacaita to be his Secretary.[29] The Neapolitan lawyer carried out this difficult task with tact and efficiency and was rewarded, on his return to England, by a KCMG. As Sir James Lacaita, his position and influence among the Whig leaders whenever Italian affairs were under discussion was second only to Panizzi's own. Panizzi never seems to have been at all jealous of his protégé's success, so similar to his own of twenty-five years before, for the two men remained good friends, though so very different in temperament and outlook.

Lacaita was never so audacious as the old Carbonaro. No one would ever have called him a Jacobin or a red as Thiers did Panizzi, even if half in jest. He successfully avoided being compromised with Orsini and shared none of his friend's passionate enthusiasm for Garibaldi. He was always far more sceptical than was Panizzi as to the ultimate success of the movement for Italian unification and in 1860 seriously considered returning home to serve the hastily reformed Bourbon monarchy.[30] Such a thing Panizzi would never have considered for one moment and he begged his friend not to accept such a compromising invitation.[31] Conversely, it was the more cautious Lacaita who advised the ever-eager Panizzi not to accept an offer to become a deputy for rebel Brescello, at a time when, had Panizzi been younger and free from official ties, he would have gladly gone to fight himself in the cause of liberty. Reluctantly, he now accepted his friend's advice, but rushed off, as soon as he was able, to visit those northern Italian provinces, which had revolted from their lawful masters.[32]

Naples once cleared of the Bourbons, it was Panizzi who now

implored Lacaita to return and, reluctantly, the other agreed. After the death of his wife, he was not really happy in England. 'I never got any justice and much less favour from the Whigs,'[33] he wrote, despite the fact, that, with his quiet ways, he fitted in better in many respects than the fiery hot-tempered Panizzi. To an increasing extent, as the years went by, Lacaita became more the Italian politician and landowner; Panizzi, like a true-born Englishman, was never anxious even to leave his beloved London.

In 1862, Lacaita joined Panizzi at Naples, where the latter was staying as a guest of Lady Holland. The two friends were horrified at much of what they saw in the newly pacified territories. Panizzi always detested any act of injustice. Chicanery and corruption aroused at once his anger and contempt and in Naples, during the aftermath of the Piedmontese victory, there was plenty of both. What particularly inflamed them, but Panizzi in particular, was the cruel and senseless policy of the Italian authorities in suppressing every religious order.[34] No man hated clericalism and the rule of priests more than did Panizzi and his Catholicism was of the most liberal kind, to say the least, but he knew that many individual priests and monks had been ardent patriots, during the struggle against Bourbon tyranny. Many had suffered harsh terms of imprisonment for their beliefs and it was a priest who, long before, in the days of his youth, had been the first victim of Francis IV of Modena. The destruction and neglect of the great monastic libraries, especially that of Monte Cassino, appalled him. Back home, Gladstone and many prominent English churchmen were protesting at the policies of the new Italian government; in Italy Panizzi acted. 'This is called liberty,' he cried, in justified disgust, and, by his efforts, secured the removal of the worst offenders.[35]

His activities on behalf of the persecuted monks and nuns aroused the hostility of certain of his acquaintances and the rumour spread that he had renounced his former opinions and had become an adherent of the Pope and of the exiled Bourbons. But no one who really knew him could believe such tales. As Hudson told him, 'How can you seriously pay attention to the chatterboxes of Naples, who had written here that you had gone over to the enemy,'[36] but nevertheless, such idle and malicious gossip deeply wounded Panizzi.

10*

In the years to come, Panizzi and Lacaita were to quarrel, but their estrangement was brief and to the last they remained good friends. It was James Lacaita who, in 1868, stayed up all night with the apparently dying Panizzi and who, at two in the morning, wrote a hurried note to tell Gladstone the happily false news that their old friend was sinking fast. In 1876 he had called on the poor old man, now half-blind and a helpless cripple, 'because it is his eightieth birthday', and still wrote to him, even when Panizzi himself was unable any longer to reply. Both men, in their own way, loved and served the Italy they had done so much to create.

A closer, far closer, friend than Lacaita, was James Hudson, probably the closest and dearest friend of all in these last years. Hudson had been British Minister at Turin and there, in alliance with Panizzi, had done much to bring about the triumph of Italian unity. Hudson, one of the most brilliant diplomats of the age, had come to Turin in 1851 and had at once won the trust and affection of Cavour. We have already seen what use the latter subsequently made of the friendship between Hudson and Panizzi to influence English opinion. Throughout the years of crisis, a constant stream of wise and witty letters flowed from 'Giacomo' in 'Mecca', as Hudson always called Turin, to his dearest Pan, the 'great god Pan', back in London. They cover every aspect of Italian and, indeed, European politics, as seen through the eyes of an experienced man of affairs and a devoted friend of liberty.

Hudson, a strikingly handsome man, had wrecked his official career by his liaison with a married Italian lady, who shared his home for many years. This scandal undoubtedly prevented Hudson from obtaining the preferment which was his due, and he bitterly resented his treatment by the authorities. Of all Panizzi's many correspondents, the letters of Hudson are easily the most delightful to read. It is a great pity that all Panizzi's own letters to his friend were destroyed after Hudson's death, together with all his other papers, by the lady who had only recently become his wife, for Hudson seems to have called out the best in everyone he came in contact with. Sunny, witty, equable of temper, despite increasingly bad health, he, almost alone among their friends, would chaff and tease the increasingly morose Panizzi and restore, for a time, the sick and ageing man to his old good humour.

In 1863, Hudson was discreetly retired by Russell. The exact circumstances are still obscure, but they seem to have involved a certain amount of double-dealing. Panizzi was furious and at once wrote off, offering what help he could, including any financial help, if such should be needed. Hudson, for once dispirited and low, answered his letter in terms of the deepest affection. 'Be assured, dear Pan,' he wrote, 'that to no human being does my heart beat more sympathetically than to yourself. You are such a good fellow that there is no other way than to love you.'[37] Hurt and embittered, Panizzi's friendship was then very precious to Hudson. 'A few words from an old chum and from a man who has suffered as you have suffered years ago, were a real balm to a wounded spirit . . . So thanks, dear old Pan. Thanks, sweet god of the glades for all you say and all you mean.'[38]

Hudson, however, soon recovered his normal good spirits and his later letters, mostly written now from his villa near Florence, to which he had retired, were always bright and cheerful. Panizzi must have longed for their arrival to comfort him in the fog and gloom of London. Hudson would dearly have loved his friend to come and settle down near him. He felt that Panizzi would greatly benefit in health from a warmer climate away from his 'old anchorage in the Square'.[39] But, by now, Panizzi's roots were too deeply laid in England and increasing infirmity soon rendered the idea impossible. Hudson tried hard. As we have seen, on the news of Panizzi's impending retirement, he urged him to get a villa near Florence and never really gave up hope that the two old friends might be neighbours, either in Florence, in Venice or, even, at the Museum itself.

They had, of course, their ups and downs. Panizzi suspected Hudson of casting aspersions on the Italian people. Hudson hurriedly explained it was their governments, and not the Italians themselves, of whom he was critical. He had never accused them 'of any other crime than that of soft-heartedness'. He would, he says, rather live in Italy than anywhere else in the world, in the midst of such honest and friendly inhabitants. Panizzi, mollified, was soon 'like your dear old self again' and the friendship pursued its normal serene course, with Hudson teasing Panizzi about not caring for Italy, since he was too busy enjoying himself in London, drinking such 'large and considerable quantities' of champagne and eating all those dinners',[40] when not gadding off to

Scotland or somewhere. The bantering tone never conceals his great affection for the other man, and his deep concern over his rapidly deteriorating health. Hudson is always giving advice to take some new cure, to travel more, to undergo a course of massage, electrical treatment or some patent medicine or other. Panizzi's health is his constant theme and this at a time when he himself was becoming a complete cripple from gout. No other man, it is safe to say, ever so loved and admired Antonio Panizzi as did this handsome, mocking, sybaritic Italianate Englishman.

So passed the years, filled for Panizzi with his ceaseless activities in the cause of Italy and the cares and responsibilities of running the Institution he so much loved. Throughout this time, his health was rapidly deteriorating and only his immense will power kept him going. As long ago as 1844, he had disclosed to Rutherfurd that he was suffering from 'a painful swelling in the right wrist that leaves me hardly strength to hold the pen. Lord Melbourne consoles me with assuring me that it is gout. I don't believe it and I will not.'[41] But, alas, it was, and as time passed, it steadily grew worse. It seems to have been combined with some form of rheumatic complaint, perhaps arthritis and, each winter, in foggy Victorian London, Panizzi suffered cruelly. The winters of 1860 and 1861 were particularly hard ones, with continual snow, frost and fog. He had had a bad cough which he was unable to throw off, and the pain in his wrist made writing very difficult. 'I have had,' he wrote, 'a bad time of it this winter'[42] and he felt he could not easily face the prospect of another such in England. In the autumn of 1860, he had gone to Homburg in the hope of finding a cure, but, 'as to my health, it is just as it was when I went to that big brothel, with a hell in the centre called Homburg',[43] and now felt that only the sun of Italy would afford him any real and lasting benefit.

Lady Holland had left for southern Italy, despite all Panizzi's entreaties to beware of dangers from war and revolution, and he longed to be there with her. To his disappointment, Museum affairs were now too pressing for him to be away long from England. The Trustees, however, were increasingly concerned at the health of their Principal Librarian. The Speaker, Denison, voiced their disquiet and assured Panizzi that they would be only too glad to grant him special leave of absence.[44] To make matters worse, to his other troubles was now added insomnia, and he feared that unless he had a break, he would be unable to carry on. Lady Holland was begging her '*carissimo Pan*' to join her in Naples and, at home, Winter Jones would cope.

So at last, on December 18, 1862, Panizzi, accompanied by young Louis Fagan, left London for Naples. In Paris, Panizzi called to pay his respects to the Emperor. Napoleon, doubtless struck by the deterioration in the old man's health, even since his visit to the Imperial family the previous summer, ordered a special carriage to be provided for the two travellers, who embarked at Marseilles, hoping to reach Naples in time for Christmas. A terrible storm delayed them and nearly cost them their lives, and it was only on Boxing Day that Panizzi and the boy, tired and weary, at last reached Naples, to be warmly welcomed by Lady Holland.

At the Palazzo Roccella, Panizzi slowly recovered his health. 'I live an idle life,' he wrote to Ellice, 'and yet I have not a moment to myself and the time passes very quickly.'[45] As he felt better, he visited the Neapolitan libraries, including those monastic ones, the treatment of which by the new government, as we have seen, aroused his anger. Gladstone wrote to tell him not to worry and that there was no need for him to return before he had intended. All was well at the Museum under Jones's watchful eye.[46] At last, however, on May 9, 1863, Panizzi returned, to struggle on, against ever-increasing odds, for three more years.

It is now time to speak of Panizzi's relationship with Lady Holland, whose guest he had been all these months and who, wherever she was, bombarded him with letters written in Italian in her sprawling, ungainly hand.

Contrary to what both Fagan and Garnett believed, it does not seem probable that Panizzi became closely acquainted with Holland House until the early forties. His name does not appear in the dinner books until 1845 and his earliest surviving letter to Elizabeth, Lady Holland, and that a very formal one, dates from March 1841. Subsequently, during the last years of old Lady Holland's life, Panizzi was a frequent guest at her house in the company of such cronies as 'Bear' Ellice, Brougham, Sidney Smith and old Samuel Rogers. When abroad, Panizzi carried out little commissions for Lady Holland and sent her the latest political gossip. It must have been a great shock to him when she died very suddenly in November 1845. As Greville wrote: 'It was the final extinction of the flickering remnant of a social light which illuminated and adorned England, and even Europe for half a century. The world never has seen and never will see anything like Holland House.'[47] Twenty years later, Hudson nostalgically recalled these days to Panizzi. Now whenever they go to Holland House . . . 'We are full of old world memories . . . C. J. Fox, old Lord & old Lady Holland and we find a knot of Bishops.'[48]

Soon Panizzi was on familiar terms with the younger members of the family and, whenever the new Lord and Lady Holland were in England, he would dine with them at Holland House. Probably in 1848, they commissioned their protégé, the painter G. F. Watts,[49] to execute a portrait of their friend and he was most grateful for the kindly thought. The dispute over the *Memoirs* clouded the friendship for a while, but neither of the Hollands ever wished to prolong a quarrel and all were soon again the best of friends. With both Holland and his wife, Panizzi carried on a long correspondence giving them the political gossip they both so much enjoyed and details of all his own hopes and plans. They are delightfully informal letters, casual and colloquial, with none of the stilted phraseology so common in letters of the period. Another still younger member of the household who now made Panizzi's acquaintance was little Marie Fox,[50] the Hollands' adopted daughter. Panizzi was as popular with her as he was with all children. To his mingled delight and annoyance, Marie's nickname for him was 'M. Catalogue', an attribute he would far rather have been without. Marie was to be his friend for many years. As Princess Liechtenstein, married and estranged from Lady Holland, she still wrote letter after letter to the lonely and ailing old man she had known so long.

In December 1859, Lord Holland died, but the friendship between his widow and Panizzi continued with, perhaps, increased affection on both sides. Whenever she was in England, Panizzi was a constant visitor, either at Holland House or, more frequently now, at St. Anne's Hill, near Chertsey, another of the family residences. In 1862 and 1863, Panizzi spent many months with her at Naples and both obviously enjoyed each other's company. But Lady Holland was a difficult woman and one who always wanted her own way. Lacaita had not been impressed, when first introduced, thinking her 'vain and vulgar-minded'[51] and several other of Panizzi's friends, especially Hudson, considered her to be self-indulgent and silly. Panizzi, too, it must be admitted, was becoming increasingly difficult. His temper, never good, was exacerbated by the pain of his rheumatism and gout and his patience was very thin.

At last, in 1866 the old friends quarrelled. It was the time of the Austro-Prussian war, in which Italy had also joined, in the hope of winning back Venice. Lady Holland had the temerity, in Panizzi's eyes, of being one of a number of ladies, 'mostly converted Catholics or catholics',[52] who had formed a committee to assist the Austrian wounded. To Panizzi, this was nothing short of treason. Austria was for him, as ever, the enemy, unforgiven and unforgotten and to think that one so dear to him as Lady Holland could now, however indirectly, assist their armies, was unthinkable. That she, the bearer of so great a Whig name, could now associate with 'Romans', 'converts' and notorious leaders of the pro-Austrian faction, was more than he could bear. In September he wrote a dignified letter to her. It was better that their friendly relationship should now cease. He would not presume to state that her opinions should be as his but hostile acts against Italy must be resented by him. Panizzi concludes, '*Addio, cara* Lady Holland. *Scrivo queste parole colle lagrime agli occhi.*' Even his beloved little Marie, 'dearer to me than most people in the world', was considering marrying an Austrian. 'Let us think of the past. Do I deserve this from you?'[53]

A long and angry reply followed from Lady Holland, 'an energetic little body in anger or love', as her brother-in-law, General Fox, had once said. Panizzi, somewhat ungallantly, circulated copies of the correspondence among his friends and asked for their comments. Lacaita, trying to smooth things over between them, was also denounced as a traitor by the now increasingly furious Panizzi.[54] Hudson commented: 'I have read the Pan, Holland, Knight of St Michael correspondence . . . I approve every word you say in it. It is like yourself, upright and to the point.'[55] Other friends, while also supporting Panizzi's point of view, remarked that if Lady Holland had not valued his opinion so highly, she would not have been so angry at losing it, which may or may not have consoled him.

For the moment, Panizzi would not be reconciled. Even the faithful Hudson was censured for being too friendly with the deceitful and treacherous Lacaita. Gradually, as tempers cooled, Panizzi recovered his good humour. Friends sought to bring them together. Gladstone, in particular, seems to have helped, thanking the irascible old man for allowing him to meddle, 'so freely and officiously in the business'[56] and, at length, congratulating him at the success of the 'grand pacification'. Panizzi, never one to bear ill-will for long, wrote to Lacaita[57] to make it up and soon Lady Holland was writing as freely as ever to her '*carissimo amico*'.

Not all, however, thought Panizzi had behaved well in the business. Lord Holland's old friend, Edward Cheney, considered 'Panizzi is very fortunate in having such kind and patient friends. He has frequently behaved to you in a way that you were not called upon to overlook . . . but he cannot exhaust your kindness.'[58] Charles Fox, too, thought that the old man had behaved 'like a rhinoceros',[59] but all were glad that the quarrel was now over. This was the last breach between the two friends and throughout Panizzi's closing years, Lady Holland looked after the now sick and tired old man with devoted care and affection.

Here, perhaps, is the place to mention a curious and still unexplained incident in Panizzi's life. He had been acquainted for some time with a Joseph McVicar, a relative of his old friend Haywood. They had corresponded, on literary and political topics, for a number of years, without, it would seem, becoming very close friends. McVicar had been living with a German lady, a Miss Exner, who had borne him a daughter. Panizzi was himself godfather to the little girl, named, after him, 'Antonia'. McVicar had for some time been in failing health and, in 1865, decided to marry and so regularize his domestic circumstances. He begged Panizzi not to mention Antonia, for the moment, to the rest of the family and to conceal the fact that Miss Exner and he had only just got married.[60] One must presume that Panizzi agreed to this deception. His own letters and comments would be most illuminating. Not long afterwards, McVicar died. After his death, his widow wrote to Panizzi what can only be described as love letters. She was now living at Wiesbaden and implored Panizzi to visit her there. She longed 'to hear you again call me your sweet pet'.[61] Both little Antonia and her mother send him many kisses, 'and her mother returns your kisses most warmly'.[62] Again she writes: 'I long very much to see you . . . send you a thousand warm kisses',[63] words which, especially in that age of formality between the sexes, could surely only denote a very intimate relationship. It is, perhaps, significant that none of his friends ever seem to refer to the McVicars. Possibly it was a discreet silence. Katherine Mc-Vicar, in a further letter, again begs Panizzi to come and see her. 'You will and dare not come . . . I care so much about you . . . Anto and myself will never find a more affectionate friend than my dear P. I know you and all your kindness . . . I long so much to see you.'[64]

In August 1868, Panizzi did, at last, go to Wiesbaden and after that, no further word from Katherine McVicar. What happened we shall probably never know. Later that year, her sister wrote that both Katherine and little Antonia were very seriously ill[65] and after that nothing, save for a curious epilogue. The next year, the younger Haywood wrote to his father's old friend concerning the McVicars. Not only had Joseph died, but also his brother and his brother's widow, both intestate. The money, therefore, had gone to Katherine and to her little daughter. Now the question was raised as to whether Antonia had been born in wedlock. If not, she was no longer the heiress and the money would come to the Haywoods.[66] Panizzi does not seem to have been very forthcoming with his information, for three months later, young Haywood informs him, as fresh news, that Antonia had been born prior to Joseph's marriage with Miss Exner, as, of course, Panizzi very well know. This fact now made young Haywood the legal next of kin and the heir to all the McVicars. In kindness, he asked Panizzi to write, at once, to warn Mrs McVicar of this fact and of what was happening, so that she can 'get her property securely settled now . . . before any proceedings can commence from the other side'.[67] Whether he did, we do not know. A further letter from Haywood told Panizzi that the family now thought that Joseph McVicar had never been married at all and asked for more details about Antonia, and if there were any other children.[68] But no more letters from the sprightly Katherine. What story lies behind it all, one cannot say. Probably nothing more than another example of Panizzi's great kindness and charity towards those lonely and in need. He had, however, not always been indifferent to the physical charms of women,[69] and it would be interesting to know the whole story.

By this time, the middle sixties, Panizzi's health was breaking up badly. In the summer of 1866, he had at long last left his beloved Museum. But before that took place, he was once more to be involved, if only indirectly, in the muddy waters of Italian politics. In the April of 1864, Giuseppe Garibaldi paid his triumphant visit to England and was given a hero's welcome, such as no foreigner has received, before or since. The romantic figure of Garibaldi had caught the imagination of Victorian England, and all, from the Prince of Wales to the great welcoming crowds in the streets, hastened to do honour to the red-shirted hero. All this enthusiasm was by no means welcome to the majority of European governments, whether Italian, French or Austrian and even the British government was worried lest the visit should give encouragement to the exiled republicans and revolutionaries, Mazzini, Louis Blanc, and others, to perpetrate new excesses.

Panizzi had always greatly admired Garibaldi, both as a man and as a soldier, differing profoundly, in this respect, from his friend Mérimée, even though he often distrusted his abilities as a politician. So Panizzi took charge of the hero of the day, welcomed him, made sure he met the right people and only the right people and protected him from what Mérimée called 'les pattes de la démocratie'.[70] On April 15, Garibaldi dined with Panizzi, together with a distinguished company, including the Duke of Sutherland, Garibaldi's London host, Lord Shaftesbury, Gladstone and many other prominent Whigs and Liberals. At the close of the banquet, Garibaldi expressed to his host a wish to visit the tomb of Foscolo in Chiswick churchyard. On April 20, therefore, at five in the morning, so as to avoid, as far as possible, the inevitable crowds, Panizzi, with young Fagan, called on the old soldier and the three set off for Chiswick in a hired carriage. During the journey, according to Fagan,[71] Panizzi passed on to Garibaldi the request of the British government that the speedy departure of their celebrated guest would save everyone needless embarrassment. Arrived at Chiswick the two stood in silence before the tomb of the man who had been Panizzi's earliest friend in England, but whose fate had been so very different from his own. Back in London, the General's departure was quickly announced.

It does indeed, however, seem that it was due more to the fatigue of the visit and to his own poor health than to pressure from the British government.

But Panizzi did not only mix with democrats and revolutionaries. He was one of those men who can be at ease in any company. His courtly manners, his wit and, when in good health, his energy and boyish sense of fun, endeared him to all classes and none more so than to the Imperial family of France. The political connections of Panizzi and Louis Napoleon have already been fully discussed. Here we must speak of him as a welcome guest, whom both the Emperor and the Empress delighted to see, not to mention their little son, with whom the big man was an especial favourite. Although he had already met the Emperor several times, it was not until 1862 that Panizzi really became friendly with the Imperial family as a whole. In that year he had passed through Paris and had been invited to dine with the Empress Eugénie at St Cloud. As he said, Panizzi scarcely knew the Empress and could only presume that he had been invited out of kindness to his friend Mérimée.[72] However, the dinner was a great success. Like so many other women, Eugénie was charmed with Panizzi and, at once, asked him to dinner again so that he could renew his acquaintance with the Emperor. Both Napoleon and Eugénie were much taken with their guest and both talked freely and confidentially to him. An invitation to Biarritz followed and in September, Panizzi went there to stay with the Imperial family. He had already been much struck with their son, then a child of six, a handsome, intelligent and charming child.[73]

It would seem that this visit to Biarritz, unlike his previous one two years before, was much more of a holiday. Affairs of state were discussed and Panizzi was once more unofficial ambassador at the Imperial court. But, primarily, he went to enjoy himself and again he seems to have made a great impression on both host and hostess. To an increasing extent, Panizzi seems to have desired to treat the Emperor and Empress as his personal friends and to leave the diplomatic side to the professionals. An impression of him on this visit has come down to us. 'A tall, stout powerful man of sixty-five to sixty-eight; his manners have a politeness which is as exquisite as it is simple and kindly; he is witty and full of information, speaks French with some difficulty and is yet very easy to talk to.'[74] No wonder Panizzi was popular and widely sought after by society hostesses! During the visit, Panizzi had caused much amusement by his expeditions on horseback to the neighbouring hills. Panizzi was no horseman and Mérimée commented sarcastically on the effect of his weight on his unfortunate mount.[75] A few weeks before, the Empress had visited England and had expressly desired to be shown the British Museum. Panizzi had been delighted to escort her round and had paid her marked attention. Now in their own villa, he could meet both husband and wife and be their guest in a happy, carefree atmosphere. After his departure, Mérimée wrote: 'Nothing is talked about . . . but yourself . . . We are all impatient for news of you. You are most popular here I can assure you among both great and small.'[76] Panizzi, too, was elated with the warm welcome he had received at Biarritz and came back to London full of his visit. He had, Ellice declared, become indeed, a regular courtier.

The Empress was always asking Mérimée for news of his friend and was disappointed when she failed to see him as he passed once more through Paris on his way back from Naples.[77] When the news of his resignation reached Paris, Eugénie was most concerned and wanted to know if there was any special reason for it, until reassured that there was none, save his failing health.[78] Panizzi again saw the Empress in January 1867, whilst on his way to Cannes to pay Mérimée what proved to be a last visit. For after this, the two friends were destined never to see each other. In 1868, Panizzi was desperately ill and quite unfit to travel, and by the following year Mérimée himself was clearly sinking. The gay Paris of the Second Empire was soon to vanish; Mérimée himself to die, as of a broken heart, at the utter collapse of all he held dear, his very house pillaged and set on fire.[79]

Panizzi always admired and respected the Empress Eugénie, despite their very different opinions on almost every matter of importance and he felt for her as the sudden terrible catastrophe overwhelmed Napoleonic France. In August 1870, he wrote to Lacaita to say that he had just received 'a most melancholy letter from Mérimée. As a Frenchman, he feels strongly the danger in which France is and as a friend of the Empress he feels for her family *and in this respect* I am very sorry too. The French deserve what they are likely to get.'[80] In his distrust of the French, Panizzi was very English, as in so many other ways, but he never forgot old friends and to those dear to him he was always loyal. When some months later, Lacaita called on the Empress, now living in exile in England, she spoke much of the old man and how she had valued his friendship. She was to see him once again. In August 1876, Lacaita took the widowed Empress round the British Museum and, afterwards, they called at 81 Bloomsbury Square to see Panizzi, who now seldom left his house. It must have been a sad reunion, so much had happened; but it is certain that they were glad to see each other and talk again over old times.[81]

These years were to see many partings. Haywood and Ellice, both very close and dear to Panizzi, were gone and by the end of the decade, many others of his old friends were to be no more. In 1862, Horne had died and in the following year, his old enemy Forshall. In 1869, within a few months of each other, those two dear old gentlemen, Ellis and Baber, had passed away peacefully both well in their nineties. To Panizzi, they were a real link with the past, with all the busy years at the Museum and with so much else besides. In 1865, Palmerston had gone, in harness to the end, and in 1870, Clarendon, both near and dear friends. But what most affected the old man, because so unexpected and so unnecessary, was the death from cholera, in Damascus, of his beloved young friend, Jane, Countess Teleki, Lady Langdale's daughter. He had known and adored her almost since her babyhood, over thirty years and it was another bitter blow in that sad year. 'My dear old friend,' wrote the stricken mother, 'God support you as I hope He will me under our common calamity.'[82] Hudson, always eager to console Panizzi when in trouble, sent a heartfelt letter of condolence.[83] Even the dying Mérimée, in the midst of his own mounting anxieties, wrote to express his sorrow. 'I only knew her slightly, but she was one of those people whom one does not forget.'[84]

But there were some compensations, even in this sad time. Safely ensconced in Bloomsbury Square, he was cared for by his devoted domestic staff and by the two young men who were now almost sons to him, Louis Fagan and Charles Cannon. After the death of his father in 1869, Louis had returned to England from South America and had, once more, become very dear to Panizzi. Cannon, who had been one of Panizzi's most valued assistants, first in Printed Books and then with him as Principal Librarian, was now at the Foreign Office and shared, with Fagan, the task of looking after the tired and weary old man. Fagan, although himself now at the Museum, in the Department of Prints and Drawings, was installed at the house in Bloomsbury Square, as a general factotum and private secretary, caring for his old friend in every way, writing his letters for him, when he could no longer hold a pen and sparing no effort to make Panizzi's last years as comfortable and as free from anxiety as it was possible to make them.

Panizzi, in gratitude for the assistance George Fagan had once given him over the Neapolitan prisoners, had done all he could to help his sons. The eldest, now in the Indian army, Louis, and the youngest, Charles, all owed much to the kind old man. Especially was this true of Louis Fagan, his future biographer. Ever since 1860, when as a small boy of fourteen, he had been sent home to school from Naples to be placed in Panizzi's care, Louis Fagan had always been near to him. All the warmth and all the love the old man was so very capable of was lavished on the boy, as if he were, indeed, his own child.

Now he was still at his side, 'still the same nice lad',[85] and with the housekeeper, the cook and Panizzi's faithful valet, Dalton, he did his utmost to care for the man, who was as dear to him as his own dead father.

From time to time, Panizzi was still consulted on Museum affairs. In December 1869, the Speaker asked for his opinion as to who should succeed Watts, whose sudden death had left vacant the Keepership of Printed Books. Did Panizzi think Rye would be suitable?[86] Panizzi, doubtless remembering all the years of patient service done by Rye, agreed that he would be most suitable and so Keeper he was. In 1871, Winter Jones wanted some information. Smirke was claiming £687 for special services in connection with the proposed reorganizations of 1862 and 1868. Could Panizzi help, at least with the former? Panizzi could, and Jones wrote to thank him, a little amazed, it would seem, that his old chief's memory was still so accurate.[87] Panizzi never ceased to be interested in what was happening at the Museum. In 1874, Lord Acton, by then a Trustee, wrote to tell him that all the plans for the better government of the Museum had received a serious setback and that Disraeli was quite useless on the Board.[88]

Honours had of course come to the proud old man, honours he had always shunned and avoided, as far as lay in his power. We have seen how, long before, he had managed to wriggle out of the *légion d'honneur*, unexpectedly thrust upon him by Louis Napoleon, but, later, with growing fame, it was not always so easy. He had succeeded in avoiding the knighthood which both Clarendon and the then Home Secretary, Cornewall Lewis, had tried very hard to get him to accept and also Russell's offer of a CB in 1866. In 1859, he had accepted with great reluctance an Hon. DCL from Oxford[89] but of less academic honours he was always very wary. Much against his will, in 1856 he had been made a cavalier of the order of St Maurice and St Lazarus by Victor Emmanuel but this, he might claim, was more a tribute to the Italian cause than to him personally. Panizzi's attitude contrasts very markedly with that of most men of his day, when the passion for honours and decorations was perhaps at its greatest. Even the gentle Ellis, back in 1832, had been furious at others getting knighthoods and not he and moved heaven and earth until he himself finally obtained one, if only a Hanoverian order.[90] Madden, too, had almost beggared himself to live up to his KH and subsequent court appointment,[91] and neither were at all unusual in their attitude.

In September 1865, Panizzi was approached as to whether he would be willing to become a Senator of the newly created Kingdom of Italy. This offer troubled him greatly. If this meant giving up his English nationality or being, in any way, disloyal to the country which had succoured him and given him so much, he would never accept. All his friends urged him to take it. Gladstone pointed out that by doing so he would be 'rendering great services to your *other* country'[92] and Mérimée cited the example of the great Duke of Wellington.[93] Panizzi, though, was unhappy and annoyed with the Italian government, for not finding out first whether he, an Englishman, might properly accept such an offer and so have avoided putting him in an embarrassing position. Hudson, as usual, summed it up: 'They offered you one of the highest honours and dignities of the state without having reflected for one moment upon the position which Fate and a long, arduous and most distinguished . . . career had *thrust* upon you, for certainly you never in your life *sought* honours.'[94]

Nevertheless, in a later letter, Hudson advised his old friend to give Italy the benefit of his great administrative ability and experience. But this was just what Panizzi felt he could no longer do. He was tired and old, worn out by the long years of struggle and controversy and wanted only peace. He could not belong to two countries and, by now, England was his own beloved land. All his memories were there; all his friends. 'He had a capital house, a comfortable income, a circle of friends and a good pension';[95] would he now want to give up all these? But it was much more than this. For all his life-long devotion to the Italian cause, he now felt he was a stranger in the new Italy. England was home and though he might travel far afield, he always longed to get back again to Bloomsbury Square. However, despite all his scruples, on March 12, 1868, Panizzi was made a Senator and in the following April, a Commander of the Order of the Crown of Italy.[96] But he never took his seat in the Senate. Probably, as he himself said, he would have done so, had not his grave illness intervened and made him give up for ever all further thought of an active life. In 1869, somewhat recovered, his old friend Gladstone, now Prime Minister, persuaded him, most reluctantly, to accept a KCB. Even this acceptance was possibly due to a misunderstanding. Panizzi was recuperating with James Hudson in Ischia. At Gladstone's request, Lacaita had written to Panizzi, asking him if he would now accept a KCB. Panizzi's reply seems to have been somewhat ambiguous, but Lacaita at once informed the Prime Minister that their old friend had agreed. Panizzi then had second thoughts and tried to withdraw. Gladstone had, however, already sent in Panizzi's name to the Queen and it was too late to do anything. Lacaita reassured Gladstone, who was distressed lest he should have offended the old man, that Panizzi would in fact be delighted once it was all settled. Hudson, too, wrote to Lacaita to say that Panizzi had shown him the letter and that 'I have advised him to accept the decoration . . .[He] cannot refuse such a distinction from such hands.'[97]

But there were still difficulties. On March 5 the summons came for Panizzi to attend the next investiture. But he was unable to go. Full of sorrow, for he would indeed have wished to thank the Queen for the honour bestowed upon him, he wrote that, since his illness he had almost entirely lost the use of his legs and could only totter a few steps, with a great risk of falling and being unable to rise.[98] The Home Office, anxious to help, let him know that he would not be expected to kneel, that a closed carriage would take him there and back and that he would be excused having to wear court dress. There would be footmen everywhere to assist him and he might take his stick. If he was unable to be present, it was pointed out, he would have to be created a knight by patent, which would cost him £120. Otherwise he would never be 'Sir Anthony'.

Panizzi was really past caring anyhow. He wrote politely but firmly to the Lord Chamberlain that he just could not nor would not go.[99] He could not even walk across a room, let alone upstairs. Gladstone, however, arranged matters. A warrant was sent, signed by the Queen, which excused him not only personal attendance at the investiture but also the payment of any fee in lieu. He was given full permission to use the appellation of his rank. Antonio Panizzi was now Sir Anthony, KCB. The insignia, dispatched by Garter King at Arms, followed in a few days and, after all, it was a very proud old man who accepted the delighted congratulations of his many friends.

In other aspects, too, 1870 was not all sorrow. Italian troops had at last occupied Rome and all Italy was united. Hudson wrote to his old ally, 'With the year 1871 that old friend of ours, the "Italian Question" comes to an end.'[100] Panizzi, unlike so many of the other patriots, had lived to see it all. In his boyhood and youth, the Napoleonic Kingdom of Italy, the bitter reaction of his early manhood, the disappointments and fears of the long years of frustration, when it must have seemed that Italy would never be free. Then the horrors of King Bomba's prisons, which he himself had done so much to make known to a shocked Europe, his desperate plans to rescue the poor wretches from their living grave and the bitter failure of all his hopes. At last, the years of triumph, the annus mirabilis of 1860, Venice and Rome liberated and all safely united. Now it all seemed a little tarnished. The Italy which had emerged from the years of struggle was no longer the Italy of his dreams. He brushed on one side Hudson's cheery optimism. He would not be comforted.

But life still went on. Once again the old man was able to visit the Ellices in Scotland. He still retained, for a little longer, his full mental powers, even if his physical strength was fading fast. Marie Fox, now Princess Liechtenstein, wrote to him long and happy letters, even though, to Panizzi's grief, she had quarrelled so bitterly with her stepmother, Lady Holland. On April 4, 1873, the Prince, her husband, wrote to tell their old friend the glad news that his wife had had a baby girl.[101] Panizzi was delighted but was too ill to write himself to congratulate the young couple. Friends still called to cheer him up. Parry, busy with the famous Tichbourne case, spared a few moments to visit his former chief. Others sent him the latest news from France, whilst Hudson, himself now desperately ill, wrote his witty and comforting letters.

For, by now, he was at last breaking up. 'As to myself,' he cried despairingly, 'I am getting worse and worse every day.'[102] Panizzi had never really recovered from that terrible illness of 1868, when it seemed to Gladstone and to all his friends that he was clearly dying. He was now very, very weary. His insomnia was worse, so much so that, in his despair, he had threatened to blow his brains out. Almost a complete cripple, half blind, he was but the wreck of the magnificent man he had once been. All he could manage was a short drive in the afternoon, accompanied usually by the faithful Fagan and, then, back to Bloomsbury Square, where a lift had been installed to ease somewhat the sick man's burden. Even now Panizzi did not forget his old acquaintances. Hearing of Hudson's grave illness, the kindly old man had called at the house of his friend's sister to see if there was any news. A little reading of the Latin poets or of Dante and if he was well enough, a dinner or, more usually, luncheon with a few guests was about as much as he could do.

But these were the last flickerings of his indomitable spirit. He made his will. He had not much to leave. His watch to Winter Jones, his books and papers to his beloved Museum, a few small bequests to friends and servants, in particular to Cannon and Fagan, and that was all.[103] On Friday, April 4, 1879, Gladstone called on Panizzi for the last time. It was plain that the poor old man, blind, almost completely paralysed, his once clear and brilliant mind now sadly clouded, was sinking fast. On the following Tuesday afternoon, April 8, 1879, he died calmly and peaceably in Louis Fagan's arms. On the Saturday the funeral took place at St. Mary's Roman Catholic Cemetery, Kensal Green. Though it was private, many of his old friends came to pay their last respects. Among them was Louis Fagan, the chief mourner, Bond, the new Principal Librarian, Major, Garnett, Cannon and other colleagues. Dr Chepmell, his medical attendant, for long the close friend of both Panizzi and of Lord and Lady Holland was there, together with representatives of the Italian Embassy and other distinguished Italians. Henry Stevens came, too, to pay his respects to the man who had done so much to foster a closer relationship between the literary world of England and of the United States. On the coffin was placed the Italian flag, a last tribute to the old patriot. A simple inscription recorded, 'Sir Antonio Panizzi, Knight Commander of the Most Honourable Order of the Bath, Civil Division, born Sept. 17, 1797, died April 8, 1879.'[104]

So passed a great man and a great librarian, mourned, loved and respected by all who knew him. In a little more than two years, his friend and disciple Winter Jones followed him to the grave. Panizzi had left but little in worldly goods – less than £3,000, even when the house and all its contents had been sold, but enough remained to settle his few small bequests. His memorial and his legacy were elsewhere, in the great Reading Room, in a thriving and world-famous library and in the gratitude of all those, both English and Italian, he had endeavoured so long to serve.

NOTES TO CHAPTER 15

1 Esdaile, p. 122.

2 Mérimée, II, p. 107. Mérimée to A.P., October 24, 1865.

3 Guglielmo Libri, 1803–1869. Mathematician, Professor of Physics at Pisa. Occupied the chair of Mathematics at the Collège de France, 1832.

4 Add. MS. 36, 721. f.316.

5 Bertram Ashburnham, Earl of Ashburnham, 1793–1878.

6 Mérimée, I, p. 224.

7 *Foreign Reminiscences* . . . *edited by his son, Henry Edward Lord Holland*, London, 1850.
Memoirs of the Whig Party during my Time by Henry Richard Lord Holland. Edited by his son, Henry Edward Lord Holland, 2 vol., London, 1852–54, 80.

8 Francis Russell, 10th Duke, 1788–1861. '. . . a good natured plausible man without enemies and really, though he does not think so, without friends.'

9 Sir Robert Adair, 1763–1853, diplomatist.

10 Add. MS. 36, 716. f.140.

11 Add. MSS. 36, 716. ff.148, 152.

12 Add. MS. 36, 716. f.157. [Edward Cheyney to A.P., January 30, 1851.]

13 Add. MS. 36, 716. f.174.

14 '. . . an invention of your correspondents,' Panizzi declares, he is not timid, 'because I had the courage not to hawk about your attack on Sir R. Adair . . . I might say much more but it is too painful . . . If you continue in your recent mood towards me, let our correspondence end here . . . in God's name let us make no more allusion . . . to sore points.' [Add. MS. 36, 716. f.179.]

15 Add. MSS. 36, 716. ff.186, 190.

16 A.P. to Lord Holland, August 9, 1851. *Holland House Papers.*

17 A.P. to Lord Holland, December 24, 1851. In the same letter Panizzi tells how he had gone to Downing Street to see Palmerston and 'found the Cabinet sitting without him'. Panizzi at once realized something was wrong, 'felt at once uneasy'. Palmerston had, in fact, just been dismissed over his act in congratulating Louis Napoleon on the success of the *coup d'état*, due to 'pressure from Windsor'. [*Holland House Papers.*]

18 Henry Bickersteth, Baron Langdale, 1783–1851. Lady Langdale was among the last descendants of Edward Harley, Earl of Oxford, one of the great early benefactors of the Museum.

19 Sir Thomas Hardy, 1804–1878. Archivist, Deputy Keeper, Public Record Office, 1861–1876.

20 *Memoirs of the Right Hon. Henry Lord Langdale*, 2 vol., London, 1852.

21 Fagan, I, p. 328.

22 Fagan, I, p. 329.

23 'Lord Brougham is here very weak and tottery but as great a busybody as ever, inquisitive to a degree . . . He has become very religious which holds out some hope for you and me when we arrive at the age of eighty-five.' Mérimée, I, p. 366.

24 Add. MS. 36, 717. f.66.

25 An attempt was made by some of his Scottish friends to teach Panizzi Scotch words and phrases, which he loved using when writing to them. He wrote to Rutherfurd: 'Altho' not a Scotchman – altho' I speak wonderfully well the Scottish language.' *Rutherfurd Correspondence*, quoted in Wicks, p. 151.

26 A.P. to Elizabeth, Lady Holland, September 11, 1844. *Holland House Papers.*

27 Thomas Dundas, 2nd Earl of Zetland, 1795–1873. In his latter years, Panizzi spent much time at Zetland's house in Yorkshire.

28 Fagan, II, p. 248.

29 Gladstone dined with Panizzi immediately before his departure. Add. MS. 44, 233. f.93.

30 As minister to the Court of St James. C. Lacaita, p. 147.

31 C. Lacaita, pp. 127, 148. Panizzi had made up his mind to accept and was only with great difficulty persuaded not to. He also received an appeal from Farini, the 'dictator' of Modena to represent the rebel provinces in England.

32 Add. MS. 42, 177. f.43.

33 C. Lacaita, pp. 128, 152.

34 Add. MS. 44, 233. f.239. 'Our friend Panizzi will already have told you how matters stand with regard to Monte Casino.' Lacaita to Gladstone, April 24, 1866.

35 Fagan, II, p. 245. Add. MSS. 36, 722. ff.89, 91, 98.

36 Add. MS. 36, 722. f.122.

37 Add. MS. 36, 722. f.180. Rutherfurd had written in a similar strain some years earlier. 'It is hard to overcome you in any contention of kindness and good feeling.' Add. MS. 36, 727. f.347.

38 Add. MS. 36, 722. f.230.

39 Add. MS. 36, 724. ff.509, 513.

40 Add. MS. 36, 725. ff.207, 232.

41 Fagan, I, p. 181.

42 Add. MS. 36, 721. f.211.

43 Add. MS. 36, 721. f.6.

44 Add. MS. 36, 726. f.116.

45 Add. MS. 36, 722. f.66.

46 Add. MS. 36, 722. f.124.

47 Greville, *Journals*, II, 307.

48 Add. MSS. 36, 724. f.167.

49 George Frederick Watts, 1817–1904.

50 Marie Fox, Princess Liechtenstein, 1851?–1878. Her parentage is unknown. For a discussion of the problem, see *Chronicles of Holland House*, pp. 400–402.

51 C. Lacaita, p. 86.

52 Add. MS. 36, 723. f.518.

53 Add. MS. 36, 724. f.39.

54 A.P. to Gladstone, November 30, 1866. Add. MS. 44, 274. f.330.

55 Add. MSS. 36, 724. f.105.

56 Add. MSS. 36, 724. f.257.

57 Add. MSS. 36, 724. f.281.

58 E. Cheyney to Lady Holland, October 5, 1866. *Holland House Papers*.

59 *Holland House*, p. 428.

60 Add. MSS. 36, 723. f.164. McVicar would seem to have been a nephew of Francis Haywood.

61 Add. MS. 36, 724. f.436.

62 Add. MS. 36, 724. f.436.

63 Add. MS. 36, 724. f.484.

64 Add. MS. 36, 724. f.488.

65 Add. MS. 36, 724. f.539.

66 Add. MS. 36, 725. f.109.

67 Add. MS. 36, 725. f.136.

68 Add. MS. 36, 725. f.215.

69 A.P. to Ellice, '. . . the game of two backs. (I have now forgotten that pleasant game for want of practice.)' [Add. MSS. 36, 722. f.199.] A.P. to Lord Holland, November 29, 1855, 'I wish I was at Paris only to see some of your ladies *sans jupons*. It is pretty nearly one of the few enjoyments left to me, except taking a glass of claret. I must confess however that I had always a taste that way and always liked simplicity.' [*Holland House Papers.*]

70 Mérimée, I, p. 389.

71 Fagan, II, p. 250.

72 A.P. to E. Ellice, August 11, 1862. Fagan, II, p. 233.

73 Panizzi was a great favourite with the young Prince. Mérimée, I, pp. 278, 281.

74 E. Barthez, p. 229.

75 Mérimée, I, p. 277.

76 Mérimée, I, p. 278.

77 He did, however, stay once more at Biarritz in September 1863. Mérimée, I, pp. 345, 346.

78 Mérimée, II, p. 76.

79 Add. MS. 36, 725. f.417.

80 Add. MS. 36, 725, f.253.

81 C. Lacaita, p. 241.

82 Add. MS. 36, 725. f.265.

83 Add. MS. 36, 725. f.274.

84 Mérimée, II, p. 366.

85 Mérimée, II, p. 330.

86 Add. MS. 36, 725. f.194.

87 Add. MS. 36, 725. ff.374, 375.

88 Add. MS. 36, 725. f.568.

89 He never used the title. *Passages*, p. 80.

90 Add. MS. 41, 312. f.144.

91 Madden, *Diary*.

92 Add. MS. 36, 723. f.222.

93 Mérimée, II, p. 101.

94 Add. MS. 36, 723. f.241.

95 Add. MS. 36, 724. f.169. Hudson also writes, 'could you abandon your lovely climate, and your fog, gas and Brooks'. Panizzi wrote to Haywood a few years before: the utmost I could expect would be to be looked upon as a crazy Angloman . . . I am a greater stranger in Italy than here.' [Fagan, II, p. 191.]

96 Add. MS. 36, 724. f.393.

97 Add. MSS. 44, 234. ff.22, 23.

98 Add. MS. 36, 725. f.241.

99 Add. MS. 36, 725. f.244.

100 Add. MS. 36, 725. f.432. In an earlier letter he says, 'I cannot imagine a greater pleasure than in entering Rome with Pan as my tutelary deity.' [Hudson to A.P., October 11, 1870. Add. MS. 36, 725. f.340.]

101 Add. MS. 36, 725. f.512. Panizzi in his dictated reply (he was now too crippled to write himself) lamented the fact that he would never be able to play with the little girl as he had with her mother when she was a child. 'It would be a great consolation to me to be able to show the moon to the young lady just born as I did at Bordeaux to her dear Mother.' He was also very hurt that Lady Holland had not told him of the baby's arrival. 'She does not even take the trouble to inquire after me, except when she wants something herself of a very confidential character.' [Add. MS. 36, 727. f.303.] This is probably only senile querulousness, for it seems generally agreed that Lady Holland was extremely good to the old man.

102 Add. MS. 36, 727. f.303.

103 Add. MS. 36, 725. f.640.

104 Newspaper cutting in Stride.

16

CONCLUSION

ONE aspect of Panizzi's many-sided personality has been, perhaps, unduly neglected: his literary achievements. His greatest contribution to scholarship was, primarily, an indirect one. He was, above all, an administrator and a very great one, by any standards. He was forced early in life to abandon the delights of academic research for more arid pastures, but, even there, he was able to leave his mark.

As has been remarked, he had early developed an interest in the Italian Romantic poets. This is well shown by notes he wrote for the course of lectures delivered at the Liverpool Royal Institution in 1825, and even more by the scholarly *Essay on the Romantic Narrative Poetry of the Italians*, which forms the first volume of Panizzi's edition of *Orlando Innamorato*. These works, which we have discussed more fully above, are undoubtedly Panizzi's chief claim to academic distinction and together with his little volume, *Chi era Francesco da Bologna?*[1] prove that, had circumstances been different, he might well have achieved distinction as a critic of taste and discernment. But it was not to be, and much of his writing is to be found in the form of articles in such periodicals as *The Quarterly* and *The Edinburgh Review*.

It is, indeed, in these, hastily written in moments snatched from the pressing cares of his official duties, that the true Panizzi, that intensely political animal, is plainly revealed. Such essays as *The Political Condition of the Italian States*, *The Congress of Verona*, *The Revolt in Lombardy*, the famous *Post Office Espionage*[2] and others, show a depth of feeling, a hatred of tyranny, a passionate desire for freedom, not only for Italy but for other oppressed nations, which spring from his deepest feelings and convictions. Naturally, Panizzi shows the limitations of his class and age.[3] Too easily, perhaps, he absorbed the prejudices of the Whigs amongst whom he lived. He could see only evil in any form of theocracy. He was blind to the glories of the Middle Ages, which he despised and hated. He detested the Jesuit order with a harsh ferocity, unmindful of its many great achievements. Italy must be free, but never Ireland, too Catholic and too backward to merit that distinction, and he had obviously, for all his warm-hearted sympathy for the lot of the poor and helpless, no conception of the horrors of the Industrial Revolution in the land of his adoption nor of the appalling social conditions, as distinct from political conditions, in the land of his birth.

But given these limitations, Panizzi's is a noble, generous outlook, akin to the best elements in the Whig tradition and very often more genuinely radical than the outlook of many latterday bearers of that name. He was in this, as in other respects, a true Whig of the old Holland House school. In the flesh he may have known it only in its declining years, spiritually he breathed the air of the great days of Charles Fox and of old Lord Holland.

Another aspect of Panizzi's complex personality, which we have touched on before, his sense of fun and his love and understanding of children, is shown in the *Works of Chichemetecatl*,[4] the humorous periodical, compiled under the 'editorship' of Jane Bickersteth, to which Panizzi, Lord Langdale and other members of the family contributed. The sunny humour of Panizzi at his best shines through the pages of the little work and though some of the political satires[5] and fables which he contributed to it were probably above the head of even such an intelligent child as Jane, she obviously loved having something to print from 'Tramper' or the 'Old Boy' or another of the pseudonyms under which he wrote. Jane Bickersteth adored Panizzi, pulling his leg unmercifully and teasing him about his many lady friends. The articles in the various reviews give us one side of Panizzi's character, the decided viewpoint, the firm, if at times, narrow outlook, the generous reaction when liberty anywhere was threatened. The happy nonsense in Jane Bickersteth's little periodicals make plain

the fun and good humour that, until pain and old age at last
dimmed them, were never far beneath the surface.

Panizzi was a man, like so many, who presented two faces to the
world. That which the public and many of his colleagues saw was
that of an efficient administrator, a stern, just and upright official,
a great stickler, perhaps too great, for small details, a strict dis-
ciplinarian, revered by many but feared by all for, in his wrath, he
was terrible.

To his real friends and intimates, he was the 'great god Pan',
'dearest, dearest Pan', 'the Prince of Good Fellows', the lover of
jokes and of a somewhat coarse humour, his great voice, in his
broken English,[6] pealing out over the room. Here was the inveterate diner-out, the epicurean lover of good food and fine
wines, the man whose company and table were eagerly sought
after by the great and by the not so great; the man whose friendship was valued and cherished by the austere Gladstone and the
sybaritic Hudson, by old Thomas Grenville, by Palmerston and
by so many more. This same man was the one around whom the
women flocked, who from youth to extreme old age was cosseted
by admiring females; the man whom children adored and who
adored them: a kind, good man, whose secret acts of charity were
legion; a man, in short, very different from the bullying ruffian
depicted in the pages of the popular press.

Panizzi, it must never be forgotten, was physically a big man, a
very big man indeed, especially for an Italian, and a man of the
most commanding and striking appearance. Almost to the end,
his friends loved to tease him about his weight and size and his
well-known reluctance to take any form of exercise and, in his
youth, he was handsome, in a rugged fashion. Even today as one
looks at the portrait by Watts on the walls of the Board Room of the
Museum, in its due place with those of so many others of the benefactors and heads of that institution he loved so much, it is an
imposing, brooding presence. Sir Henry Ellis stares out of his
portrait in mild astonishment; Panizzi's successor, the kindly
Winter Jones, gazes calmly and patiently, the devoted follower
rather than the inspired leader. Sir Anthony sits and watches, as if
guarding still the Museum he cherished for so long with such
'savage tenderness'.[7] One feels there, also 'the steam roller',[8] if not
the thorough-going tyrant of popular belief, feared yet respected

11*

by his younger colleagues. It gives an impression of great latent strength and firmness of purpose, a powerful, almost menacing figure, whom one would hesitate to cross.

For Antonio Panizzi was, indeed, hot-tempered, few more so. In this, if in nothing else, he was a true son of Italy. Stupidity, especially if combined with a certain shiftiness and unwarranted arrogance, particularly infuriated him. It was this element, which he found in Edwards and even more so in others with whom he crossed swords, that always aroused his wrath. Any officiousness or overweening self-satisfaction, such as it seemed to him he detected in Carlyle and in many a politician or foreign potentate, was equally abhorrent to him. But for the most part his rage was soon over. He never bore malice for any personal insult or reflection on his own character, though he would spare no pains to hunt down and destroy anyone that seemed to him to be harming in some way his beloved Museum. He would go out of his way to seek to make peace with those, such as Madden and Gray, who had sought to do him an injury. Almost never did Panizzi himself initiate a quarrel. When threatened, he counter-attacked with consummate skill and energy and the attention to detail of a great commander, overwhelming his opponents by the vigour and ability of his thrusts. He was undoubtedly over-sensitive and, especially in his later years, far too ready to take offence where none was intended. But it must not be forgotten that Panizzi had had to endure long years of calumny and misrepresentation which would have soured a man of much more equable temper. Few men in public life have ever had to bear such mean and petty attacks as did Panizzi, not only on his official conduct and on the running of the Museum, but also on his private life. He was an exile and a refugee, and despite his success, his almost complete absorption into English society, he was never allowed to forget his foreign origin.

As we have seen, in one thing only was he ready to pick a quarrel, even with his dearest friends, and that was over any reflection against, any slur upon, his native Italy. To cast doubts on the nobility of the Italian cause and on the integrity of the Italian people was to arouse his speedy anger. Even though he himself, in old age, was less sure than he had been, such hesitations must never be expressed by others. His lifelong devotion to the Whig cause, his hearty espousal of its principles stemmed mainly from his devotion to Italy as did, contrariwise, his contempt for and distrust of the Tories. Any party or person who openly advocated a friendly policy towards Austria, the cowardly tyrant which had for so long enslaved his people. the object of his sustained and bitter hatred throughout his long life, was anathema to him. His dear Lady Holland was cast off for no greater offence than of joining a committee formed to succour the Austrian wounded and it deeply distressed him that Marie Fox had married an Austrian nobleman. Panizzi could, of course, play the courtier as well as any other man and seek the assistance of the pro-Austrian Prince Consort in his efforts to become Principal Librarian and, in his official capacity, entertain visiting Austrian Archdukes. But it was his unshaken opinion, that it was to 'friends of order' such as these that the sufferings of his beloved Italy were largely due. It was due to them, or to those like them, that brave men had died on the scaffold, spent long years in filthy dungeons or pined in exile. Whatever his official duties might cause him to do, such could never be his friends.[9]

Panizzi, in many ways, the mildest of Whigs and certainly not such a born rebel as his friend Hudson, was, in other respects, far more of a radical than many realized. He would not, indeed, go all the way with such men as Orsini or Mazzini, far from it, but this was, to a very large extent, not, as with Mérimée, from fear of their radicalism, but in the belief that, by their activities, they did more harm than good to the Italian cause. 'May [Italy] be preserved from such friends as [Mazzini and Gallenga],'[10] he cried and this was his constant theme. It did not necessarily imply any marked hostility to them as individuals. Indeed, according to Fagan, Panizzi saved Mazzini from certain capture and possible death,[11] and Parry, one of Mazzini's most faithful English supporters, was Panizzi's lifelong friend.

Nevertheless, his opinion of Mazzini, in particular, as a politician was very low. He distrusted his visionary schemes, 'his wicked absurdities', which had cost so many men their lives, but he always respected Mazzini's genuine devotion to their common motherland. Despite his love of high society, Panizzi would never pay lip service to views which he did not nor could not support. He could never be so passively amenable to the opinions of others as was Lacaita, for example, whose great aim was, in Panizzi's eyes, 'to be well with everybody and to make money'.[12] In his own words, he was one 'who never begged or humbled himself',[13] a proud man in whatever circles he was mixing, conscious of his own integrity, perhaps, at times, too fond of parading that particular virtue, in whom there was always a passion for justice and for the rule of law.

Panizzi was, above all, proud of what he had achieved, proud that he, who had come to England penniless, should have raised himself, almost entirely by his own efforts, to a position of such authority and responsibility. He had made enemies; no man who had done what he had done could have failed to do so. His unsuccessful attempts to get into the Athenaeum, which Lacaita entered so easily, were particularly galling and there were some who would never forgive him for his reputed attitude towards scientists, already, by the sixties, a power to be reckoned with. Yet by the end of his life, Panizzi was a national institution, all criticism stilled, as so often with the British, by the mere fact of longevity.

Panizzi never formally renounced the faith of his youth, as did Lacaita, even though it became, what Mérimée sarcastically called 'second-rate Catholicism'.[14] Whenever discussion arose, whenever there was any controversy, he would simply say 'I am a Roman Catholic', and the matter would drop. His sympathies, however, were rarely with his co-religionists.[15] He had in him all the engrained anti-clericalism of the continental liberal, combined with much of the scepticism in religious matters of the Whig circles in which he moved, sharing their deep distrust of all ecclesiastical pretensions and religious enthusiasm. Panizzi would have undoubtedly agreed with the opinion of his friend Russell that all creeds were much the same as long as they were not enforced; most doctrines inoffensive as long as they were optional. He had none of Gladstone's consuming interest in theological questions, but, also, little of the zealous agnosticism of Huxley and the post-Darwinian scientists. Panizzi would never hesitate to use the religious opinions of others to further the aims nearest to his heart, the Catholicism of Shrewsbury or the evangelical Protestantism of Shaftesbury, the one to influence clerical circles in Naples, the other to rouse British indignation against Papal pretensions

He had few friends among his fellow Catholics in England. He got on well with Wiseman,[16] both before and after the latter had become a Cardinal and, in later years, he enjoyed Acton's[17] company. Such friends as he had then among Catholics were from the old families, Erastian in their beliefs and mostly hostile, as he was, to the ultramontane policies of the new converts. Such men as Manning and Faber aroused his strong dislike and he was as hotly opposed to the Tractarians and their 'Newmania', as the most rabid Protestant. His views on religion were undoubtedly greatly influenced by the Papal claims to the temporal sovereignty of central Italy, and by the support given by many of the clergy, though not, he freely admitted, by all, to the despotism of the Bourbon monarchs of Naples and to the reactionary rulers of northern Italy.[18] Any extension of Papal pretensions aroused his immediate anger. Thus the restoration of the Catholic hierarchy in England, the 'Papal Aggression' of 1851, alarmed Panizzi as much as it did that heir of the 'Glorious Revolution', Lord John Russell. Both as an Italian patriot and as an English Whig, he bitterly attacked the reactionary government set up in the Papal States after the downfall of Mazzini's Roman Republic of 1848.[19] He feared and detested the Concordat of 1855 between Austria and the Holy See. To him, it was a device to curtail the freedom of Italy and to undermine what little freedom was still left within the Austrian dominions, a diabolical pact between a treacherous and unworthy Italian government and the hereditary enemy of all free men. To Panizzi, England was the 'citadel of free inquiry, of civil and religious liberty against passive obedience and spiritual as well as temporal despotism'[20] and he looked fearfully for signs of any cracks or of any weakening of its ancient defences. Absolutism in any guise was abhorrent to him. He would never admit that the Church had anything but a minimal interest in temporal affairs and to him, as to any other Whig, the demands of temporal affairs were always paramount. Like Russell, he too would say, 'Above all, no dogma!'

'Whoever believes in spiritual despotism,' wrote Panizzi, 'will readily submit to a temporal despot,'[21] and Antonio Panizzi would never in this world submit to either, hating, above all, what he described to Gladstone as the '*scelerata tirannida dei preti*".[22] No wonder then, when in 1868, as he lay, apparently dying, an unknown priest forced his way into the house to administer the last rites, on his recovery, Panizzi's rage knew no bounds. To his Voltairian mind, such conduct was indefensible. He issued strict instructions that in no circumstances was such a thing ever to happen again.[23] With individual priests or clergymen, provided they were men of broad views, he could be friends. To all forms of organized religion he was fundamentally hostile and the greater the spiritual claims of the faith upon the minds of men, the greater his hostility. In this, of course, Panizzi was typical of his age and upbringing. Though his own cousin was a bishop,[24] such was exceptional in the bourgeois families of early nineteenth-century Europe. Panizzi and the great majority of those born at the turn of the century were real children of the Enlightenment and had none of the passionate, and even morbid, interest in matters of religion of the next generation, particularly, of course, in England. Panizzi would have undoubtedly cried with his old friend Lord Melbourne, 'This damned morality will undo us all.'

It must be admitted that even granted his gifts of industry and acumen, Panizzi was most fortunate in his age. In the political world of England, the reign of the great Whig families was, at last, coming to an end. A generation earlier, he would have scarcely been accepted, a generation later it would have mattered little if he had been. No longer would it have been possible to change the course of history through a personal relationship with half a dozen Whig grandees. As early as 1846, Clarendon, that acute observer, had remarked that the exclusive aristocratic group of a few Whig noblemen was beginning to break up. By 1867, when Gladstone took over from Russell, their influence had become almost negligible. During these comparatively few years, by knowing the right people, by his powers of persuasion, by his wit and social graces, by his appeal, not only to the Whig love of liberty, but also to their love of scholarship, Panizzi achieved for his beloved Italy much which could never have been achieved, at least by these means, at any other period.

Again, his meteoric rise was facilitated by the still widespread interest in Italian literature among educated people. The young Panizzi could depend upon the knowledge of and enthusiasm for things Italian of such men as Roscoe and Grenville. At no other period since the sixteenth century was an understanding of Italian language and literature held to be indispensable for any truly well-educated man or woman. To them, Panizzi was not one from among a remote, barbarous, or, worst of all, merely comic, people. He was, on the contrary, a not unworthy representative of the nation which had produced both Dante and the giants of the Renaissance. Ariosto, Petrarch, Tasso, Boiardo and many others were familiar names, such as they had not been fifty years before and, certainly, were not fifty years later. It was the high tide of Italian studies in England and many, such as Gladstone, came to a knowledge of contemporary Italy through a love for her literature and for her past. Panizzi was able to take full advantage of this interest. It started him on his career; it furthered his advancement and secured for him many friends from every class of society. Almost all his life, chance acquaintances as well as close friends wrote to him on subjects connected with Italian language and literature. It was not a remote esoteric subject, the preserve of academic specialists and scholars. It was part of the mental equipment of every educated Englishman.

Then, too, in his Museum career, he was again most fortunate. His long reign as Keeper of Printed Books coincided with a new and more widespread interest in every aspect of knowledge. The new spirit of the age would never have been content with the old easy-going, slothful Museum of the early years of the century. Reformed, willy-nilly, it would have to have been. It was its supreme good fortune to have been reformed, from within, by an administrator of genius, such as Panizzi, so much of whose work still endures in the institution he so much loved.

For with the exception of the laid-down printed catalogue introduced shortly after his death,[25] there is scarcely a feature in the day-to-day procedure and administration of his old department that does not owe its origin to the fertile mind of Antonio Panizzi. Printed reading-room tickets; labels on books; press-marks; the placing system; staff diaries; copyright administration, adequate readers' reference books, even the staff canteen, all are due in their original form to the great Modenese. The ninety-one rules, the basis of all Museum cataloguing for more than a hundred years, was primarily his work and that alone would ensure his place in bibliographical history.

Throughout every activity of the Department, his influence can be traced. Panizzi started or greatly enlarged every division of the present Department of Printed Books: Maps, Music, State Papers, Slavonic, Newspapers, all derive, in a very large part, from his own endeavours or from those directly inspired by him. To him, too, are due the start of the American collections and a great increase in the number of works in oriental languages. Panizzi had, above all, the true librarian's belief that no work, however apparently trivial, was valueless. Even the most ephemeral publication might be of inestimable importance to future historians. Panizzi was in every respect a librarian of librarians, perhaps the greatest we have yet seen. The world of learning, both of his own and of all subsequent generations, owes him an inestimable debt of gratitude. A volcano in a Dutch garden,[26] he very well may have been, but despite every criticism, his monument endures. Every day hundreds of scholars, from every land, pass beneath the bust of Panizzi above the entrance to his great Reading Room. Few stop to think of the debt they all owe to the genius of this most remarkable man.

NOTES TO CHAPTER 16

1 *Chi era Francesco da Bologna?* London, 1858. Dedicated to the Duc d'Aumale.

2 Among the more important of Panizzi's contributions to various periodicals are:

> *Edinburgh Review*
> July 1824 *The Holy Alliance.*
> July 1832 *The Political Condition of the Italian States.*
> July 1848 *The Revolt in Lombardy.*
> July–October 1851 *Neapolitan Justice.*

> *British and Foreign Review*
> October 1838 *The Congress of Verona*
> 1843 *The Spanish Question*

> *North British Review*
> November 1844 *Post Office Espionage*
> May 1845 *Prince Polignac and the French Carlists*

> There were, in addition, several articles on literary themes.

3 His reaction to the news of the Indian Mutiny was: 'Woe to us, if all the army should revolt.' [A.P. to Lord Holland, July 30, 1857.] His opinions on Ireland and on the American Civil War were equally conventional.

4 *Works of C. Chichemetecatl. Part the First. The Elf*, April 17–December 18, 1848; *Part the Second. The Fairy*, April 2–July 8, 1849; *The Mite*, September 24, 1849–March 31, 1851.

5 For example, *The Fable of the Cocks, The Mite*, January 27–February 17, 1851. In the B.M. copy of *The Elf*, a key in Panizzi's handwriting to this earlier *Animal Farm* has been inserted.

6 Charles Lacaita remembered him as a very ugly and stout old man, who, when the young Lacaita declined a glass of wine and expressed a preference for beer, roared, 'Wine is ze drink of ze gods, beer is ze drink of ze Goths.' Brooks, p. 161.

7 Hudson to A.P., December 29, 1863. Add. MS. 36, 722. f.566.

8 Percy Gardner of the Department of Coins and Medals. Quoted in Esdaile, p. 123.

9 'I have always thought and think that all despotic governments join in trying to put down England. In fact they must do so. The Crusade against civil and religious liberty will be a failure so long as this citadel of both stands.' [A.P. to Lord Holland, March 18, 1853.] [*Holland House Papers.*]

10 Add. MS. 36, 727. f.299.

11 Fagan, I, p. 186.

12 Add. MS. 44, 274. f.384.

13 Add. MS. 36, 723. f.321.

14 Mérimée, I, p. 171.

15 A.P. to Gladstone, November 22, 1874. 'I am in very bad odour with the priests and I thought you knew it . . . I never concealed my opinions and all the Roman Catholics are aware of it.' [Add. MS. 44, 274. f.388.]

16 Nicholas Wiseman, Cardinal, 1802–1865.

17 John Acton, first Baron Acton, 1834–1902. Historian.

18 'The Bourbons are a damned set of cut-throats and parjurors [sic] and I hope to live long enough to see them scattered over the face of the earth.' [A.P. to Lord Holland, March 12, 1856.] [Holland House Papers.]

19 Add. MS. 44, 274. f.12. [A.P. to Gladstone, October 8, 1849.]

20 Add. MS. 44, 274. f.146. In Panizzi's opinion both Russia and Austria would only be too glad to bring about 'the humiliation and destruction of England' and so enthusiastically supported the Crimean War. [A.P. to Gladstone, November 30, 1855.]

21 Add. MS. 44, 274. f.146.

22 Add. MS. 44, 274. f.178.

23 Add. MS. 36, 724. ff.438, 439.

24 Emilio Cugini, Bishop of Modena.

25 The printing of the catalogue began in 1881 under Garnett's direction. The first part appeared the following year, the last in 1905.

26 Esdaile, p. 123.

ABBREVIATIONS
USED IN THE NOTES

Add. MS.   *Additional Manuscripts*, Department of Manuscripts, British Museum.

Bacchi   I. Bacchi, *La giovinezza di A.P.*

Boselli   A. Boselli, *Angelo Pezzana e A.P.*

Brooks   C. Brooks, *A.P., scholar and patriot.*

Brougham MSS.   Manuscripts relating to Lord Brougham at University College, London.

Cary, Memoir   H. Cary, *Memoir of the Rev. F. Cary.*

Committee Minutes   Minutes of the Committee of the Board of Trustees, British Museum.

Cowtan   R. Cowtan, *Memories of the British Museum.*

Dei Processi   A. Panizzi, *Dei processi e dello sentenze contra gli imputati di lesa Maestra.*

Dito   O. Dito, *Masoneria, Carboneria, e altre societa segrete.*

Edwards, Diary   E. Edwards, *Manuscript diary*, Department of Printed Books, British Museum.

Episodes   A. Gallenga, *Episodes of my second life.*

Epistolario   U. Foscolo, *Opere*, vol. 3. *Epistolario.*

Esdaile   A. Esdaile, *The British Museum Library.*

Espinasse   F. Espinasse, *Literary Recollections.*

Fagan   L. Fagan, *The life of Sir A.P.*

Friggeri   E. Friggeri, *La vita, le opere e i tempi di A.P.*

Garnett, John Winter Jones   R. Garnett, *The late J.W.J.*

Halévy   E. Halévy, *The Age of Peel and Cobden.*

Hobhouse Recollections   J. C. Hobhouse, *Recollections of a long life.*

Holland House   G. Fox-Strangways, Earl of Ilchester, *Chronicles of Holland House.*

Holland House Papers   Letters and other papers from Holland House in the Department of Manuscripts, British Museum.

Jones, Introduction	British Museum, *A list of the books of reference in the Reading Room.* [With an introduction by J.W.J.]
C. Lacaita	C. Lacaita, *An Italian Englishman, Sir J. Lacaita.*
Letter	W. Gladstone, *A letter to the Earl of Aberdeen.*
Lettere ad A.P.	L. Fagan, *Lettere ad A.P. di uomini illustre.*
Mérimée	L. Fagan, *Letters of P. Mérimée to A.P.*
Madden Collection	F. Madden [*A collection of newspaper cuttings relating to the British Museum*].
Morley	J. Morley, *Life of Gladstone.*
Munford, Edwards	W. Munford, *E. Edwards, 1812–1886.*
Passages	A. Panizzi, *Passages in my official life.*
Pecchio, Semi-Serious Observations	G. Pecchio, *Semi-serious observations of an Italian exile.*
P.P.	Official papers of A.P. in the Department of Printed Books, British Museum.
Royal Commission	*Commission appointed to inquire into the Constitution and Government of the British Museum.*
Report, Appendix	*Report, Appendix to the Report.*
Select Committee 1835	*Select Committee to inquire into the condition, management and affairs of the British Museum.*
Select Committee 1836	*Select Committee on the same subject the following session.*
Select Committee 1838	*Select Committee on Plans and Estimates for the British Museum.*
Select Committee 1850	*Select Committee on Public Libraries, 1850.*
Shepherd MSS.	Manuscripts of the Rev. W. Sheppherd, Manchester College, Oxford.
Stride	E. Stride [*A collection of newspaper cuttings, etc. relating to A.P.*]
To the Assignees.	A. Panizzi. *To the Assignees of Messrs. Richter*, etc.
Wicks	M. Wicks, *The Italian Exiles in London.*

BIBLIOGRAPHY

A. PRIMARY SOURCES

BRITISH MUSEUM.
　　Board of Trustees. *Committee Minutes.* Vol. 27–31 1856–1866.
DEPARTMENT OF MANUSCRIPTS.
　　Panizzi (Sir Anthony).
　　Correspondence and papers, 1797–1877. Add. MSS. 36, 714–36, 729.
　　Correspondence with Count Cavour, 1854–1860. Add. MSS. 39, 757 ff. 9–29.
　　Correspondence with Sir A. H. Layard, 1859–1865. Add. MSS. 38986 ff. 184, 292, 301–383, 38987 ff. 57, 132, 38988 f. 172, 38991 f. 256, *etc.*
　　Correspondence with Sir F. Madden, 1840–1866. Egerton 2842 ff. 233, 320, 322, 2843 f. 287, 2846 ff. 145, 150, 207, 211–13, 227, 2847 ff. 202, *etc.*
　　Correspondence with Elizabeth, Lady Holland, 1841–1845. Holland House Papers. In Add. MSS. 51, 318–52, 254.
　　Correspondence with Henry Edward, fourth Lord Holland, 1849–1859. Holland House Papers. Add. MSS. 52,008, 52,009.
　　Correspondence with Mary, Lady Holland, 1852–1856. Holland House Papers.
　　Correspondence with Sir J. Lacaita, 1852–1875. Add. MSS. 42,177.
　　Correspondence with W. E. Gladstone, 1844–1878. *Gladstone Papers.* Vol. 189. Add. MSS. 44,274.
　　Miscellaneous letters to Panizzi, 1832–1873. Egerton 3677/F.
　　Miscellaneous letters to Panizzi, 1853–1863. Add. MSS. 49,596.
　　Letter to Duke of Sussex requesting the post of Librarian to the Royal Society, 1835. Fair copy not in Panizzi's hand. Add. MSS. 41667m.
　　Lacaita (Sir James).
　　Correspondence with W. E. Gladstone, 1851–1874. Gladstone

Papers. Vol. 149. Add. MSS. 44,233, 44,234.
Ellis (Sir Henry).
Correspondence and papers. Add. MSS. 41,312.
Cheyney (Edward).
Correspondence with Mary, Lady Holland (Letters referring to Panizzi, February 3, 1860, October 5, 1866, April 19, 1879).
Holland Papers.
Madden (Sir Frederic).
Journal (Photographic reproduction up to 1835 of original in Bodleian Library, Oxford). MS. Eng.hist. c.148.
Gladstone (William E.).
Dinner Books, 1851-1874. Gladstone Papers. Vol. 697-9. Add. MSS. 44, 782-784.
Hobhouse (John C.), Lord Broughton.
Broughton Papers. Add. MSS. 36,459. ff. 330-347b.

DEPARTMENT OF PRINTED BOOKS.
Panizzi (Sir Anthony).
Official correspondence and papers, 1837-1855. (Together with a few additional papers, 1856-1866).
Madden (Sir Frederic).
[*A collection of newspaper cuttings, etc., relating to the British Museum*] 4 vol. (Those relating to Panizzi consist for the most part of attacks on him from the popular press.)
Edwards (Edward).
Manuscript Diary, 1844-1884.
Stride (Edward).
[*A collection of press cuttings, photographs and other documents relating to Sir A. Panizzi.*] [1859-1884.]

MANCHESTER COLLEGE, OXFORD.
Panizzi (Sir Anthony).
Correspondence with Rev. William Shepherd.

MUSEO DI RISORGIMENTO, MODENA.
Panizzi (Luigi).
A letter describing the flight of A. Panizzi.

NATIONAL LIBRARY OF SCOTLAND.
Panizzi (Sir Anthony).
Correspondence with Andrew, Lord Rutherfurd.

UNIVERSITY COLLEGE, LONDON.
Panizzi (Sir Anthony).
Correspondence.
Minutes and proceedings of Council.
Brougham MSS.

B. SECONDARY SOURCES

GENERAL

BROOKS (CONSTANCE). *Antonio Panizzi, scholar and patriot.* University Press, Manchester, 1931. [*Publications of the University of Manchester,* no. CCVIII. *Italian series,* no. 1].

CAPRIN (GIULIO). *L'esule fortunato, Antonio Panizzi,* Firenze [1945].

COWTAN (ROBERT). *A biographical sketch of Sir Anthony Panizzi.* Asher, London, 1873.

FAGAN (LOUIS). *The Life of Sir Anthony Panizzi, etc.,* 2 vol. Remington, London, 1880.

FRIGGERI (ENRICO). *La vita, le opere e i tempi di Antonio Panizzi.* Belluno, 1897.

REGGIO NELL'EMILIA. Comitato par le Celebrazione del Centocinquantesimo Anniversario . . . di Antonio Panizzi. *Antonio Panizzi.* MDCCXCVII–MCMXLVII. *Racolta di scritti,* etc. Reggio, 1947.

WICKS (MARGARET C.). *The Italian exiles in London, 1816–1848.* University Press, Manchester, 1937. [*Publications of the University of Manchester,* no. CCLV. *Italian series,* no. 11].

ITALY, 1797–1822

ACTON (HAROLD). *The Bourbons of Naples, 1734–1825.* Methuen, London, 1956.

BACCHI (IGINO). *La giovinezza di Antonio Panizzi.* Reggio-Emilia, 1932.

BIANCHI (NICOMEDE). *I Ducati Estensi.* 2 vol., Torino, 1852.

BOSELLI (ANTONIO). *Angelo Pezzana e Antonio Panizzi, maestro e discepolo,* Parma [1933].

DITO (ORESTE). *Massoneria, Carboneria e daltre società segrete nella storica del risorgimento italiano.* Torino, Roma, 1905.

FANO (CLELIA). *Francesco IV. Documenti e aspetti di vita reggiana.* Reggio-Emilia, 1932.

MODENA, PROVINCE OF. *Documenti risguardanti il governo degli Austro-Estensi in Modena dal 1814 al 1859.* Modena, 1859.

PANIZZI (SIR ANTHONY). K.C.B. *Dei processi e delle sentenze contra gli imputati di lesa Maestà . . . Notizie, scritte da Antonio Panizzi pubblicate da xxx,* Madrid, 1823. The imprint is false; printed in Lugano.

RATH (REUBEN J.). 'The Carbonari. Their origins, initiation rites and aims.' [*American Historical Review*. Vol. XLIX, No. 2, January, 1964].

ROGERS (SAMUEL). *The Italian Journals of Samuel Rogers*. Edited by J. R. Hale. Faber & Faber, London, 1956.

VAUSSARD (MAURICE). *Daily Life in 18th century Italy*. Translated by M. Heron. Allen & Unwin, 1962. [*Daily Life* series. No. 8].

WHYTE (ARTHUR J.). *The Evolution of Modern Italy*. Blackwell, Oxford, 1944.

ENGLAND 1823–1831

Annual Register. 'The King v. Edward Gibbon Wakefield.' *Annual Register, 1827. Law Cases*, p. 316.

BEATTIE (WILLIAM). *Life and Letters of T. Campbell*. 3 vol. Moxon, London, 1849.

BROOKS (CONSTANCE). 'Una lettera inedita di Ugo Foscolo.' [*Giornale storico della letteratura italiana*. Vol. XCII, pp. 214, 215].

BRUCE (MARY L.). *Anna Swanick. A memoir and recollections*. T. Fisher Unwin, London. 1903.

CHANDLER (GEORGE). *Liverpool*, Batsford, London, 1957.

CHANDLER (GEORGE). *William Roscoe of Liverpool*. Batsford, London, 1953.

CLARK (GEORGE K.). *The Making of Victorian England*. Methuen, London, 1962.

CREEVEY (THOMAS). *Creevey's Life and Times. A further selection from the correspondence* . . . Edited by J. Gore. Murray, London, 1934.

FOSCOLO (NICCOLO U.). *Opere, edite e postume*, etc. 12 vol. Firenze, 1850–90.

GALLENGA (ANTONIO). *Episodes of my Second Life*. 2 vol. Chapman & Hall, London, 1884.

GORE'S *Liverpool Directory*, etc., 1825

Liverpool Mercury, March 8, 1825; November 11, 1825.

NEW (CHESTER W.). *The Life of Henry Brougham to 1830*. Clarendon Press, Oxford, 1961.

PECCHIO (GIUSEPPE). *Count. Semi-serious observations of an Italian exile during his residence in England*. Effingham Wilson, London, 1833.

REDDING (CYRUS). *Literary reminiscences and memoirs of Thomas Campbell.* 2 vol. Skeat, London, 1860.

ROSCOE (HENRY). *Life of William Roscoe.* 2 vol. T. Cadell & W. Blackwood, London. Edinburgh, 1833.

Times Literary Supplement. 'Letter from T. Campbell to W. Roscoe, Junior. Roscoe Papers in Picton Library, Liverpool.' [T.L.S., July 8, 1944].

VIGLIONE (FRANCESCO). *Ugo Foscolo in Inghilterra.* Catania, 1910.

VINCENT (ERIC R.). *Byron, Hobhouse and Foscolo.* University Press, Cambridge, 1949.

THE BRITISH MUSEUM

BARWICK (GEORGE F.). *The Reading Room of the British Museum.* Benn, London, 1929.

BRITISH MUSEUM. *A List of the books of reference in the Reading Room, etc.* [With an introduction on the building of the Reading Room by J. Winter Jones.] London, 1859.

CARY (HENRY). *Memoir of the Rev. Henry Francis Cary . . . with his literary journals and letters.* 2 vol. Moxon, London, 1847.

COLLIER (JOHN P.). *A Letter to the Earl of Ellesmere on the subject of a new alphabetical catalogue of printed books in the British Museum.* Privately printed [London], 1849.

COLLIER (JOHN P.). *A supplementary Letter to the Earl of Ellesmere, occasioned by certain interrogatories from the Keeper of Printed Books in the British Museum.* Privately printed, London, 1849.

COWTAN (ROBERT). *Memories of the British Museum.* Bentley, London, 1872.

EDWARDS (EDWARD). *A Letter to the . . . Earl of Ellesmere . . . on the desirability of a better provision for public libraries, etc.* London, 1848.

EDWARDS (EDWARD). *Lives of the Founders of the British Museum, etc.* Trubner & Co., London, 1870.

EDWARDS (EDWARD). *Remarks on the paucity of libraries . . . A letter to the Earl of Ellesmere.* Privately printed, London, 1849.

ESDAILE (ARUNDELL). *The British Museum Library. A short history and survey.* Allen & Unwin, London, 1946.

ESPINASSE (FRANCIS). *Literary Recollections and Sketches.* Hodder & Stoughton, London, 1893.

FERGUSSON (JAMES). *Observations on the British Museum, National Gallery . . . with suggestions for their improvement.* Weale, London, 1849.

GARNETT (RICHARD). *The late John Winter Jones, Principal Librarian,* etc. (Library Association, 1882.) Chiswick Press, London. 1882.
  On the printing of the British Museum Catalogue. A paper read at the Cambridge meeting of the Library Association. London [1882].

GEMMER (FREDERIC W.). *Memorial addressed to the Trustees of the British Museum.* Privately printed, London, 1864.

GRAY (JOHN E.). *A Letter to the Earl of Ellesmere on the management of the Library of Printed Books in the British Museum.* Privately printed, London, 1849.

GRAY (JOHN E.). *A Second Letter to the Earl of Ellesmere on the management of the Library of Printed Books, etc.* Privately printed, London, 1849.

HEILBRUN (CAROLYN). *The Garnett Family.* Allen & Unwin, London, 1961.

LIBRARY ASSOCIATION. *Transactions and proceedings . . .* 7th Annual Meeting . . . September . . . 1884. [London, 1884].

Mechanics Magazine, Museum Register, Journal and Gazette.
  'The New Buildings at the British Museum.' By P.P.C.R. (Thomas Watts). Vol. 36. October 1, 1836–March 31, 1837, p. 454.
  'The British Museum and its Library.' By P.P.C.R. (Thomas Watts). Vol. 36, p. 291. A review of the report of the Select Committee of 1836.

MUNFORD (WILLIAM A.). *Edward Edwards, 1812–1886. Portrait of a Librarian.* Library Association, London, 1963.

NICOLAS (SIR NICHOLAS H.). *Aminadversions on the Library and Catalogues of the British Museum. A reply to Mr. Panizzi's statement.* Bentley, London, 1846.

OLDMAN (CECIL B.). *Sir Anthony Panizzi and the British Museum Library.* [*English Libraries.* 1800–1850, *etc.*], H. K. Lewis, London, 1958.

PANIZZI (SIR ANTHONY). *A Letter to His Royal Highness the President of the Royal Society on the new catalogue of the library of that institution now in the press.* Privately printed, London [1837].

PANIZZI (SIR ANTHONY). *Observations on the address by the President and on the statement by the Council . . . respecting Mr*

Panizzi . . . at their general meeting, Nov. 30, 1837. Privately printed, London, 1838.

PANIZZI (SIR ANTHONY). *On the supply of printed books from the Library to the Reading Room of the British Museum.* [London,] 1846.

PANIZZI (SIR ANTHONY). *Passages in my official life.* Privately printed, London, 1871.

PANIZZI (SIR ANTHONY), and BOND (SIR EDWARD A.). *Remarks on a 'Memorial addressed to the Trustees . . . by Frederic W. Gemmer.'* London, 1864.

PARLIAMENTARY PAPERS, HOUSE OF COMMONS.

Accounts relating the the Income and Expenditure, etc., 1831–1865 [British Museum Annual Reports].

Report from the Select Committee to inquire into the Condition, Management and Affairs of the British Museum. Session 1835. Vol. VII, p. 1.

Report from the Select Committee appointed in the following session to consider the same subject. Session 1836. Vol. X, p. 1.

Resolutions of the Trustees on Report of the Committee of the House of Commons. Session 1836. Vol. XLVII, p. 39.

Minutes made by the Trustees since July 1836 with reference to the resolutions of the Select Committee of the House of Commons. Session 1837. Vol. XXXIX, p. 181.

Report from the Select Committee appointed to inquire into the plans and estimates from the completion of the buildings of the British Museum. Session 1837–38. Vol. XXIII, p. 1.

Monies, salaries and emoluments of persons employed in the British Museum. Session 1840. Vol. XXIX, p. 279.

Representations from the Trustees of the British Museum to the Treasury on the subject of an enlarged scale of expenditure for the supply of printed books . . . and of the Minute of the Board of Treasury thereon. Session 1846. Vol. XXV, p. 229.

Names, salaries, etc. of persons employed by the Trustees . . . and of the promotions and discharges since January 1, 1841. Session 1847. Vol. XXXIV, p. 243.

Memorial to the First Lord of the Treasury, presented on March 10, 1847, by members of the British Association for the advancement of science . . . respecting the management of the British Museum, etc. Session 1847. Vol. XXXIV, p. 253.

Commission issued by Her Majesty to inquire into the affairs of the British Museum, dated June 17, 1847. Session 1847. Vol. XXXIV, p. 257.

Sums expended on the Library of the British Museum . . . 1763 to the year 1848, etc. Session 1849. Vol. XVII, p. 1.

Reports from the Select Committee on Public Libraries. Session 1849. Vol. XVII, p. 1; 1850, Vol. XVIII, p. 1; 1851, Vol. X, p. 793; 1852, Vol. V, p. 461.

Report of the Commissioners appointed to inquire into the constitution and government of the British Museum. Session 1850. Vol. XXIV, p. 1.

Appendix to the Report, etc.

Answers to queries contained in a circular sent to foreign libraries as to the regulations under which they are accessible to the public. Session 1850. Vol. XVIII, p. 85.

Communications addressed to the Treasury by the Trustees of the British Museum with reference to the report of the Commissioners appointed to inquire into the constitution and management of the British Museum. Session 1850. Vol. XXXIII, p. 247.

Communications made by the architect and officers of the British Museum to the Trustees respecting the enlargement of the building, etc. Session 1852. Vol. XXVIII, p. 201; 1852–53, Vol. LVII, p. 317; 1857–58, Vol. XXXIII, p. 373.

Letter from Mr Panizzi to the Treasury in 1858 relative to want of space in the British Museum. Session 1857–58. Vol. XXXIV, p. 195.

Report of the Select Committee on the British Museum. Session 1860. Vol. XVI, p. 173.

Correspondence between the Treasury and the British Museum as to providing additional accommodation. Session 1862. Vol. XXIX, p. 169; 1864, Vol. XXXII, p. 167.

Correspondence subsequent to October 1, 1864, between the Civil Service Commissioners and the Librarian respecting the examination of candidates for situations in the department. Session 1866. Vol. XXXIX, p. 241.

Quarterly Review. 'Report from the Select Committee, 1835.' (A review of this and subsequent Parliamentary Committees and Commissions and related documents.) Vol. 88, no. CLXXV. December 1850. Art. VI.

Quarterly Review. 'Observations on the British Museum,' etc. (Review of Fergusson's proposals for the rebuilding of the Museum and of other similar publications.) Vol. 92, no. CLXXXIII. December 1852. March 1853. Art. VII.

ROYAL SOCIETY. *Defence of the resolution for omitting Mr Panizzi's bibliographical notes from the catalogue of the Royal Society.*

SMITH (SIMON N.). *Carlyle and the London Library.* [English Libraries, 1800–1850.] H. K. Lewis, London, 1958.

LITERARY

Foreign Quarterly Review. 'Review of *Orlando Innamorato di Bojardo*,' etc., Vol. 15, no. 29. Art. II.

PANIZZI (SIR ANTHONY). *Chi era Francesco da Bologna?* Whittingham, London, 1858.

PANIZZI (SIR ANTHONY). *Orlando Innamorato di Bojardo. Orlando Furioso di Ariosto. With an essay on the romantic poetry of the Italians. Memoirs and notes.* W. Pickering, London, 1830–34.

PANIZZI (SIR ANTHONY). *To the Assignees of Messrs. Richter . . . Publishers and proprietors of the Foreign Quarterly Review.* Whittingham, London [1835].

Quarterly Review. (Review of L. Fagan's '*Life*' and '*Letters of Prosper Mérimée*'). Vol. 151, p. 463.

ROSSETTI (GABRIELE). *Opere inedite e rare di Gabriele Rossetti. La vita mia. Il testamento*, etc. Lanciano, 1910.

POLITICAL AND SOCIAL

ACTON (HAROLD). *The Last Bourbons of Naples, 1825–1861.* Methuen, London, 1961.

BALLEYDIER (ALPHONSE). *La vérité sur les affaires de Naples.* Paris 1851.

BARTHEZ (ANTOINE E. C.). *The Empress Eugénie and her circle.* Fisher Unwin, London, 1912.

BATTISCOMBE (ESTHER G.). *Mrs. Gladstone. The portrait of a marriage.* Constable, London, 1956.

BROOKS'S CLUB. *Memorials of Brooks's from the foundation of the club to the close of the nineteenth century.* Ballantyne & Co., London. 1907.

BUSTICO (GUIDO). *Antonio Panizzi, il Passano e il duca d'Aumale, con lettere inedite.* Genova, 1913.

FAGAN (LOUIS). *Letters of Prosper Mérimée to Panizzi.* Remington & Co., London, 1881.

FAGAN (LOUIS). *Lettere ad Antonio Panizzi di uomini illustri e di amici italiani, 1823–1870.* Firenze, 1880.

FILON (AUGUSTIN). *Mérimée et ses amis.* Paris, 1894.

GLADSTONE (WILLIAM E.). *A Letter to the Earl of Aberdeen on the state prosecutions of the Neapolitan government.* Murray, London, 1851.

GLADSTONE (WILLIAM E.). *A second letter to the Earl of Aberdeen on the state prosecutions of the Neapolitan government.* Murray, London, 1851.

GLADSTONE (WILLIAM E.). *An examination of the official reply of the Neapolitan government.* Murray, London, 1852.

HALÉVY (ELIE). *The Age of Peel and Cobden. A History of the English people, 1841–1852.* Benn, London, 1947.

HENNESSY (JAMES P.). *Monckton Milnes. The flight of youth.* Constable, London, 1951.

HOLLAND (SABA) LADY. *A memoir of the Reverend Sydney Smith . . . with a selection of his letters edited by Mrs. Austin.* 2 vol. Longmans, London, 1855.

HOUGHTON (WALTER E.). *The Victorian frame of mind, 1830–1870.* Yale University Press, Newhaven, 1957.

HOWARTH (THOMAS E. B.). *Citizen-King. The Life of Louis Philippe, King of the French.* Eyre & Spottiswoode, London, 1961.

JONES (WILBUR D.). *Lord Derby and Victorian Conservatism.* Blackwell, Oxford, 1956.

JOYCE (MICHAEL). *'My Friend H.' John Cam Hobhouse.* Murray, London, 1948.

LACAITA (CHARLES). *An Italian Englishman. Sir James Lacaita, K.C.M.G. 1813–1895, etc.* Grant Richards, London, 1933.

LIECHTENSTEIN (MARIE) PRINCESS. *Holland House.* 2 vol. Macmillan, London, 1874.

MAXWELL (SIR HERBERT). *The Life and Letters of George William Frederick, fourth Earl of Clarendon, etc.* 2 vol. Arnold, London, 1913.

MORELLI (EMILIA). *L'Inghilterra di Mazzini.* Roma, 1965. [*Istituto per la storia del risorgimento italiano. Biblioteca scientifica.* Serie II. Memorie. Vol. XXI].

MORLEY (JOHN), *Viscount Morley. The Life of W. E. Gladstone.* 3 vol. Macmillan, London, 1903.

MUNFORD (WILLIAM A.). *William Ewart, M.P., 1798–1867. Portrait of a radical.* Grafton & Co., London, 1960.

North British Review. 'Report from the Select Committee on the Post Office.' (Review by Panizzi of these reports.) Vol. 2. November 1844–February 1845. No. III. Art. VIII.

PACKE (MICHAEL ST. J.). *The Bombs of Orsini.* Secker & Warburg, London, 1957.

PARRY (ERNEST J.). *The Spanish Marriages, 1841–1846. A study of the influence of dynastic ambition upon foreign policy.*

Macmillan, London, 1936. [*London School of Economics. Studies in International History and Relations.* No. 1].

PEMBERTON (NOEL W. B.). *Lord Palmerston.* Batchworth Press, London. 1954.

ROBINSON (HENRY C.). *Diary, reminiscences and correspondence of Henry Crabb Robinson* . . . Edited by T. Sadler. Macmillan, London, 1872.

RUSSELL (ODO W. L.). *Baron Ampthill. The Roman Question. Extracts from the despatches of O. Russell from Rome, 1858–1870.* Edited by M. Blakiston. Chapman & Hall, London, 1962.

SETTEMBRINI (LUIGI). *Ricordanze della mia vita.* 2 vol. Napoli, 1881.

SMITH (SYDNEY). *The Letters of S. Smith.* Edited by S. N. Smith. 2 vol. Clarendon Press, Oxford, 1953.

STRANGWAYS (GILES S. H. F.). *Earl of Ilchester. Chronicles of Holland House, 1820–1900.* Murray, London, 1937.

TREVELYAN (GEORGE M.). *Garibaldi's Defence of the Roman Republic.* Longmans, London, 1907.
Garibaldi and the Thousand. Longmans, London, 1909.
Garibaldi and the Making of Italy. Longmans, London, 1911.

TREVELYAN (SIR GEORGE O.). *Life and Letters of Lord Macaulay.* London, 1876.

VILLIERS (GEORGE W. F.), *Earl of Clarendon. 'My Dear Duchess.' Social and political letters to the Duchess of Manchester.* Edited by A. L. Kennedy. Murray, London, 1956.

INDEX